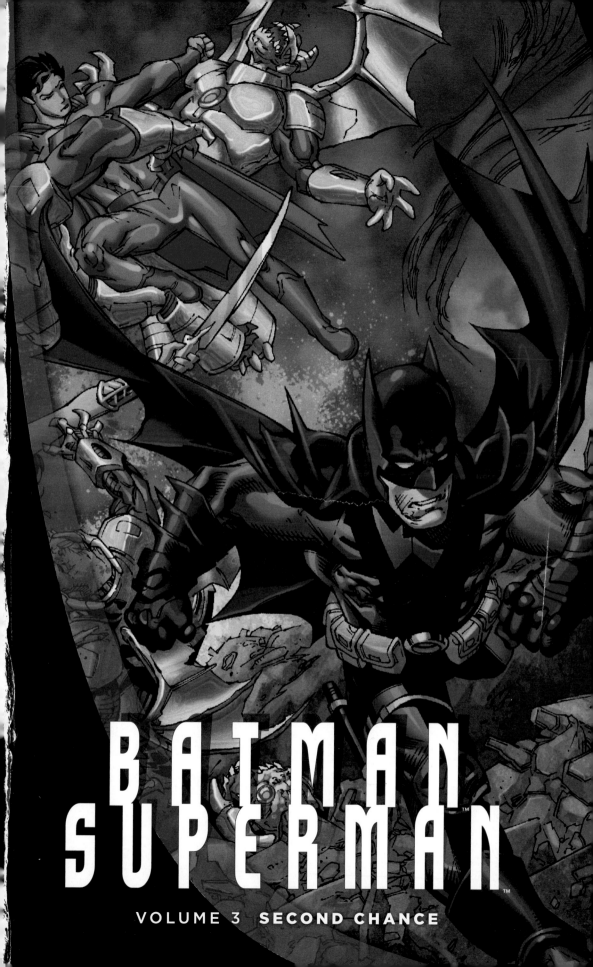

BATMAN
SUPERMAN

VOLUME 3   SECOND CHANCE

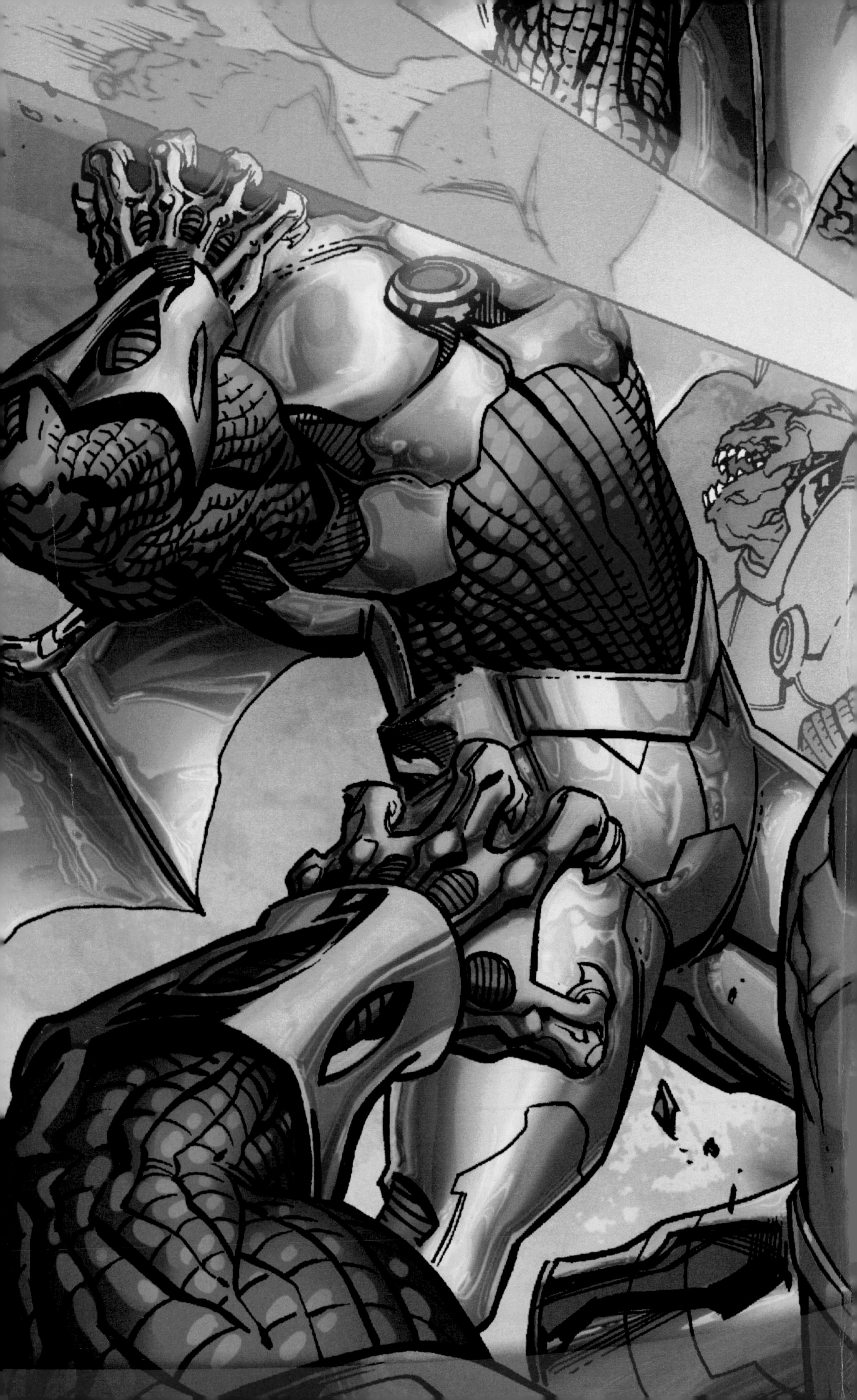

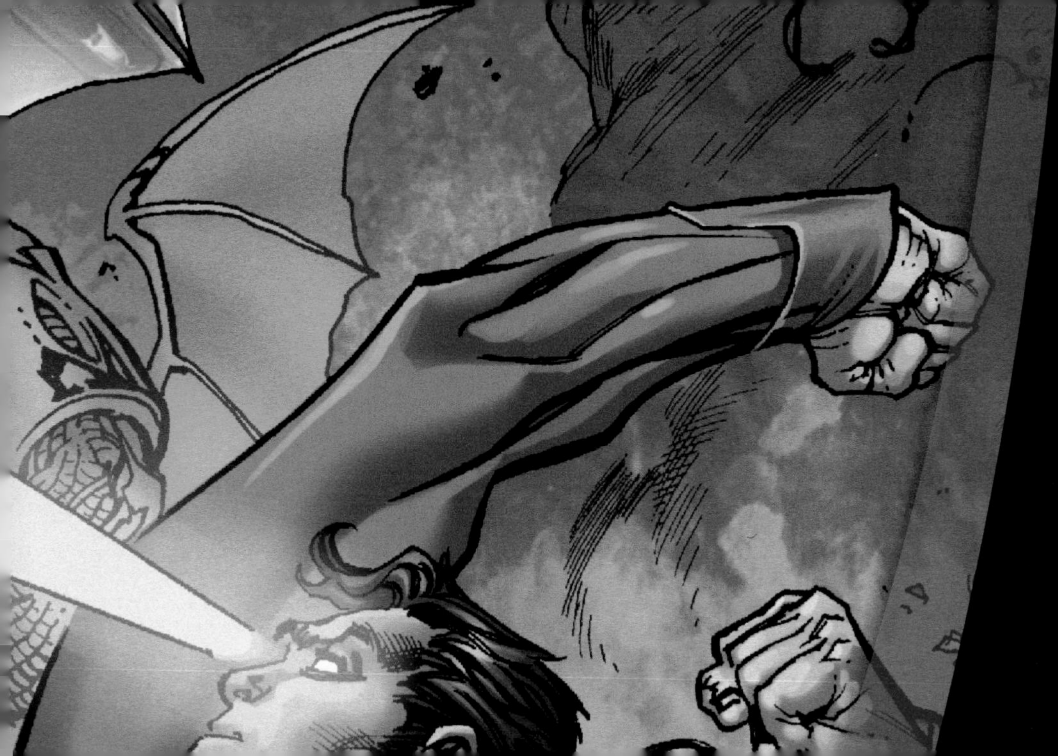

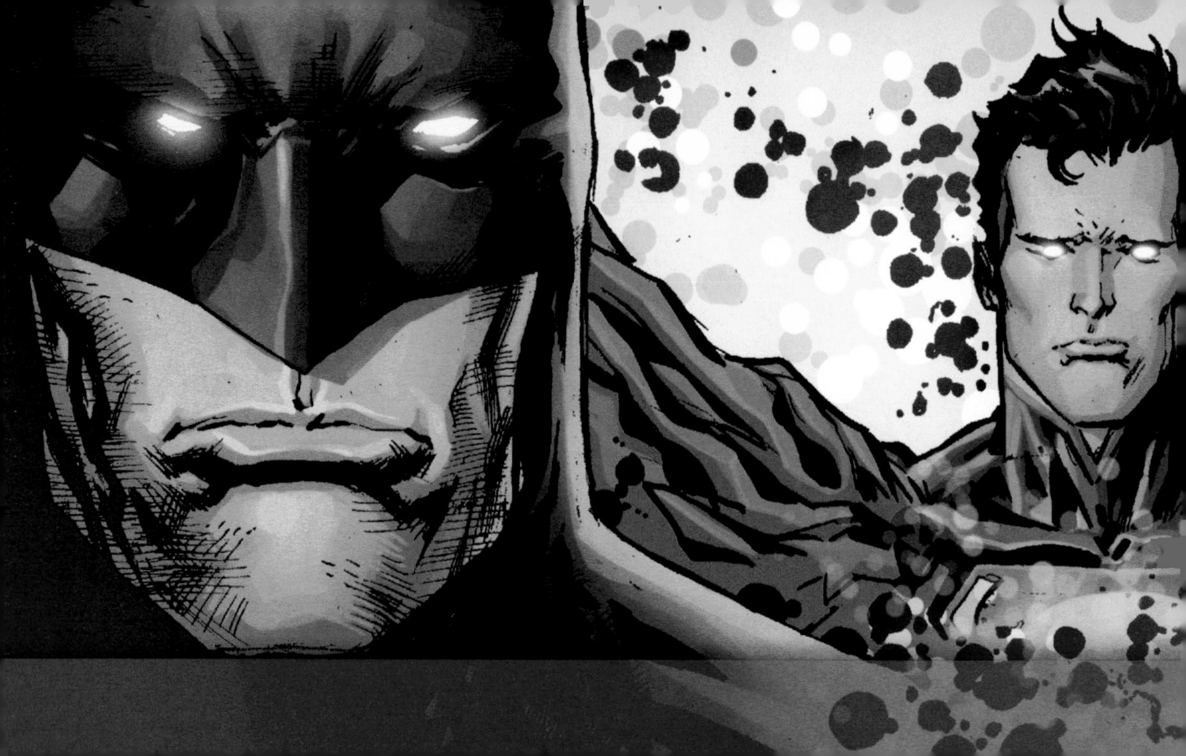

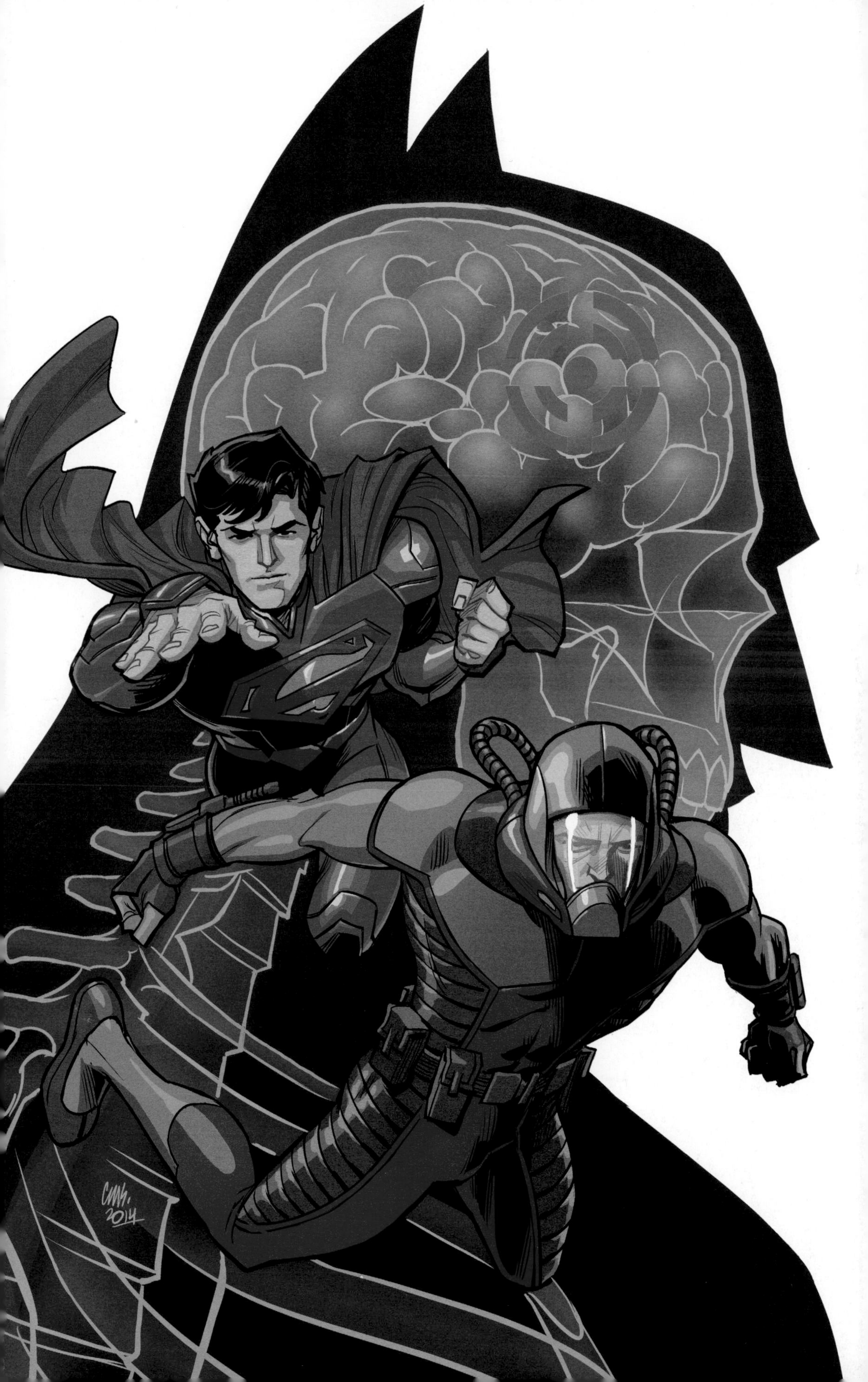

ENTER THE MICROVERSE

JEFF LEMIRE writer **KARL KERSCHL SCOTT HEPBURN** (pgs 12-15, 17-19, 22, 24) artists **GABE ELTAEB** colorist **ROB LEIGH** letterer
cover by **CAMERON STEWART**

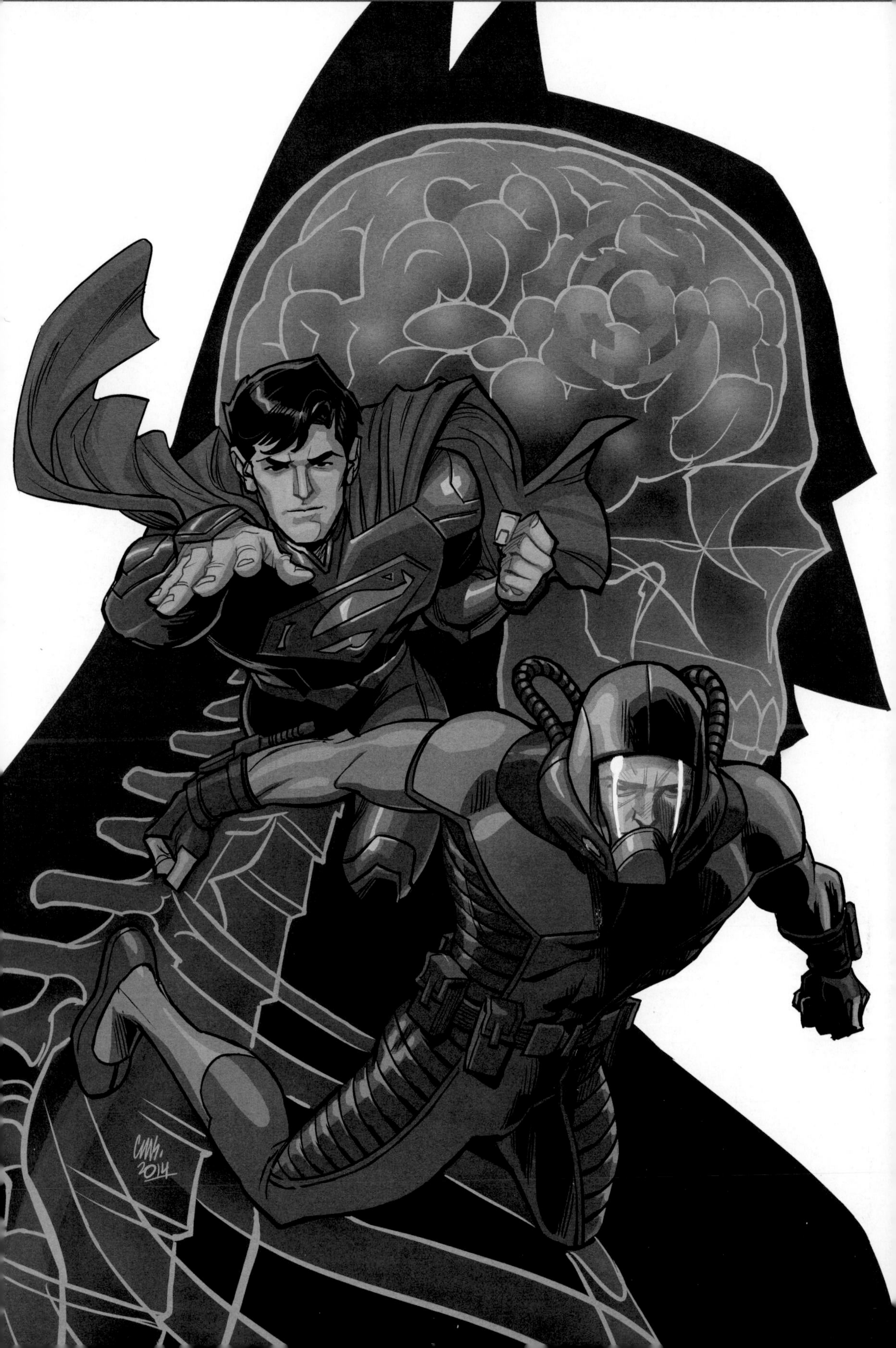

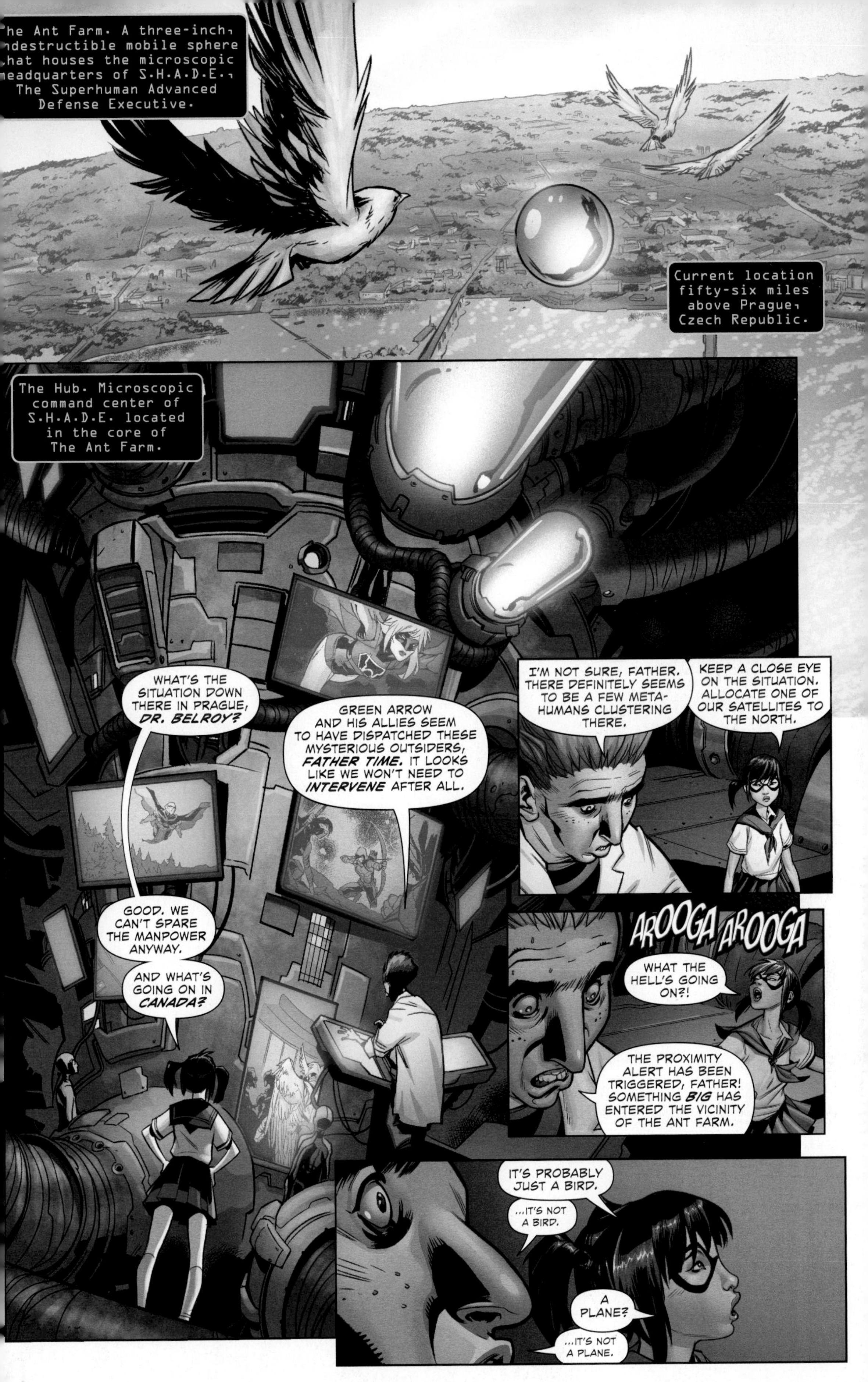
he Ant Farm. A three-inch, ndestructible mobile sphere hat houses the microscopic eadquarters of S.H.A.D.E., The Superhuman Advanced Defense Executive.
Current location fifty-six miles above Prague, Czech Republic.
The Hub. Microscopic command center of S.H.A.D.E. located in the core of The Ant Farm.
WHAT'S THE SITUATION DOWN THERE IN PRAGUE, DR. BELROY?
GREEN ARROW AND HIS ALLIES SEEM TO HAVE DISPATCHED THESE MYSTERIOUS OUTSIDERS, FATHER TIME. IT LOOKS LIKE WE WON'T NEED TO INTERVENE AFTER ALL.
GOOD. WE CAN'T SPARE THE MANPOWER ANYWAY.
AND WHAT'S GOING ON IN CANADA?
I'M NOT SURE, FATHER. THERE DEFINITELY SEEMS TO BE A FEW META-HUMANS CLUSTERING THERE.
KEEP A CLOSE EYE ON THE SITUATION. ALLOCATE ONE OF OUR SATELLITES TO THE NORTH.
AROOGA AROOGA
WHAT THE HELL'S GOING ON?!
THE PROXIMITY ALERT HAS BEEN TRIGGERED, FATHER! SOMETHING BIG HAS ENTERED THE VICINITY OF THE ANT FARM.
IT'S PROBABLY JUST A BIRD.
...IT'S NOT A BIRD.
A PLANE?
...IT'S NOT A PLANE.

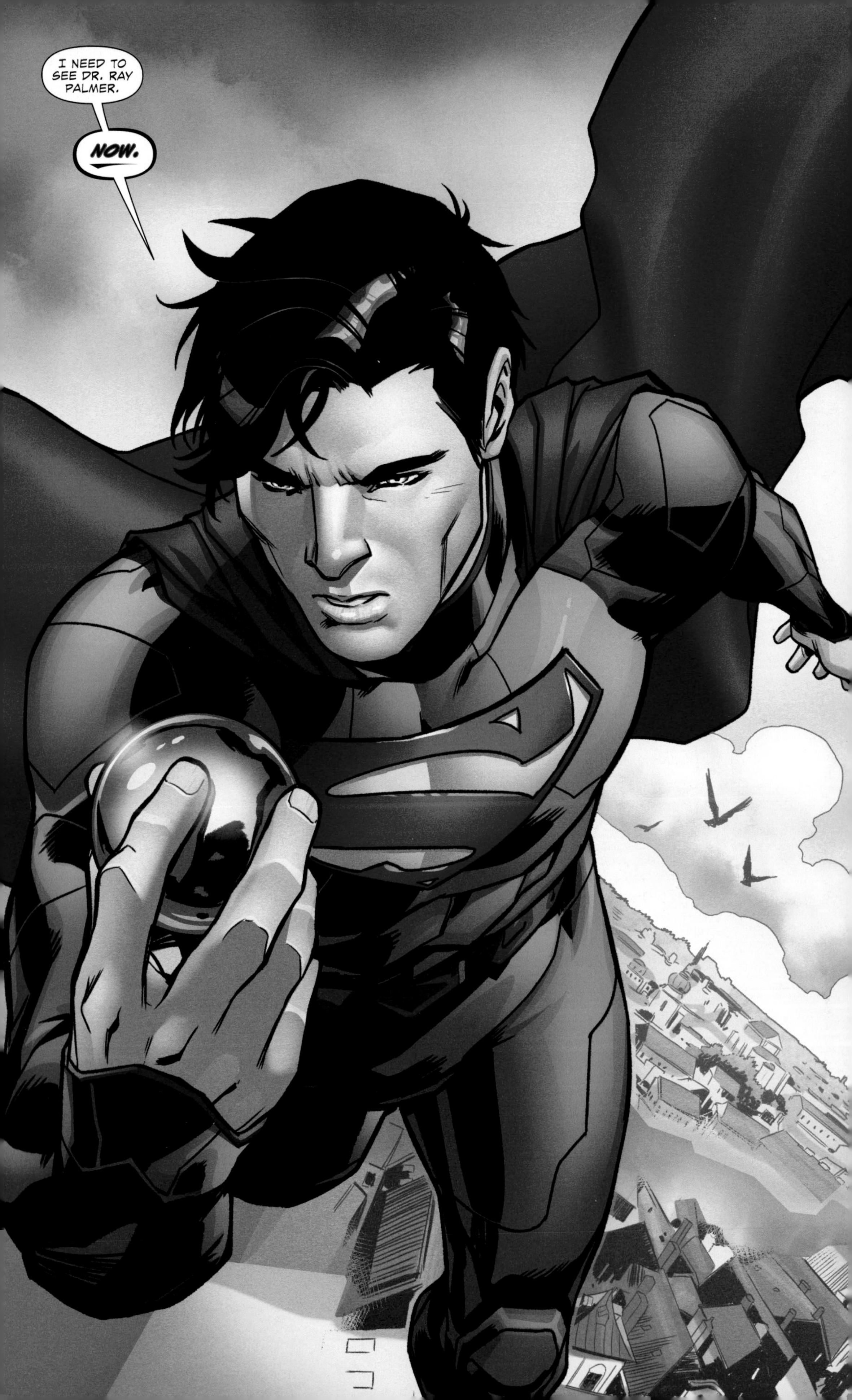
I NEED TO SEE DR. RAY PALMER.
NOW.

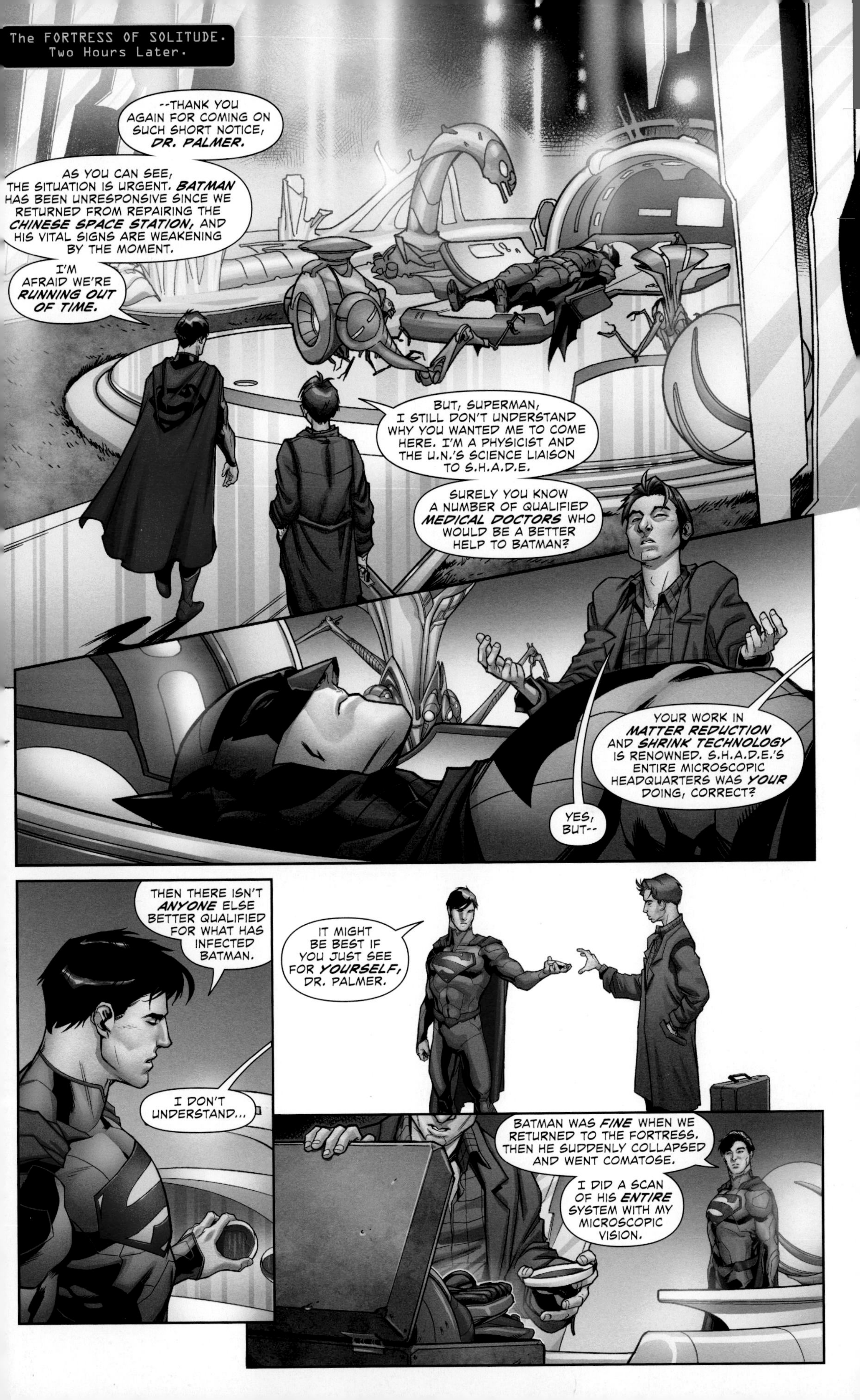
The FORTRESS OF SOLITUDE. Two Hours Later.
--THANK YOU AGAIN FOR COMING ON SUCH SHORT NOTICE, DR. PALMER.
AS YOU CAN SEE, THE SITUATION IS URGENT. BATMAN HAS BEEN UNRESPONSIVE SINCE WE RETURNED FROM REPAIRING THE CHINESE SPACE STATION, AND HIS VITAL SIGNS ARE WEAKENING BY THE MOMENT.
I'M AFRAID WE'RE RUNNING OUT OF TIME.
BUT, SUPERMAN, I STILL DON'T UNDERSTAND WHY YOU WANTED ME TO COME HERE. I'M A PHYSICIST AND THE U.N.'S SCIENCE LIAISON TO S.H.A.D.E.
SURELY YOU KNOW A NUMBER OF QUALIFIED MEDICAL DOCTORS WHO WOULD BE A BETTER HELP TO BATMAN?
YOUR WORK IN MATTER REDUCTION AND SHRINK TECHNOLOGY IS RENOWNED. S.H.A.D.E.'S ENTIRE MICROSCOPIC HEADQUARTERS WAS YOUR DOING, CORRECT?
YES, BUT--
THEN THERE ISN'T ANYONE ELSE BETTER QUALIFIED FOR WHAT HAS INFECTED BATMAN.
I DON'T UNDERSTAND...
IT MIGHT BE BEST IF YOU JUST SEE FOR YOURSELF, DR. PALMER.
BATMAN WAS FINE WHEN WE RETURNED TO THE FORTRESS. THEN HE SUDDENLY COLLAPSED AND WENT COMATOSE.
I DID A SCAN OF HIS ENTIRE SYSTEM WITH MY MICROSCOPIC VISION.

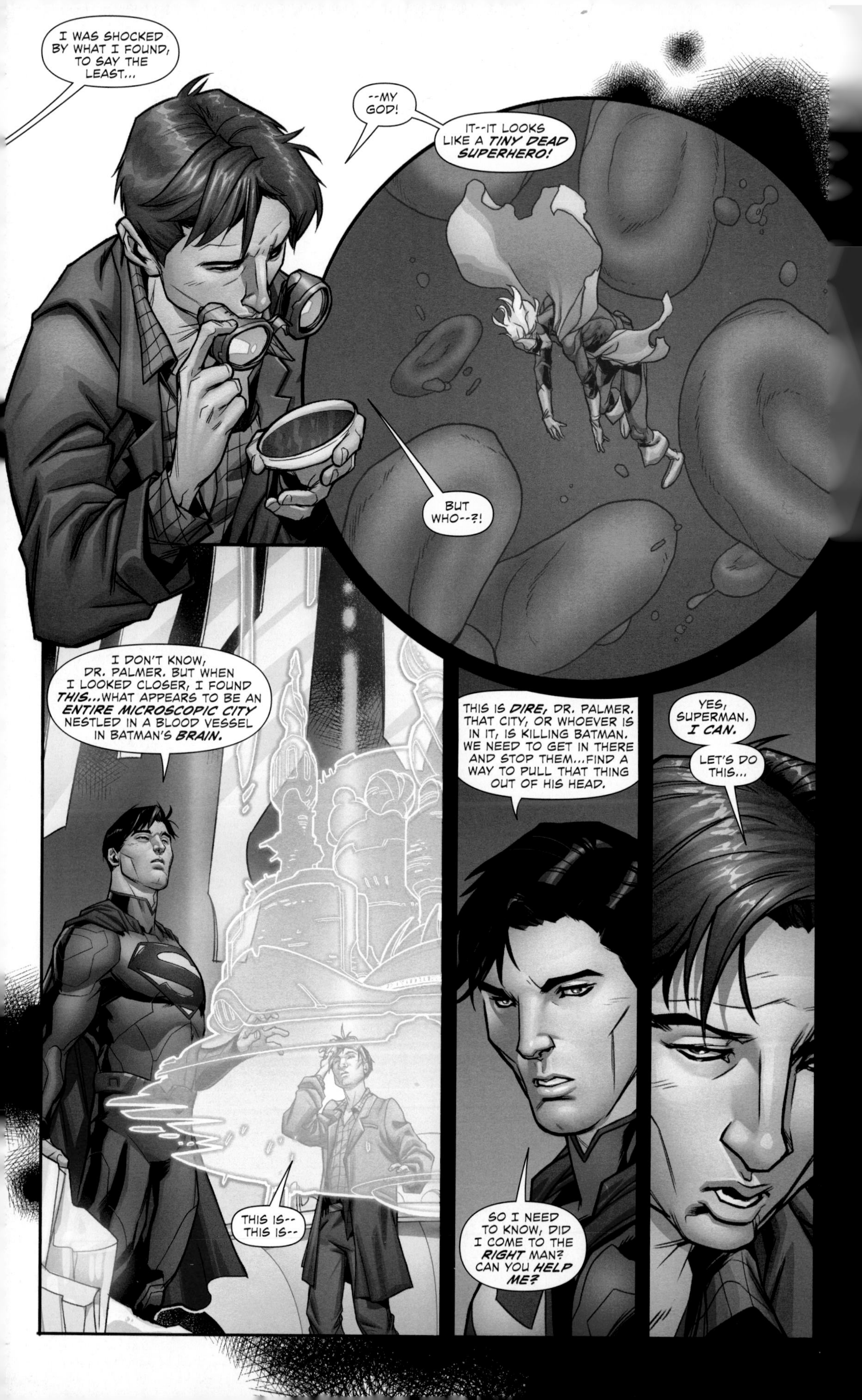
I WAS SHOCKED BY WHAT I FOUND, TO SAY THE LEAST...
--MY GOD!
IT--IT LOOKS LIKE A TINY DEAD SUPERHERO!
BUT WHO--?!
I DON'T KNOW, DR. PALMER. BUT WHEN I LOOKED CLOSER, I FOUND THIS...WHAT APPEARS TO BE AN ENTIRE MICROSCOPIC CITY NESTLED IN A BLOOD VESSEL IN BATMAN'S BRAIN.
THIS IS-- THIS IS--
THIS IS DIRE, DR. PALMER. THAT CITY, OR WHOEVER IS IN IT, IS KILLING BATMAN. WE NEED TO GET IN THERE AND STOP THEM...FIND A WAY TO PULL THAT THING OUT OF HIS HEAD.
SO I NEED TO KNOW, DID I COME TO THE RIGHT MAN? CAN YOU HELP ME?
YES, SUPERMAN. I CAN.
LET'S DO THIS...

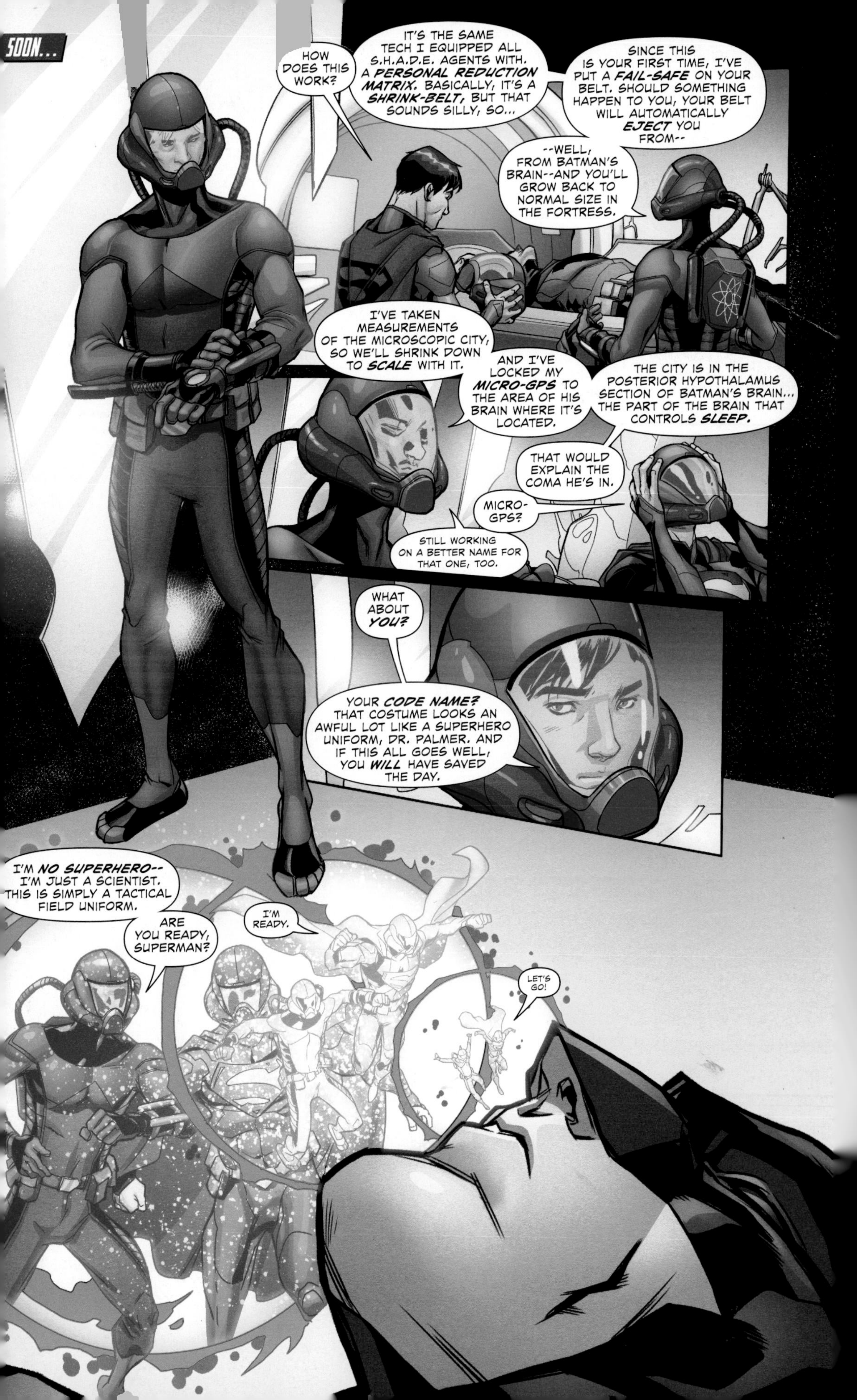
SOON...
HOW DOES THIS WORK?
IT'S THE SAME TECH I EQUIPPED ALL S.H.A.D.E. AGENTS WITH. A PERSONAL REDUCTION MATRIX. BASICALLY, IT'S A SHRINK-BELT, BUT THAT SOUNDS SILLY, SO...
SINCE THIS IS YOUR FIRST TIME, I'VE PUT A FAIL-SAFE ON YOUR BELT. SHOULD SOMETHING HAPPEN TO YOU, YOUR BELT WILL AUTOMATICALLY EJECT YOU FROM--
--WELL, FROM BATMAN'S BRAIN--AND YOU'LL GROW BACK TO NORMAL SIZE IN THE FORTRESS.
I'VE TAKEN MEASUREMENTS OF THE MICROSCOPIC CITY, SO WE'LL SHRINK DOWN TO SCALE WITH IT.
AND I'VE LOCKED MY MICRO-GPS TO THE AREA OF HIS BRAIN WHERE IT'S LOCATED.
THE CITY IS IN THE POSTERIOR HYPOTHALAMUS SECTION OF BATMAN'S BRAIN... THE PART OF THE BRAIN THAT CONTROLS SLEEP.
THAT WOULD EXPLAIN THE COMA HE'S IN.
MICRO-GPS?
STILL WORKING ON A BETTER NAME FOR THAT ONE, TOO.
WHAT ABOUT YOU?
YOUR CODE NAME? THAT COSTUME LOOKS AN AWFUL LOT LIKE A SUPERHERO UNIFORM, DR. PALMER. AND IF THIS ALL GOES WELL, YOU WILL HAVE SAVED THE DAY.
I'M NO SUPERHERO-- I'M JUST A SCIENTIST. THIS IS SIMPLY A TACTICAL FIELD UNIFORM.
ARE YOU READY, SUPERMAN?
I'M READY.
LET'S GO!

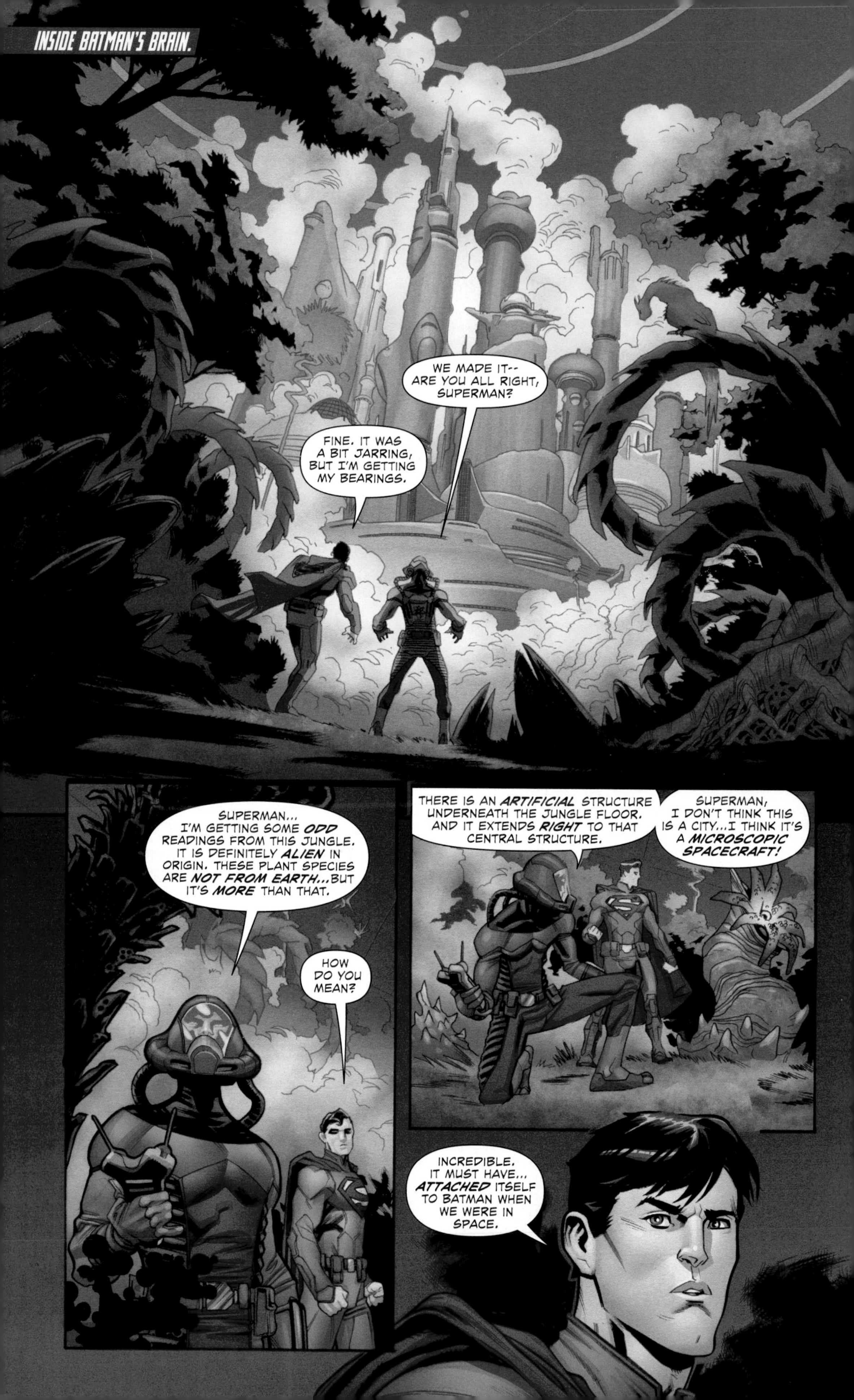
INSIDE BATMAN'S BRAIN.
WE MADE IT-- ARE YOU ALL RIGHT, SUPERMAN?
FINE. IT WAS A BIT JARRING, BUT I'M GETTING MY BEARINGS.
SUPERMAN... I'M GETTING SOME ODD READINGS FROM THIS JUNGLE. IT IS DEFINITELY ALIEN IN ORIGIN. THESE PLANT SPECIES ARE NOT FROM EARTH...BUT IT'S MORE THAN THAT.
HOW DO YOU MEAN?
THERE IS AN ARTIFICIAL STRUCTURE UNDERNEATH THE JUNGLE FLOOR. AND IT EXTENDS RIGHT TO THAT CENTRAL STRUCTURE.
SUPERMAN, I DON'T THINK THIS IS A CITY...I THINK IT'S A MICROSCOPIC SPACECRAFT!
INCREDIBLE. IT MUST HAVE... ATTACHED ITSELF TO BATMAN WHEN WE WERE IN SPACE.

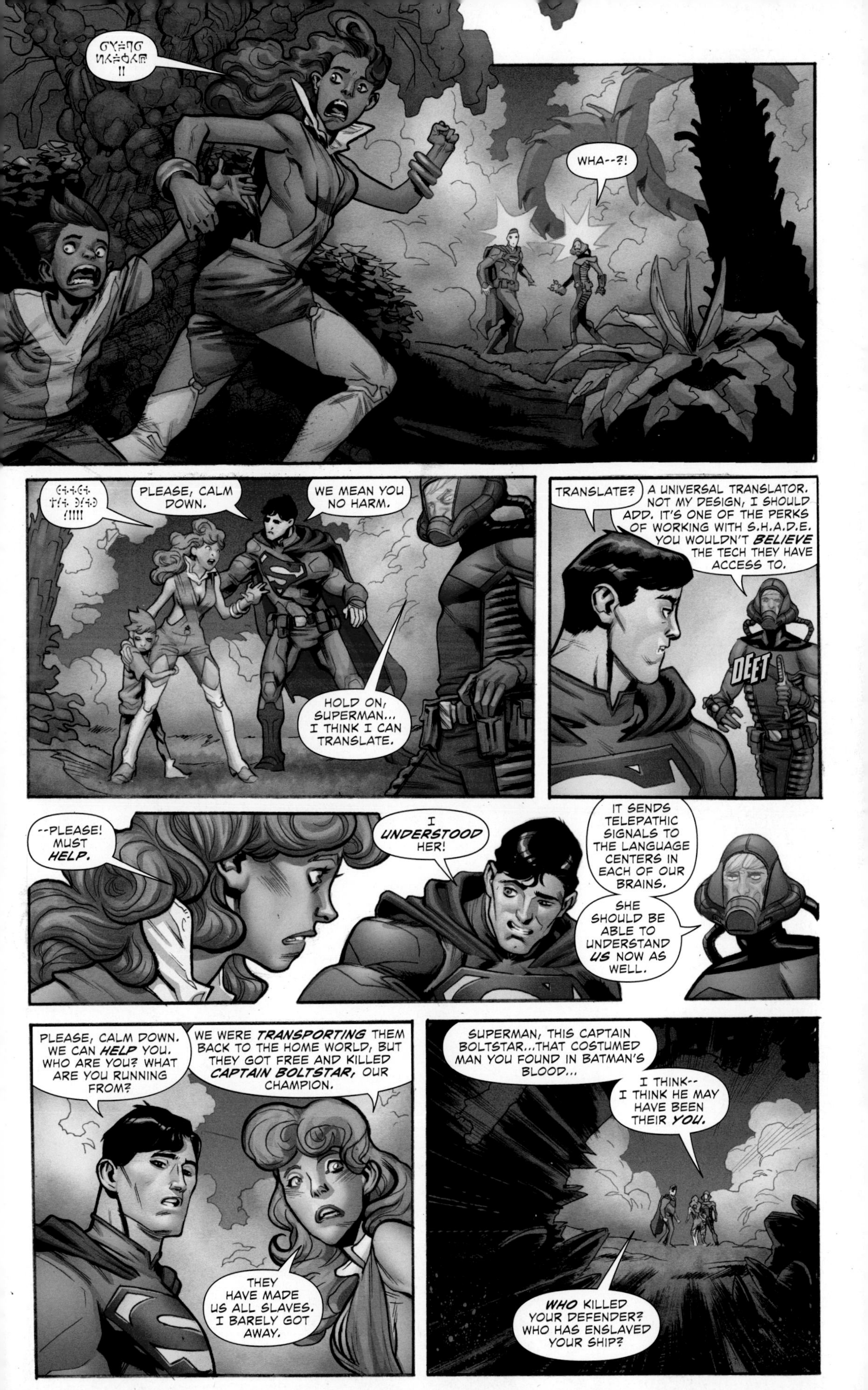
WHA--?!
PLEASE, CALM DOWN.
WE MEAN YOU NO HARM.
HOLD ON, SUPERMAN... I THINK I CAN TRANSLATE.
TRANSLATE?
A UNIVERSAL TRANSLATOR. NOT MY DESIGN, I SHOULD ADD. IT'S ONE OF THE PERKS OF WORKING WITH S.H.A.D.E. YOU WOULDN'T BELIEVE THE TECH THEY HAVE ACCESS TO.
DEET
--PLEASE! MUST HELP.
I UNDERSTOOD HER!
IT SENDS TELEPATHIC SIGNALS TO THE LANGUAGE CENTERS IN EACH OF OUR BRAINS.
SHE SHOULD BE ABLE TO UNDERSTAND US NOW AS WELL.
PLEASE, CALM DOWN. WE CAN HELP YOU. WHO ARE YOU? WHAT ARE YOU RUNNING FROM?
WE WERE TRANSPORTING THEM BACK TO THE HOME WORLD, BUT THEY GOT FREE AND KILLED CAPTAIN BOLTSTAR, OUR CHAMPION.
THEY HAVE MADE US ALL SLAVES. I BARELY GOT AWAY.
SUPERMAN, THIS CAPTAIN BOLTSTAR...THAT COSTUMED MAN YOU FOUND IN BATMAN'S BLOOD...
I THINK-- I THINK HE MAY HAVE BEEN THEIR YOU.
WHO KILLED YOUR DEFENDER? WHO HAS ENSLAVED YOUR SHIP?

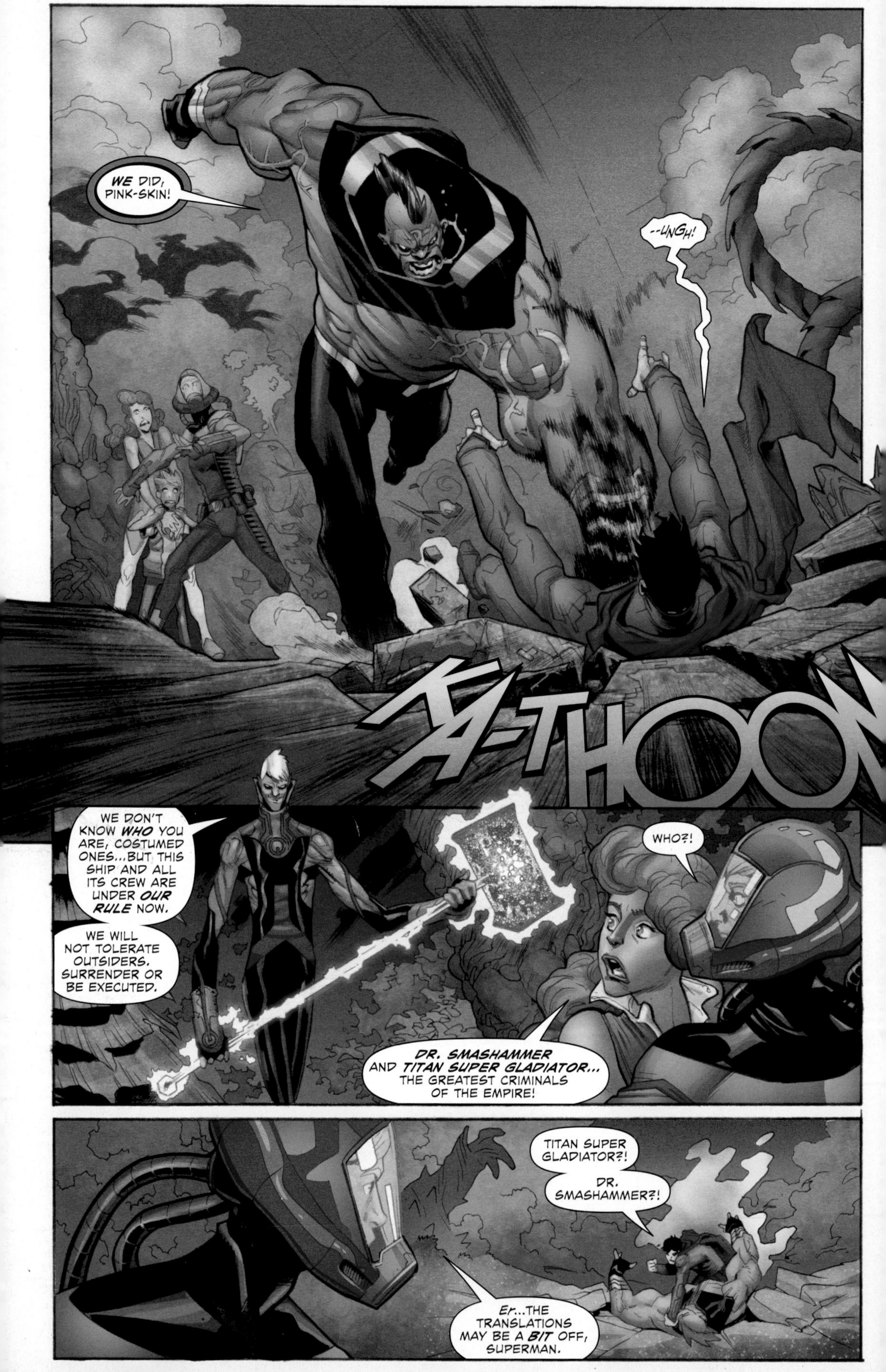
WE DID, PINK-SKIN!
--UNGH!
KA-THOOM
WE DON'T KNOW WHO YOU ARE, COSTUMED ONES...BUT THIS SHIP AND ALL ITS CREW ARE UNDER OUR RULE NOW.
WE WILL NOT TOLERATE OUTSIDERS. SURRENDER OR BE EXECUTED.
WHO?!
DR. SMASHAMMER AND TITAN SUPER GLADIATOR... THE GREATEST CRIMINALS OF THE EMPIRE!
TITAN SUPER GLADIATOR?!
DR. SMASHAMMER?!
Er...THE TRANSLATIONS MAY BE A BIT OFF, SUPERMAN.

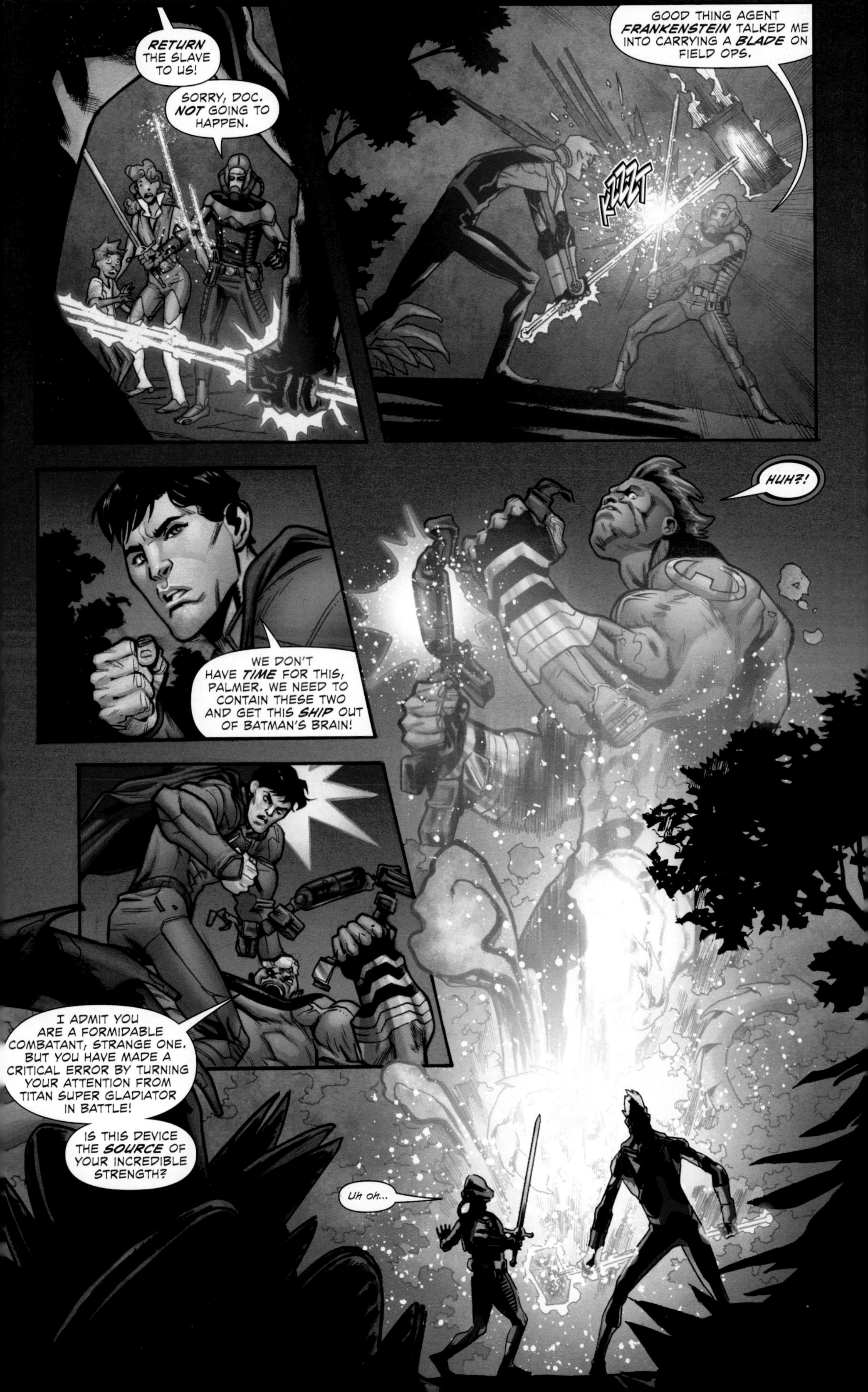

RETURN THE SLAVE TO US!
SORRY, DOC. NOT GOING TO HAPPEN.
GOOD THING AGENT FRANKENSTEIN TALKED ME INTO CARRYING A BLADE ON FIELD OPS.
KZZZT
WE DON'T HAVE TIME FOR THIS, PALMER. WE NEED TO CONTAIN THESE TWO AND GET THIS SHIP OUT OF BATMAN'S BRAIN!
HUH?!
I ADMIT YOU ARE A FORMIDABLE COMBATANT, STRANGE ONE. BUT YOU HAVE MADE A CRITICAL ERROR BY TURNING YOUR ATTENTION FROM TITAN SUPER GLADIATOR IN BATTLE!
IS THIS DEVICE THE SOURCE OF YOUR INCREDIBLE STRENGTH?
Uh oh...

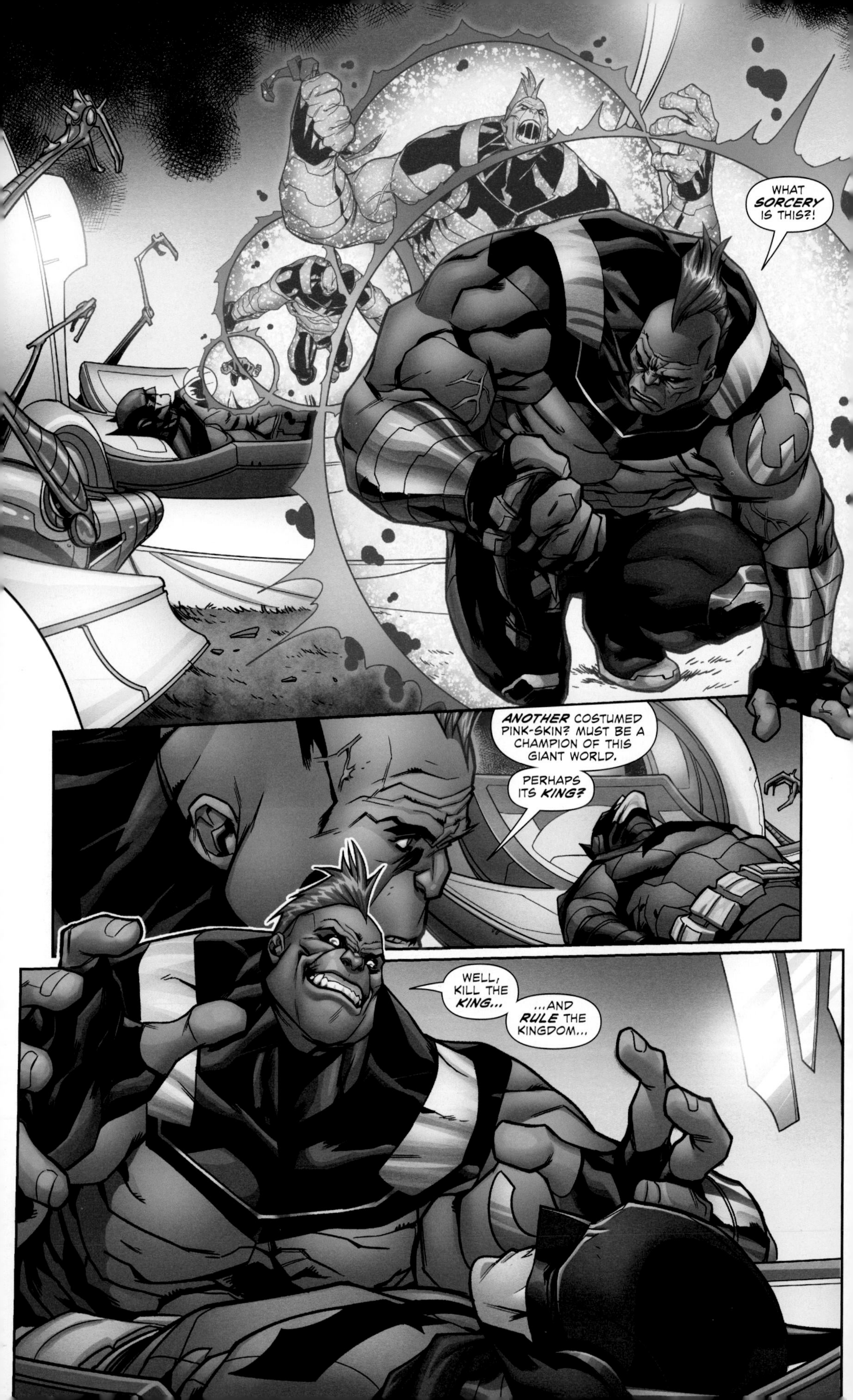
WHAT SORCERY IS THIS?!
ANOTHER COSTUMED PINK-SKIN? MUST BE A CHAMPION OF THIS GIANT WORLD.
PERHAPS ITS KING?
WELL, KILL THE KING...
...AND RULE THE KINGDOM...

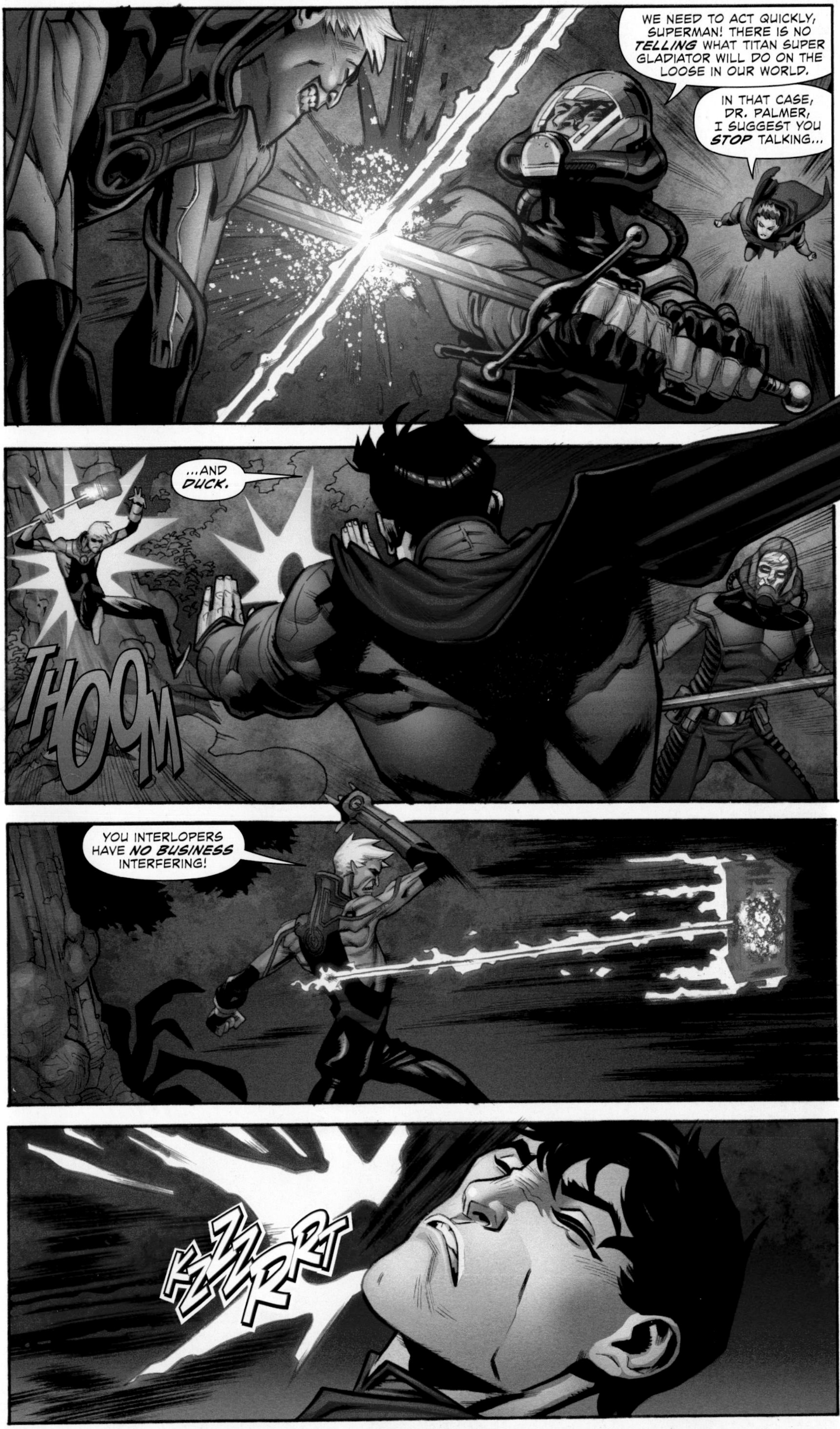
WE NEED TO ACT QUICKLY, SUPERMAN! THERE IS NO TELLING WHAT TITAN SUPER GLADIATOR WILL DO ON THE LOOSE IN OUR WORLD.
IN THAT CASE, DR. PALMER, I SUGGEST YOU STOP TALKING...
...AND DUCK.
THOOM
YOU INTERLOPERS HAVE NO BUSINESS INTERFERING!
KZZZRRRT

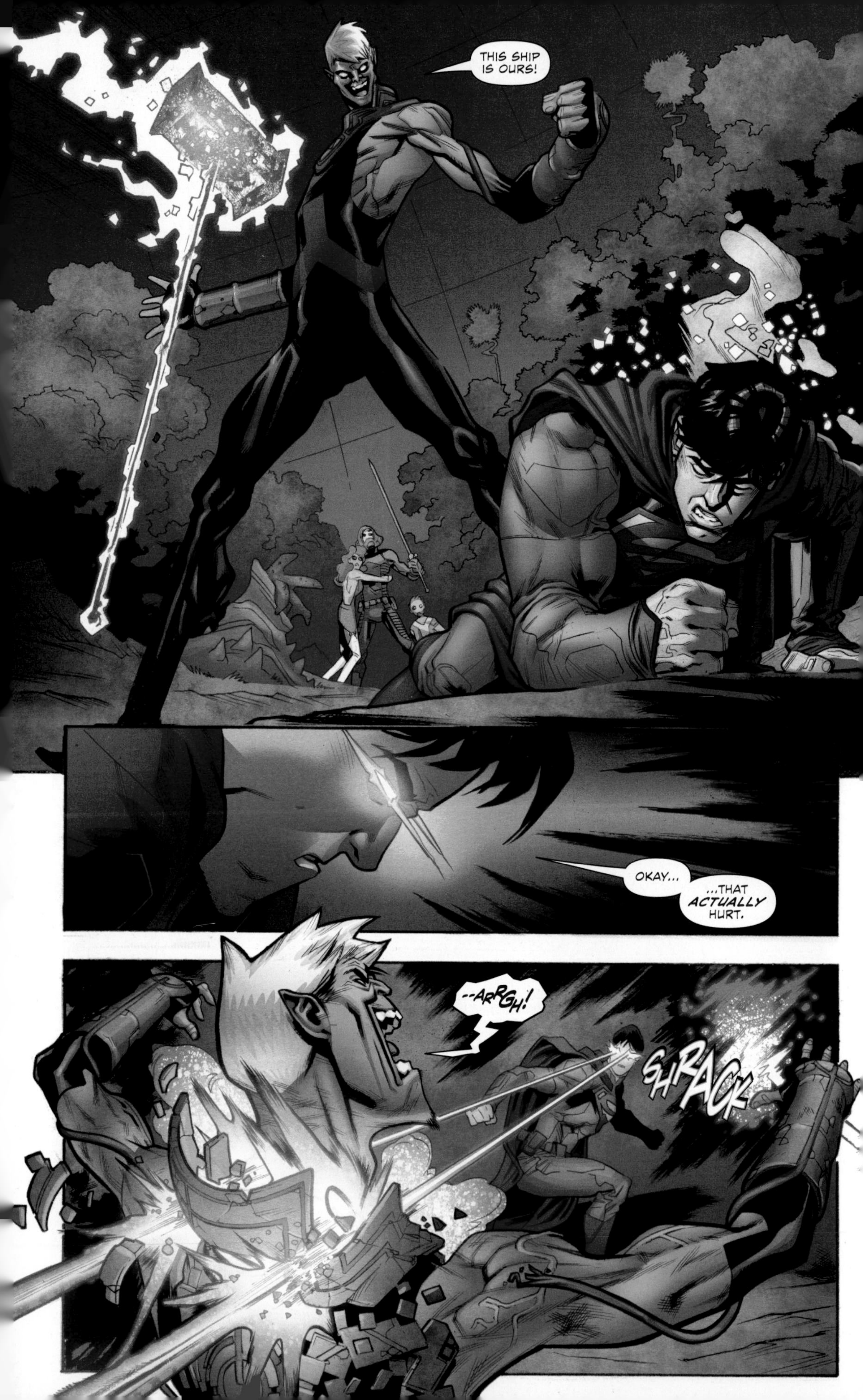
THIS SHIP IS OURS!
OKAY...
...THAT ACTUALLY HURT.
--ARRGH!
SHRACK

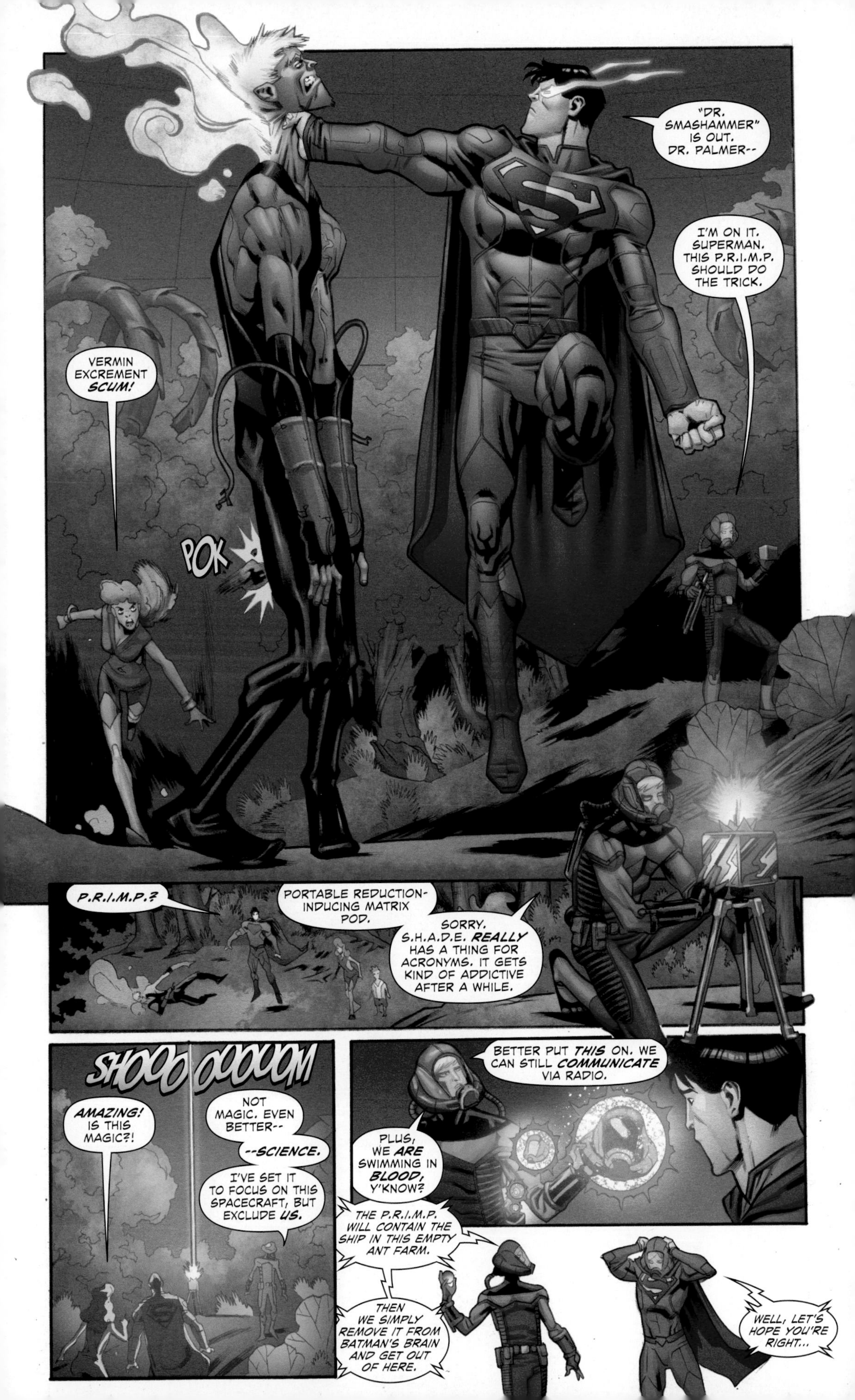
"DR. SMASHAMMER" IS OUT. DR. PALMER--
I'M ON IT. SUPERMAN. THIS P.R.I.M.P. SHOULD DO THE TRICK.
VERMIN EXCREMENT SCUM!
POK
P.R.I.M.P.?
PORTABLE REDUCTION-INDUCING MATRIX POD.
SORRY. S.H.A.D.E. REALLY HAS A THING FOR ACRONYMS. IT GETS KIND OF ADDICTIVE AFTER A WHILE.
SHOOOOOOOOM
AMAZING! IS THIS MAGIC?!
NOT MAGIC. EVEN BETTER--
--SCIENCE.
I'VE SET IT TO FOCUS ON THIS SPACECRAFT, BUT EXCLUDE US.
BETTER PUT THIS ON. WE CAN STILL COMMUNICATE VIA RADIO.
PLUS, WE ARE SWIMMING IN BLOOD, Y'KNOW?
THE P.R.I.M.P. WILL CONTAIN THE SHIP IN THIS EMPTY ANT FARM.
THEN WE SIMPLY REMOVE IT FROM BATMAN'S BRAIN AND GET OUT OF HERE.
WELL, LET'S HOPE YOU'RE RIGHT...

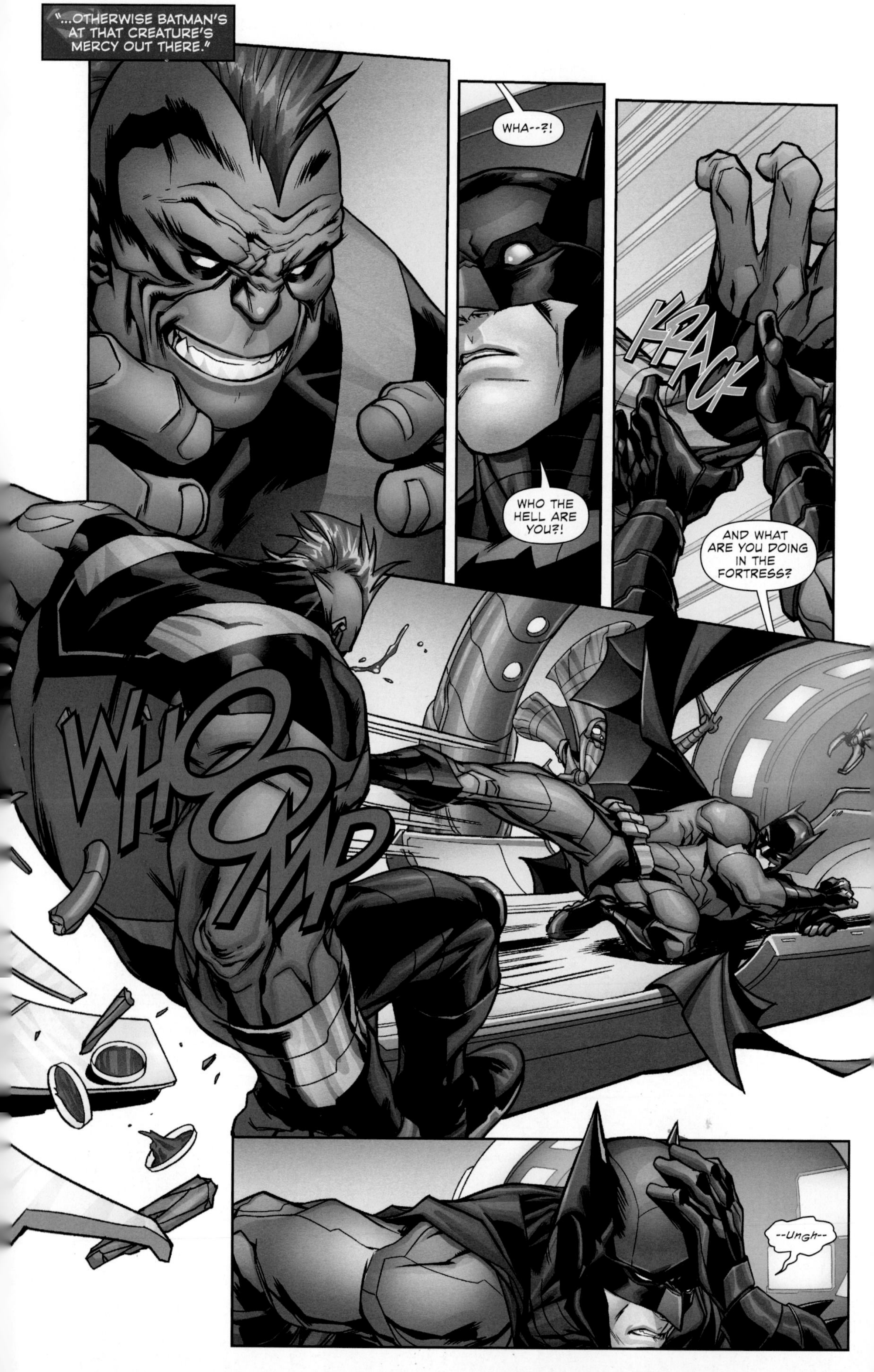
"...OTHERWISE BATMAN'S AT THAT CREATURE'S MERCY OUT THERE."
WHA--?!
KRACK
WHO THE HELL ARE YOU?!
AND WHAT ARE YOU DOING IN THE FORTRESS?
WHOOMP
--Ungh--

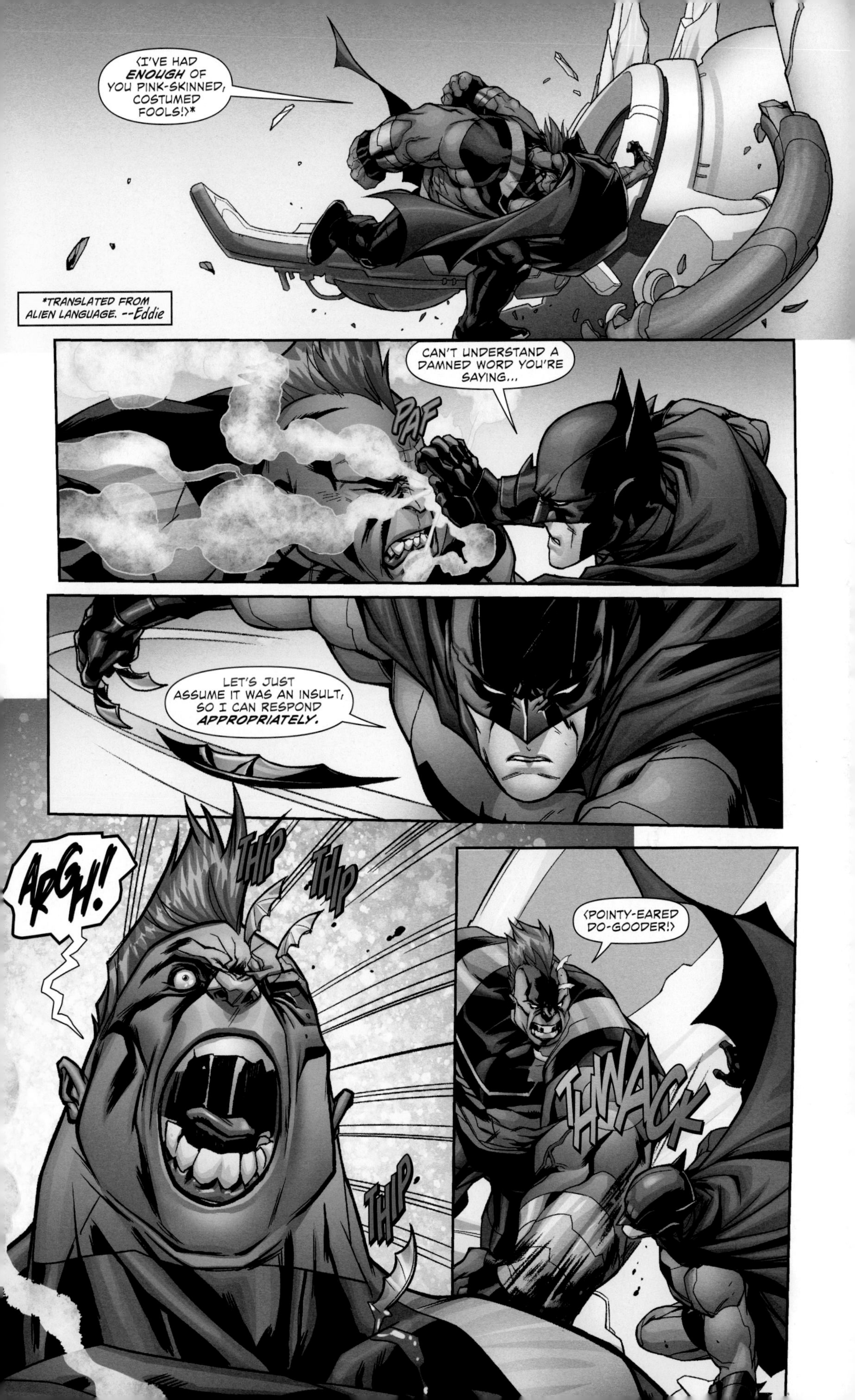

‹I'VE HAD ENOUGH OF YOU PINK-SKINNED, COSTUMED FOOLS!›*
*TRANSLATED FROM ALIEN LANGUAGE. --Eddie
CAN'T UNDERSTAND A DAMNED WORD YOU'RE SAYING...
PAF
LET'S JUST ASSUME IT WAS AN INSULT, SO I CAN RESPOND APPROPRIATELY.
ARGH!
THIP
THIP
THIP
‹POINTY-EARED DO-GOODER!›
THWACK

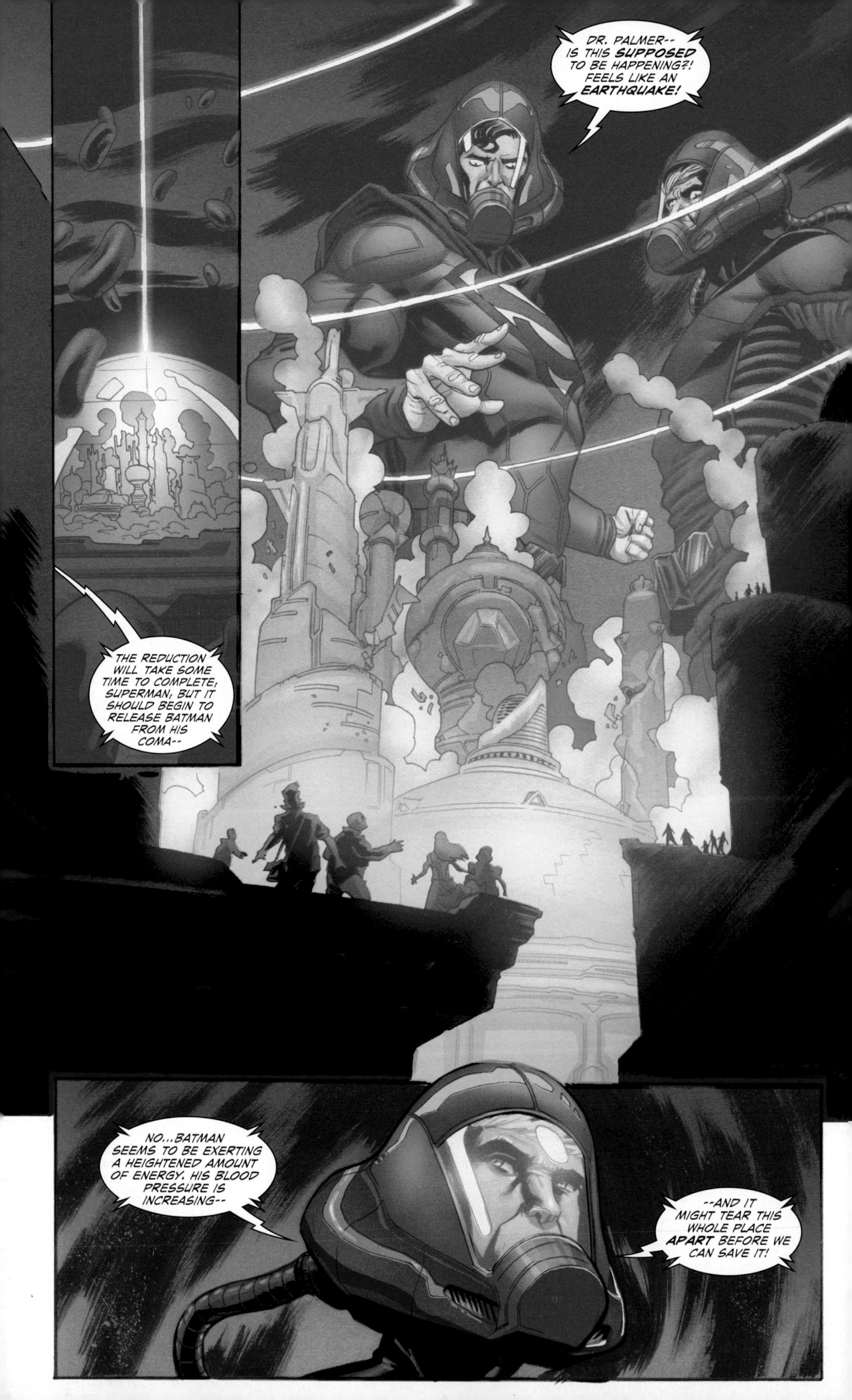
DR. PALMER-- IS THIS **SUPPOSED** TO BE HAPPENING?! FEELS LIKE AN **EARTHQUAKE!**
THE REDUCTION WILL TAKE SOME TIME TO COMPLETE, SUPERMAN, BUT IT SHOULD BEGIN TO RELEASE BATMAN FROM HIS COMA--
NO...BATMAN SEEMS TO BE EXERTING A HEIGHTENED AMOUNT OF ENERGY. HIS BLOOD PRESSURE IS INCREASING--
--AND IT MIGHT TEAR THIS WHOLE PLACE **APART** BEFORE WE CAN SAVE IT!

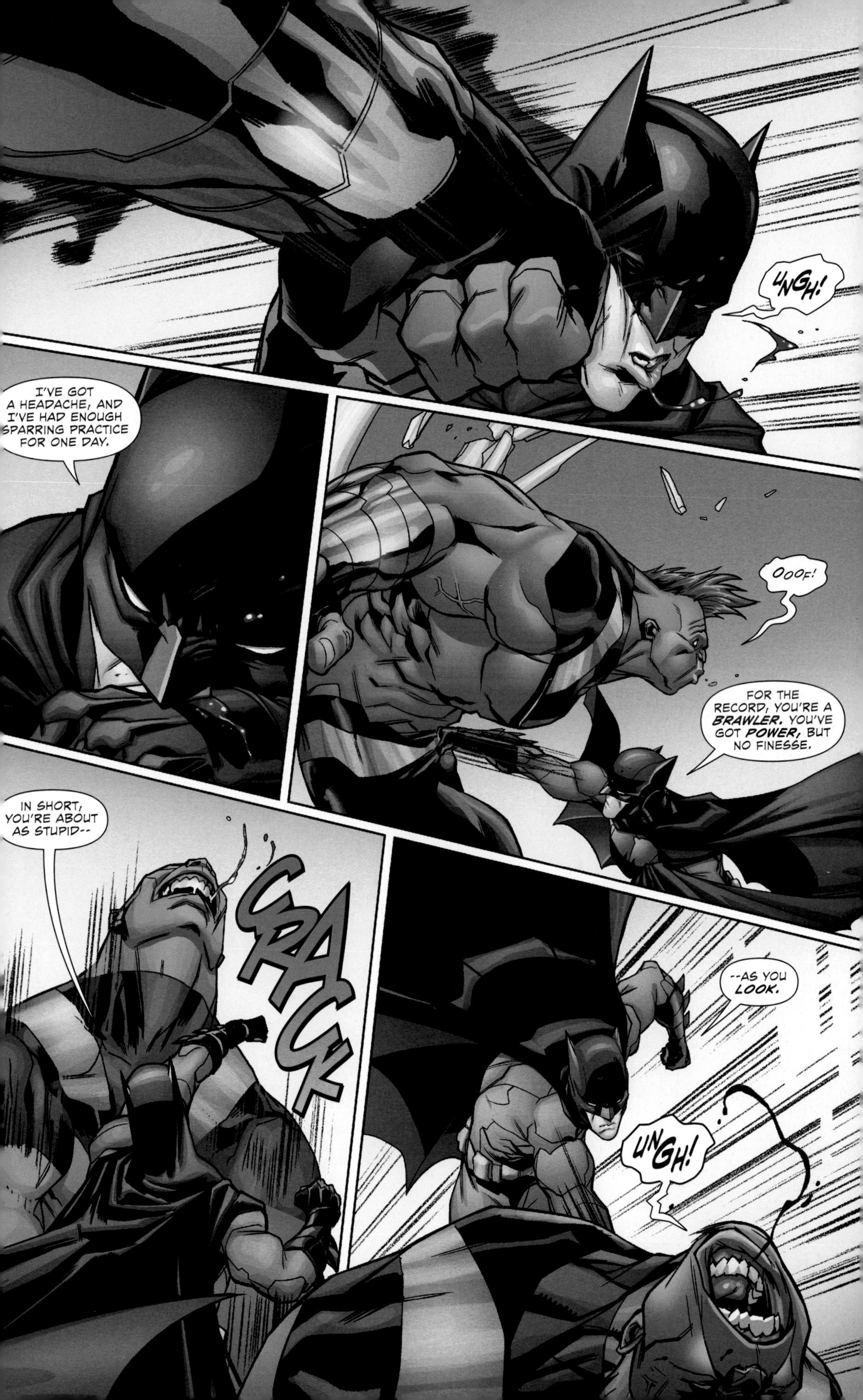
UNGH!
I'VE GOT A HEADACHE, AND I'VE HAD ENOUGH SPARRING PRACTICE FOR ONE DAY.
OOOF!
FOR THE RECORD, YOU'RE A **BRAWLER.** YOU'VE GOT **POWER,** BUT NO FINESSE.
IN SHORT, YOU'RE ABOUT AS STUPID--
CRACK
--AS YOU **LOOK.**
UNGH!

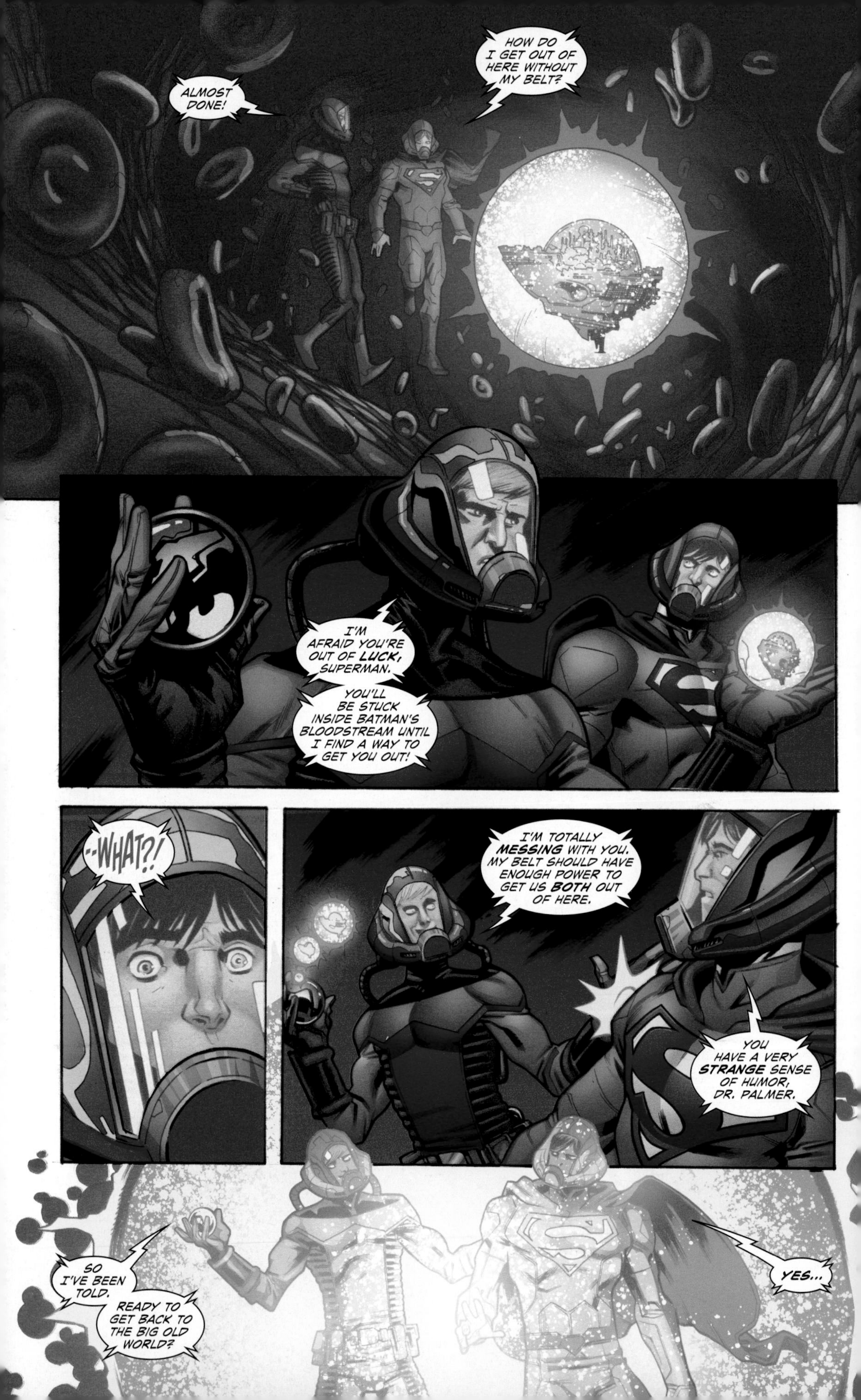
ALMOST DONE!
HOW DO I GET OUT OF HERE WITHOUT MY BELT?
I'M AFRAID YOU'RE OUT OF LUCK, SUPERMAN.
YOU'LL BE STUCK INSIDE BATMAN'S BLOODSTREAM UNTIL I FIND A WAY TO GET YOU OUT!
--WHAT?!
I'M TOTALLY MESSING WITH YOU. MY BELT SHOULD HAVE ENOUGH POWER TO GET US BOTH OUT OF HERE.
YOU HAVE A VERY STRANGE SENSE OF HUMOR, DR. PALMER.
SO I'VE BEEN TOLD.
READY TO GET BACK TO THE BIG OLD WORLD?
YES...

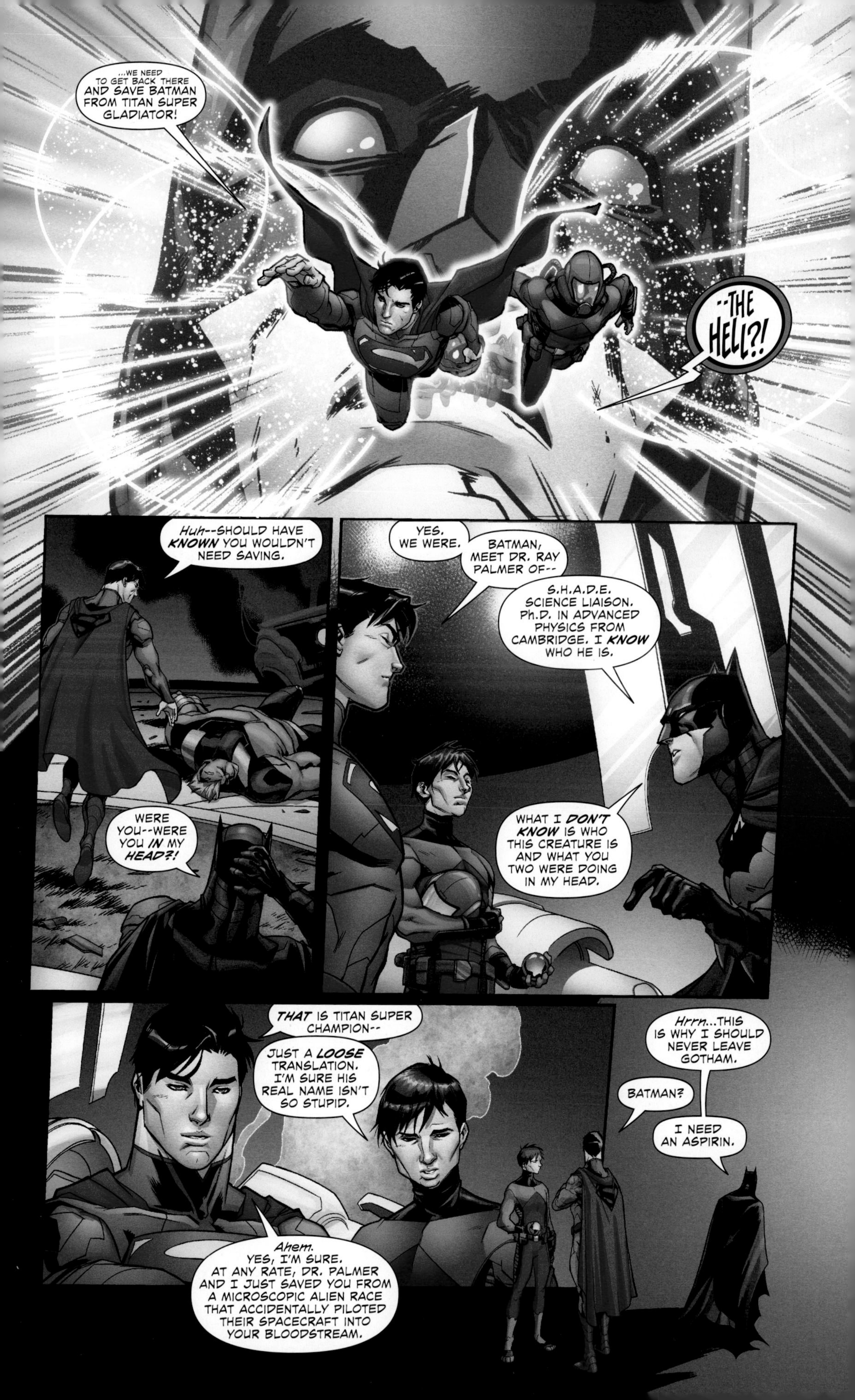
...WE NEED TO GET BACK THERE AND SAVE BATMAN FROM TITAN SUPER GLADIATOR!
--THE HELL?!
Huh--SHOULD HAVE ***KNOWN*** YOU WOULDN'T NEED SAVING.
WERE YOU--WERE YOU ***IN*** MY ***HEAD?!***
YES. WE WERE.
BATMAN, MEET DR. RAY PALMER OF--
S.H.A.D.E. SCIENCE LIAISON. Ph.D. IN ADVANCED PHYSICS FROM CAMBRIDGE. I ***KNOW*** WHO HE IS.
WHAT I ***DON'T KNOW*** IS WHO THIS CREATURE IS AND WHAT YOU TWO WERE DOING IN MY HEAD.
THAT IS TITAN SUPER CHAMPION--
JUST A ***LOOSE*** TRANSLATION. I'M SURE HIS REAL NAME ISN'T SO STUPID.
Ahem. YES, I'M SURE. AT ANY RATE, DR. PALMER AND I JUST SAVED YOU FROM A MICROSCOPIC ALIEN RACE THAT ACCIDENTALLY PILOTED THEIR SPACECRAFT INTO YOUR BLOODSTREAM.
Hrrn...THIS IS WHY I SHOULD NEVER LEAVE GOTHAM.
BATMAN?
I NEED AN ASPIRIN.

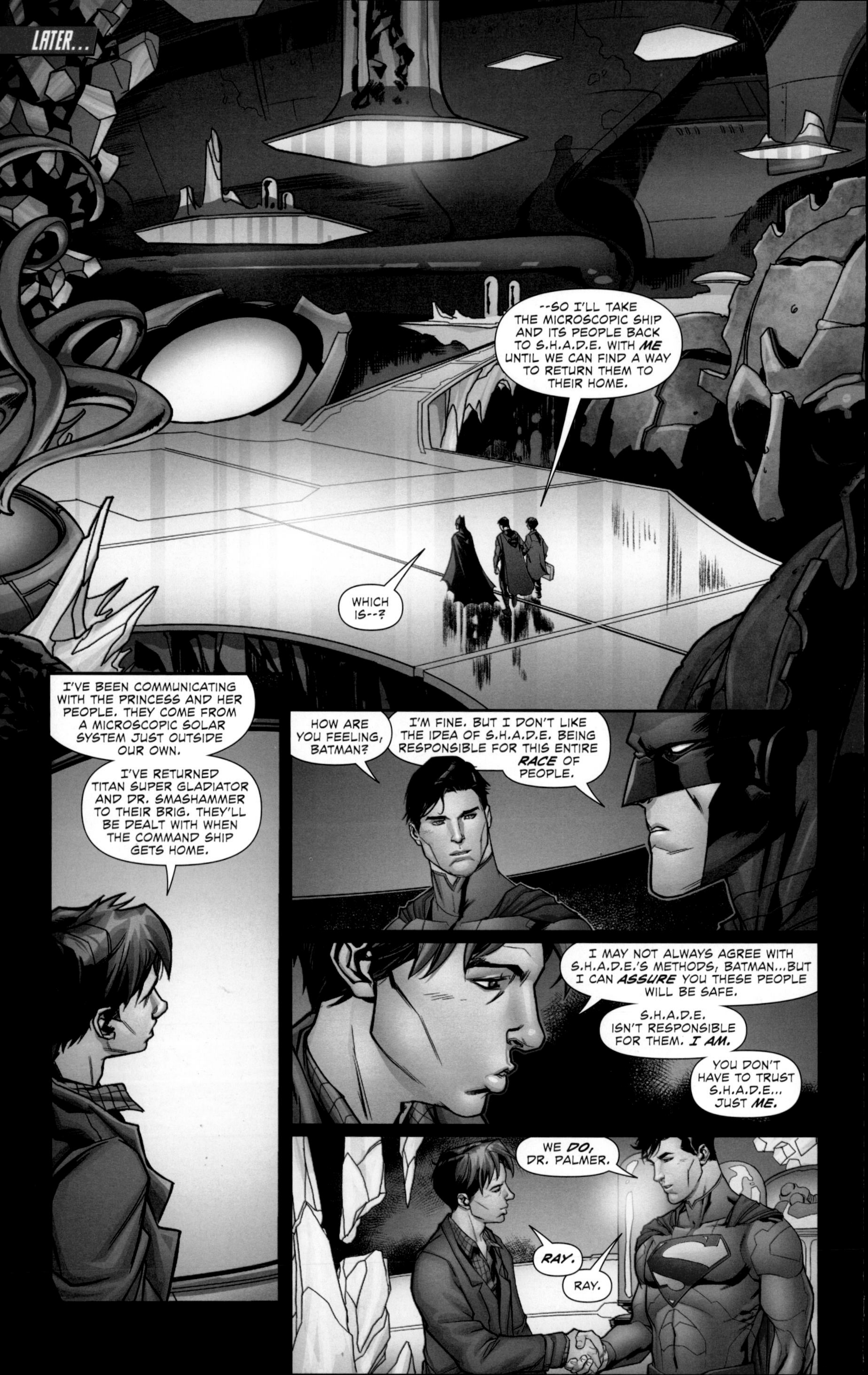
LATER...
--SO I'LL TAKE THE MICROSCOPIC SHIP AND ITS PEOPLE BACK TO S.H.A.D.E. WITH ME UNTIL WE CAN FIND A WAY TO RETURN THEM TO THEIR HOME.
WHICH IS--?
I'VE BEEN COMMUNICATING WITH THE PRINCESS AND HER PEOPLE. THEY COME FROM A MICROSCOPIC SOLAR SYSTEM JUST OUTSIDE OUR OWN.
I'VE RETURNED TITAN SUPER GLADIATOR AND DR. SMASHAMMER TO THEIR BRIG. THEY'LL BE DEALT WITH WHEN THE COMMAND SHIP GETS HOME.
HOW ARE YOU FEELING, BATMAN?
I'M FINE. BUT I DON'T LIKE THE IDEA OF S.H.A.D.E. BEING RESPONSIBLE FOR THIS ENTIRE RACE OF PEOPLE.
I MAY NOT ALWAYS AGREE WITH S.H.A.D.E.'S METHODS, BATMAN...BUT I CAN ASSURE YOU THESE PEOPLE WILL BE SAFE.
S.H.A.D.E. ISN'T RESPONSIBLE FOR THEM. I AM.
YOU DON'T HAVE TO TRUST S.H.A.D.E... JUST ME.
WE DO, DR. PALMER.
RAY.
RAY.

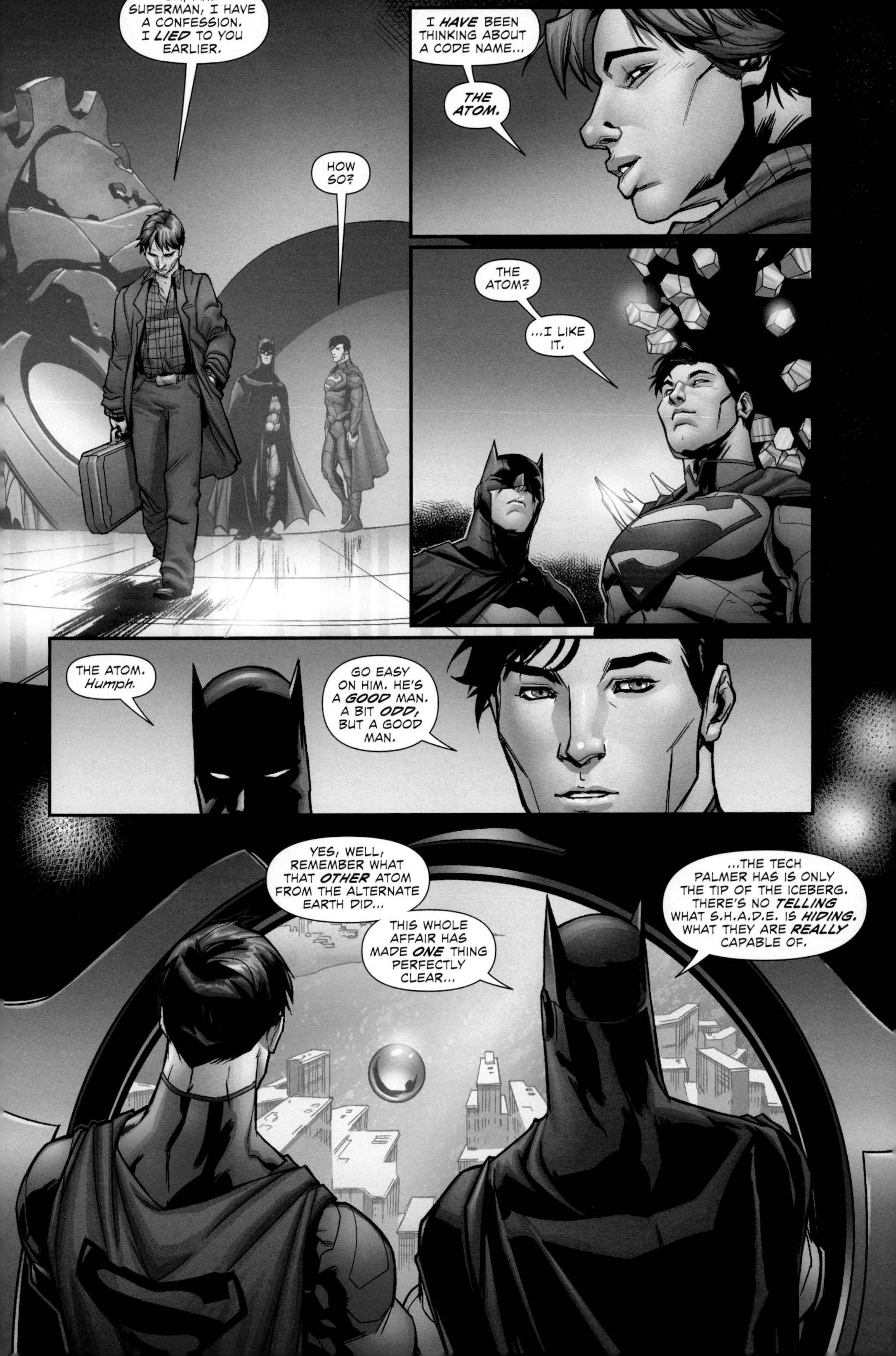
OH, AND SUPERMAN, I HAVE A CONFESSION. I LIED TO YOU EARLIER.
HOW SO?
I HAVE BEEN THINKING ABOUT A CODE NAME...
THE ATOM.
THE ATOM?
...I LIKE IT.
THE ATOM. Humph.
GO EASY ON HIM. HE'S A GOOD MAN. A BIT ODD, BUT A GOOD MAN.
YES, WELL, REMEMBER WHAT THAT OTHER ATOM FROM THE ALTERNATE EARTH DID...
THIS WHOLE AFFAIR HAS MADE ONE THING PERFECTLY CLEAR...
...THE TECH PALMER HAS IS ONLY THE TIP OF THE ICEBERG. THERE'S NO TELLING WHAT S.H.A.D.E. IS HIDING. WHAT THEY ARE REALLY CAPABLE OF.

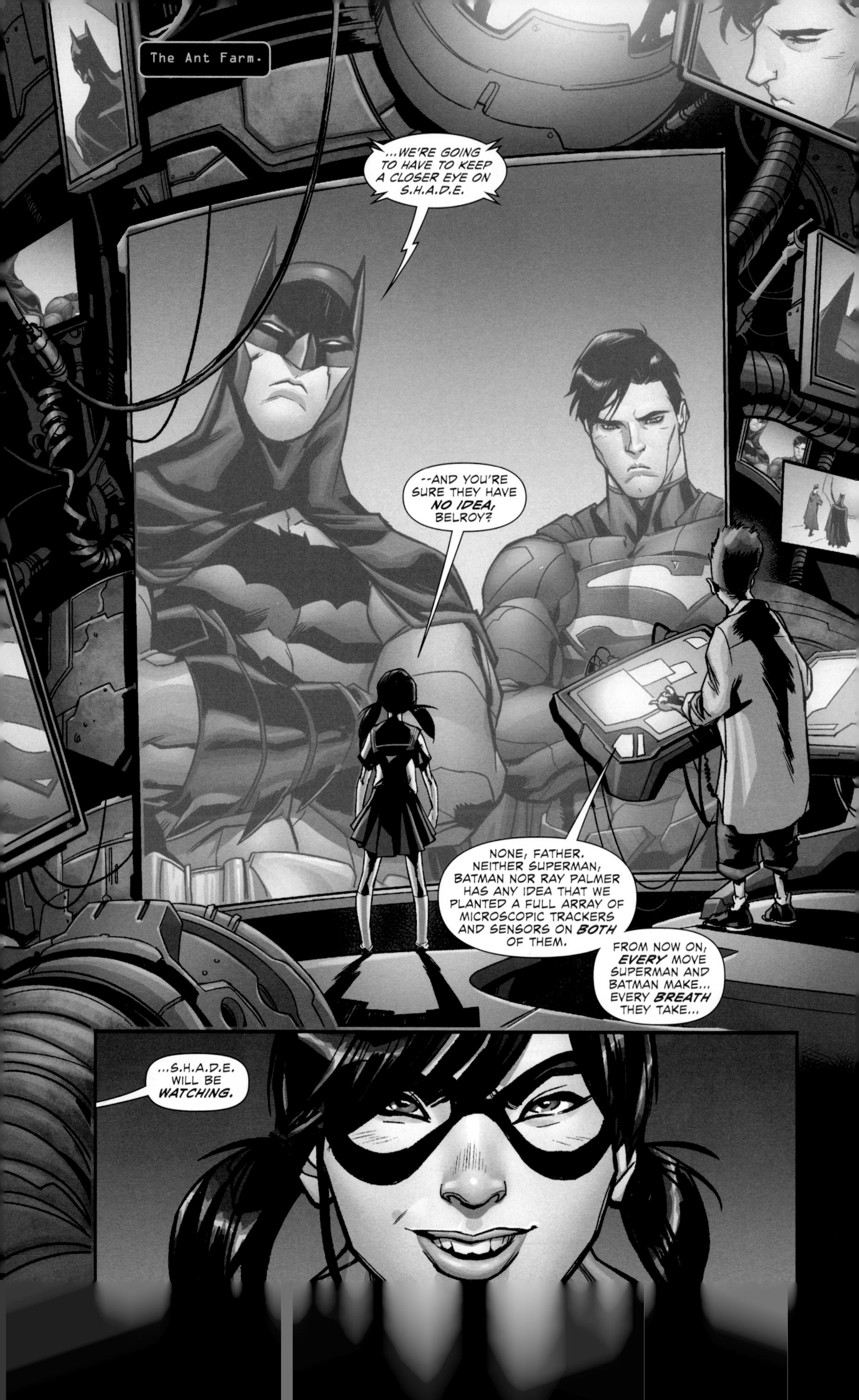
The Ant Farm.
...WE'RE GOING TO HAVE TO KEEP A CLOSER EYE ON S.H.A.D.E.
--AND YOU'RE SURE THEY HAVE NO IDEA, BELROY?
NONE, FATHER. NEITHER SUPERMAN, BATMAN NOR RAY PALMER HAS ANY IDEA THAT WE PLANTED A FULL ARRAY OF MICROSCOPIC TRACKERS AND SENSORS ON BOTH OF THEM.
FROM NOW ON, EVERY MOVE SUPERMAN AND BATMAN MAKE... EVERY BREATH THEY TAKE...
...S.H.A.D.E. WILL BE WATCHING.

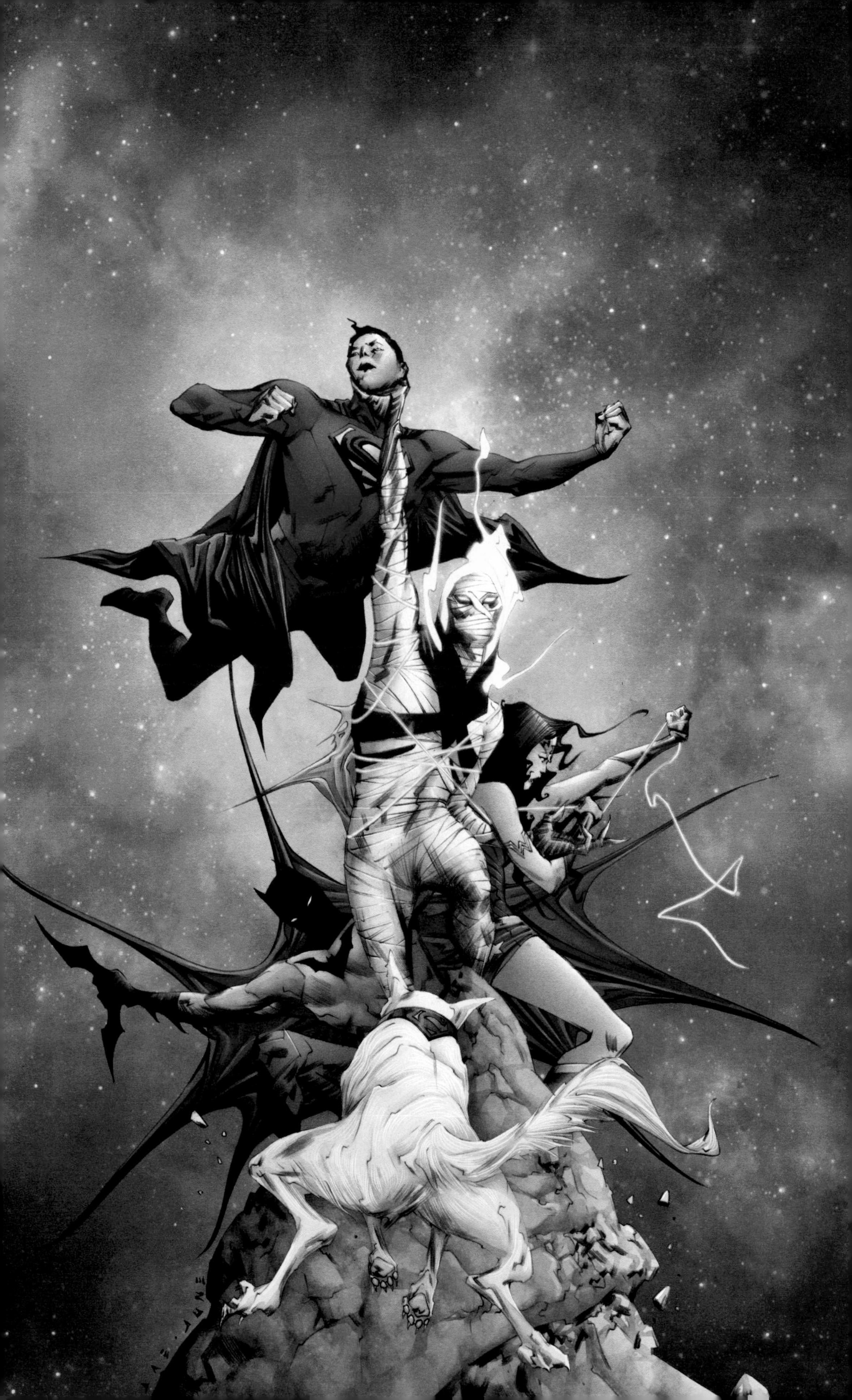

DANGER ZONE

GREG PAK writer **KARL KERSCHL TOM DERENICK DANIEL SAMPERE** pencillers **KARL KERSCHL VICENTE CIFUENTES MARC DEERING WAYNE FAUCHER DANIEL SAMPERE** inkers **HI-FI** colorist **ROB LEIGH** letterer cover by **JAE LEE** with **JUNE CHUNG**

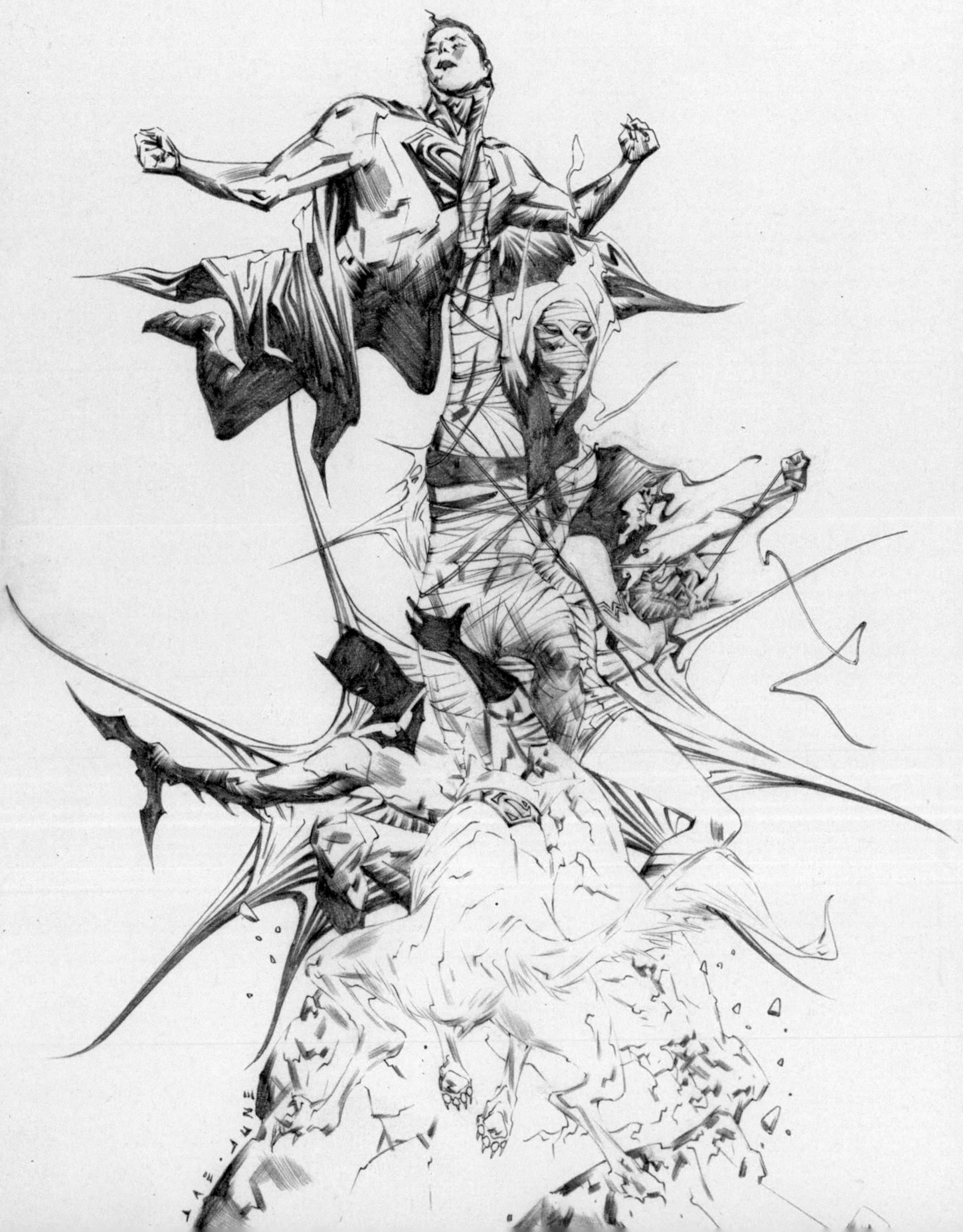

WORLD   U.S.   METROPOLIS   BUSINESS   OPINION   SPORTS   ARTS   STYLE   VIDEO

May 21, 2014

Daily Planet

DAILY PLANET

SUPER-MENACE!

Photo by James Olsen

By Lois Lane

It was the Boom heard around the world. Everyone's worst fears have come true as Superman seems to be infected with what S.T.A.R. Labs officials can only speculate is a virus from the creature the world has come to know as Doomsday.

The Kryptonian's affliction became public knowledge after fellow Justice Leaguers Wonder Woman and Batman tried to contain him in a battle that shook the entirety of New Troy island in Metropolis.

Miraculously, no one was hurt, but many residents on Clinton Street report severe property damage from the fight.

At present, it seems that Superman has turned himself in to authorities, and at the behest of Senator Samuel Lane many prominent scientists have been brought in to study the case, among them Dr. Ray Palmer, Dr. Shay Veritas and Lex Luthor, who just had this to say: "We do not know what is happening to Superman. We hope for the best, but none of us have ever faced anything like this," adding, "Unfortunately, we do know what this could evolve into, and we have to be prepared to contain it, or exterminate it in any way possible."

Watch exclusive video footage of the destruction in the Bahamas.

Metropolis Mayhem, locals report their Super-encounters

"Doomsday" origins recovery in the northwestern Indies

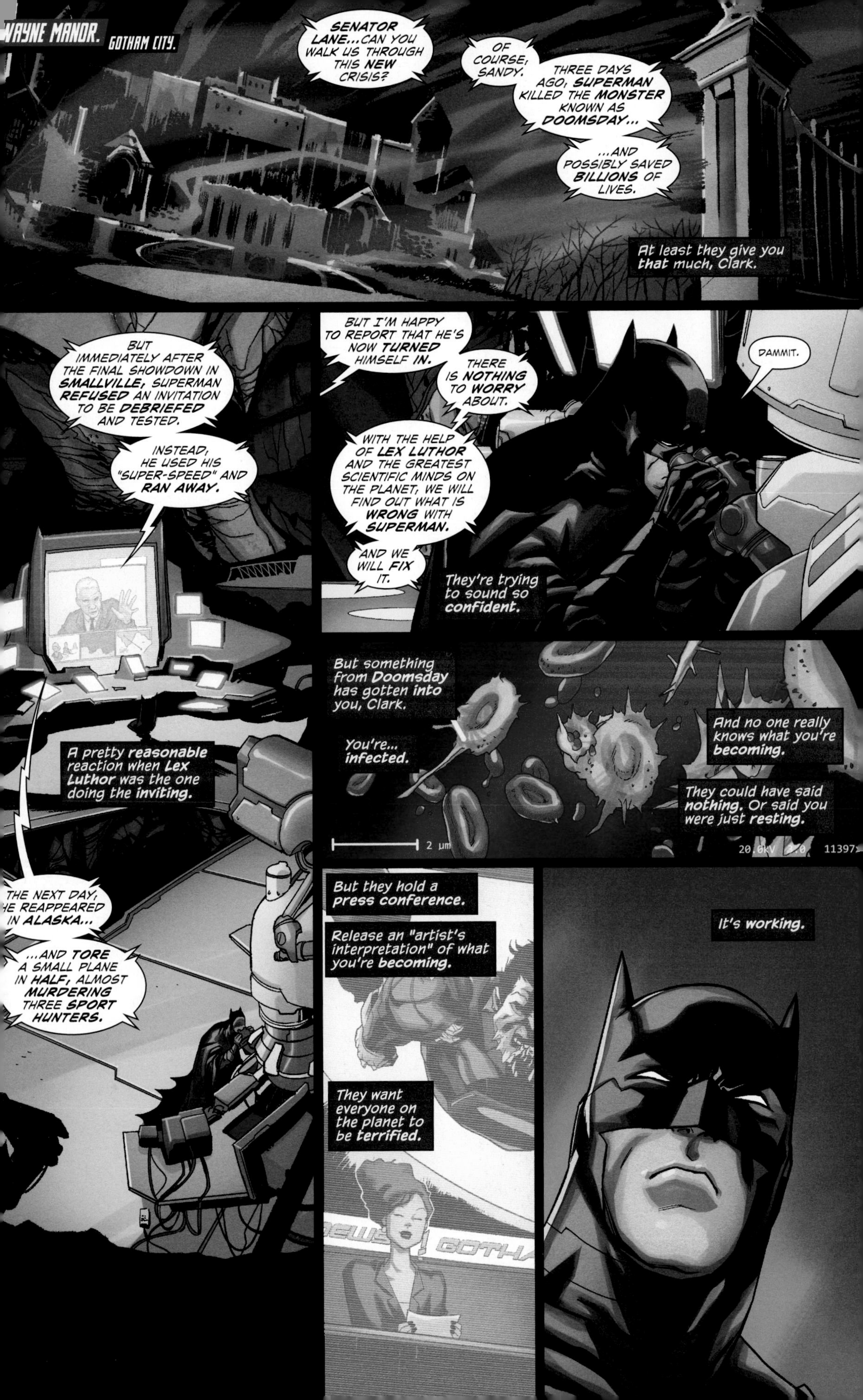
WAYNE MANOR. GOTHAM CITY.
SENATOR LANE...CAN YOU WALK US THROUGH THIS NEW CRISIS?
OF COURSE, SANDY.
THREE DAYS AGO, SUPERMAN KILLED THE MONSTER KNOWN AS DOOMSDAY...
...AND POSSIBLY SAVED BILLIONS OF LIVES.
At least they give you that much, Clark.
BUT IMMEDIATELY AFTER THE FINAL SHOWDOWN IN SMALLVILLE, SUPERMAN REFUSED AN INVITATION TO BE DEBRIEFED AND TESTED.
INSTEAD, HE USED HIS "SUPER-SPEED" AND RAN AWAY.
A pretty reasonable reaction when Lex Luthor was the one doing the inviting.
THE NEXT DAY, HE REAPPEARED IN ALASKA...
...AND TORE A SMALL PLANE IN HALF, ALMOST MURDERING THREE SPORT HUNTERS.
BUT I'M HAPPY TO REPORT THAT HE'S NOW TURNED HIMSELF IN.
THERE IS NOTHING TO WORRY ABOUT.
WITH THE HELP OF LEX LUTHOR AND THE GREATEST SCIENTIFIC MINDS ON THE PLANET, WE WILL FIND OUT WHAT IS WRONG WITH SUPERMAN.
AND WE WILL FIX IT.
DAMMIT.
They're trying to sound so confident.
But something from Doomsday has gotten into you, Clark.
You're... infected.
And no one really knows what you're becoming.
They could have said nothing. Or said you were just resting.
2 μm
But they hold a press conference.
Release an "artist's interpretation" of what you're becoming.
They want everyone on the planet to be terrified.
It's working.

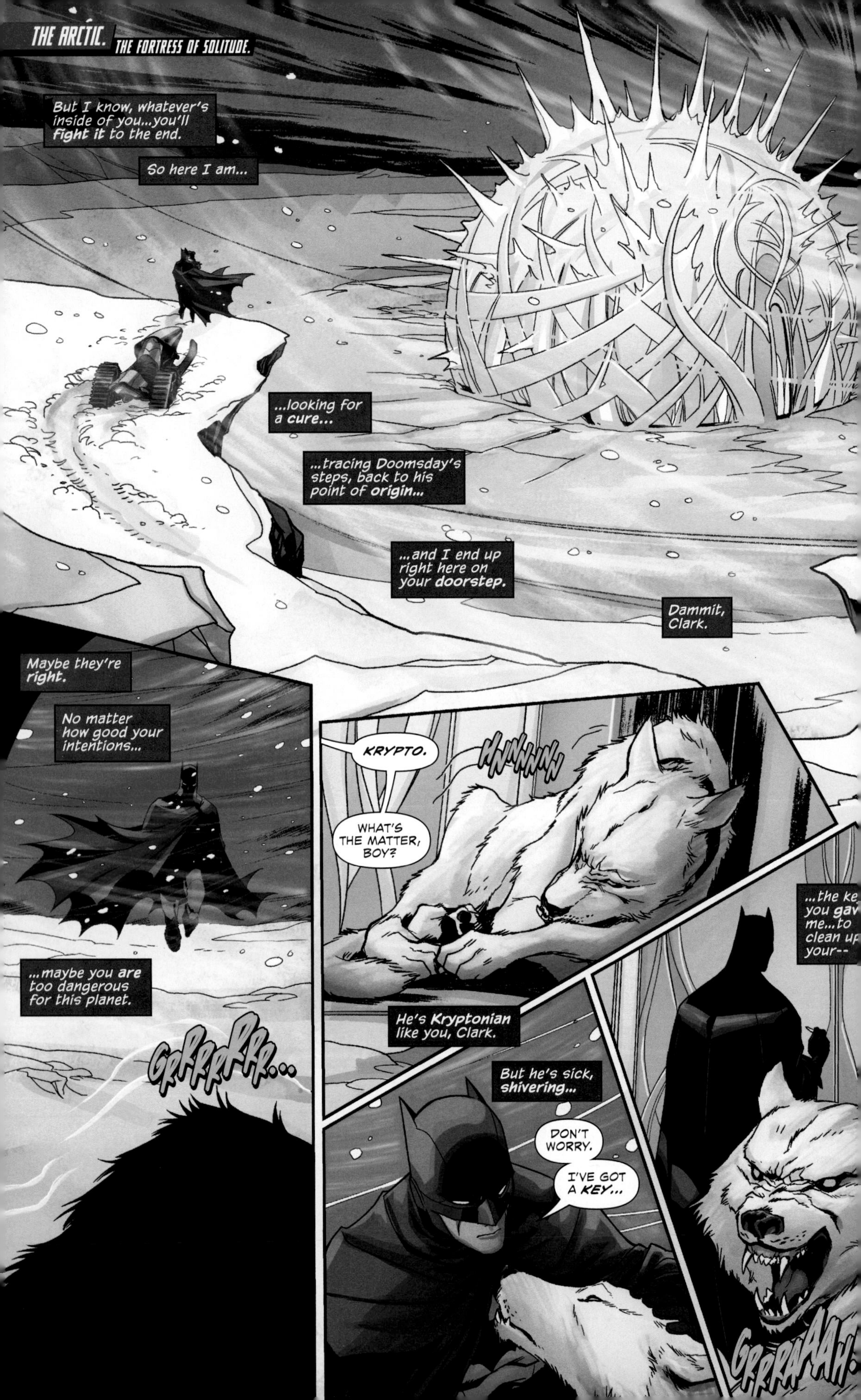
THE ARCTIC.
THE FORTRESS OF SOLITUDE.
But I know, whatever's inside of you...you'll fight it to the end.
So here I am...
...looking for a cure...
...tracing Doomsday's steps, back to his point of origin...
...and I end up right here on your doorstep.
Dammit, Clark.
Maybe they're right.
No matter how good your intentions...
...maybe you are too dangerous for this planet.
GRRRRRR...
KRYPTO.
HNNNNNN
WHAT'S THE MATTER, BOY?
He's Kryptonian like you, Clark.
But he's sick, shivering...
DON'T WORRY.
I'VE GOT A KEY...
GRRRAAAH!

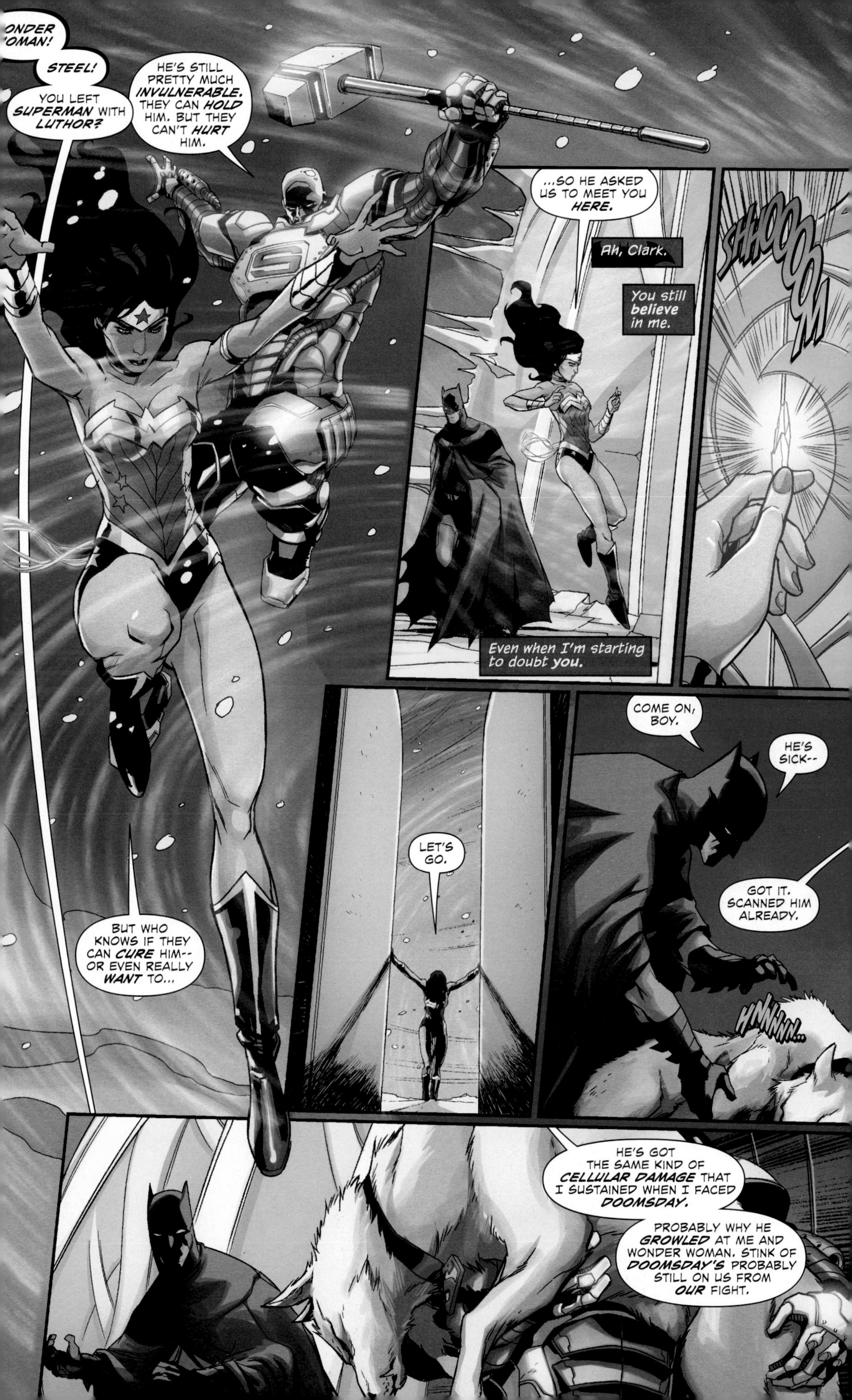

ONDER
OMAN!
STEEL!
YOU LEFT SUPERMAN WITH LUTHOR?
HE'S STILL PRETTY MUCH INVULNERABLE. THEY CAN HOLD HIM. BUT THEY CAN'T HURT HIM.
BUT WHO KNOWS IF THEY CAN CURE HIM-- OR EVEN REALLY WANT TO...
...SO HE ASKED US TO MEET YOU HERE.
Ah, Clark.
You still believe in me.
Even when I'm starting to doubt you.
SHHOOOOM
LET'S GO.
COME ON, BOY.
HE'S SICK--
GOT IT. SCANNED HIM ALREADY.
HNNNNN...
HE'S GOT THE SAME KIND OF CELLULAR DAMAGE THAT I SUSTAINED WHEN I FACED DOOMSDAY.
PROBABLY WHY HE GROWLED AT ME AND WONDER WOMAN. STINK OF DOOMSDAY'S PROBABLY STILL ON US FROM OUR FIGHT.

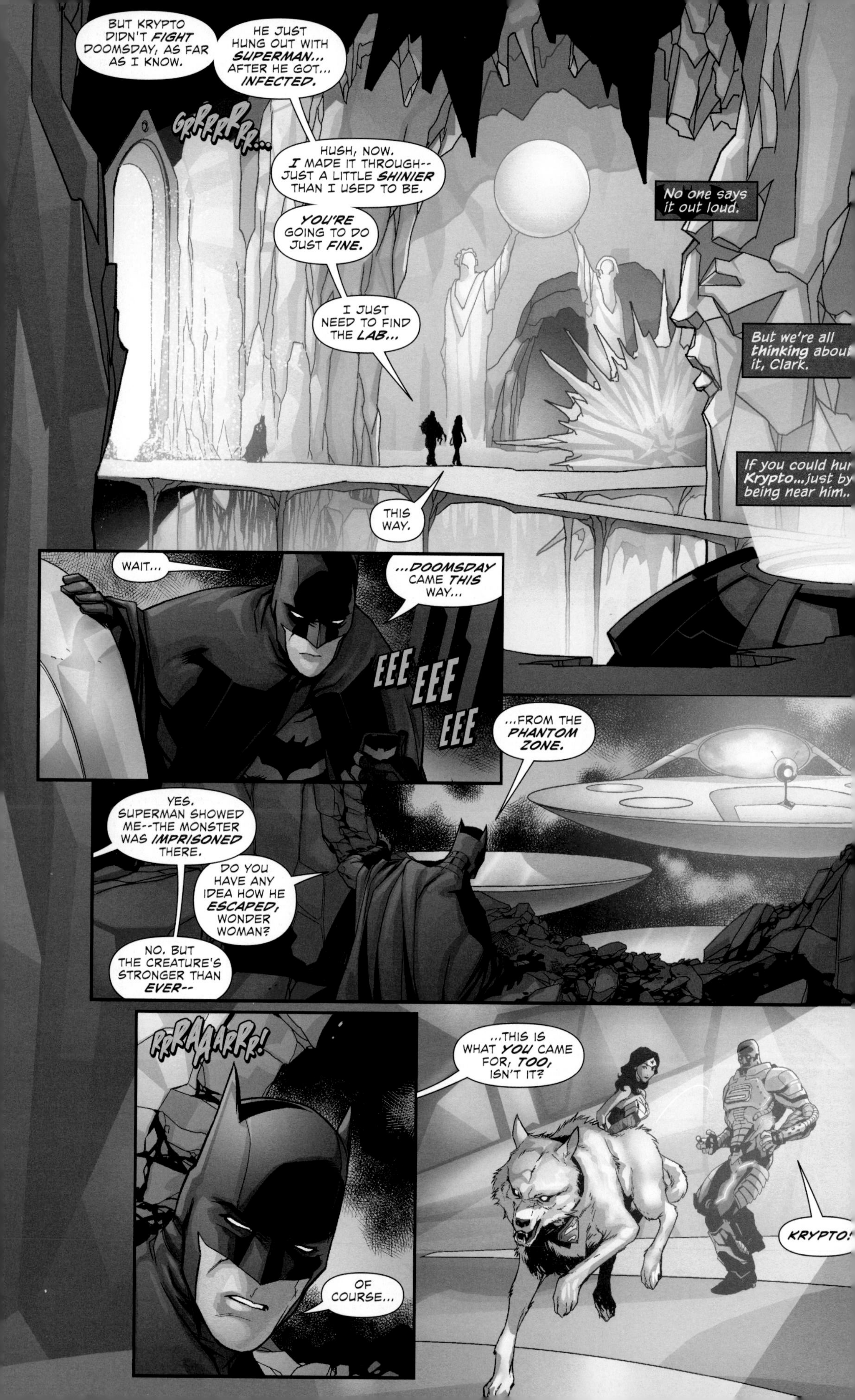
BUT KRYPTO DIDN'T FIGHT DOOMSDAY, AS FAR AS I KNOW.
HE JUST HUNG OUT WITH SUPERMAN... AFTER HE GOT... INFECTED.
GRRRRRR...
HUSH, NOW. I MADE IT THROUGH--JUST A LITTLE SHINIER THAN I USED TO BE.
YOU'RE GOING TO DO JUST FINE.
I JUST NEED TO FIND THE LAB...
THIS WAY.
No one says it out loud.
But we're all thinking about it, Clark.
If you could hurt Krypto...just by being near him..
WAIT...
...DOOMSDAY CAME THIS WAY...
EEE EEE EEE
...FROM THE PHANTOM ZONE.
YES. SUPERMAN SHOWED ME--THE MONSTER WAS IMPRISONED THERE.
DO YOU HAVE ANY IDEA HOW HE ESCAPED, WONDER WOMAN?
NO. BUT THE CREATURE'S STRONGER THAN EVER--
RRRAAARRR!
...THIS IS WHAT YOU CAME FOR, TOO, ISN'T IT?
OF COURSE...
KRYPTO!

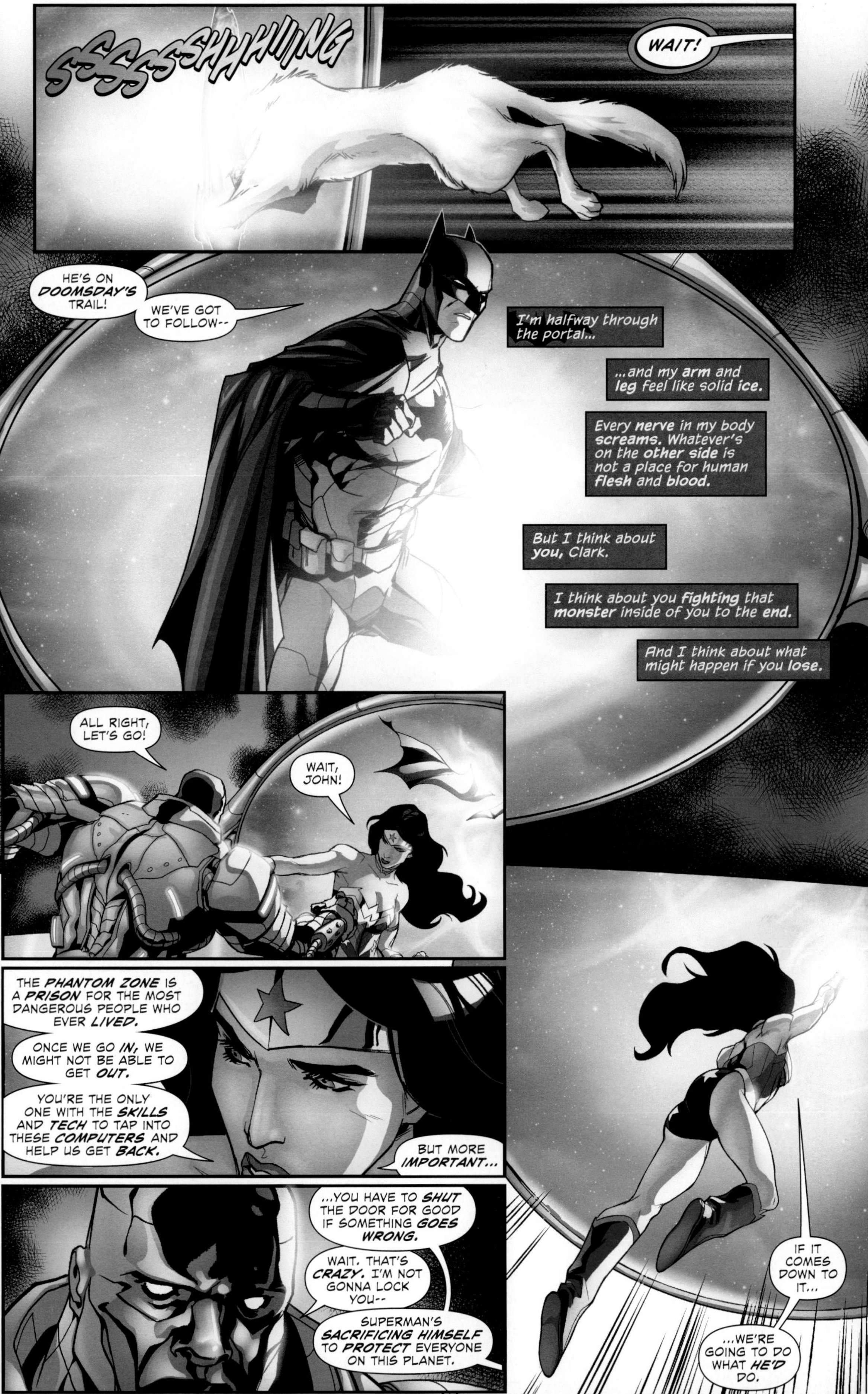
SSSSSSHHHHING
WAIT!
HE'S ON DOOMSDAY'S TRAIL!
WE'VE GOT TO FOLLOW--
I'm halfway through the portal...
...and my arm and leg feel like solid ice.
Every nerve in my body screams. Whatever's on the other side is not a place for human flesh and blood.
But I think about you, Clark.
I think about you fighting that monster inside of you to the end.
And I think about what might happen if you lose.
ALL RIGHT, LET'S GO!
WAIT, JOHN!
THE PHANTOM ZONE IS A PRISON FOR THE MOST DANGEROUS PEOPLE WHO EVER LIVED.
ONCE WE GO IN, WE MIGHT NOT BE ABLE TO GET OUT.
YOU'RE THE ONLY ONE WITH THE SKILLS AND TECH TO TAP INTO THESE COMPUTERS AND HELP US GET BACK.
BUT MORE IMPORTANT...
...YOU HAVE TO SHUT THE DOOR FOR GOOD IF SOMETHING GOES WRONG.
WAIT. THAT'S CRAZY. I'M NOT GONNA LOCK YOU--
SUPERMAN'S SACRIFICING HIMSELF TO PROTECT EVERYONE ON THIS PLANET.
IF IT COMES DOWN TO IT...
...WE'RE GOING TO DO WHAT HE'D DO.

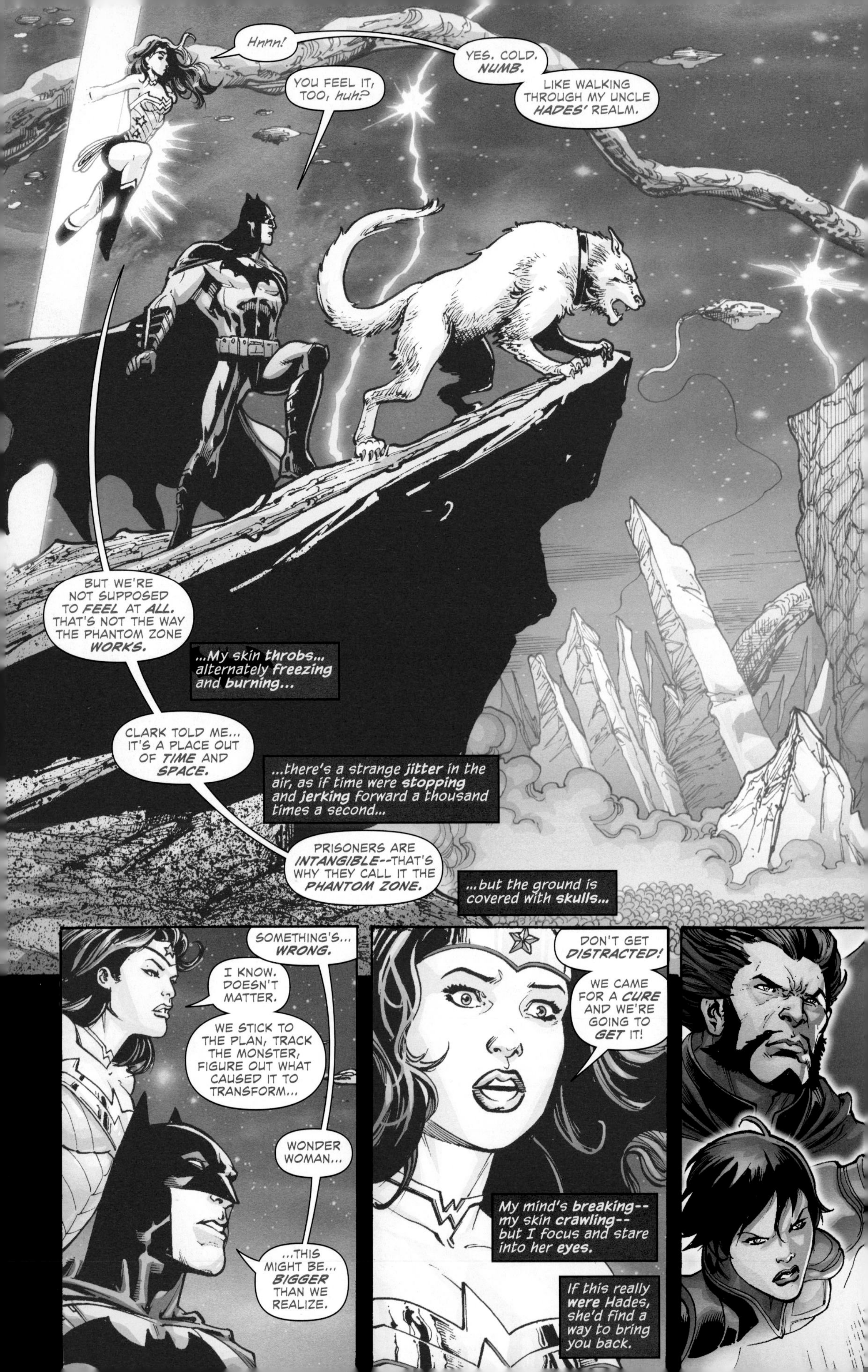
Hnnn!
YOU FEEL IT, TOO, huh?
YES. COLD. NUMB.
LIKE WALKING THROUGH MY UNCLE HADES' REALM.
BUT WE'RE NOT SUPPOSED TO FEEL AT ALL. THAT'S NOT THE WAY THE PHANTOM ZONE WORKS.
...My skin throbs... alternately freezing and burning...
CLARK TOLD ME... IT'S A PLACE OUT OF TIME AND SPACE.
...there's a strange jitter in the air, as if time were stopping and jerking forward a thousand times a second...
PRISONERS ARE INTANGIBLE--THAT'S WHY THEY CALL IT THE PHANTOM ZONE.
...but the ground is covered with skulls...
SOMETHING'S... WRONG.
I KNOW. DOESN'T MATTER.
WE STICK TO THE PLAN, TRACK THE MONSTER, FIGURE OUT WHAT CAUSED IT TO TRANSFORM...
WONDER WOMAN...
...THIS MIGHT BE... BIGGER THAN WE REALIZE.
DON'T GET DISTRACTED!
WE CAME FOR A CURE AND WE'RE GOING TO GET IT!
My mind's breaking--my skin crawling--but I focus and stare into her eyes.
If this really were Hades, she'd find a way to bring you back.

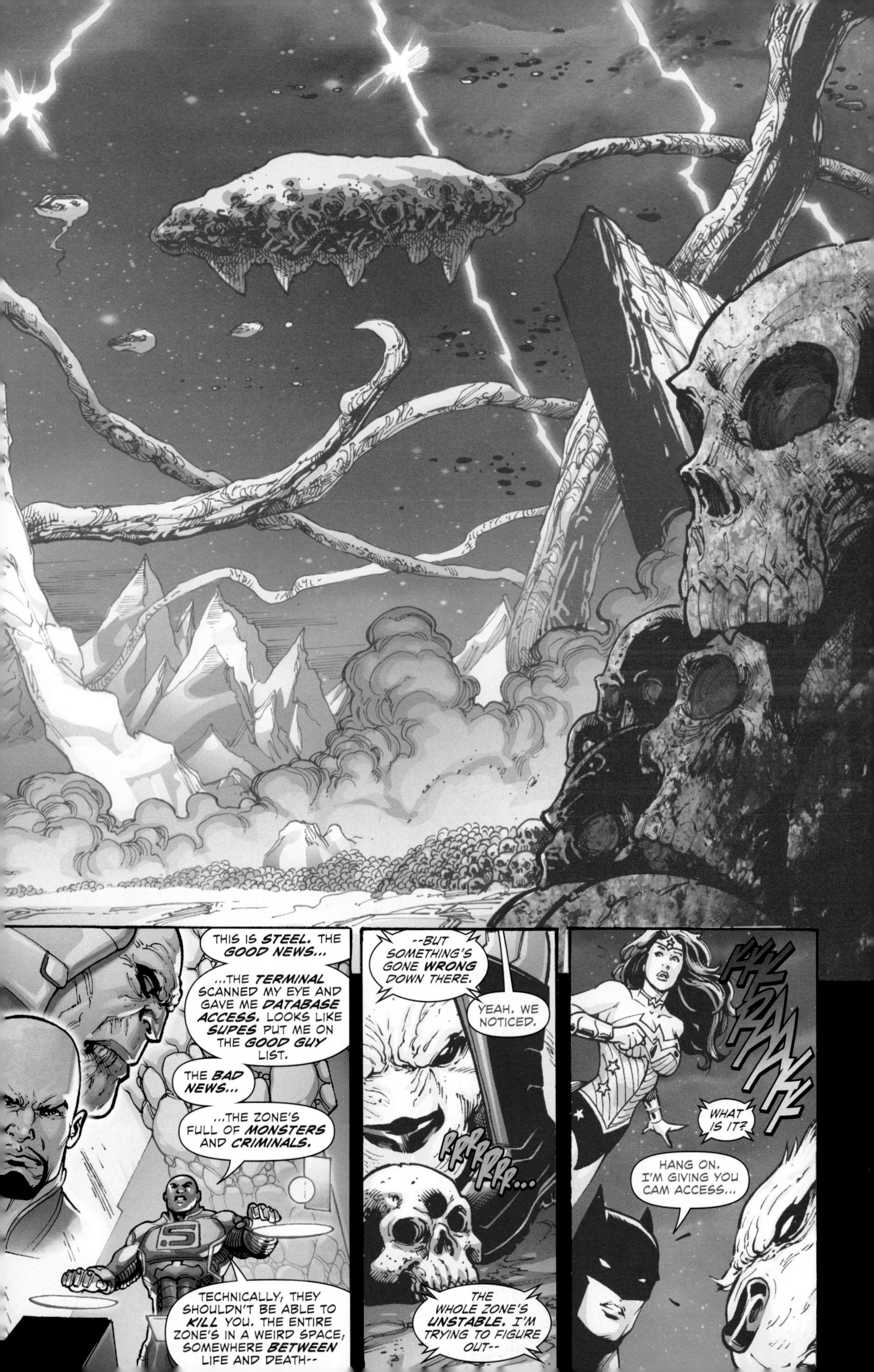
THIS IS STEEL. THE GOOD NEWS...
...THE TERMINAL SCANNED MY EYE AND GAVE ME DATABASE ACCESS. LOOKS LIKE SUPES PUT ME ON THE GOOD GUY LIST.
THE BAD NEWS...
...THE ZONE'S FULL OF MONSTERS AND CRIMINALS.
TECHNICALLY, THEY SHOULDN'T BE ABLE TO KILL YOU. THE ENTIRE ZONE'S IN A WEIRD SPACE, SOMEWHERE BETWEEN LIFE AND DEATH--
--BUT SOMETHING'S GONE WRONG DOWN THERE.
YEAH. WE NOTICED.
RRRRRRR...
THE WHOLE ZONE'S UNSTABLE. I'M TRYING TO FIGURE OUT--
KKRAKK
WHAT IS IT?
HANG ON. I'M GIVING YOU CAM ACCESS...

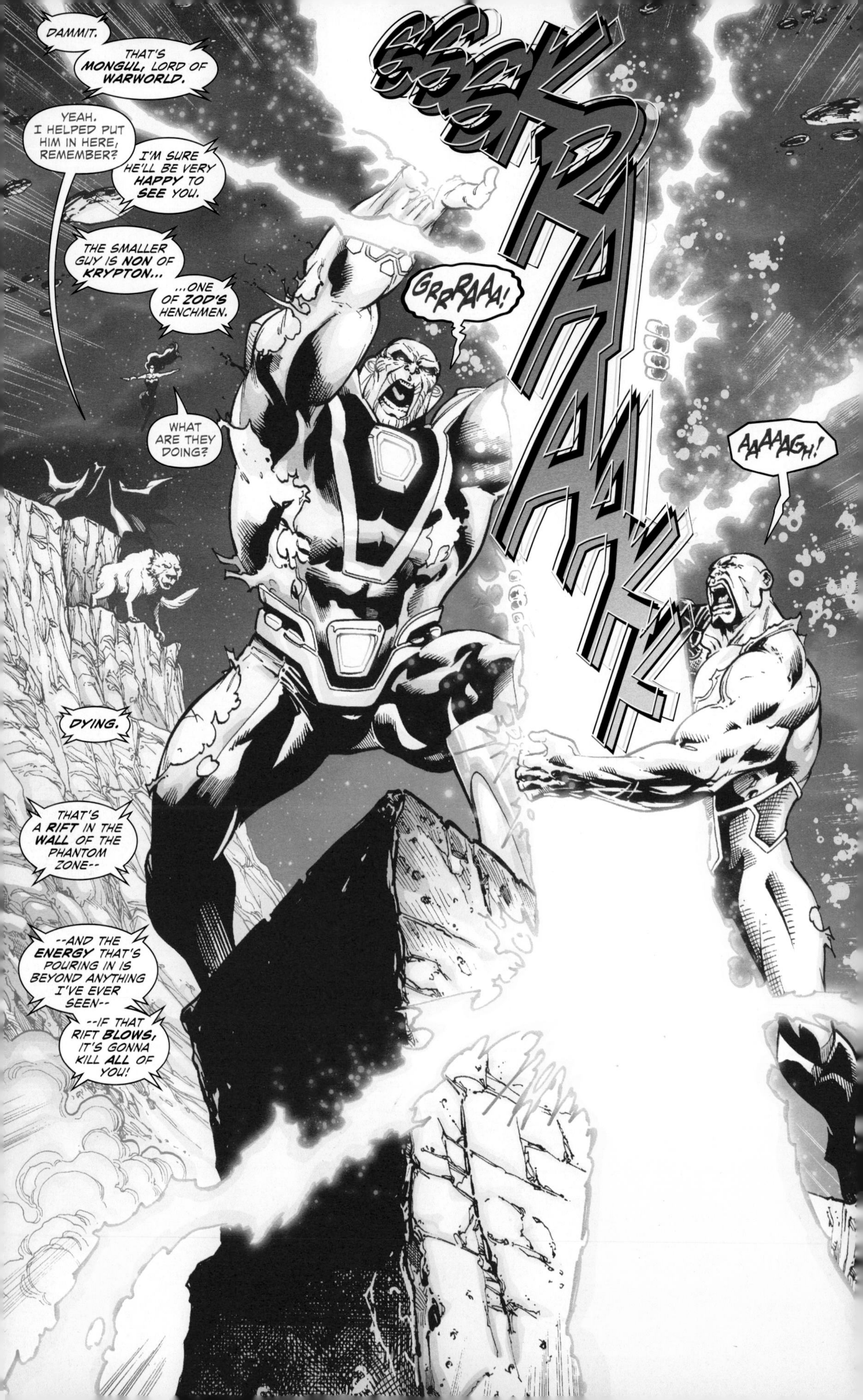

DAMMIT.
THAT'S MONGUL, LORD OF WARWORLD.
YEAH. I HELPED PUT HIM IN HERE, REMEMBER?
I'M SURE HE'LL BE VERY HAPPY TO SEE YOU.
THE SMALLER GUY IS NON OF KRYPTON...
...ONE OF ZOD'S HENCHMEN.
WHAT ARE THEY DOING?
GRRRAAAA!
SSSKRAKAKAKK
AAAAAGH!
DYING.
THAT'S A RIFT IN THE WALL OF THE PHANTOM ZONE--
--AND THE ENERGY THAT'S POURING IN IS BEYOND ANYTHING I'VE EVER SEEN--
--IF THAT RIFT BLOWS, IT'S GONNA KILL ALL OF YOU!

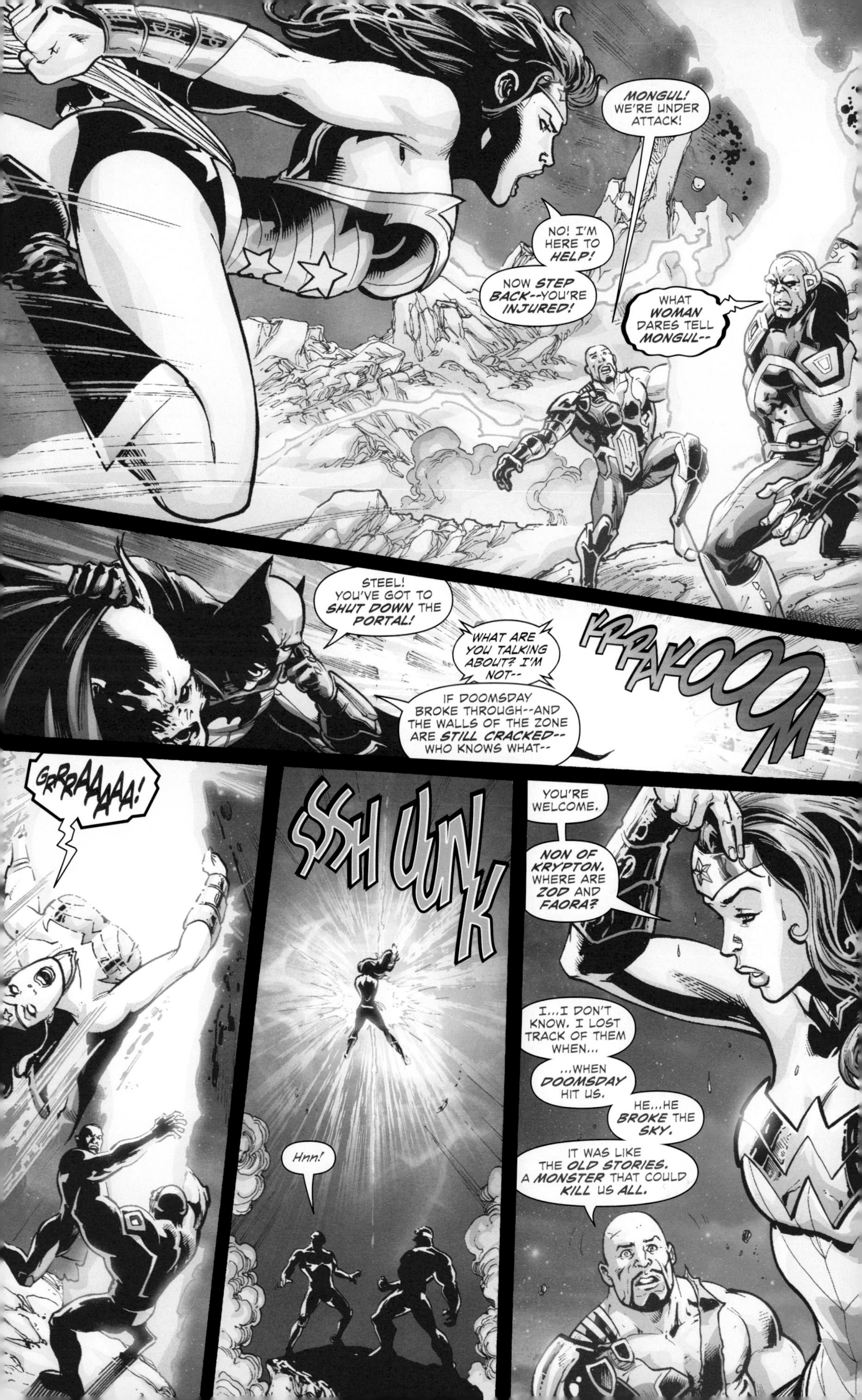
MONGUL! WE'RE UNDER ATTACK!
NO! I'M HERE TO HELP!
NOW STEP BACK--YOU'RE INJURED!
WHAT WOMAN DARES TELL MONGUL--
STEEL! YOU'VE GOT TO SHUT DOWN THE PORTAL!
WHAT ARE YOU TALKING ABOUT? I'M NOT--
IF DOOMSDAY BROKE THROUGH--AND THE WALLS OF THE ZONE ARE STILL CRACKED--WHO KNOWS WHAT--
KRRAKOOOM
GRRRAAAAAA!
SSHUUNK
Hnn!
YOU'RE WELCOME.
NON OF KRYPTON. WHERE ARE ZOD AND FAORA?
I...I DON'T KNOW. I LOST TRACK OF THEM WHEN...
...WHEN DOOMSDAY HIT US.
HE...HE BROKE THE SKY.
IT WAS LIKE THE OLD STORIES. A MONSTER THAT COULD KILL US ALL.

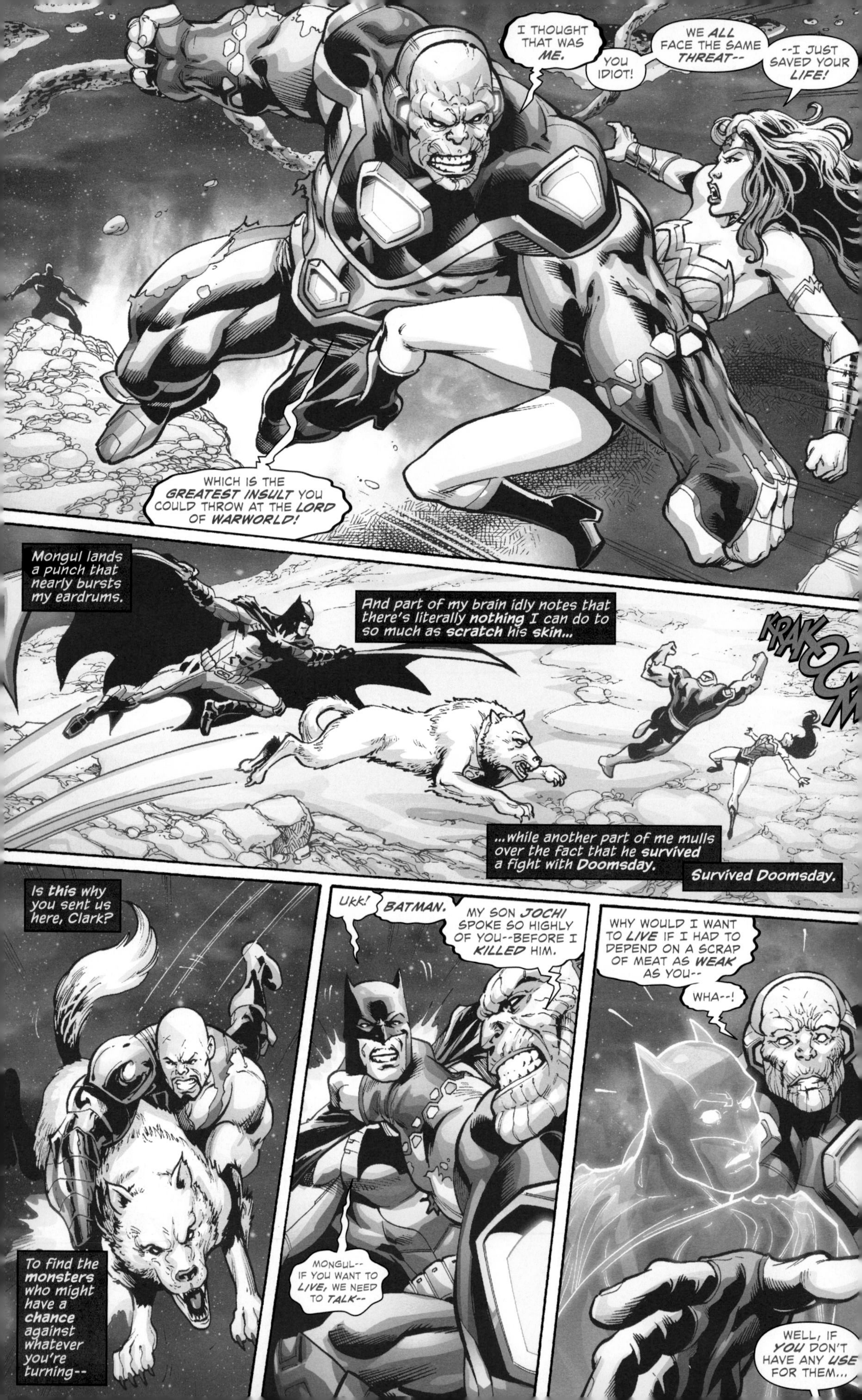
I THOUGHT THAT WAS ME.
YOU IDIOT!
WE ALL FACE THE SAME THREAT--
--I JUST SAVED YOUR LIFE!
WHICH IS THE GREATEST INSULT YOU COULD THROW AT THE LORD OF WARWORLD!
Mongul lands a punch that nearly bursts my eardrums.
And part of my brain idly notes that there's literally nothing I can do to so much as scratch his skin...
KRAKOOM
...while another part of me mulls over the fact that he survived a fight with Doomsday.
Survived Doomsday.
Is this why you sent us here, Clark?
To find the monsters who might have a chance against whatever you're turning--
Ukk!
BATMAN.
MY SON JOCHI SPOKE SO HIGHLY OF YOU--BEFORE I KILLED HIM.
MONGUL-- IF YOU WANT TO LIVE, WE NEED TO TALK--
WHY WOULD I WANT TO LIVE IF I HAD TO DEPEND ON A SCRAP OF MEAT AS WEAK AS YOU--
WHA--!
WELL, IF YOU DON'T HAVE ANY USE FOR THEM...

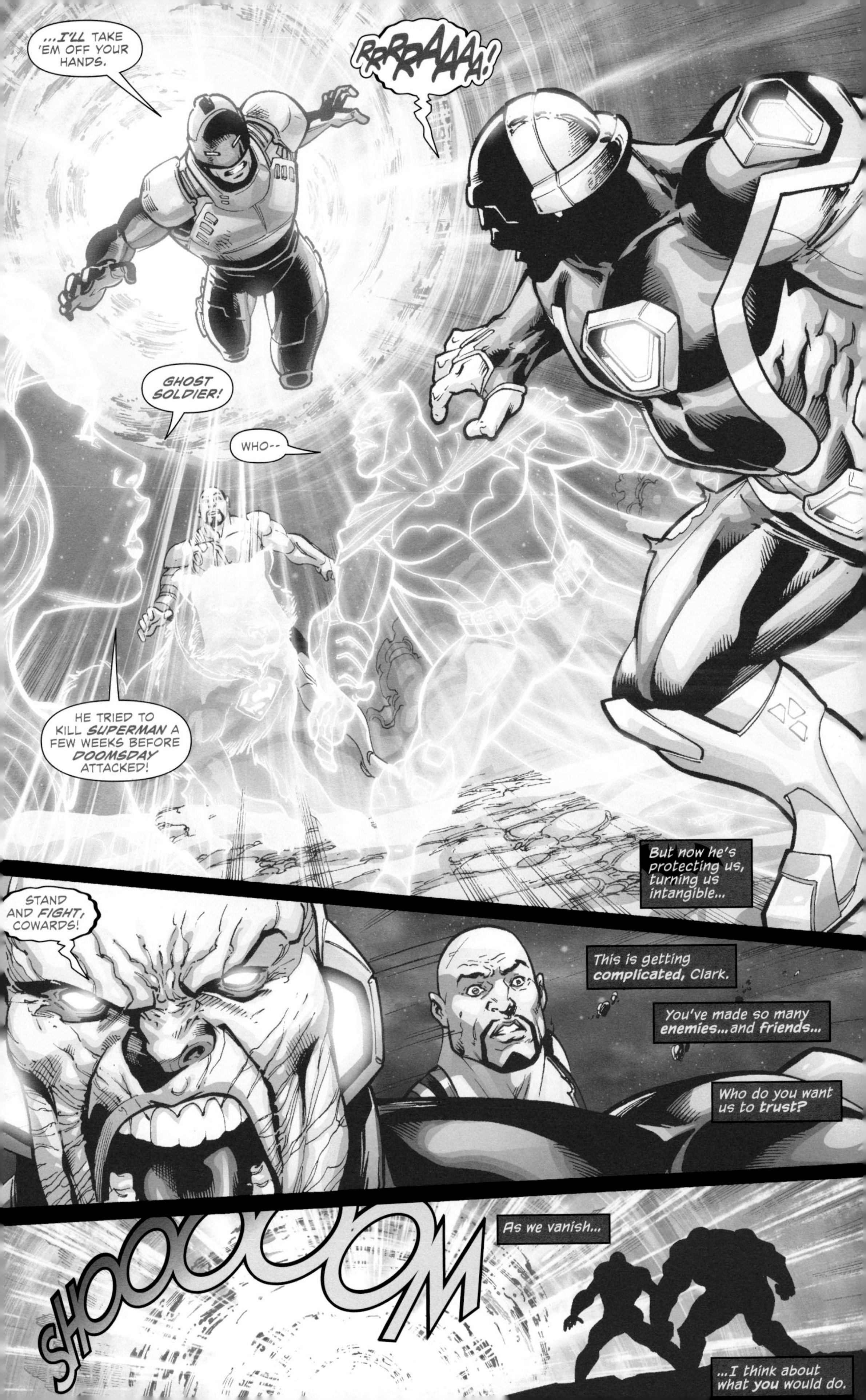

...I'LL TAKE 'EM OFF YOUR HANDS.
RRRRAAAA!
GHOST SOLDIER!
WHO--
HE TRIED TO KILL SUPERMAN A FEW WEEKS BEFORE DOOMSDAY ATTACKED!
But now he's protecting us, turning us intangible...
STAND AND FIGHT, COWARDS!
This is getting complicated, Clark.
You've made so many enemies...and friends...
Who do you want us to trust?
SHOOOOOM
As we vanish...
...I think about what you would do.

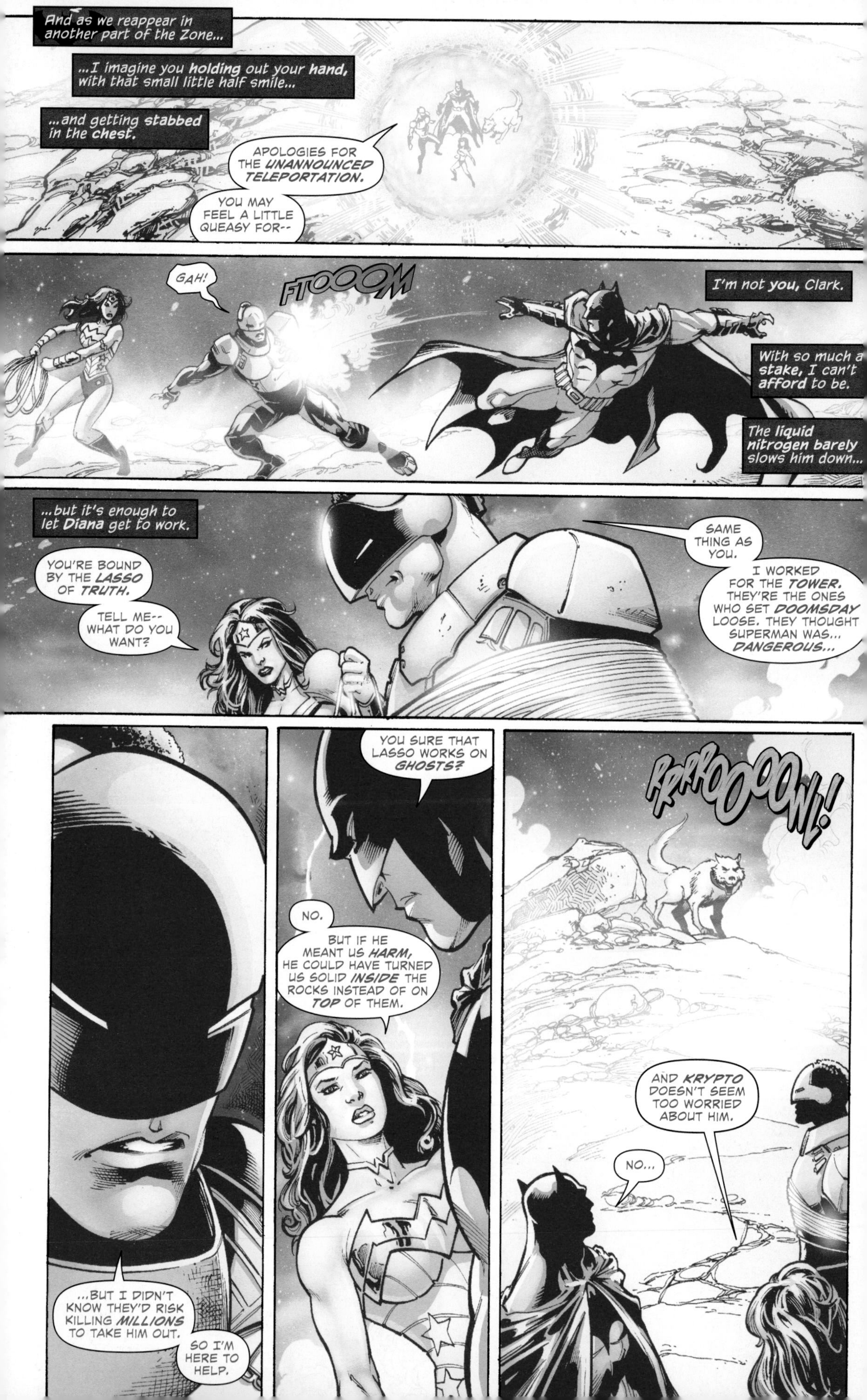

And as we reappear in another part of the Zone...
...I imagine you holding out your hand, with that small little half smile...
...and getting stabbed in the chest.
APOLOGIES FOR THE UNANNOUNCED TELEPORTATION.
YOU MAY FEEL A LITTLE QUEASY FOR--
GAH!
FTOOOM
I'm not you, Clark.
With so much at stake, I can't afford to be.
The liquid nitrogen barely slows him down...
...but it's enough to let Diana get to work.
YOU'RE BOUND BY THE LASSO OF TRUTH.
TELL ME-- WHAT DO YOU WANT?
SAME THING AS YOU.
I WORKED FOR THE TOWER. THEY'RE THE ONES WHO SET DOOMSDAY LOOSE. THEY THOUGHT SUPERMAN WAS... DANGEROUS...
...BUT I DIDN'T KNOW THEY'D RISK KILLING MILLIONS TO TAKE HIM OUT.
SO I'M HERE TO HELP.
YOU SURE THAT LASSO WORKS ON GHOSTS?
NO.
BUT IF HE MEANT US HARM, HE COULD HAVE TURNED US SOLID INSIDE THE ROCKS INSTEAD OF ON TOP OF THEM.
RRRROOOOOWL!
AND KRYPTO DOESN'T SEEM TOO WORRIED ABOUT HIM.
NO...

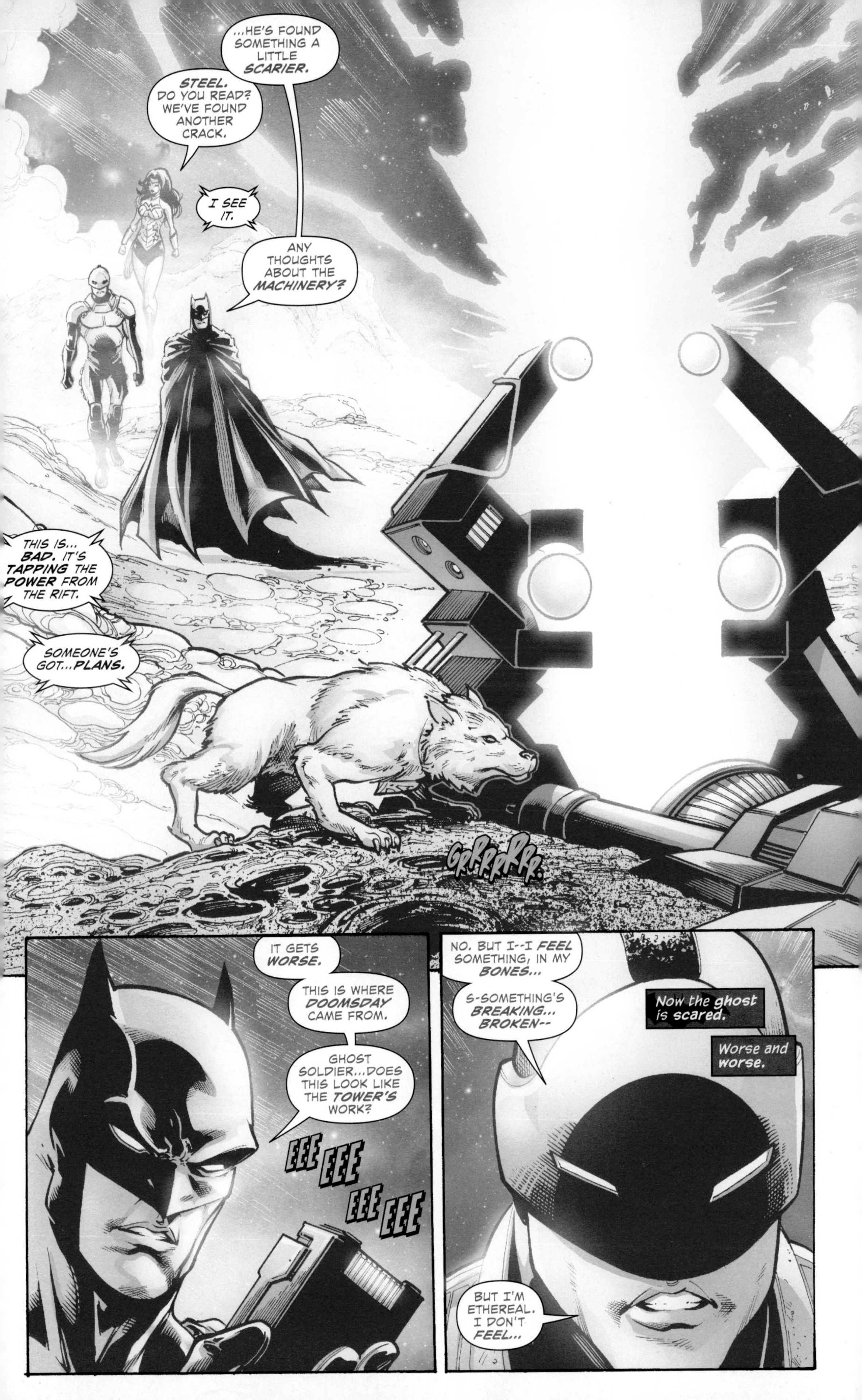
STEEL. DO YOU READ? WE'VE FOUND ANOTHER CRACK.
...HE'S FOUND SOMETHING A LITTLE SCARIER.
I SEE IT.
ANY THOUGHTS ABOUT THE MACHINERY?
THIS IS... BAD. IT'S TAPPING THE POWER FROM THE RIFT.
SOMEONE'S GOT...PLANS.
GRRRRRRR.
IT GETS WORSE.
THIS IS WHERE DOOMSDAY CAME FROM.
GHOST SOLDIER...DOES THIS LOOK LIKE THE TOWER'S WORK?
EEE EEE EEE EEE
NO. BUT I--I FEEL SOMETHING, IN MY BONES...
S-SOMETHING'S BREAKING... BROKEN--
Now the ghost is scared.
Worse and worse.
BUT I'M ETHEREAL. I DON'T FEEL...

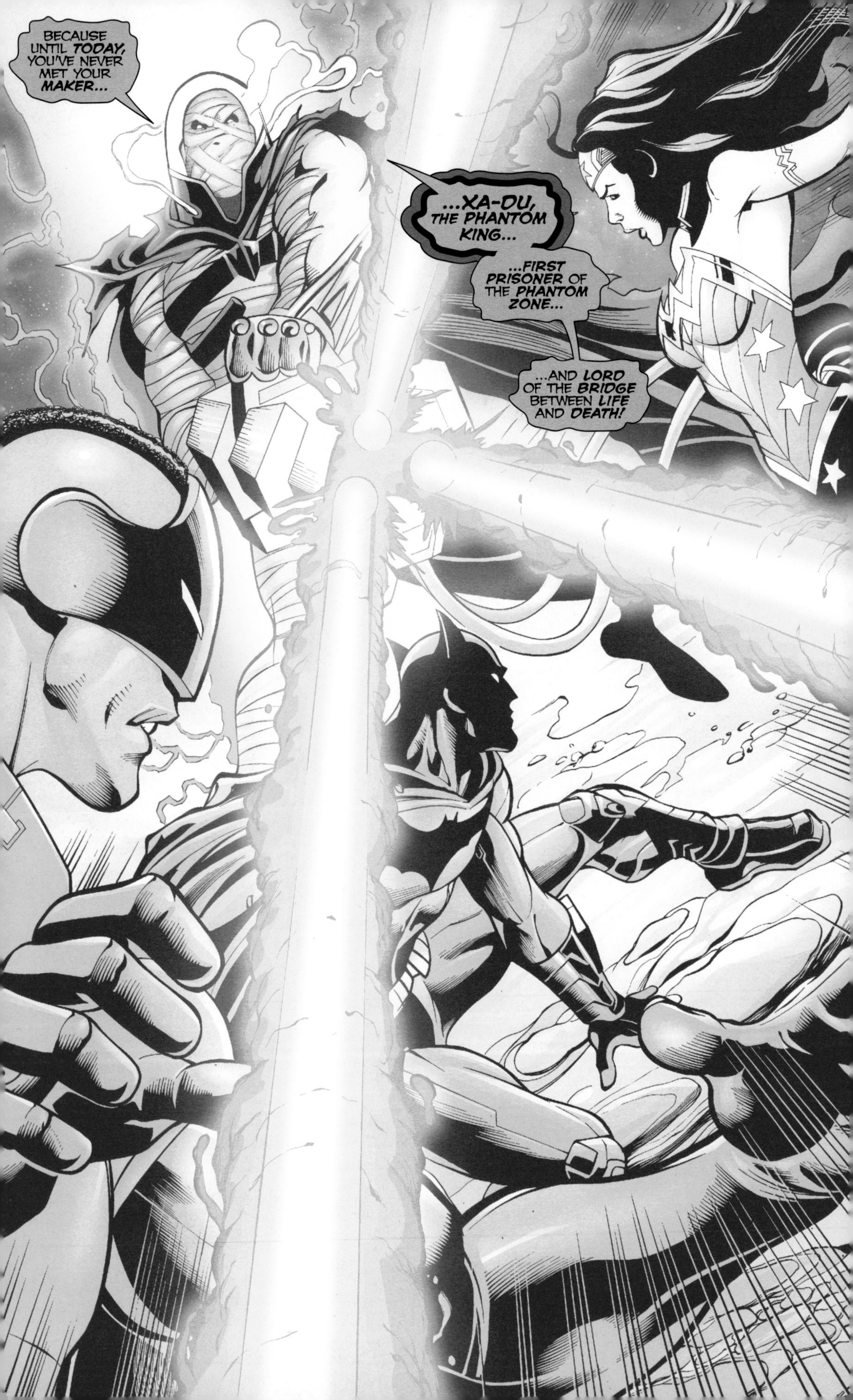
BECAUSE UNTIL TODAY, YOU'VE NEVER MET YOUR MAKER...
...XA-DU, THE PHANTOM KING...
...FIRST PRISONER OF THE PHANTOM ZONE...
...AND LORD OF THE BRIDGE BETWEEN LIFE AND DEATH!

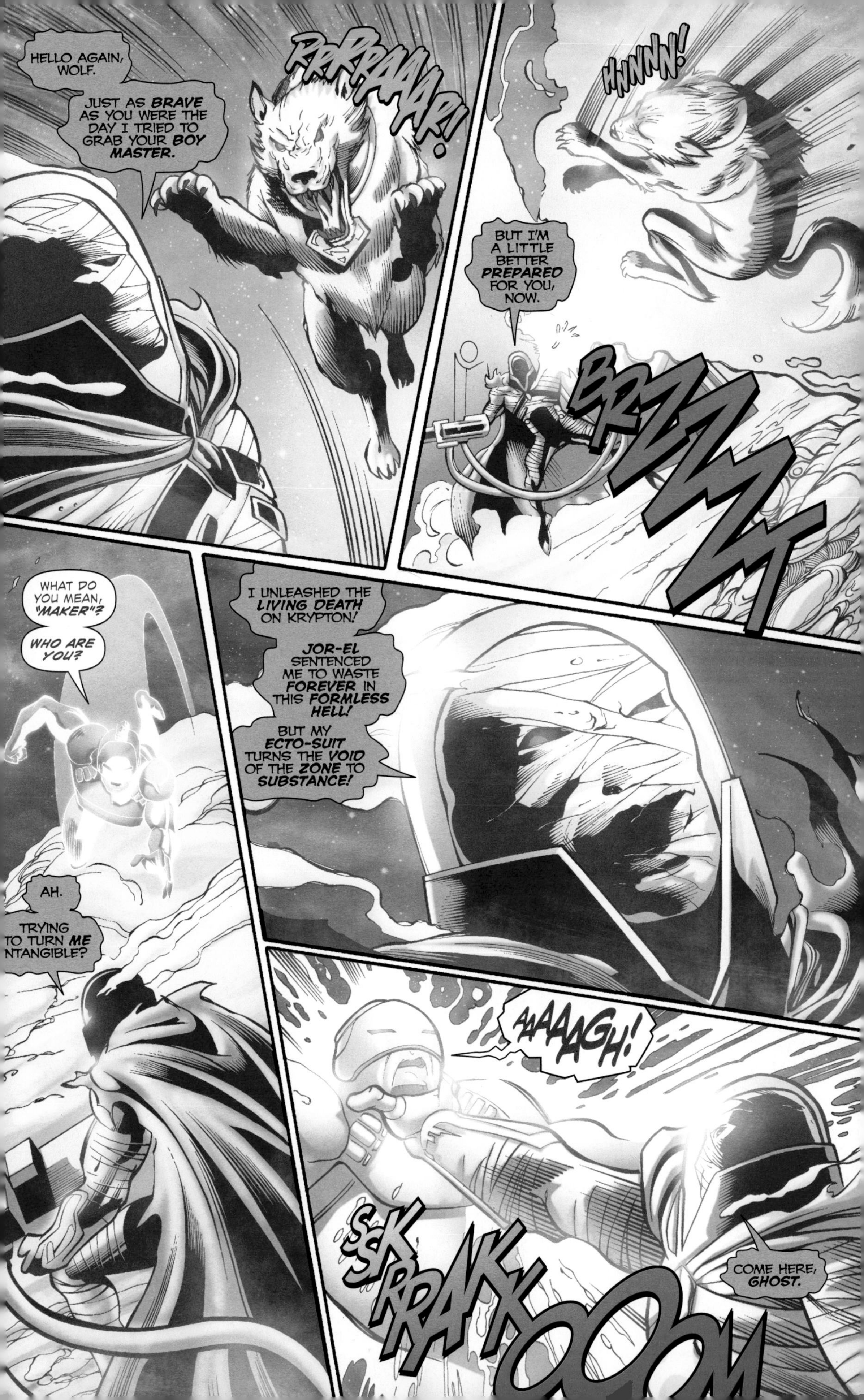
HELLO AGAIN, WOLF.
JUST AS BRAVE AS YOU WERE THE DAY I TRIED TO GRAB YOUR BOY MASTER.
RRRRAAAAAR!
HNNNNN!
BUT I'M A LITTLE BETTER PREPARED FOR YOU, NOW.
BRZZZM
WHAT DO YOU MEAN, "MAKER"?
WHO ARE YOU?
I UNLEASHED THE LIVING DEATH ON KRYPTON!
JOR-EL SENTENCED ME TO WASTE FOREVER IN THIS FORMLESS HELL!
BUT MY ECTO-SUIT TURNS THE VOID OF THE ZONE TO SUBSTANCE!
AH.
TRYING TO TURN ME NTANGIBLE?
AAAAAGH!
COME HERE, GHOST.
SSKRRAKK
OOOM

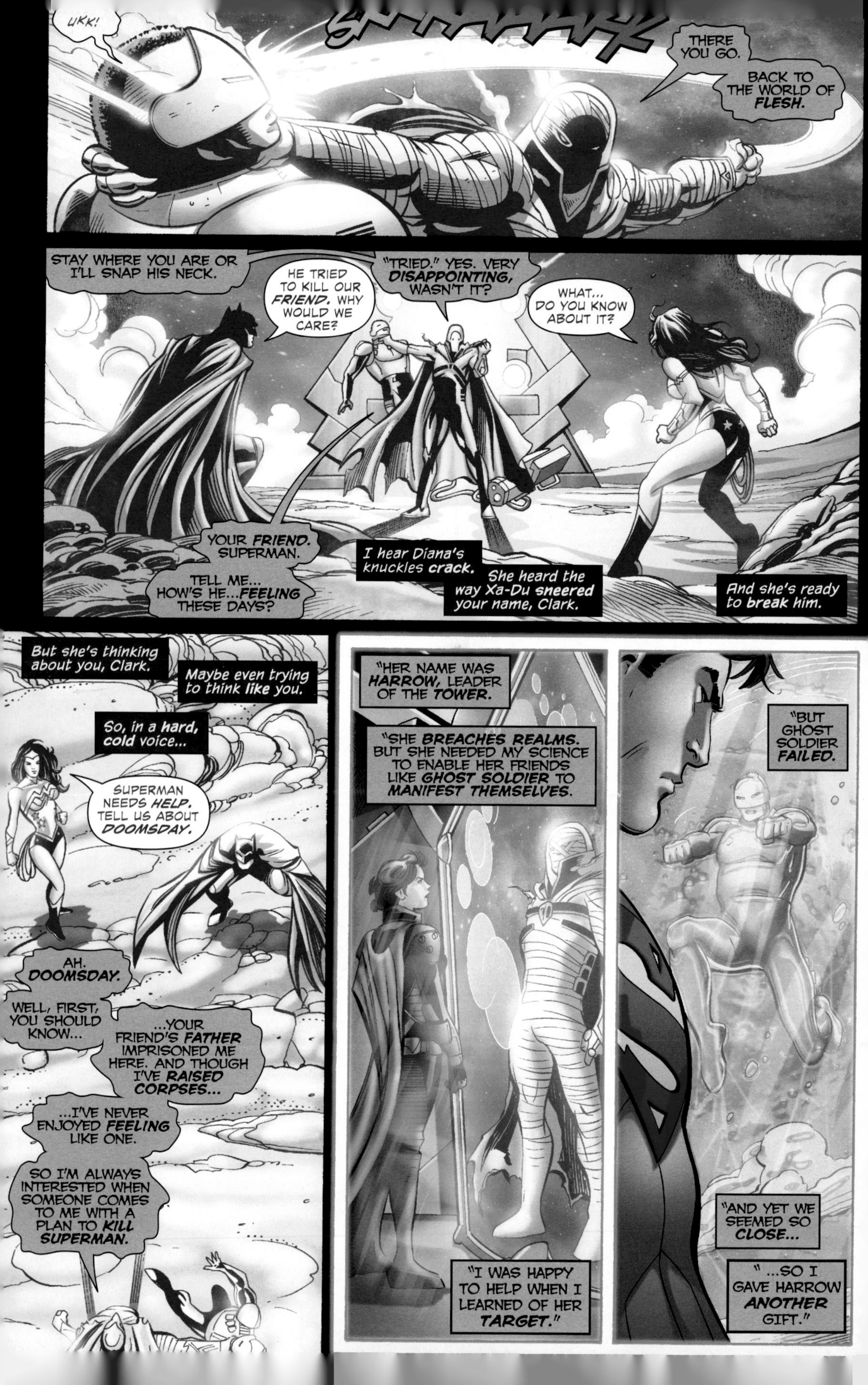
UKK!
SHHHHHHK
THERE YOU GO.
BACK TO THE WORLD OF FLESH.
STAY WHERE YOU ARE OR I'LL SNAP HIS NECK.
HE TRIED TO KILL OUR FRIEND. WHY WOULD WE CARE?
"TRIED." YES. VERY DISAPPOINTING, WASN'T IT?
WHAT... DO YOU KNOW ABOUT IT?
YOUR FRIEND. SUPERMAN.
TELL ME... HOW'S HE...FEELING THESE DAYS?
I hear Diana's knuckles crack.
She heard the way Xa-Du sneered your name, Clark.
And she's ready to break him.
But she's thinking about you, Clark.
Maybe even trying to think like you.
So, in a hard, cold voice...
SUPERMAN NEEDS HELP. TELL US ABOUT DOOMSDAY.
AH. DOOMSDAY.
WELL, FIRST, YOU SHOULD KNOW...
...YOUR FRIEND'S FATHER IMPRISONED ME HERE. AND THOUGH I'VE RAISED CORPSES...
...I'VE NEVER ENJOYED FEELING LIKE ONE.
SO I'M ALWAYS INTERESTED WHEN SOMEONE COMES TO ME WITH A PLAN TO KILL SUPERMAN.
"HER NAME WAS HARROW, LEADER OF THE TOWER.
"SHE BREACHES REALMS. BUT SHE NEEDED MY SCIENCE TO ENABLE HER FRIENDS LIKE GHOST SOLDIER TO MANIFEST THEMSELVES.
"I WAS HAPPY TO HELP WHEN I LEARNED OF HER TARGET."
"BUT GHOST SOLDIER FAILED.
"AND YET WE SEEMED SO CLOSE...
"...SO I GAVE HARROW ANOTHER GIFT."

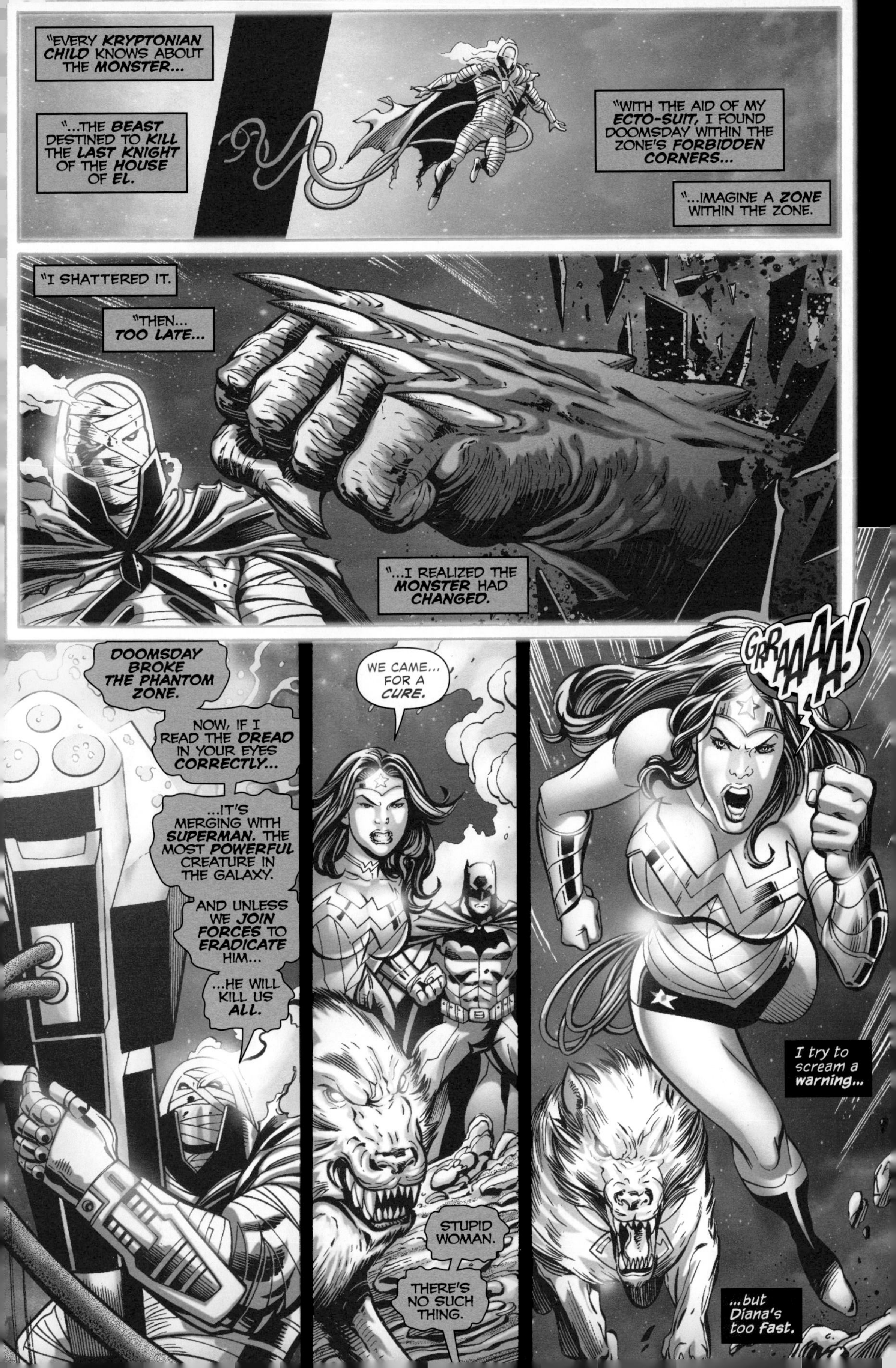
"EVERY KRYPTONIAN CHILD KNOWS ABOUT THE MONSTER...
"...THE BEAST DESTINED TO KILL THE LAST KNIGHT OF THE HOUSE OF EL.
"WITH THE AID OF MY ECTO-SUIT, I FOUND DOOMSDAY WITHIN THE ZONE'S FORBIDDEN CORNERS...
"...IMAGINE A ZONE WITHIN THE ZONE.
"I SHATTERED IT.
"THEN... TOO LATE...
"...I REALIZED THE MONSTER HAD CHANGED.
DOOMSDAY BROKE THE PHANTOM ZONE.
NOW, IF I READ THE DREAD IN YOUR EYES CORRECTLY...
...IT'S MERGING WITH SUPERMAN. THE MOST POWERFUL CREATURE IN THE GALAXY.
AND UNLESS WE JOIN FORCES TO ERADICATE HIM...
...HE WILL KILL US ALL.
WE CAME... FOR A CURE.
STUPID WOMAN.
THERE'S NO SUCH THING.
GRRAAAA!
I try to scream a warning...
...but Diana's too fast.

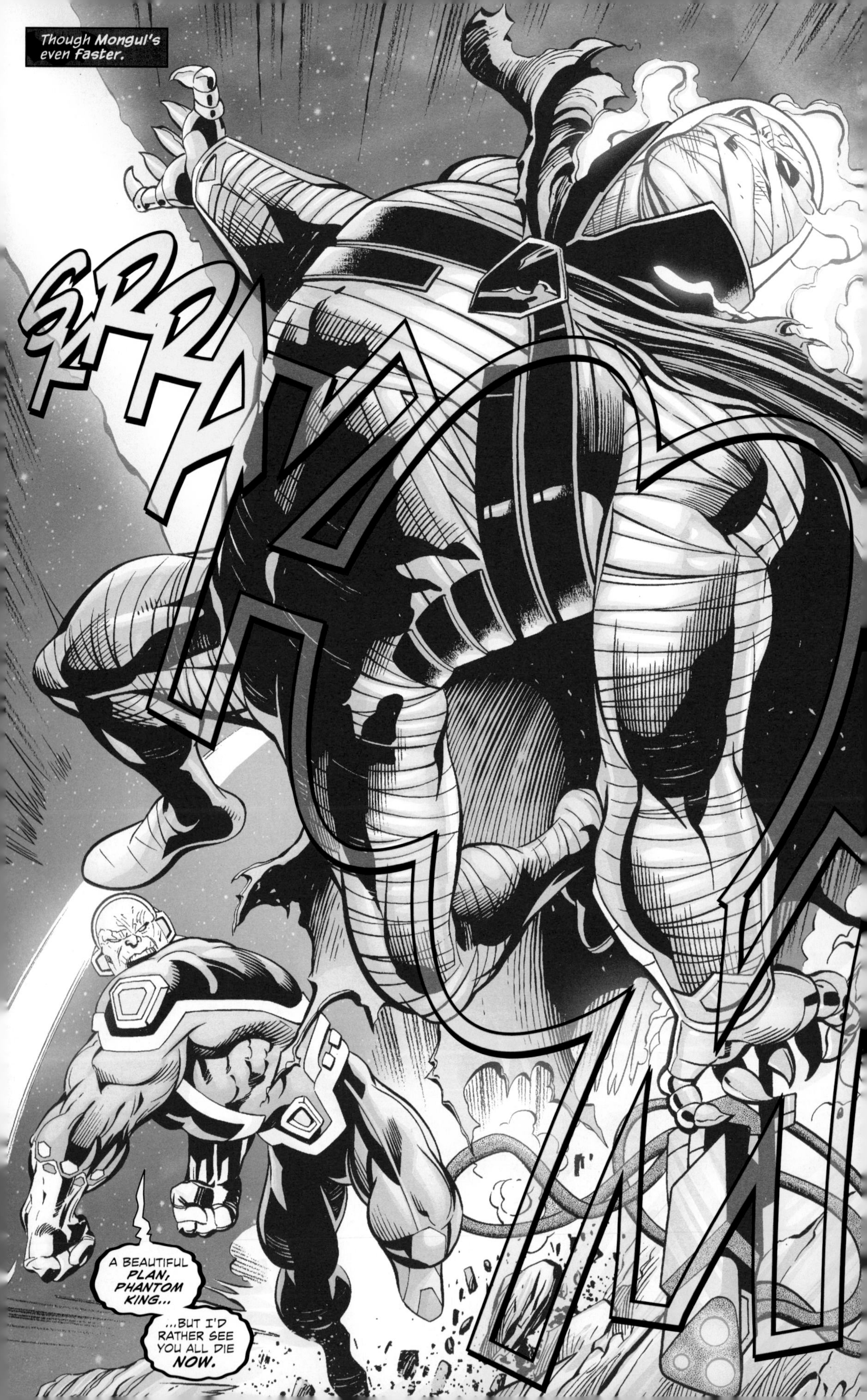
Though Mongul's even faster.
A BEAUTIFUL PLAN, PHANTOM KING...
...BUT I'D RATHER SEE YOU ALL DIE NOW.

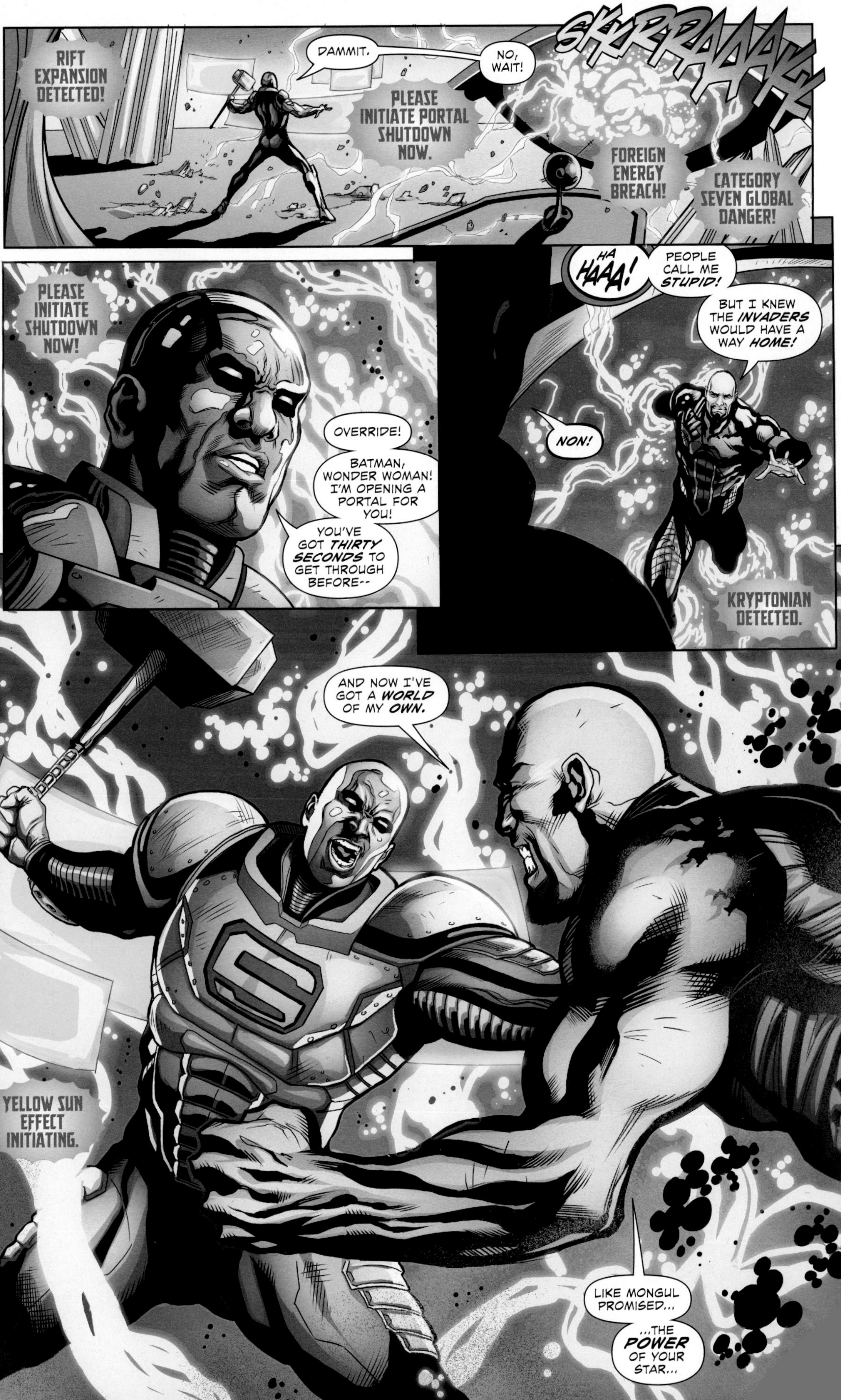
RIFT EXPANSION DETECTED!
DAMMIT.
NO, WAIT!
PLEASE INITIATE PORTAL SHUTDOWN NOW.
SKRRAAAAK
FOREIGN ENERGY BREACH!
CATEGORY SEVEN GLOBAL DANGER!
PLEASE INITIATE SHUTDOWN NOW!
OVERRIDE!
BATMAN, WONDER WOMAN! I'M OPENING A PORTAL FOR YOU!
YOU'VE GOT THIRTY SECONDS TO GET THROUGH BEFORE--
HA HAAA!
PEOPLE CALL ME STUPID!
BUT I KNEW THE INVADERS WOULD HAVE A WAY HOME!
NON!
KRYPTONIAN DETECTED.
AND NOW I'VE GOT A WORLD OF MY OWN.
YELLOW SUN EFFECT INITIATING.
LIKE MONGUL PROMISED...
...THE POWER OF YOUR STAR...

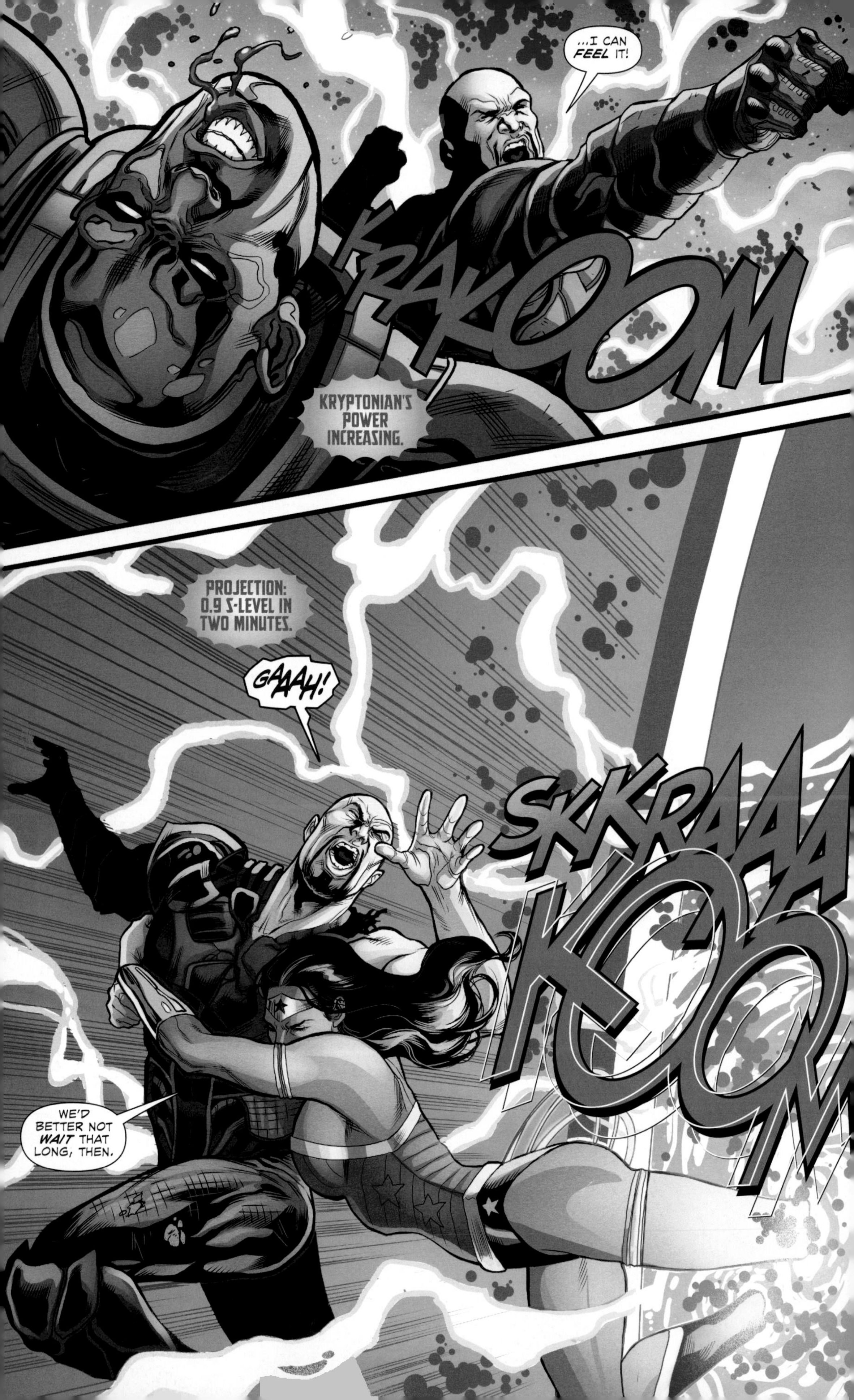
...I CAN FEEL IT!
KRAKOOM
KRYPTONIAN'S POWER INCREASING.
PROJECTION: 0.9 S-LEVEL IN TWO MINUTES.
GAAAH!
SKKRAAA
KOOM
WE'D BETTER NOT WAIT THAT LONG, THEN.

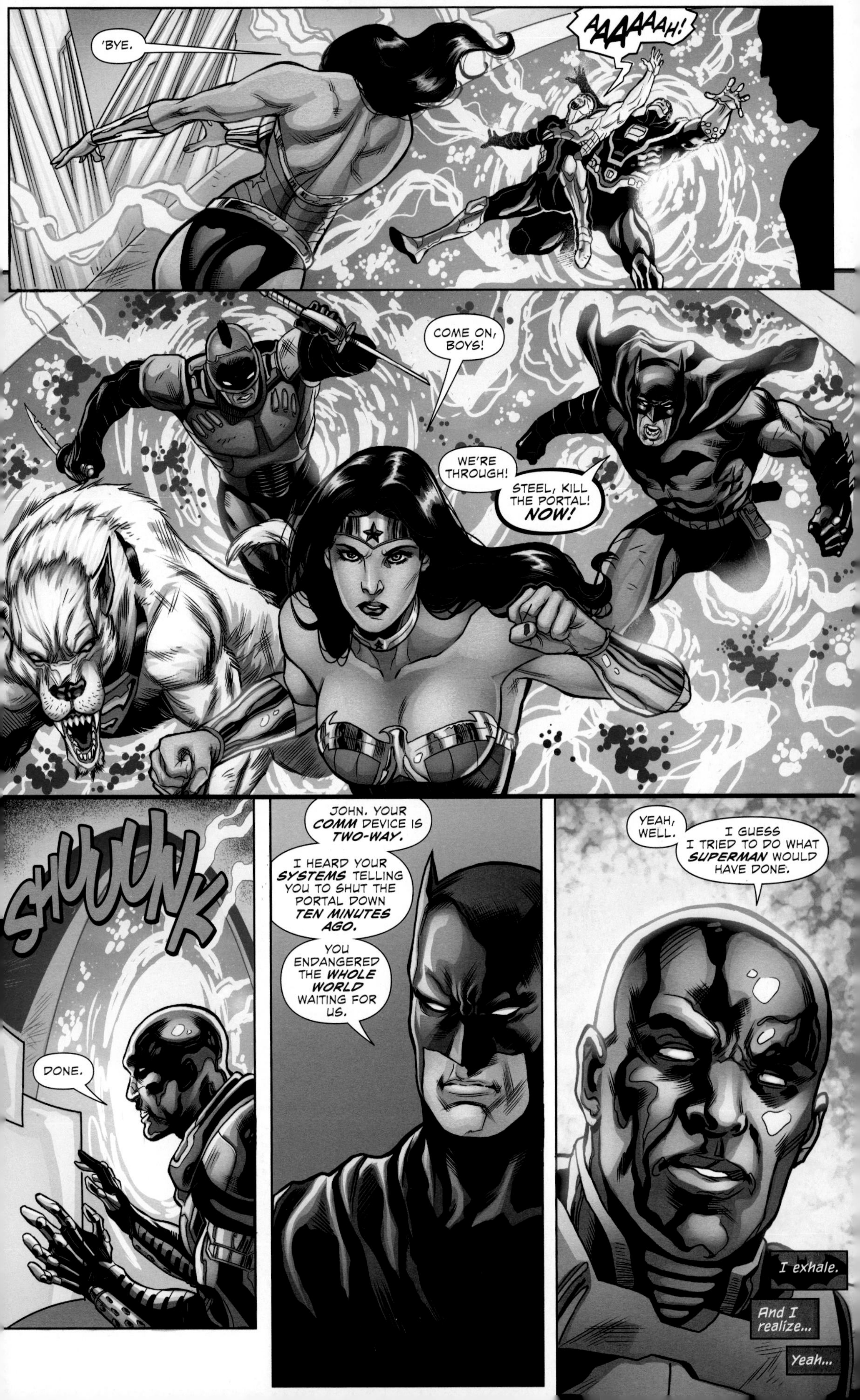
'BYE.
AAAAAAH!
COME ON, BOYS!
WE'RE THROUGH!
STEEL, KILL THE PORTAL! NOW!
SHUUUNK
DONE.
JOHN. YOUR COMM DEVICE IS TWO-WAY.
I HEARD YOUR SYSTEMS TELLING YOU TO SHUT THE PORTAL DOWN TEN MINUTES AGO.
YOU ENDANGERED THE WHOLE WORLD WAITING FOR US.
YEAH, WELL.
I GUESS I TRIED TO DO WHAT SUPERMAN WOULD HAVE DONE.
I exhale.
And I realize...
Yeah...

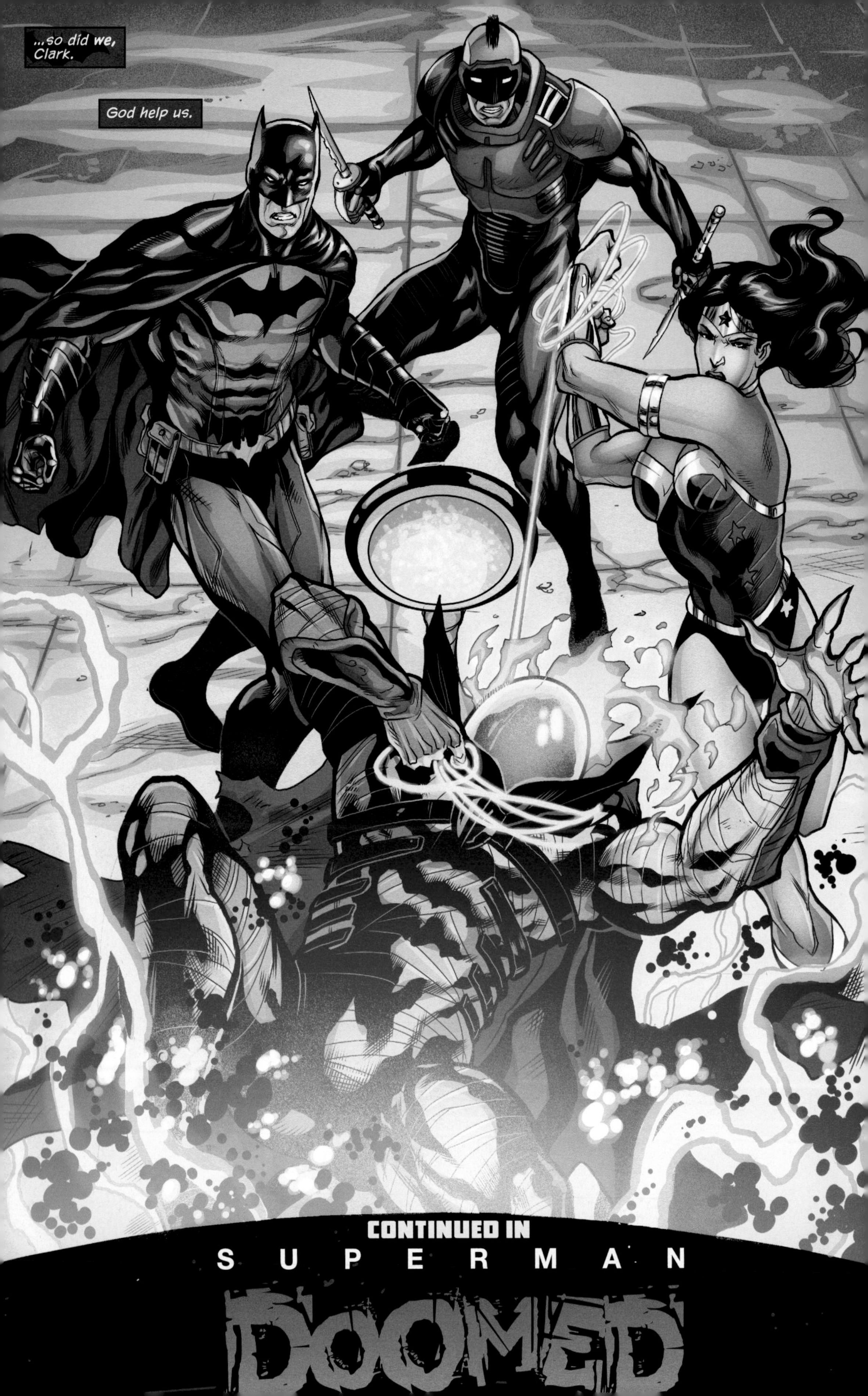
...so did we, Clark.
God help us.
CONTINUED IN
SUPERMAN
DOOMED

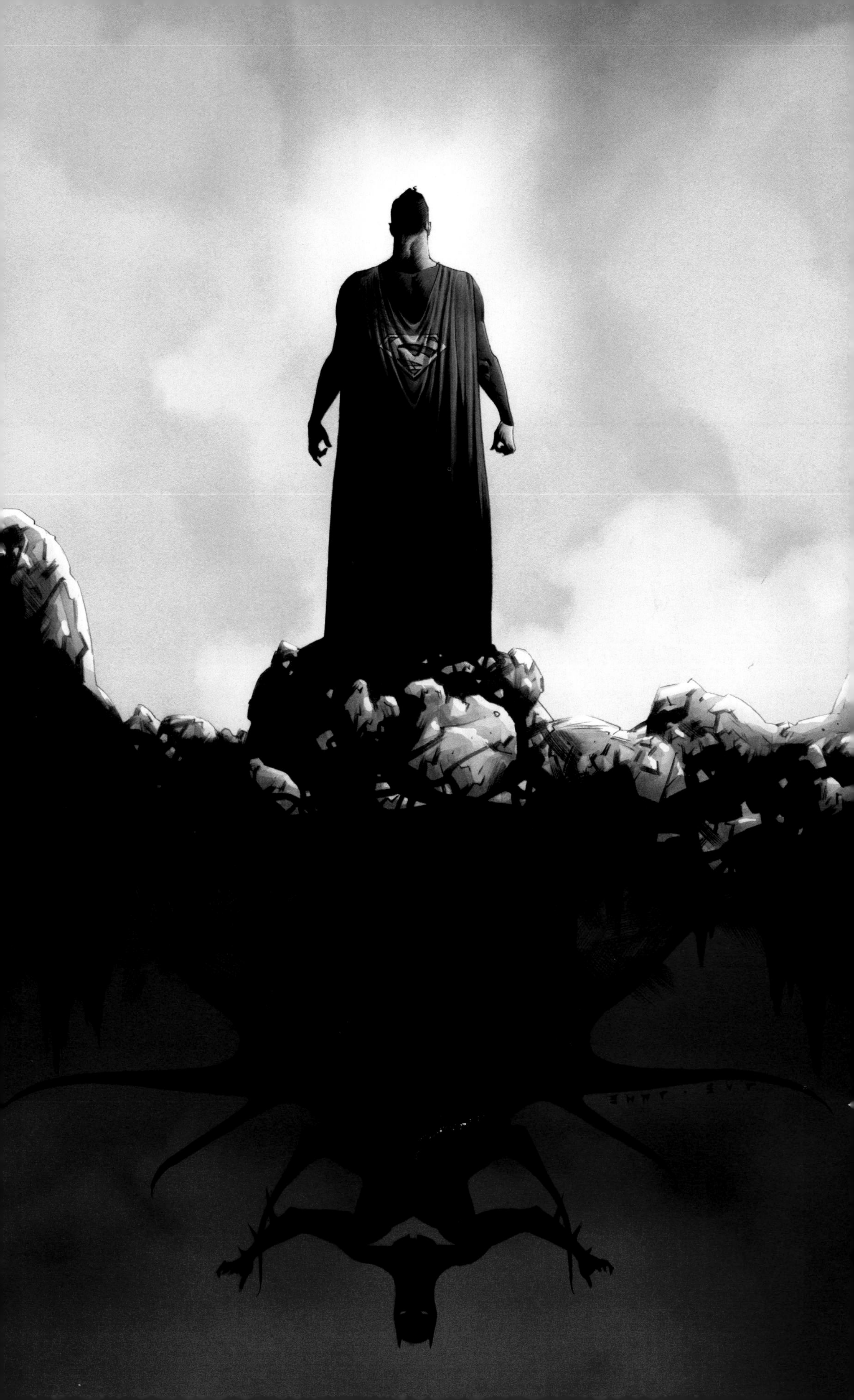

SECOND CHANCE

GREG PAK writer **TOM RANEY** **KEN LASHLEY** (pgs 75-78) pencillers **JAIME MENDOZA** (pgs 61-63, 66-74) **TOM RANEY** (pgs 57-60, 64-65) **KEN LASHLEY** (75-78) inkers **JASON WRIGHT** colorist **ROB LEIGH** letterer cover by **JAE LEE** with **JUNE CHUNG**

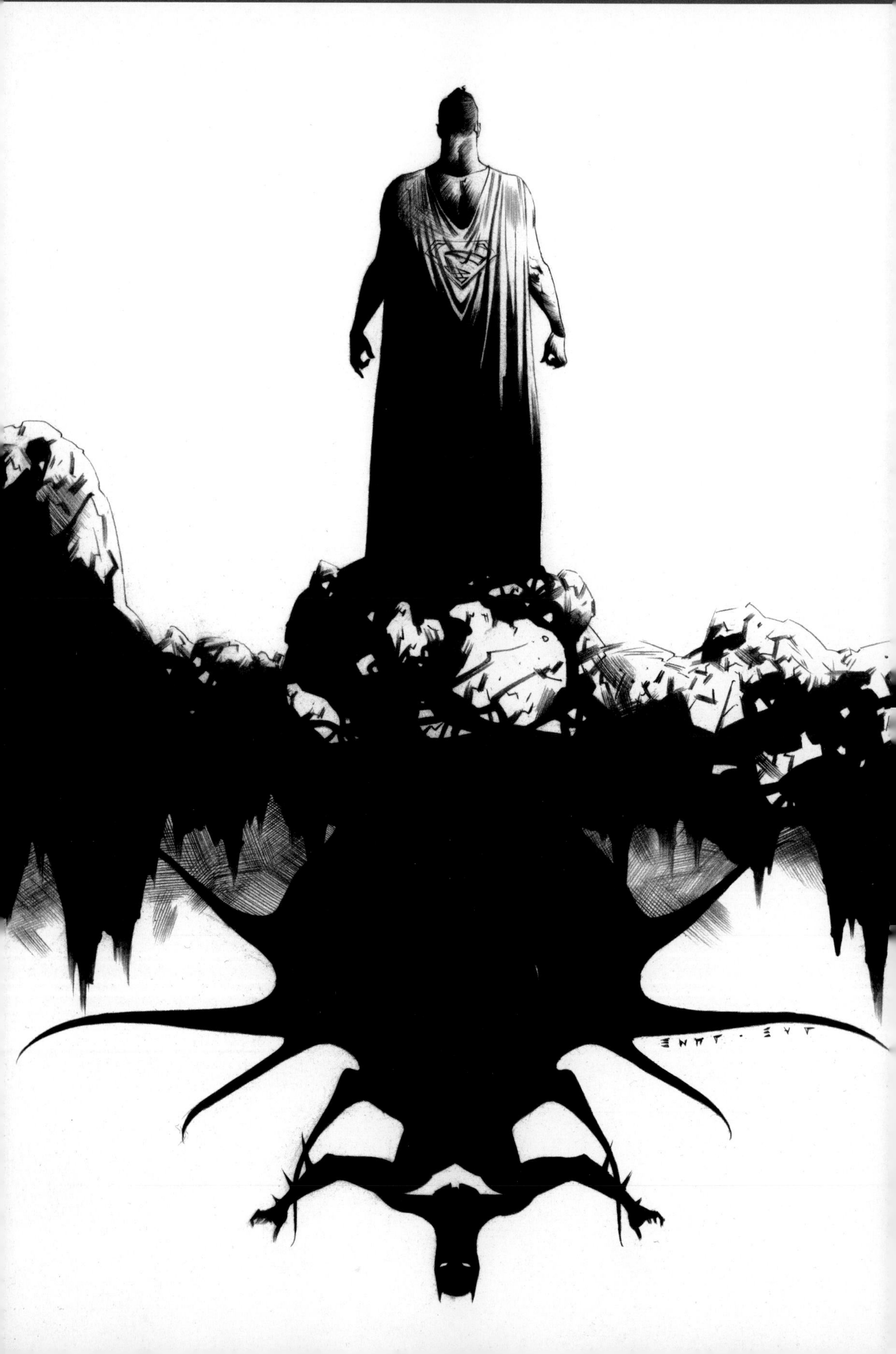

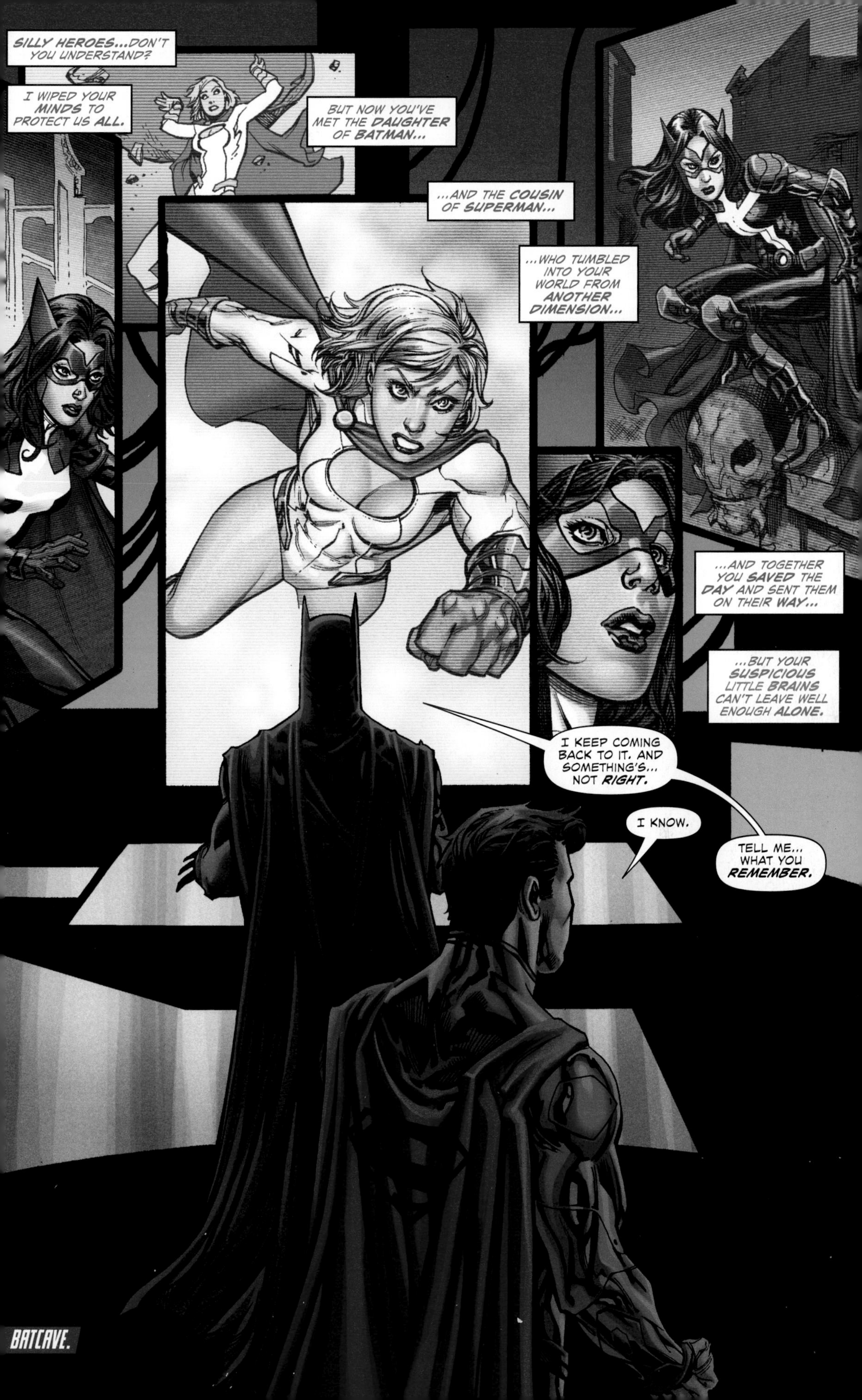
SILLY HEROES...DON'T YOU UNDERSTAND?
I WIPED YOUR MINDS TO PROTECT US ALL.
BUT NOW YOU'VE MET THE DAUGHTER OF BATMAN...
...AND THE COUSIN OF SUPERMAN...
...WHO TUMBLED INTO YOUR WORLD FROM ANOTHER DIMENSION...
...AND TOGETHER YOU SAVED THE DAY AND SENT THEM ON THEIR WAY...
...BUT YOUR SUSPICIOUS LITTLE BRAINS CAN'T LEAVE WELL ENOUGH ALONE.
BATCAVE.
I KEEP COMING BACK TO IT. AND SOMETHING'S... NOT RIGHT.
I KNOW.
TELL ME... WHAT YOU REMEMBER.

WE WERE *YOUNG.* MAYBE FIVE YEARS AGO...

...MEETING FOR THE *FIRST TIME.*

I THOUGHT YOU WERE A...

"MONSTER."

"...MADMAN."

"AND THEN SUDDENLY WE WERE IN *ANOTHER WORLD.*"

"FACING *OLDER VERSIONS* OF OURSELVES.

"AND WE *FOUGHT* THEM."

"*BEAT* THEM."

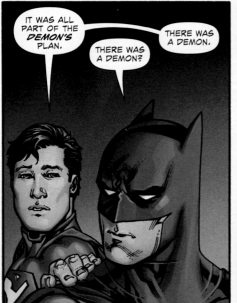

IT WAS ALL PART OF THE *DEMON'S* PLAN.

THERE WAS A DEMON.

THERE WAS A DEMON?

"KAIYO...THE *CHAOS BRINGER.*"

"THAT'S RIGHT. SHE TOLD US THAT *DARKSEID* WOULD COME..."

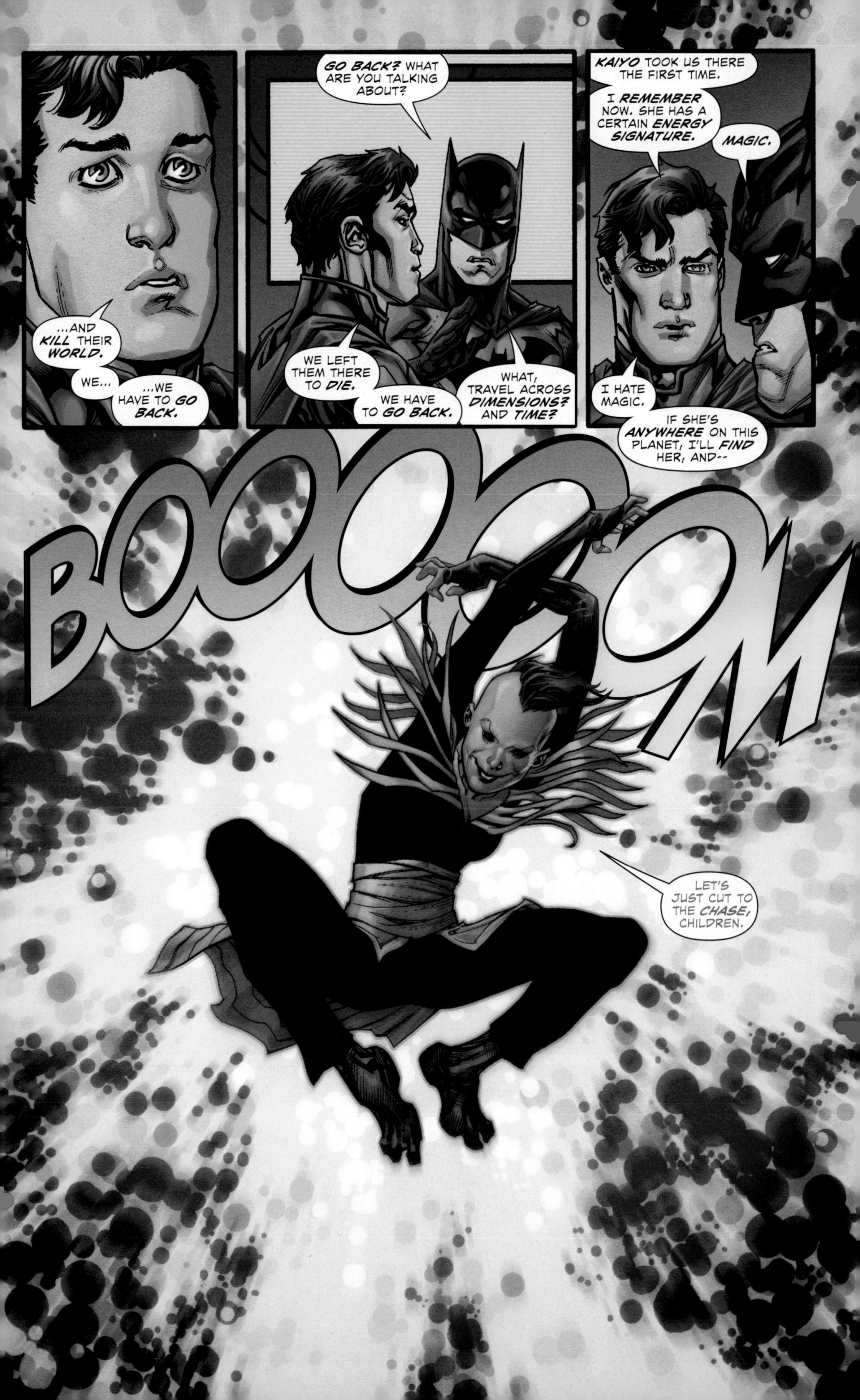
...AND KILL THEIR WORLD.
WE...
...WE HAVE TO GO BACK.
GO BACK? WHAT ARE YOU TALKING ABOUT?
WE LEFT THEM THERE TO DIE.
WE HAVE TO GO BACK.
WHAT, TRAVEL ACROSS DIMENSIONS? AND TIME?
KAIYO TOOK US THERE THE FIRST TIME.
I REMEMBER NOW. SHE HAS A CERTAIN ENERGY SIGNATURE.
MAGIC.
I HATE MAGIC.
IF SHE'S ANYWHERE ON THIS PLANET, I'LL FIND HER, AND--
BOOOOOM
LET'S JUST CUT TO THE CHASE, CHILDREN.

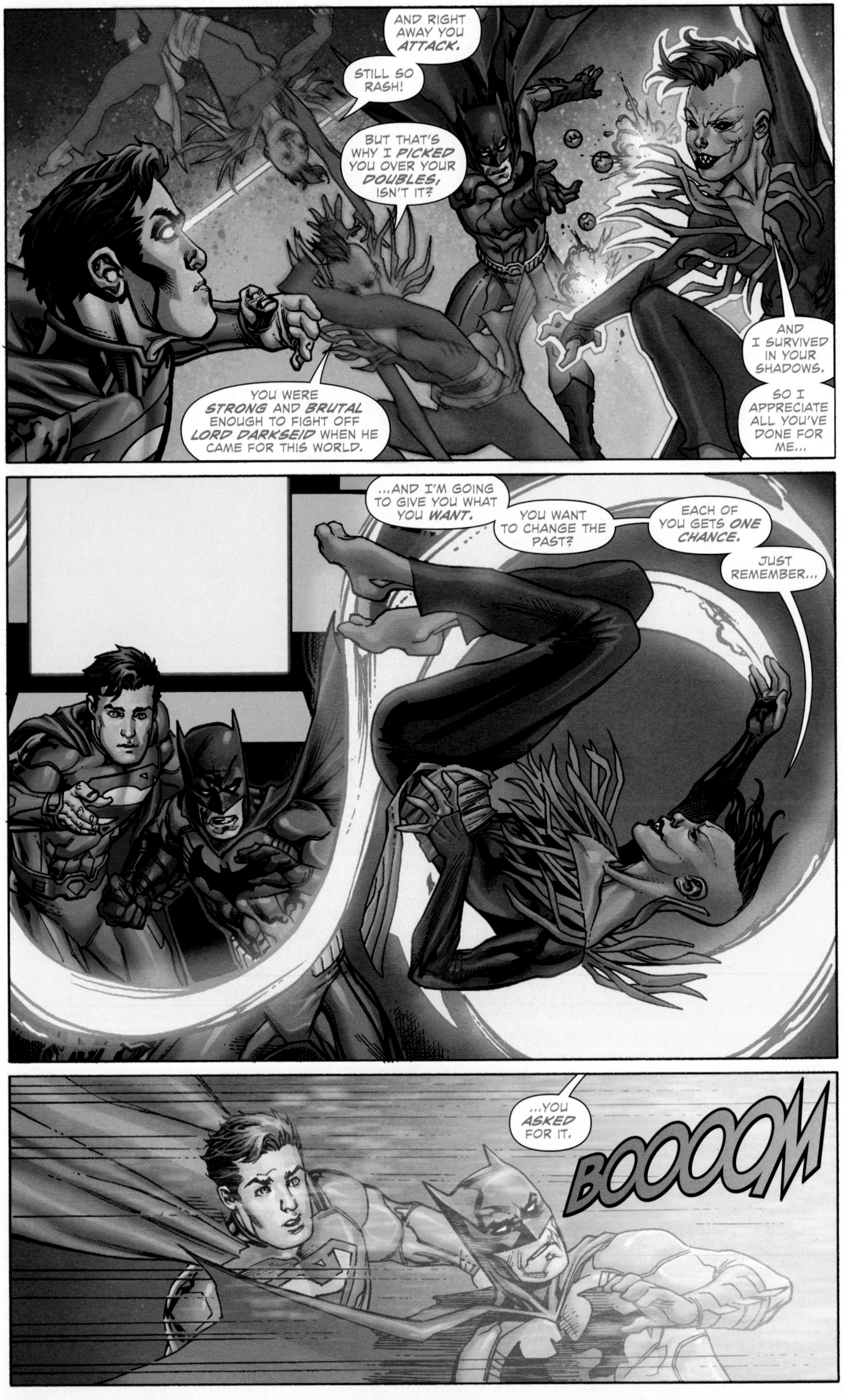
AND RIGHT AWAY YOU ATTACK.
STILL SO RASH!
BUT THAT'S WHY I PICKED YOU OVER YOUR DOUBLES, ISN'T IT?
YOU WERE STRONG AND BRUTAL ENOUGH TO FIGHT OFF LORD DARKSEID WHEN HE CAME FOR THIS WORLD.
AND I SURVIVED IN YOUR SHADOWS.
SO I APPRECIATE ALL YOU'VE DONE FOR ME...
...AND I'M GOING TO GIVE YOU WHAT YOU WANT.
YOU WANT TO CHANGE THE PAST?
EACH OF YOU GETS ONE CHANCE.
JUST REMEMBER...
...YOU ASKED FOR IT.
BOOOOOM

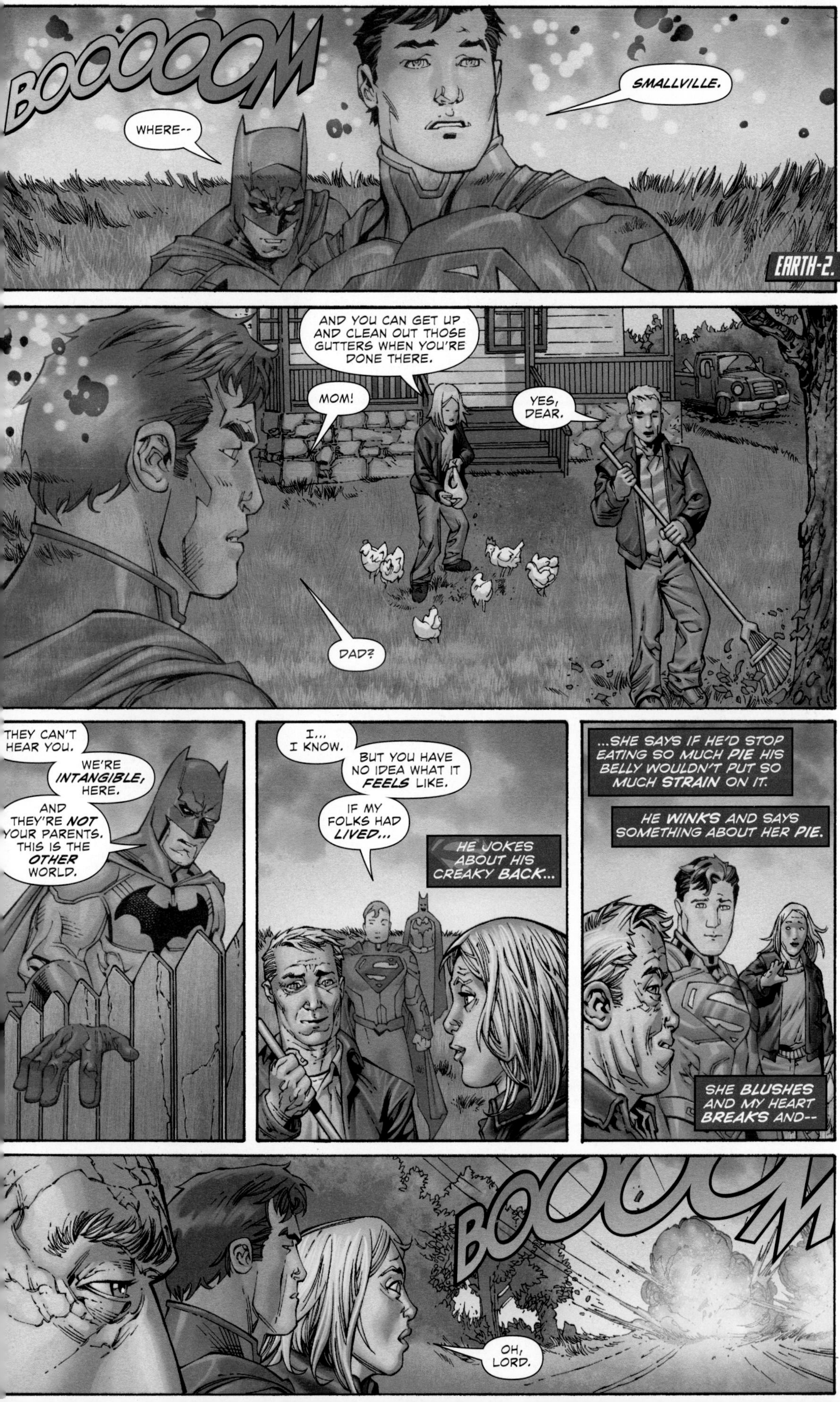
BOOOOOM
WHERE--
SMALLVILLE.
EARTH-2.
AND YOU CAN GET UP AND CLEAN OUT THOSE GUTTERS WHEN YOU'RE DONE THERE.
MOM!
YES, DEAR.
DAD?
THEY CAN'T HEAR YOU.
WE'RE INTANGIBLE, HERE.
AND THEY'RE NOT YOUR PARENTS. THIS IS THE OTHER WORLD.
I... I KNOW.
BUT YOU HAVE NO IDEA WHAT IT FEELS LIKE.
IF MY FOLKS HAD LIVED...
HE JOKES ABOUT HIS CREAKY BACK...
...SHE SAYS IF HE'D STOP EATING SO MUCH PIE HIS BELLY WOULDN'T PUT SO MUCH STRAIN ON IT.
HE WINKS AND SAYS SOMETHING ABOUT HER PIE.
SHE BLUSHES AND MY HEART BREAKS AND--
BOOOOM
OH, LORD.

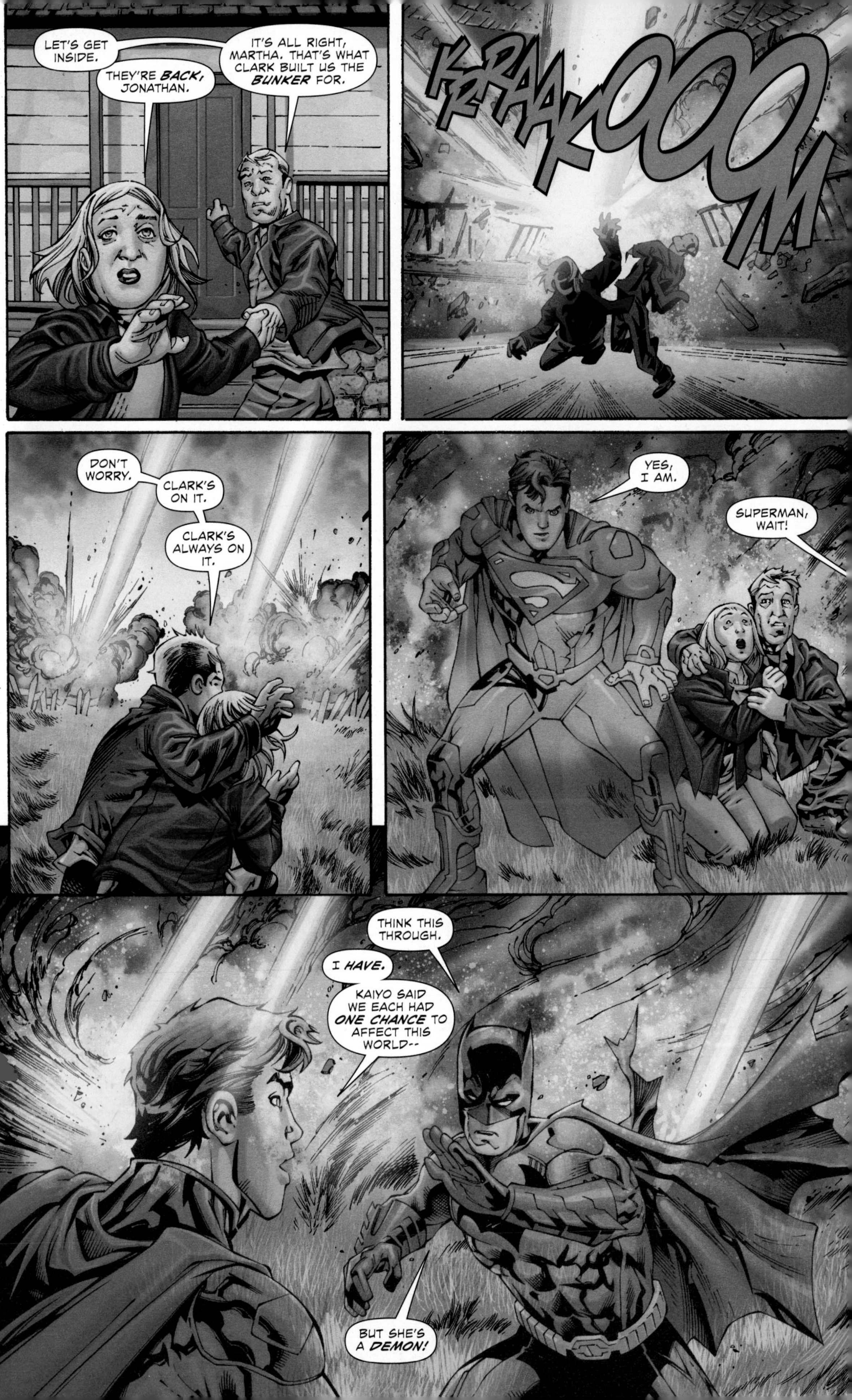
LET'S GET INSIDE.
THEY'RE BACK, JONATHAN.
IT'S ALL RIGHT, MARTHA. THAT'S WHAT CLARK BUILT US THE BUNKER FOR.
KRRAAKOOOM
DON'T WORRY.
CLARK'S ON IT.
CLARK'S ALWAYS ON IT.
YES, I AM.
SUPERMAN, WAIT!
THINK THIS THROUGH.
I HAVE.
KAIYO SAID WE EACH HAD ONE CHANCE TO AFFECT THIS WORLD--
BUT SHE'S A DEMON!

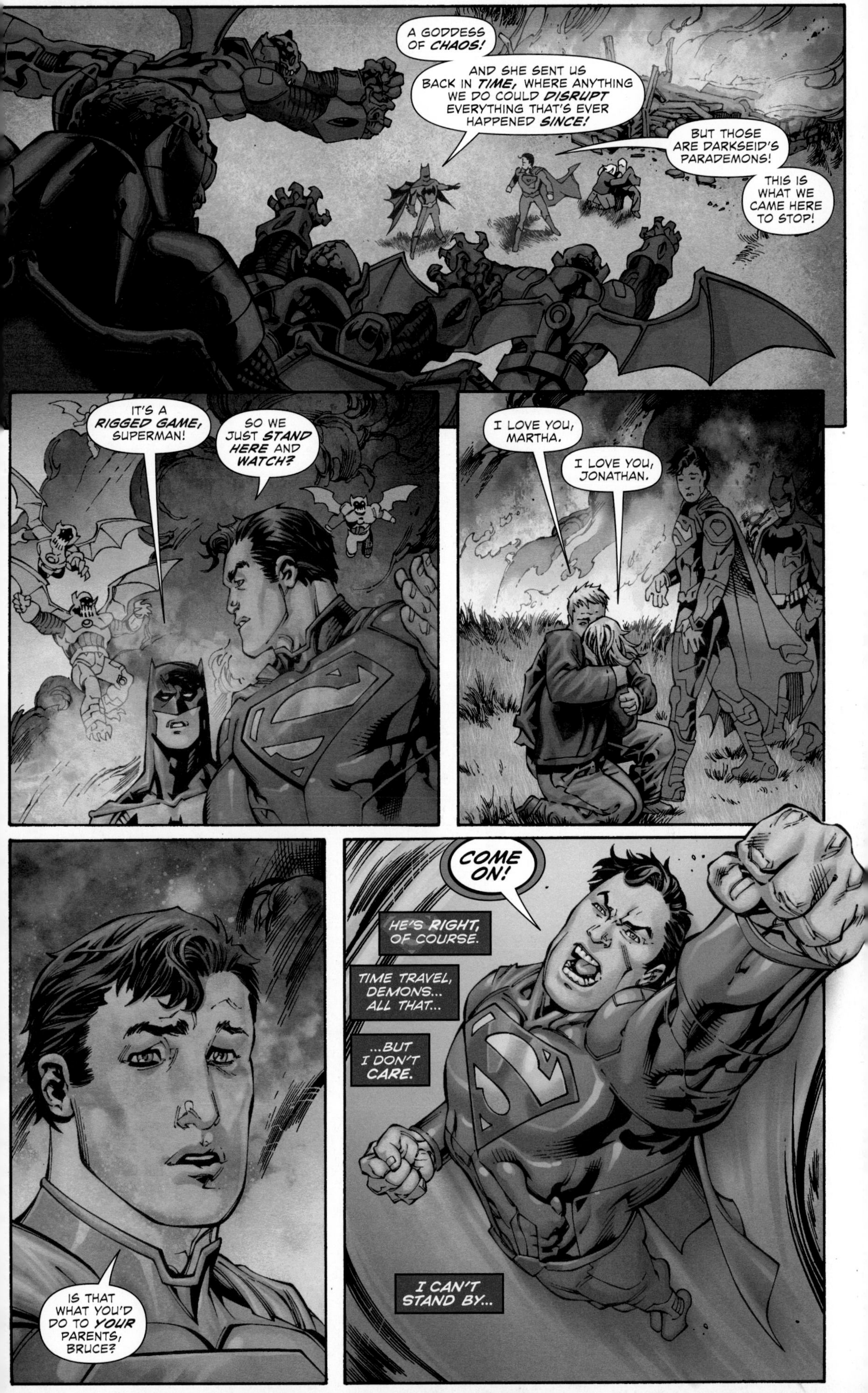
A GODDESS OF CHAOS!
AND SHE SENT US BACK IN TIME, WHERE ANYTHING WE DO COULD DISRUPT EVERYTHING THAT'S EVER HAPPENED SINCE!
BUT THOSE ARE DARKSEID'S PARADEMONS!
THIS IS WHAT WE CAME HERE TO STOP!
IT'S A RIGGED GAME, SUPERMAN!
SO WE JUST STAND HERE AND WATCH?
I LOVE YOU, MARTHA.
I LOVE YOU, JONATHAN.
IS THAT WHAT YOU'D DO TO YOUR PARENTS, BRUCE?
COME ON!
HE'S RIGHT, OF COURSE.
TIME TRAVEL, DEMONS... ALL THAT...
...BUT I DON'T CARE.
I CAN'T STAND BY...

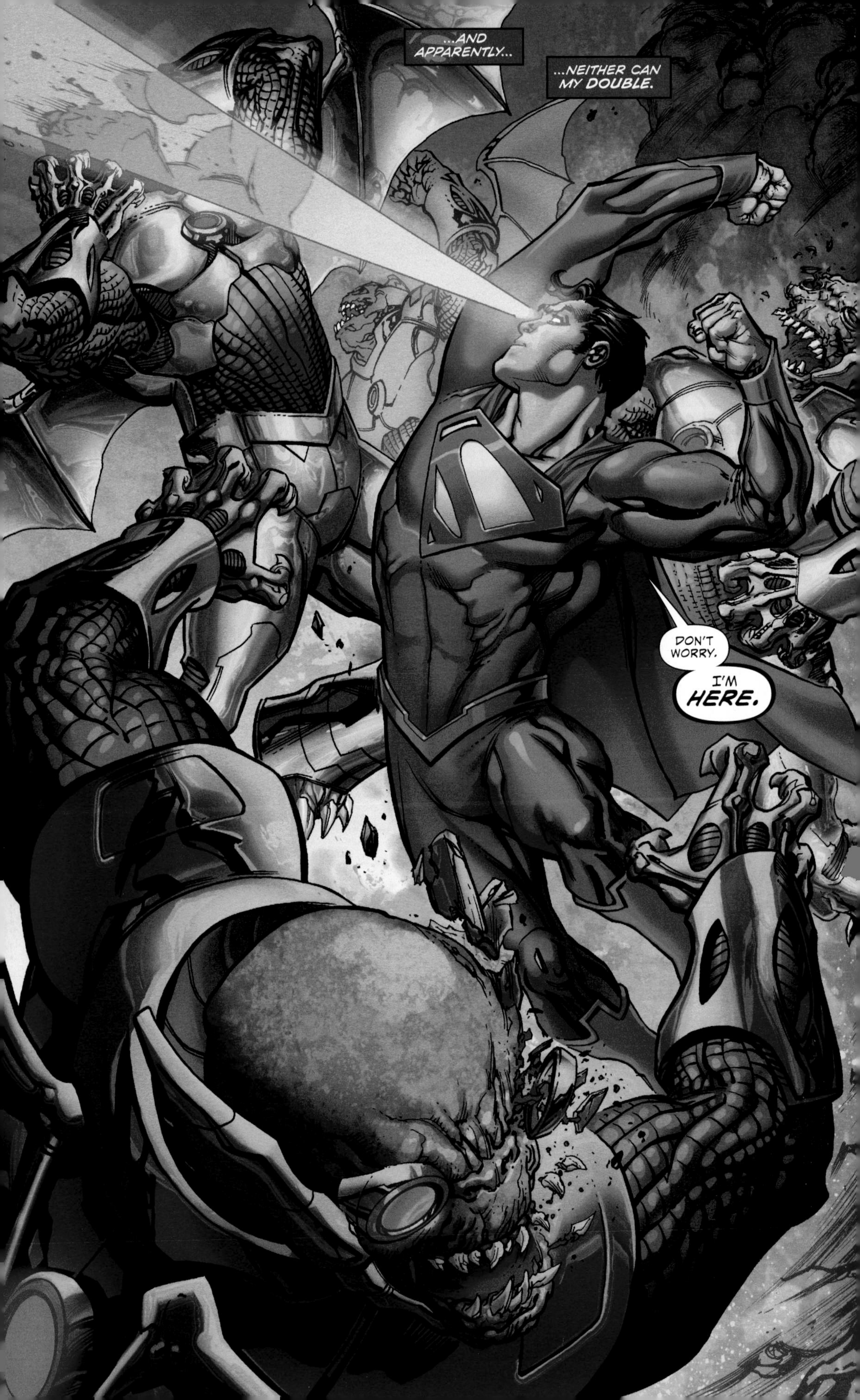
...AND APPARENTLY...
...NEITHER CAN MY DOUBLE.
DON'T WORRY.
I'M HERE.

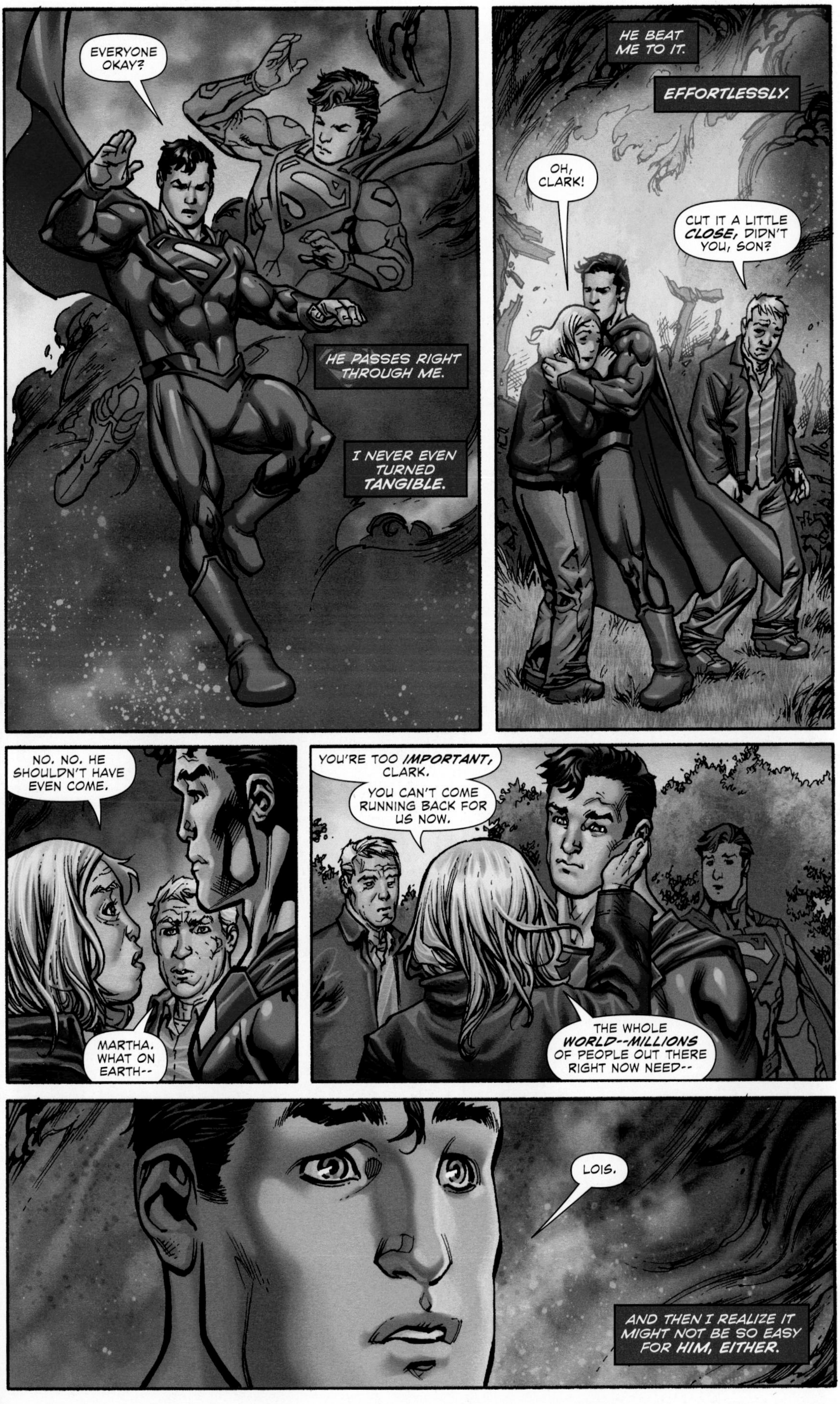
EVERYONE OKAY?
HE PASSES RIGHT THROUGH ME.
I NEVER EVEN TURNED TANGIBLE.
HE BEAT ME TO IT.
EFFORTLESSLY.
OH, CLARK!
CUT IT A LITTLE CLOSE, DIDN'T YOU, SON?
NO. NO. HE SHOULDN'T HAVE EVEN COME.
MARTHA. WHAT ON EARTH--
YOU'RE TOO IMPORTANT, CLARK.
YOU CAN'T COME RUNNING BACK FOR US NOW.
THE WHOLE WORLD--MILLIONS OF PEOPLE OUT THERE RIGHT NOW NEED--
LOIS.
AND THEN I REALIZE IT MIGHT NOT BE SO EASY FOR HIM, EITHER.

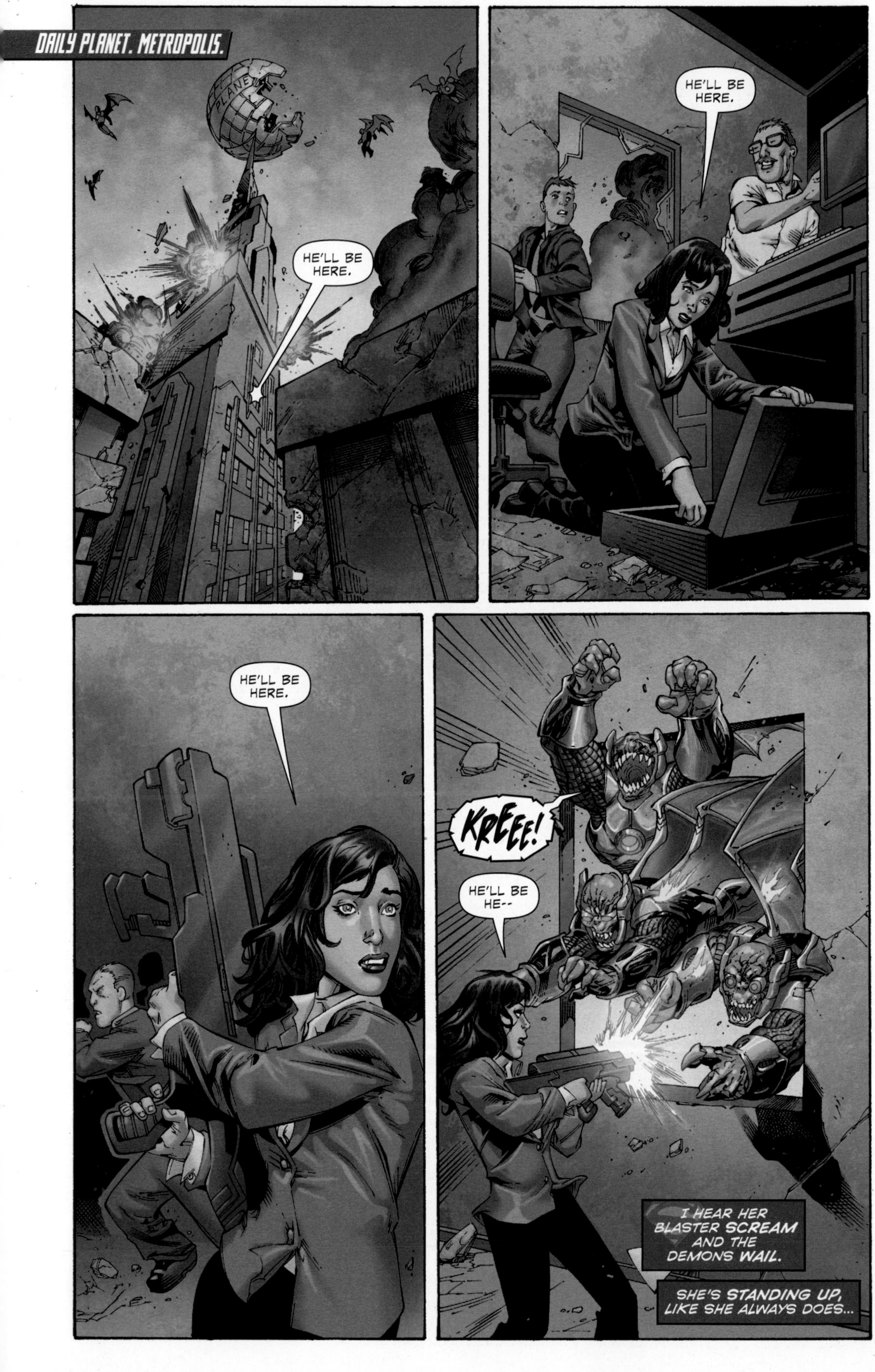
DAILY PLANET. METROPOLIS.
PLANET
HE'LL BE HERE.
HE'LL BE HERE.
HE'LL BE HERE.
KREEE!
HE'LL BE HE--
I HEAR HER BLASTER SCREAM AND THE DEMONS WAIL.
SHE'S STANDING UP, LIKE SHE ALWAYS DOES...

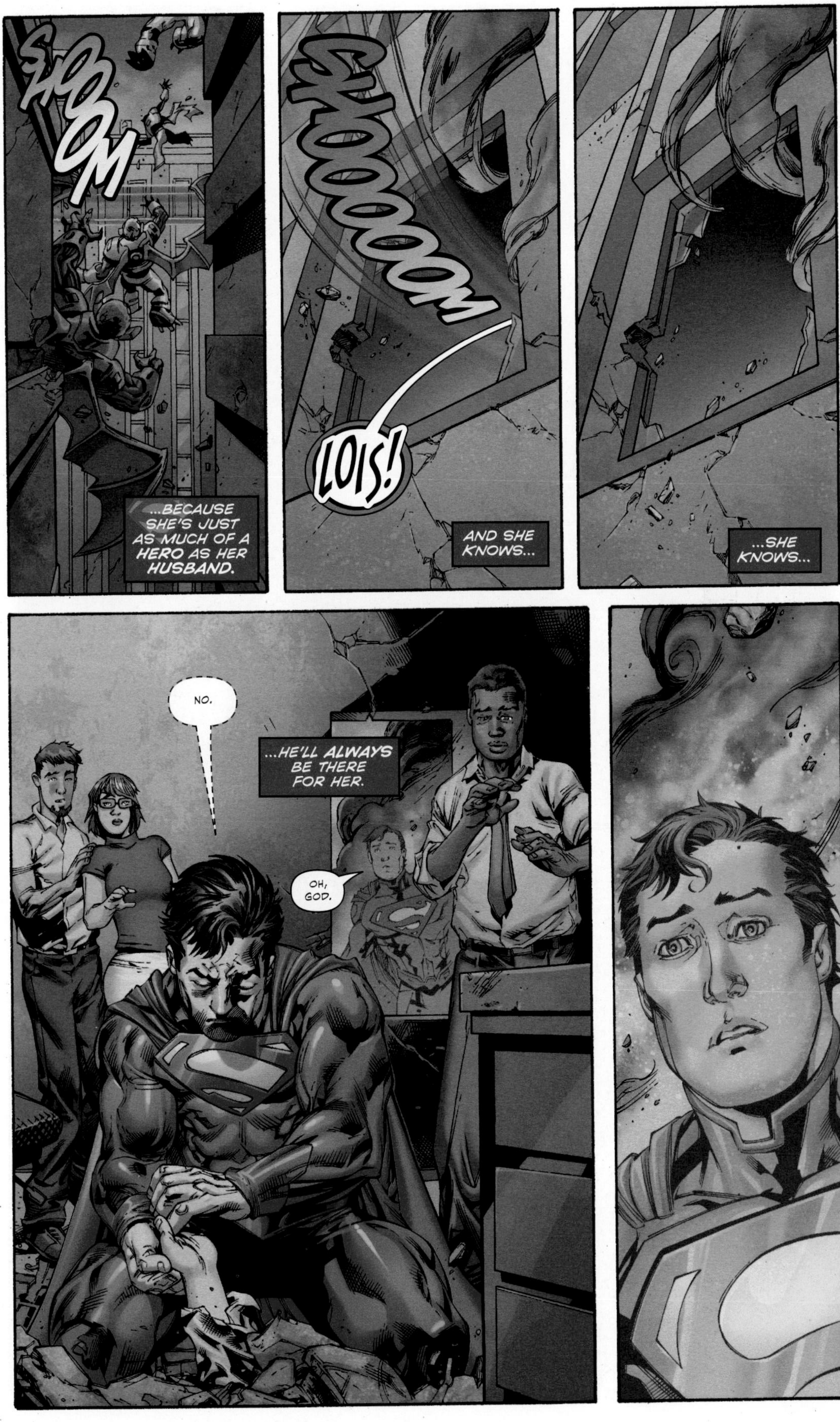
SHOOOM
...BECAUSE SHE'S JUST AS MUCH OF A HERO AS HER HUSBAND.
SHOOOOOOM
LOIS!
AND SHE KNOWS...
...SHE KNOWS...
NO.
...HE'LL ALWAYS BE THERE FOR HER.
OH, GOD.

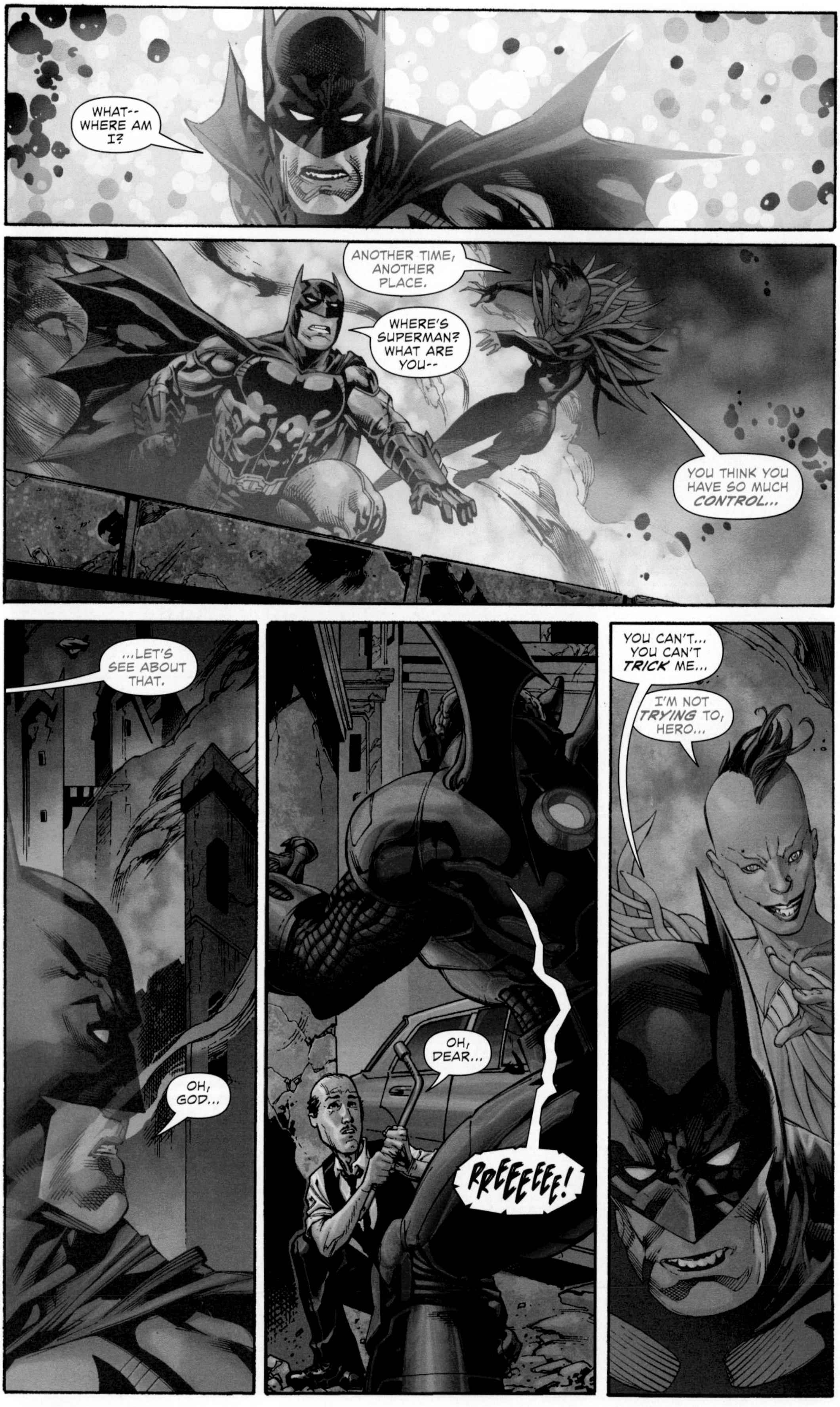
WHAT--
WHERE AM I?
ANOTHER TIME, ANOTHER PLACE.
WHERE'S SUPERMAN? WHAT ARE YOU--
YOU THINK YOU HAVE SO MUCH CONTROL...
...LET'S SEE ABOUT THAT.
OH, GOD...
OH, DEAR...
RREEEEEE!
YOU CAN'T... YOU CAN'T TRICK ME...
I'M NOT TRYING TO, HERO...

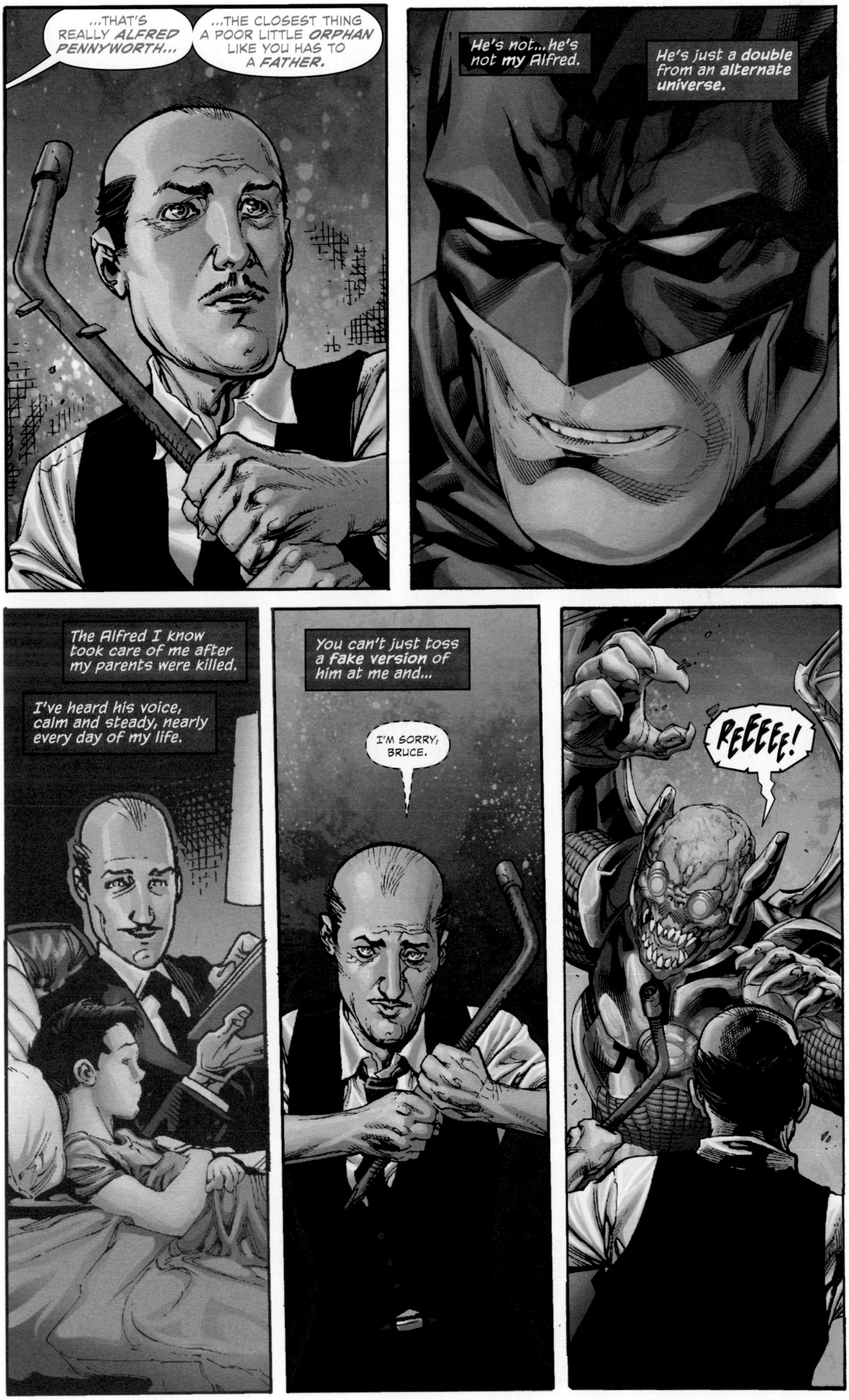
...THAT'S REALLY ALFRED PENNYWORTH...
...THE CLOSEST THING A POOR LITTLE ORPHAN LIKE YOU HAS TO A FATHER.
He's not...he's not my Alfred.
He's just a double from an alternate universe.
The Alfred I know took care of me after my parents were killed.
I've heard his voice, calm and steady, nearly every day of my life.
You can't just toss a fake version of him at me and...
I'M SORRY, BRUCE.
REEEEE!

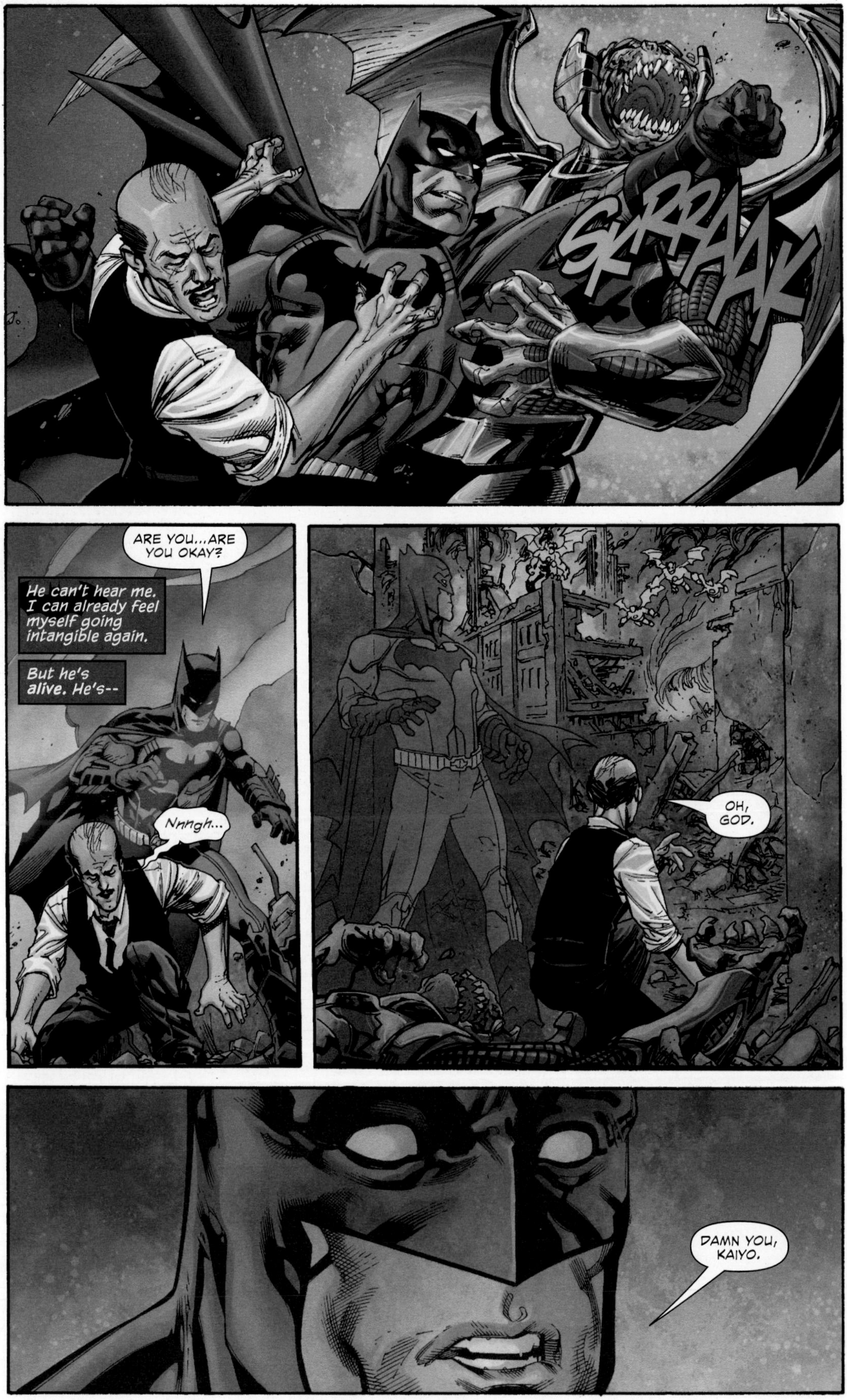
SKRRAAK
ARE YOU...ARE YOU OKAY?
He can't hear me. I can already feel myself going intangible again.
But he's alive. He's--
Nnngh...
OH, GOD.
DAMN YOU, KAIYO.

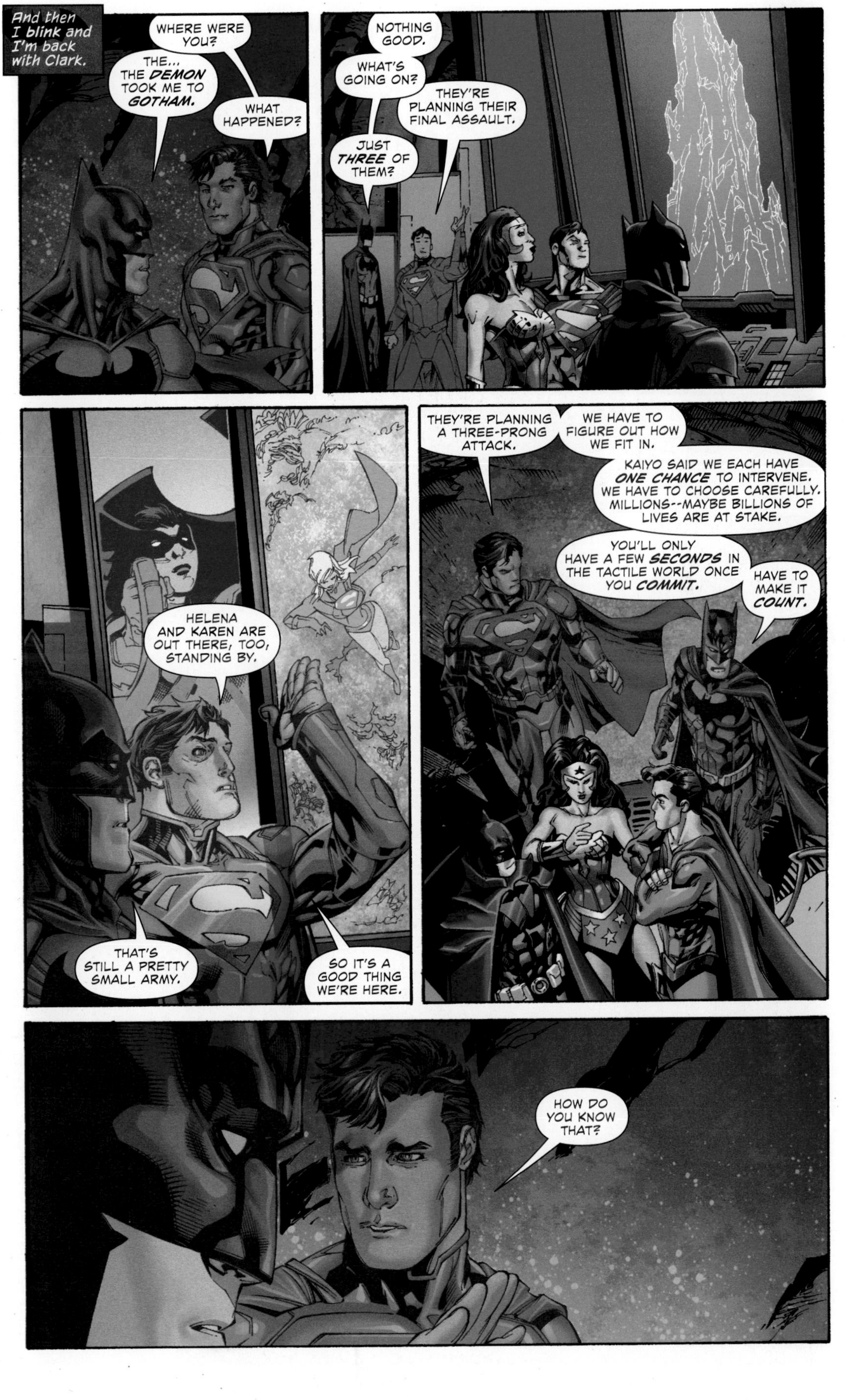
And then I blink and I'm back with Clark.
WHERE WERE YOU?
THE... THE DEMON TOOK ME TO GOTHAM.
WHAT HAPPENED?
NOTHING GOOD.
WHAT'S GOING ON?
THEY'RE PLANNING THEIR FINAL ASSAULT.
JUST THREE OF THEM?
HELENA AND KAREN ARE OUT THERE, TOO, STANDING BY.
THAT'S STILL A PRETTY SMALL ARMY.
SO IT'S A GOOD THING WE'RE HERE.
THEY'RE PLANNING A THREE-PRONG ATTACK.
WE HAVE TO FIGURE OUT HOW WE FIT IN.
KAIYO SAID WE EACH HAVE ONE CHANCE TO INTERVENE. WE HAVE TO CHOOSE CAREFULLY. MILLIONS--MAYBE BILLIONS OF LIVES ARE AT STAKE.
YOU'LL ONLY HAVE A FEW SECONDS IN THE TACTILE WORLD ONCE YOU COMMIT.
HAVE TO MAKE IT COUNT.
HOW DO YOU KNOW THAT?

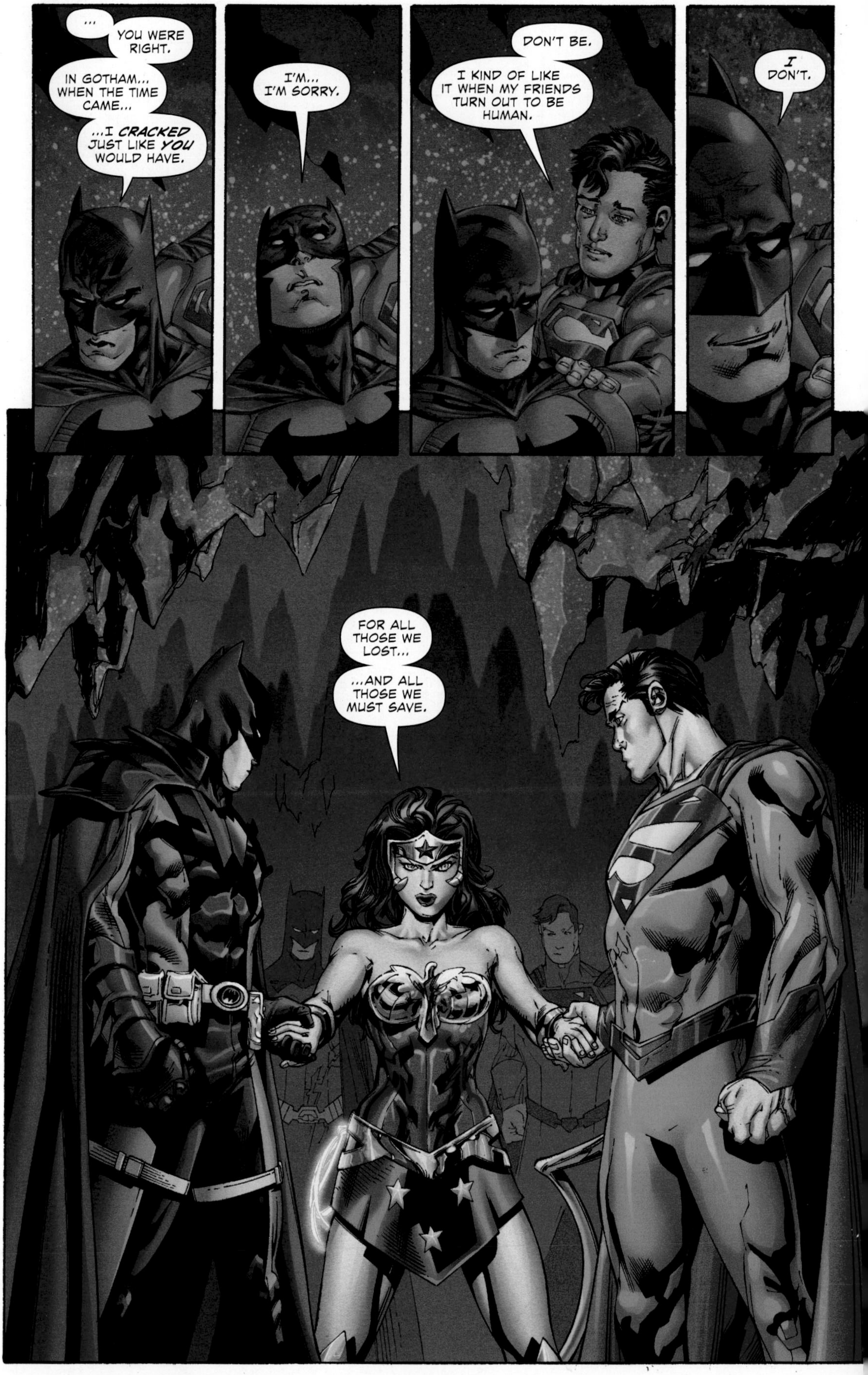
...
YOU WERE RIGHT.
IN GOTHAM... WHEN THE TIME CAME...
...I CRACKED JUST LIKE YOU WOULD HAVE.
I'M... I'M SORRY.
DON'T BE.
I KIND OF LIKE IT WHEN MY FRIENDS TURN OUT TO BE HUMAN.
I DON'T.
FOR ALL THOSE WE LOST...
...AND ALL THOSE WE MUST SAVE.

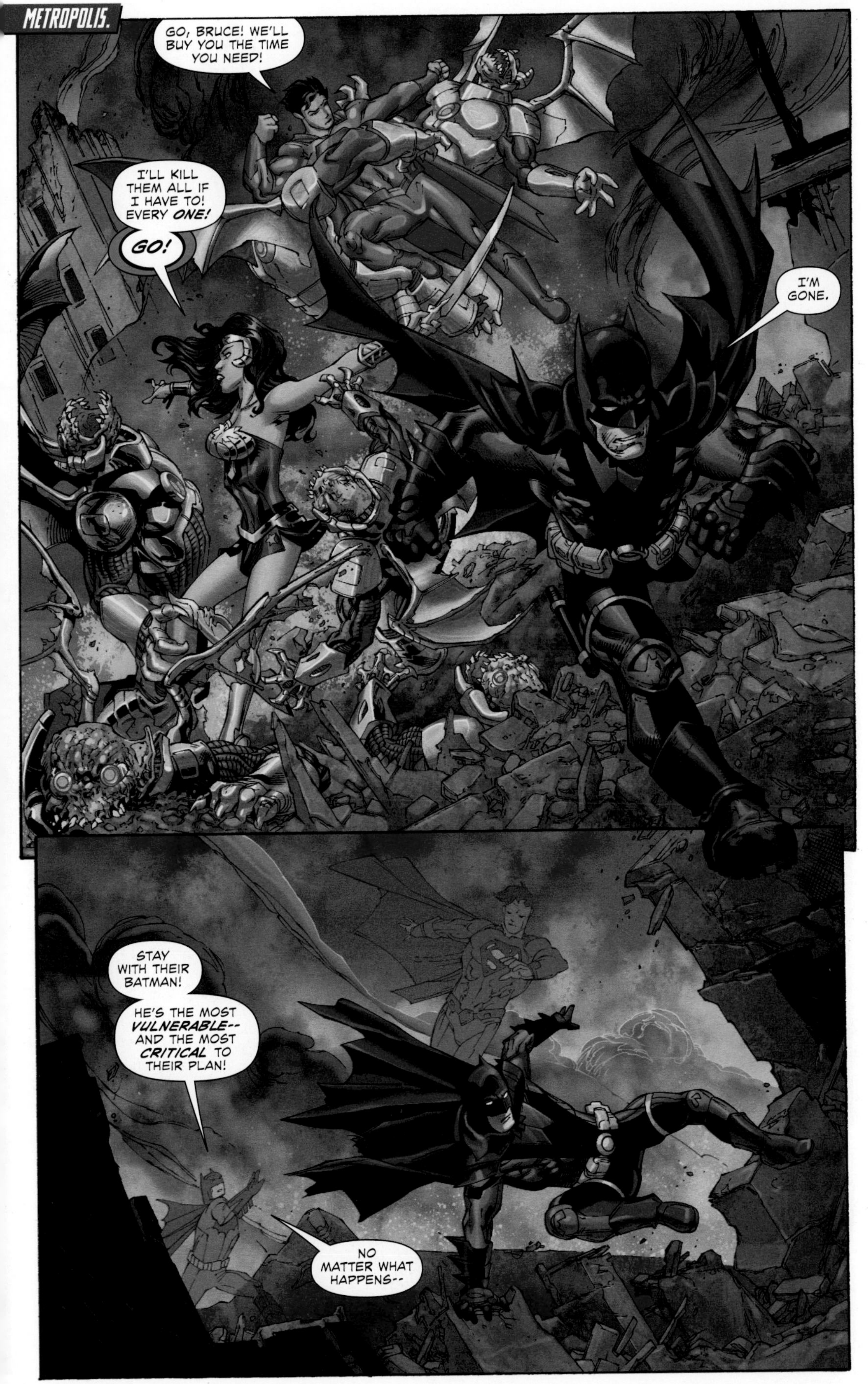
METROPOLIS.
GO, BRUCE! WE'LL BUY YOU THE TIME YOU NEED!
I'LL KILL THEM ALL IF I HAVE TO! EVERY ONE!
GO!
I'M GONE.
STAY WITH THEIR BATMAN!
HE'S THE MOST VULNERABLE-- AND THE MOST CRITICAL TO THEIR PLAN!
NO MATTER WHAT HAPPENS--

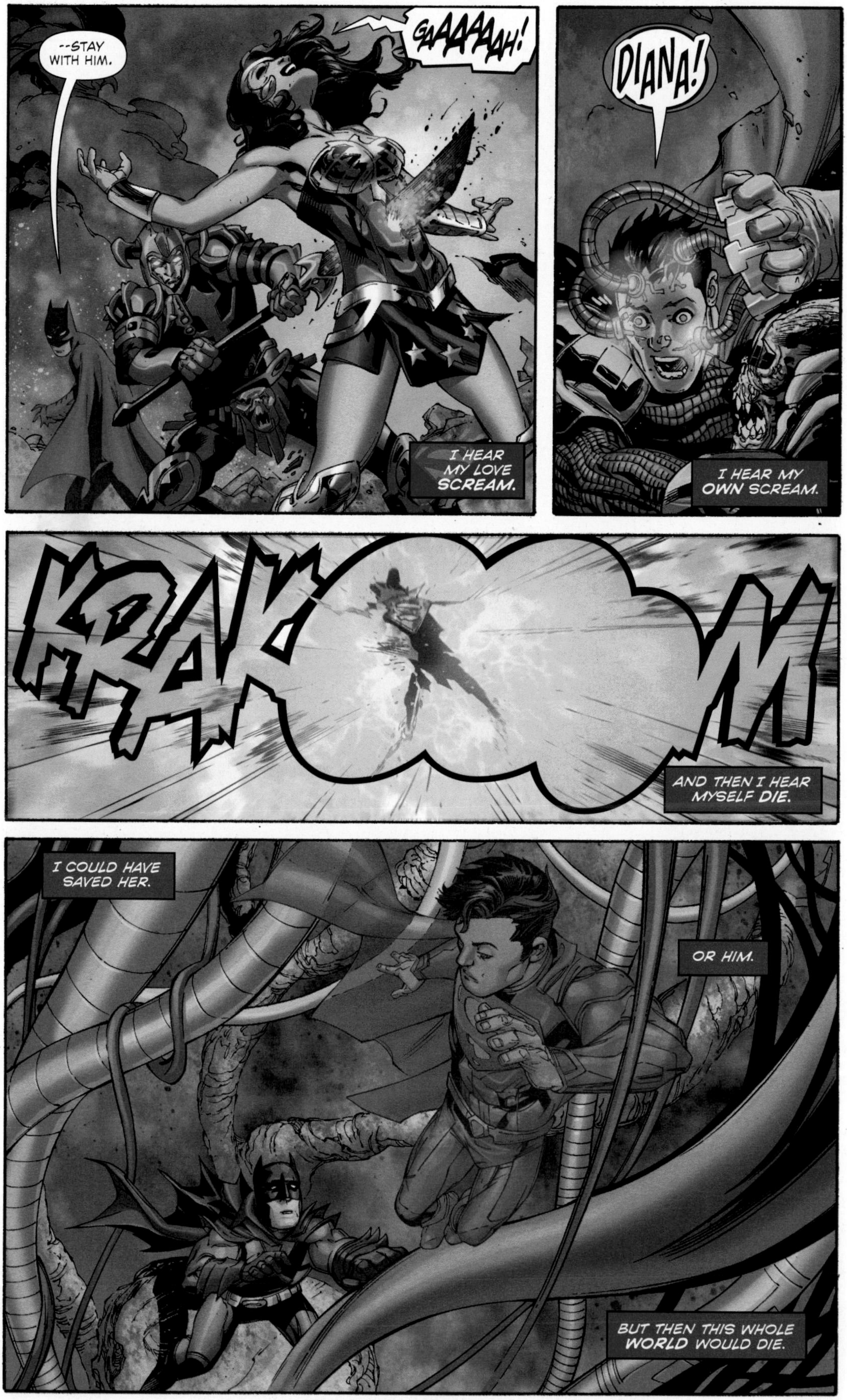
--STAY WITH HIM.
GAAAAAAH!
I HEAR MY LOVE SCREAM.
DIANA!
I HEAR MY OWN SCREAM.
KRAKOOOM
AND THEN I HEAR MYSELF DIE.
I COULD HAVE SAVED HER.
OR HIM.
BUT THEN THIS WHOLE WORLD WOULD DIE.

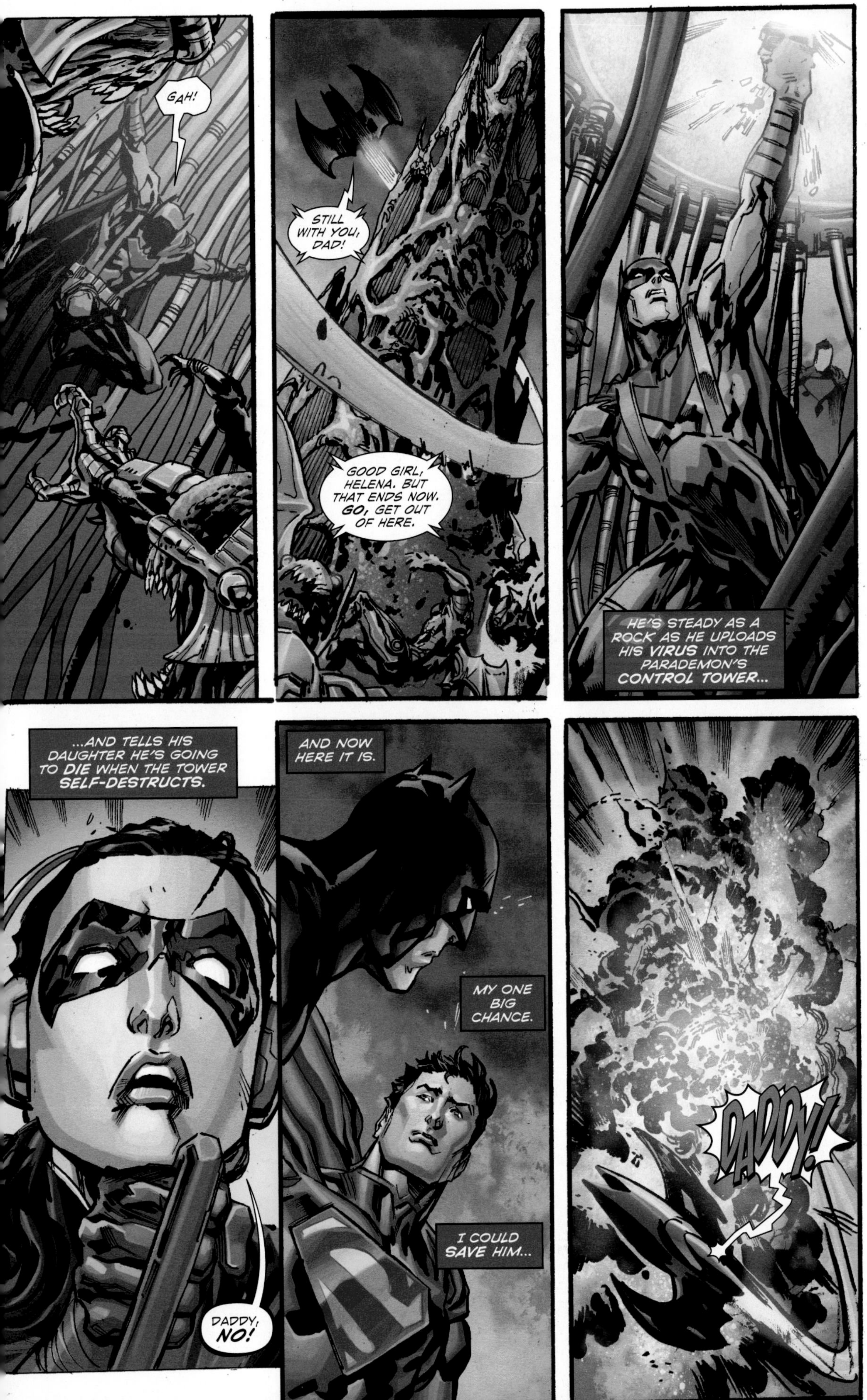
GAH!
STILL WITH YOU, DAD!
GOOD GIRL, HELENA. BUT THAT ENDS NOW. GO, GET OUT OF HERE.
HE'S STEADY AS A ROCK AS HE UPLOADS HIS VIRUS INTO THE PARADEMON'S CONTROL TOWER...
...AND TELLS HIS DAUGHTER HE'S GOING TO DIE WHEN THE TOWER SELF-DESTRUCTS.
DADDY, NO!
AND NOW HERE IT IS.
MY ONE BIG CHANCE.
I COULD SAVE HIM...
DADDY!

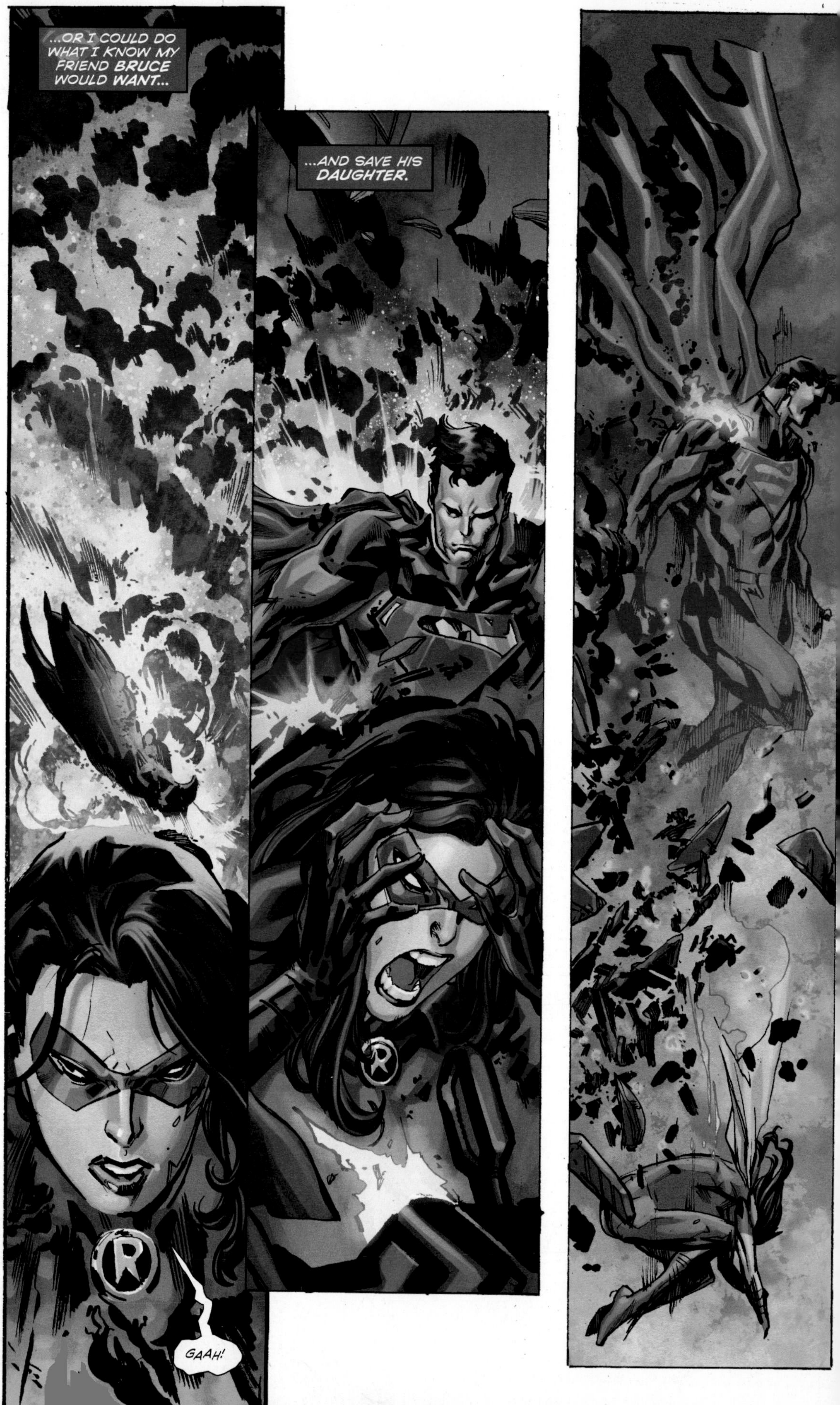
...OR I COULD DO WHAT I KNOW MY FRIEND BRUCE WOULD WANT...
...AND SAVE HIS DAUGHTER.
GAAH!

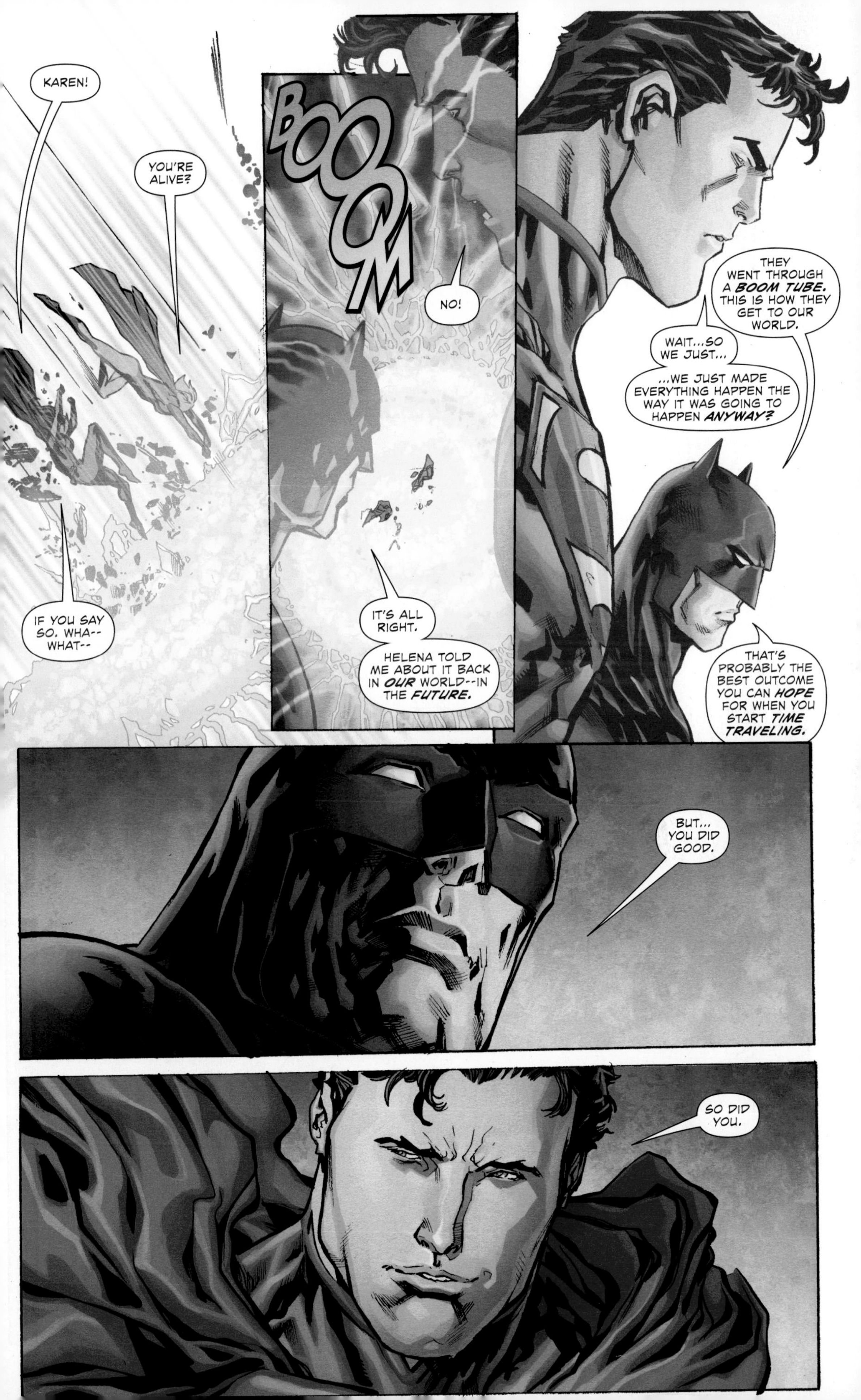
KAREN!
YOU'RE ALIVE?
IF YOU SAY SO. WHA-- WHAT--
BOOOM
NO!
IT'S ALL RIGHT.
HELENA TOLD ME ABOUT IT BACK IN OUR WORLD--IN THE FUTURE.
THEY WENT THROUGH A BOOM TUBE. THIS IS HOW THEY GET TO OUR WORLD.
WAIT...SO WE JUST...
...WE JUST MADE EVERYTHING HAPPEN THE WAY IT WAS GOING TO HAPPEN ANYWAY?
THAT'S PROBABLY THE BEST OUTCOME YOU CAN HOPE FOR WHEN YOU START TIME TRAVELING.
BUT... YOU DID GOOD.
SO DID YOU.

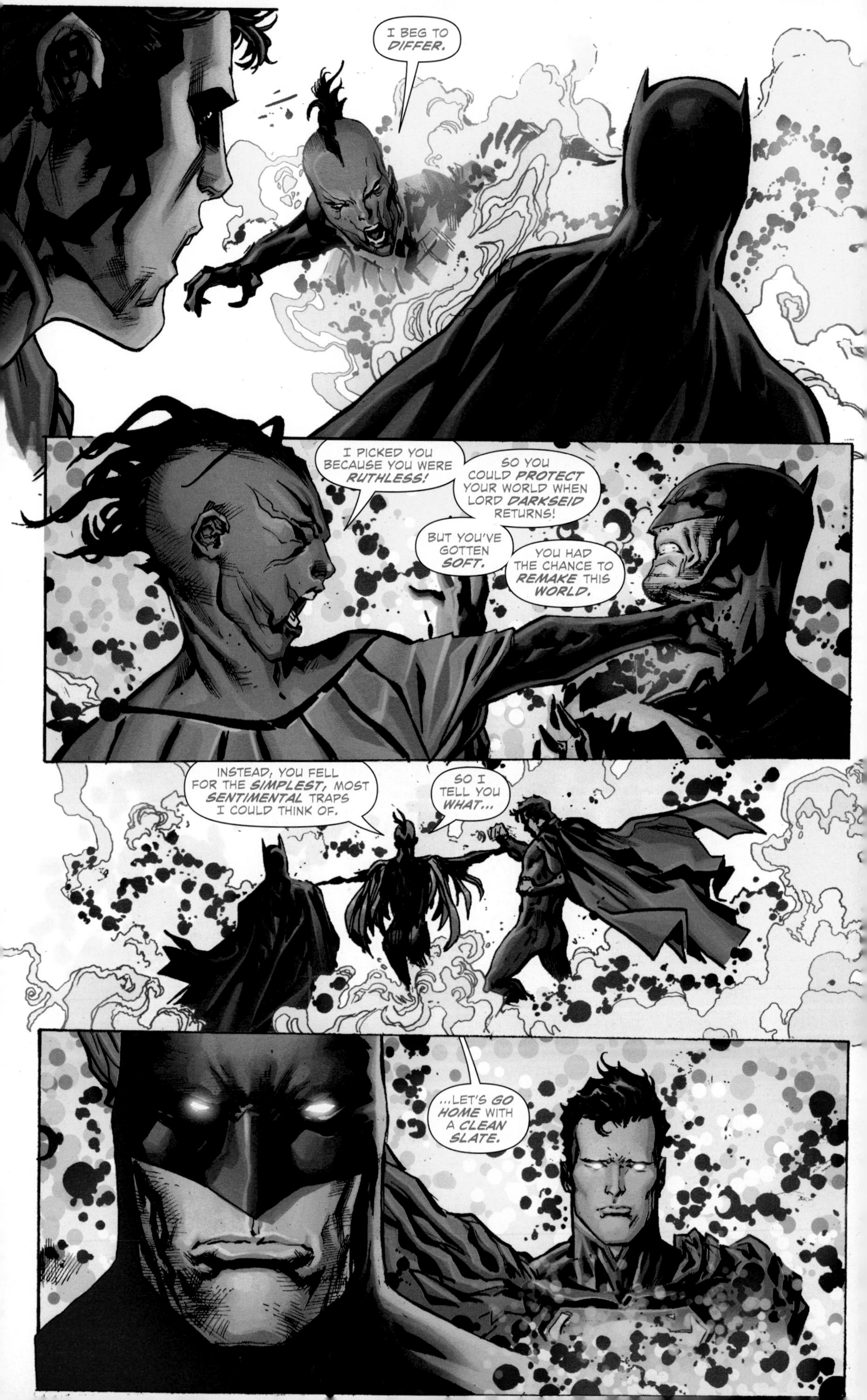
I BEG TO DIFFER.
I PICKED YOU BECAUSE YOU WERE RUTHLESS!
SO YOU COULD PROTECT YOUR WORLD WHEN LORD DARKSEID RETURNS!
BUT YOU'VE GOTTEN SOFT.
YOU HAD THE CHANCE TO REMAKE THIS WORLD.
INSTEAD, YOU FELL FOR THE SIMPLEST, MOST SENTIMENTAL TRAPS I COULD THINK OF.
SO I TELL YOU WHAT...
...LET'S GO HOME WITH A CLEAN SLATE.

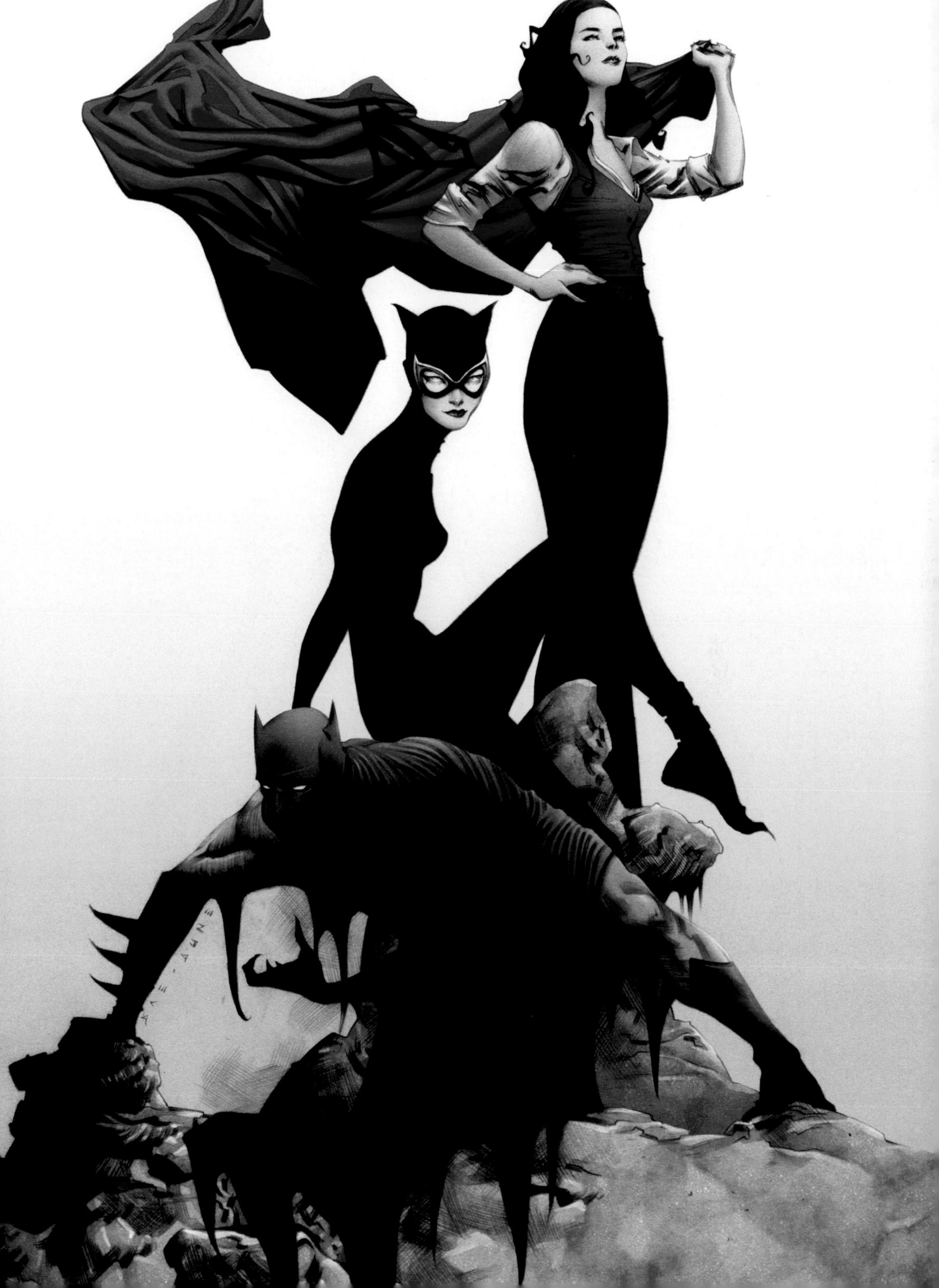

EYE OF SATANUS

GREG PAK writer **JAE LEE** artist **JUNE CHUNG** colorist **ROB LEIGH** letterer cover by **JAE LEE** with **JUNE CHUNG**

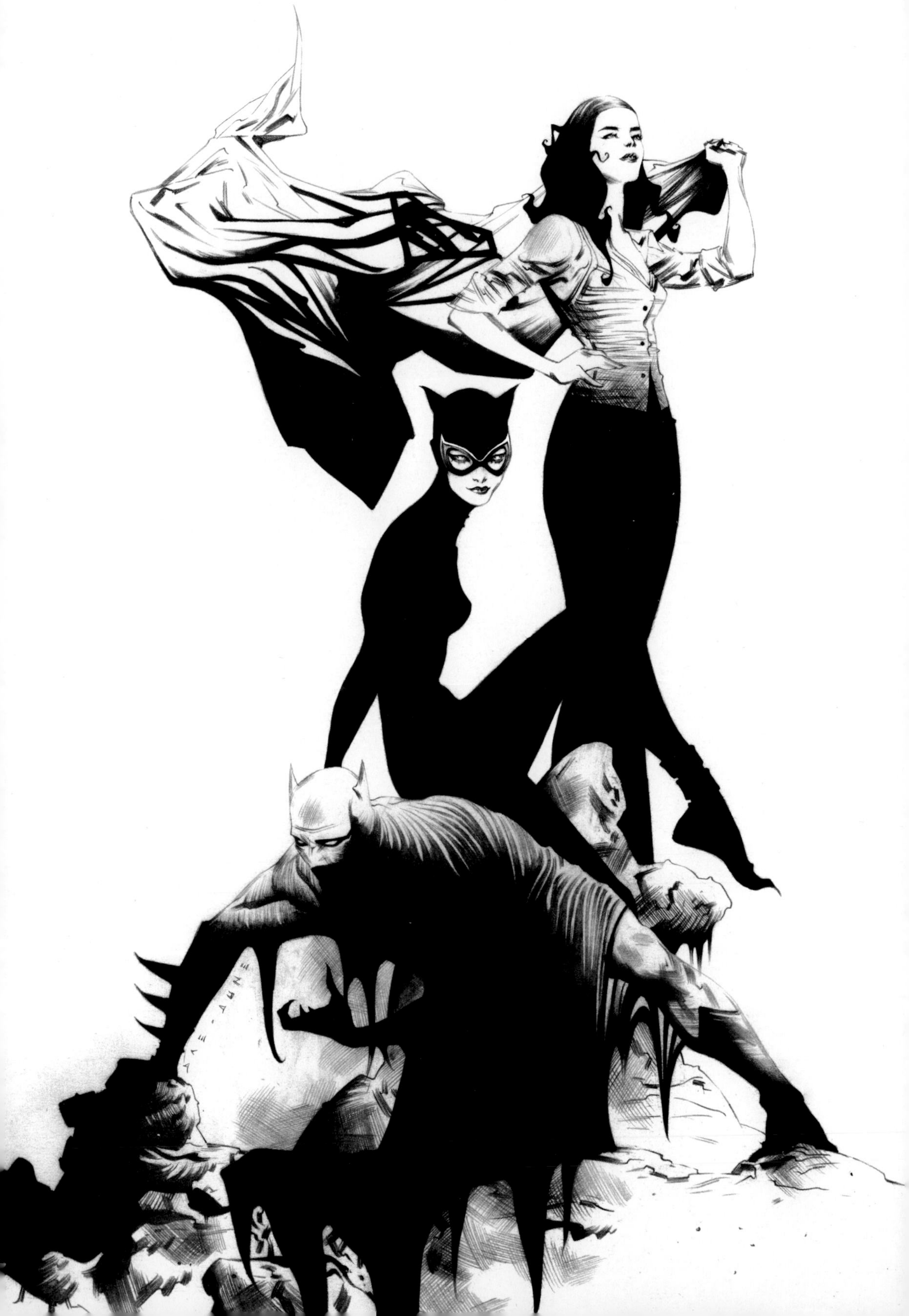

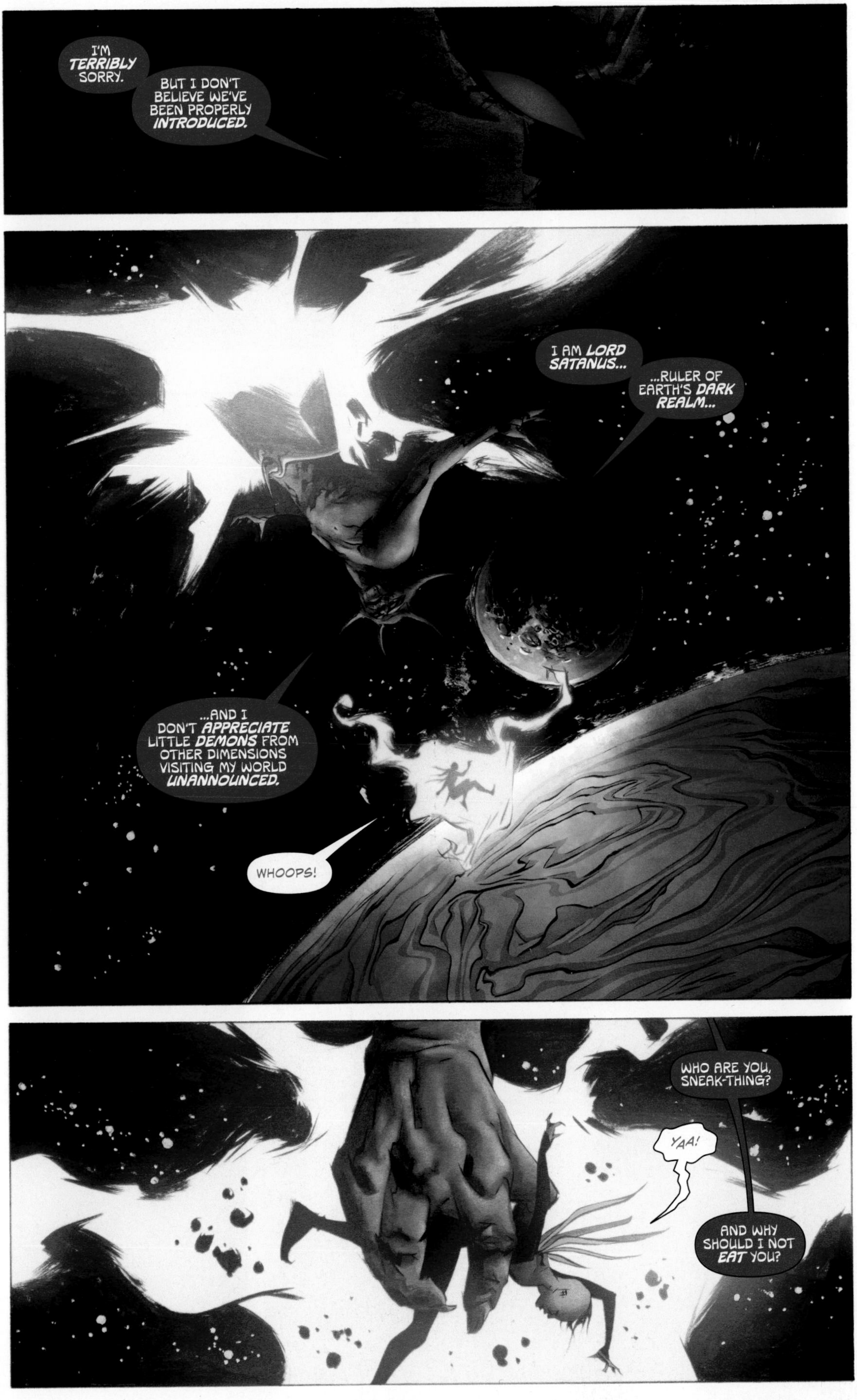
I'M TERRIBLY SORRY.
BUT I DON'T BELIEVE WE'VE BEEN PROPERLY INTRODUCED.
I AM LORD SATANUS...
...RULER OF EARTH'S DARK REALM...
...AND I DON'T APPRECIATE LITTLE DEMONS FROM OTHER DIMENSIONS VISITING MY WORLD UNANNOUNCED.
WHOOPS!
WHO ARE YOU, SNEAK-THING?
YAA!
AND WHY SHOULD I NOT EAT YOU?

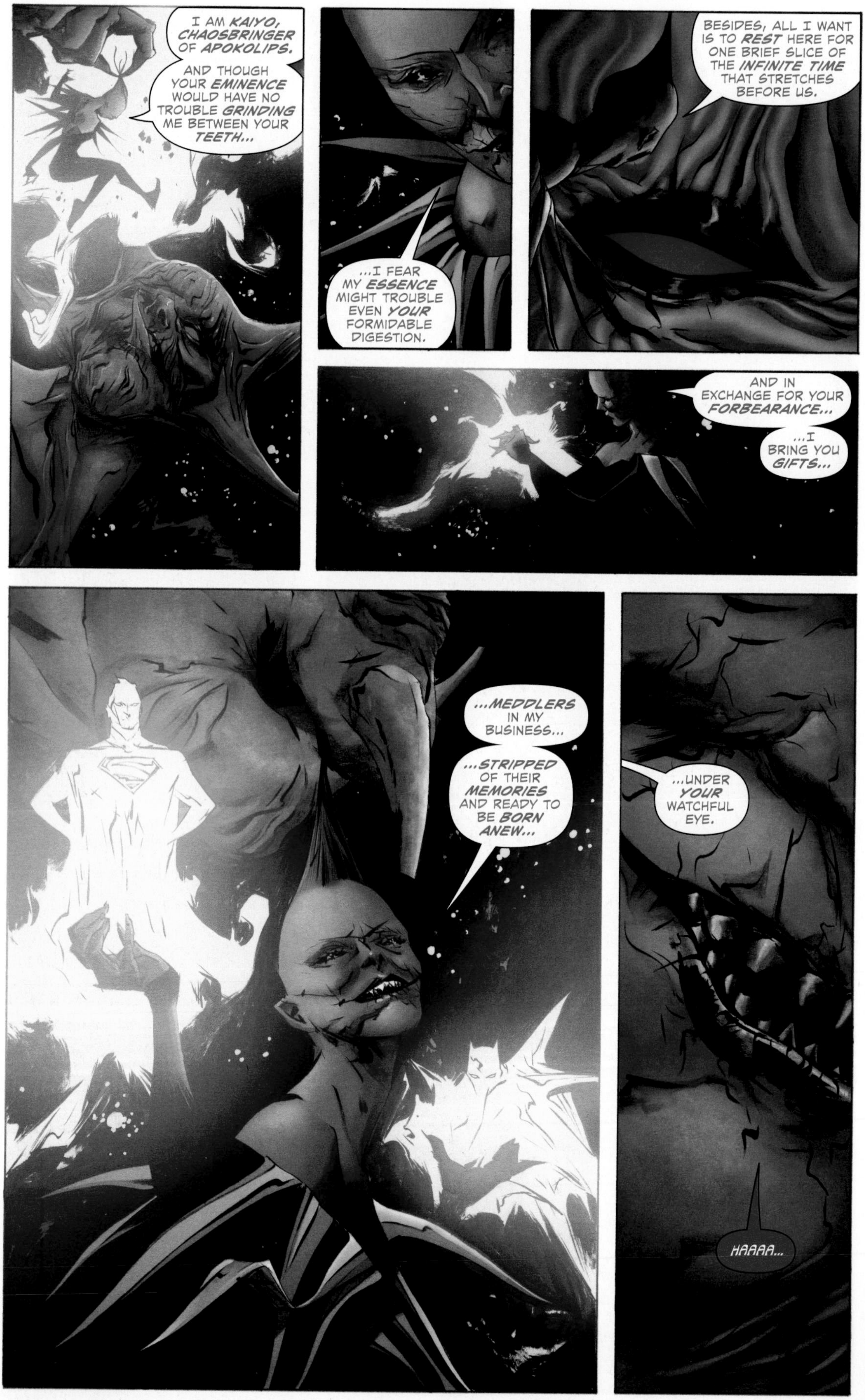

I AM KAIYO, CHAOSBRINGER OF APOKOLIPS.
AND THOUGH YOUR EMINENCE WOULD HAVE NO TROUBLE GRINDING ME BETWEEN YOUR TEETH...
...I FEAR MY ESSENCE MIGHT TROUBLE EVEN YOUR FORMIDABLE DIGESTION.
BESIDES, ALL I WANT IS TO REST HERE FOR ONE BRIEF SLICE OF THE INFINITE TIME THAT STRETCHES BEFORE US.
AND IN EXCHANGE FOR YOUR FORBEARANCE...
...I BRING YOU GIFTS...
...MEDDLERS IN MY BUSINESS...
...STRIPPED OF THEIR MEMORIES AND READY TO BE BORN ANEW...
...UNDER YOUR WATCHFUL EYE.
HAAAA...

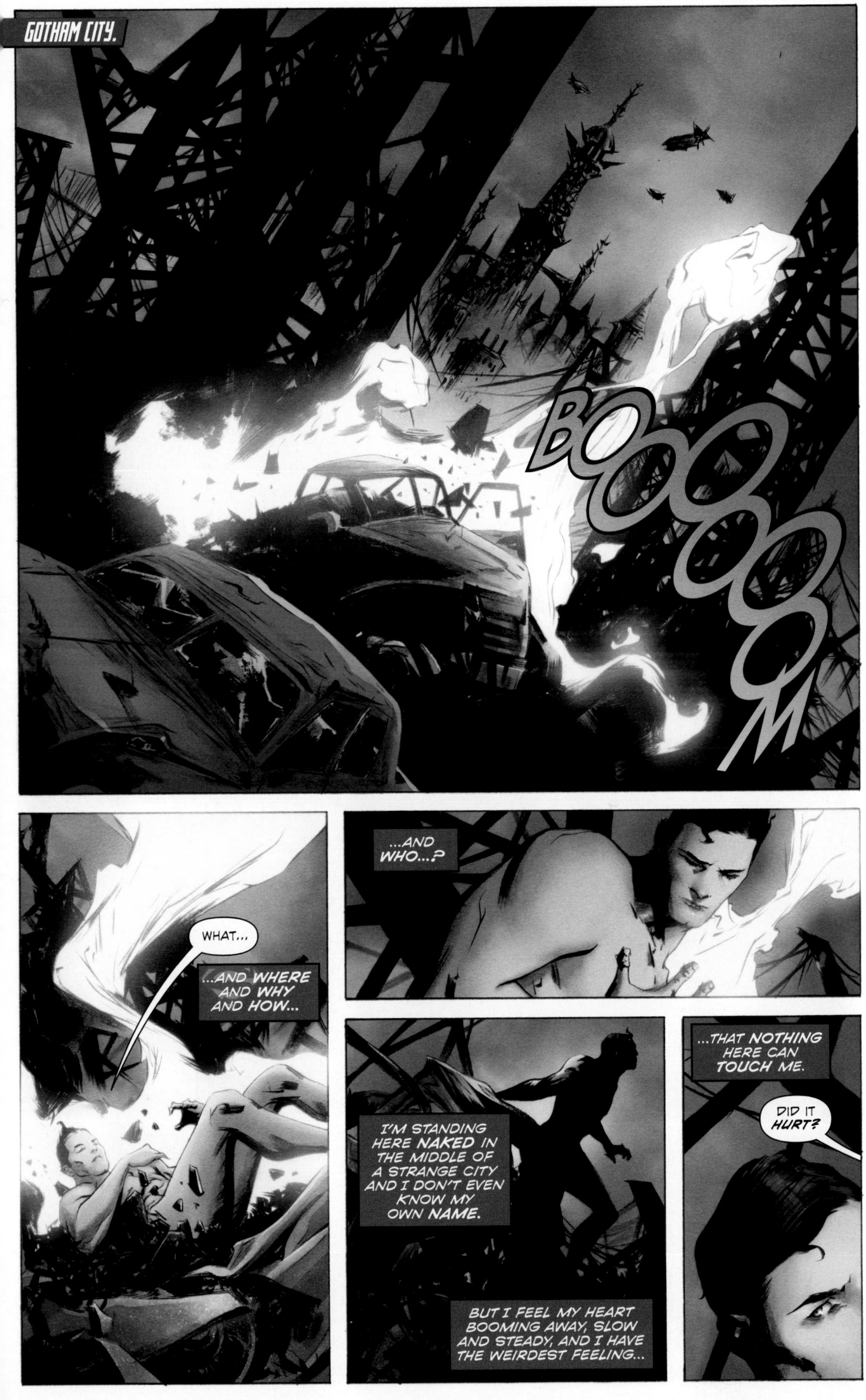
GOTHAM CITY.
BOOOOOOM
WHAT...
...AND WHERE AND WHY AND HOW...
...AND WHO...?
I'M STANDING HERE NAKED IN THE MIDDLE OF A STRANGE CITY AND I DON'T EVEN KNOW MY OWN NAME.
BUT I FEEL MY HEART BOOMING AWAY, SLOW AND STEADY, AND I HAVE THE WEIRDEST FEELING...
...THAT NOTHING HERE CAN TOUCH ME.
DID IT HURT?

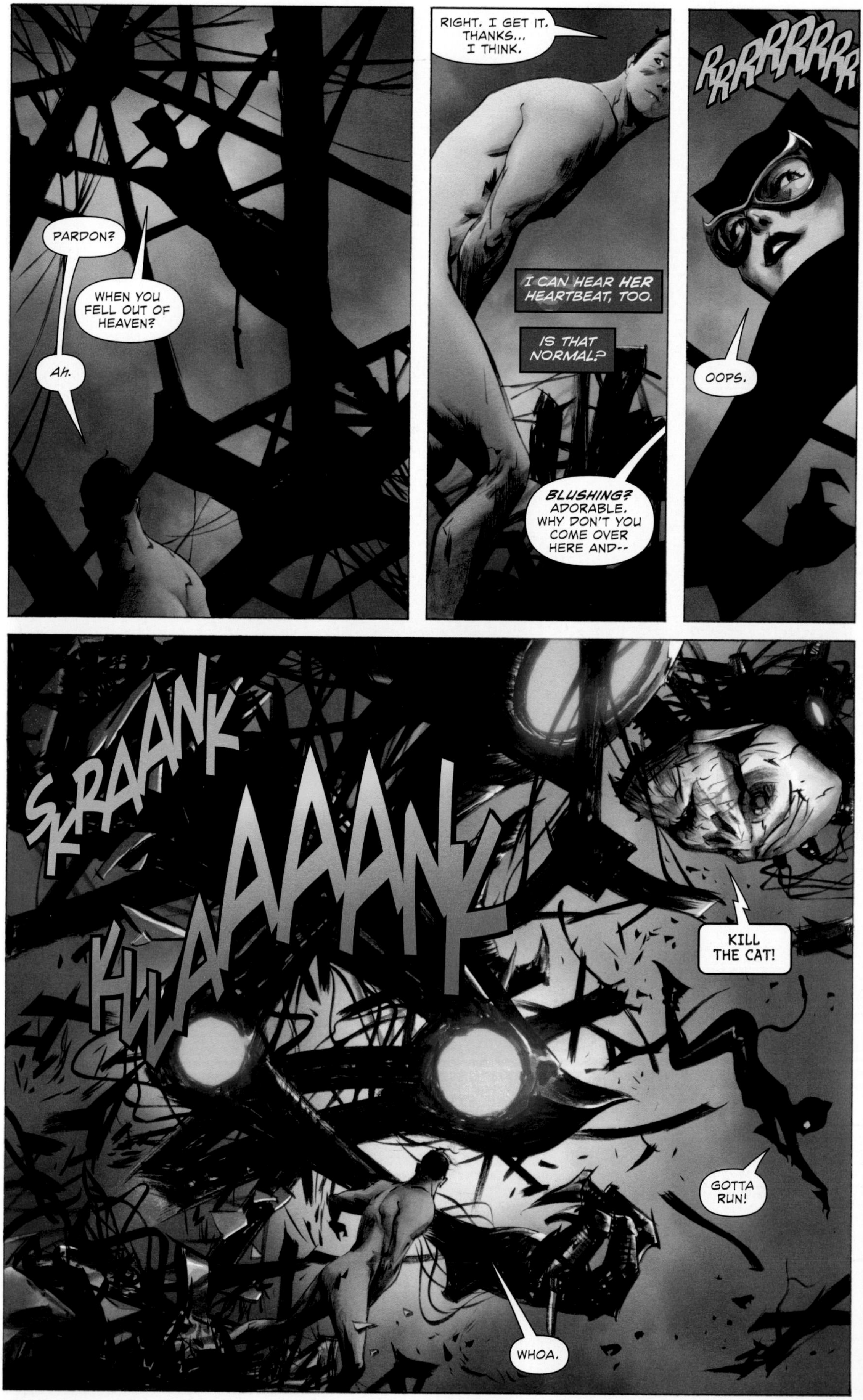

PARDON?
WHEN YOU FELL OUT OF HEAVEN?
Ah.
RIGHT. I GET IT. THANKS... I THINK.
I CAN HEAR HER HEARTBEAT, TOO.
IS THAT NORMAL?
BLUSHING? ADORABLE. WHY DON'T YOU COME OVER HERE AND--
RRRRRRRR
OOPS.
SKRAANK
KLLAAAANK
KILL THE CAT!
GOTTA RUN!
WHOA.

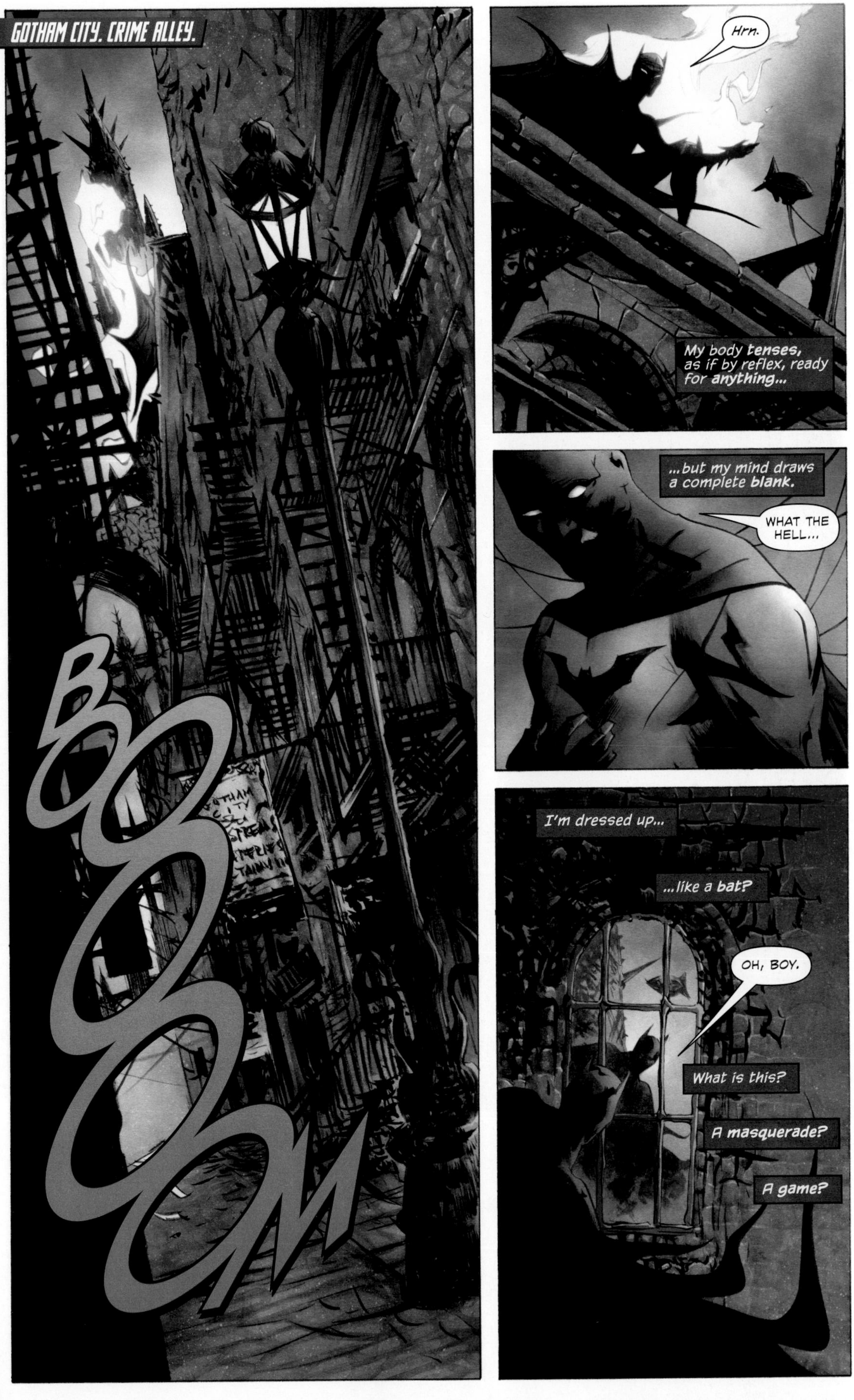
GOTHAM CITY. CRIME ALLEY.
BOOOOOOM
Hrn.
My body tenses, as if by reflex, ready for anything...
...but my mind draws a complete blank.
WHAT THE HELL...
I'm dressed up...
...like a bat?
OH, BOY.
What is this?
A masquerade?
A game?

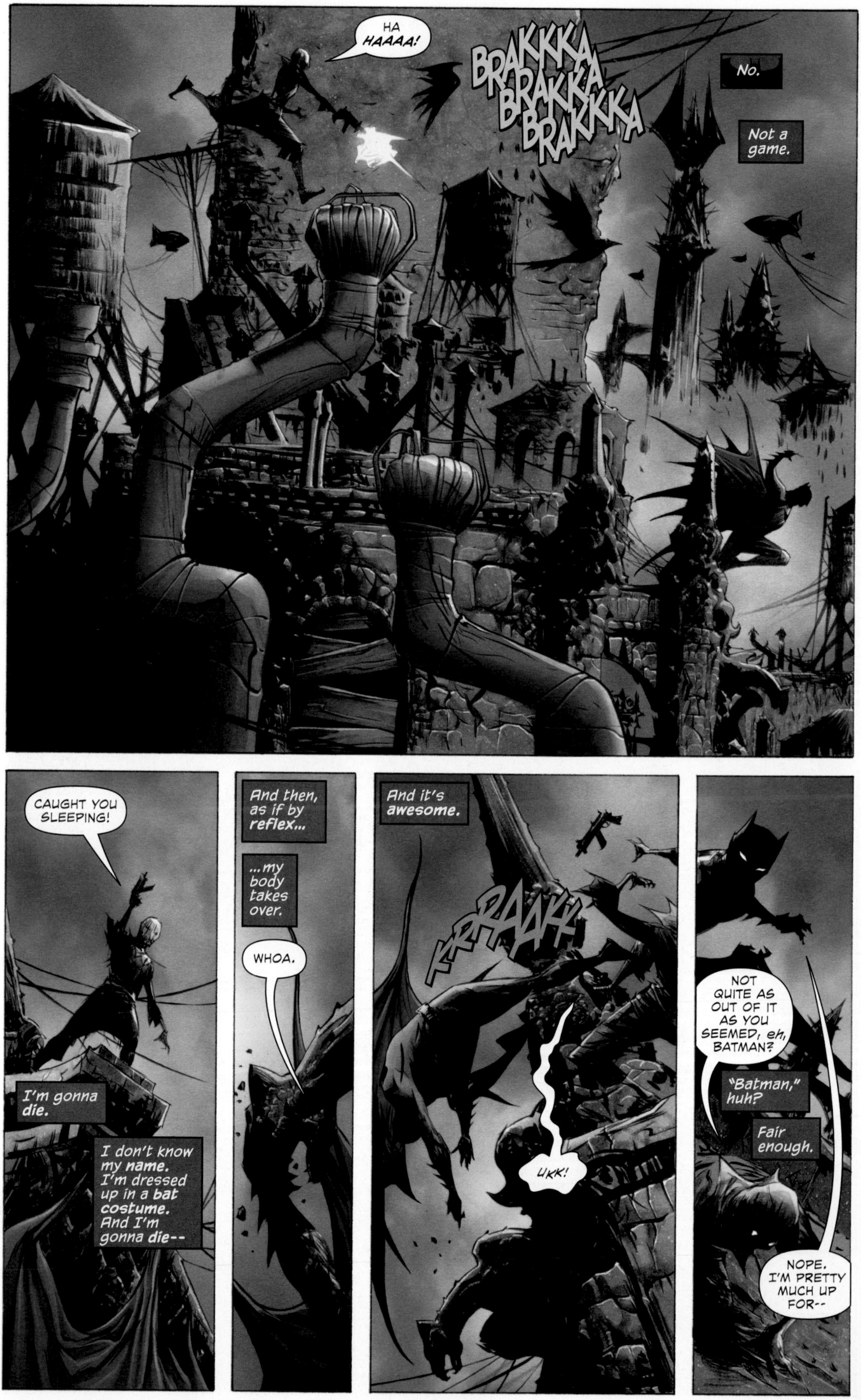

HA HAAAA!
BRAKKKA BRAKKKA BRAKKKA
No.
Not a game.
CAUGHT YOU SLEEPING!
I'm gonna die.
I don't know my name. I'm dressed up in a bat costume. And I'm gonna die--
And then, as if by reflex...
...my body takes over.
WHOA.
And it's awesome.
KRRAAKK
UKK!
NOT QUITE AS OUT OF IT AS YOU SEEMED, eh, BATMAN?
"Batman," huh?
Fair enough.
NOPE. I'M PRETTY MUCH UP FOR--

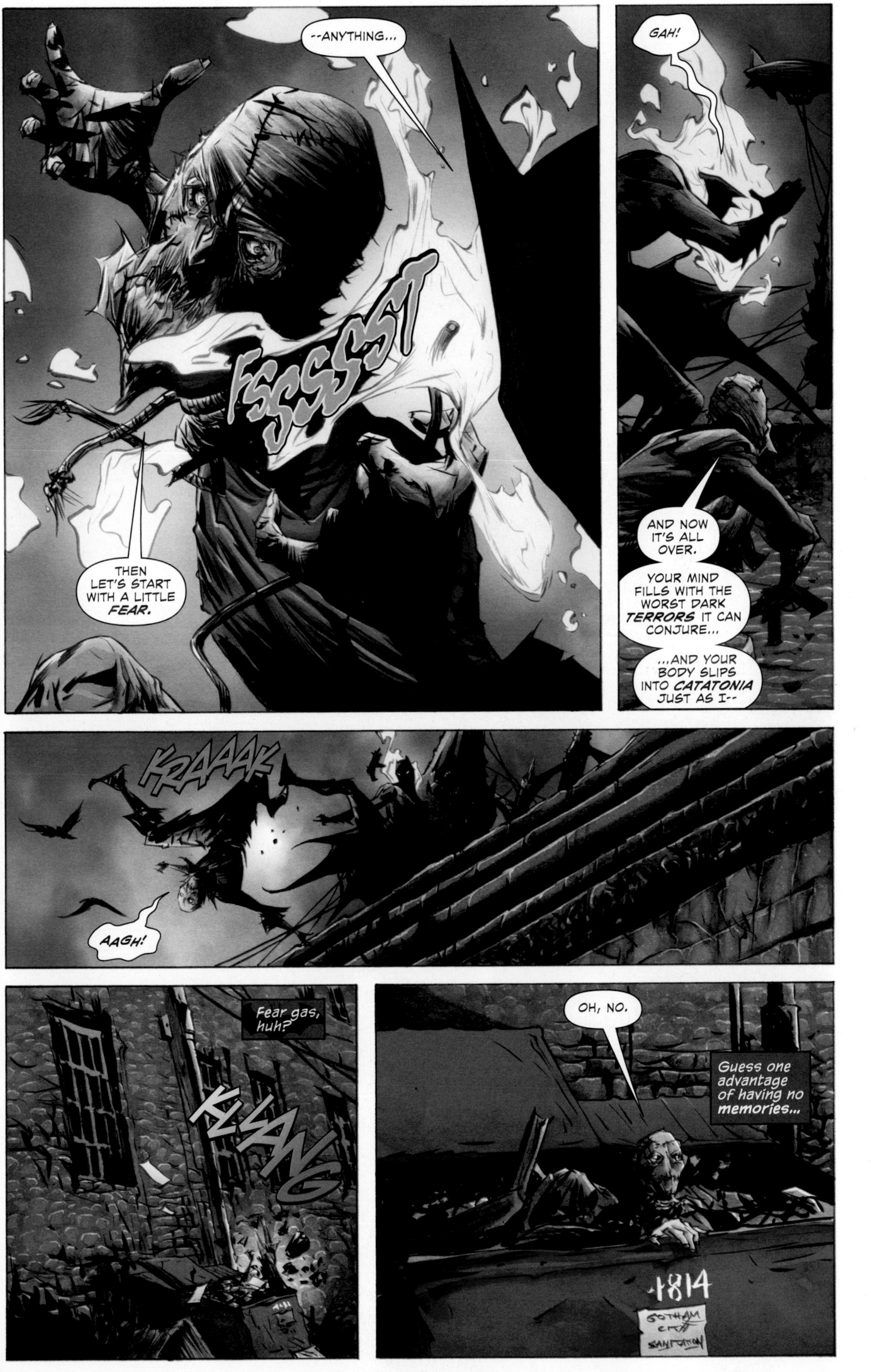
--ANYTHING...
THEN LET'S START WITH A LITTLE FEAR.
FSSSSST
GAH!
AND NOW IT'S ALL OVER.
YOUR MIND FILLS WITH THE WORST DARK TERRORS IT CAN CONJURE...
...AND YOUR BODY SLIPS INTO CATATONIA JUST AS I--
KRAAAK
AAGH!
Fear gas, huh?
KLANG
OH, NO.
Guess one advantage of having no memories...
1814
GOTHAM CITY SANITATION

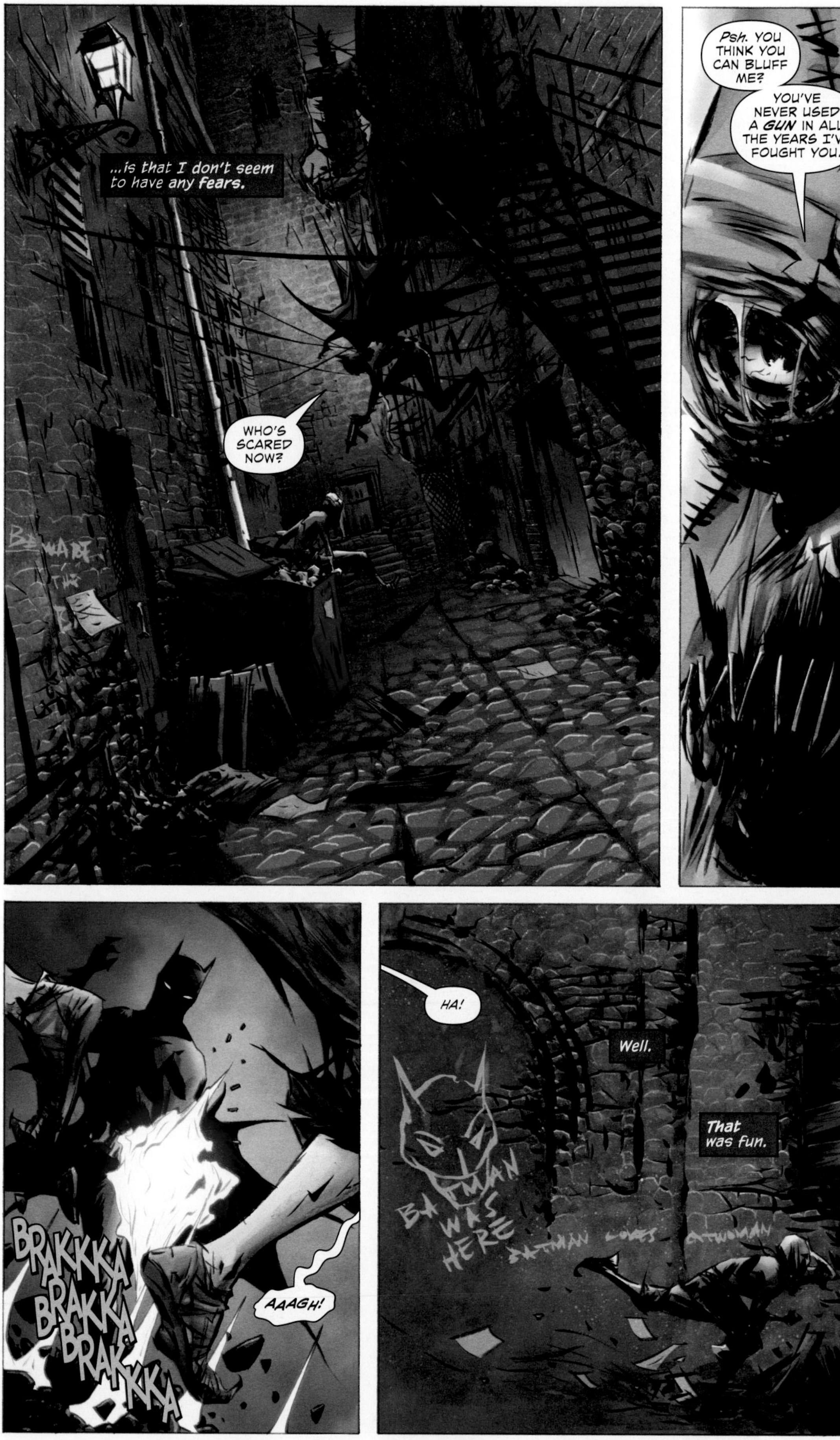
...is that I don't seem to have any fears.
WHO'S SCARED NOW?
Psh. YOU THINK YOU CAN BLUFF ME?
YOU'VE NEVER USED A GUN IN ALL THE YEARS I'VE FOUGHT YOU.
BRAKKKA BRAKKKA BRAKKKA
AAAGH!
HA!
Well.
That was fun.
BATMAN WAS HERE
BATMAN LOVES CATWOMAN

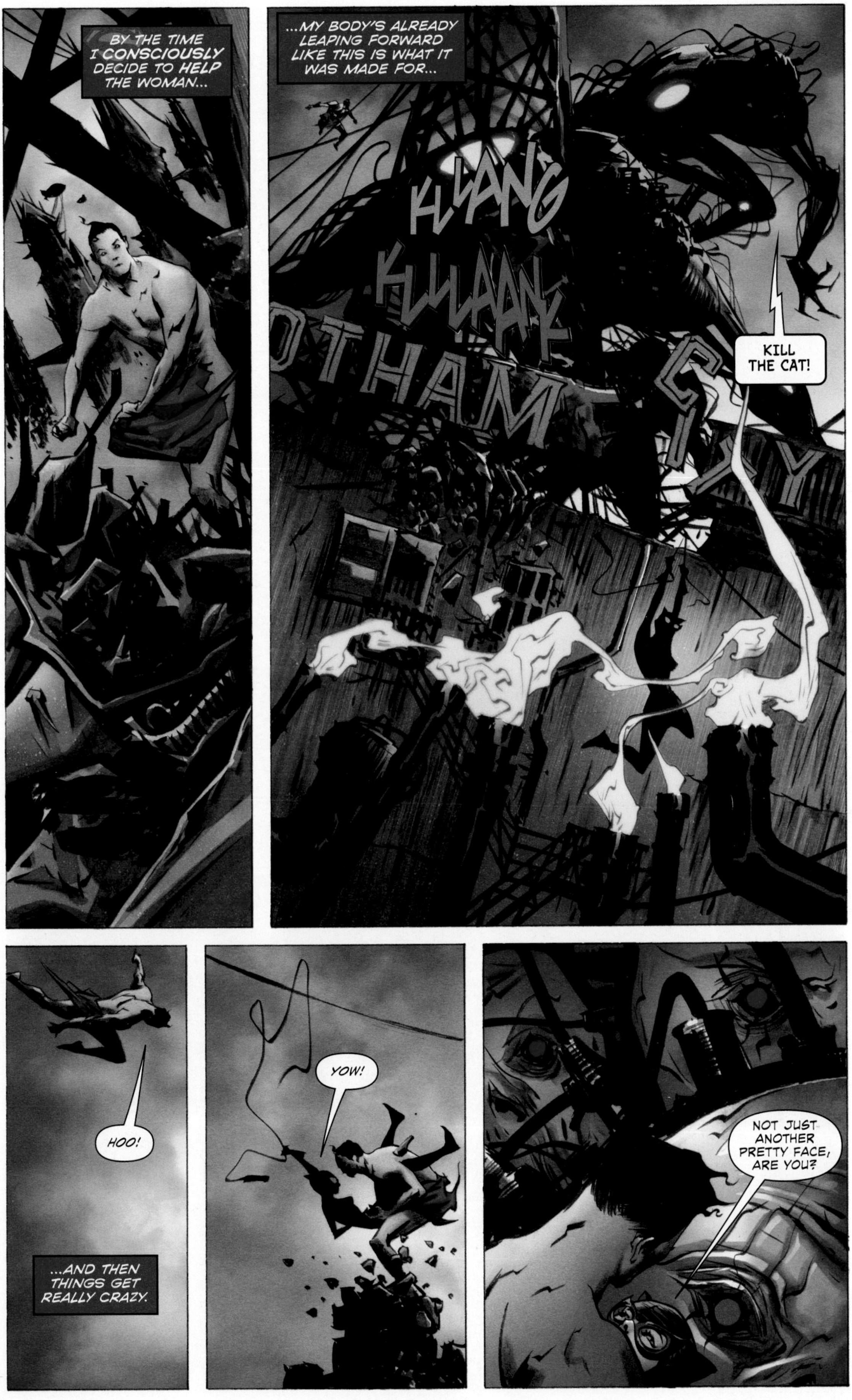
BY THE TIME I CONSCIOUSLY DECIDE TO HELP THE WOMAN...
...MY BODY'S ALREADY LEAPING FORWARD LIKE THIS IS WHAT IT WAS MADE FOR...
KLLANG
KLLAANK
OTHAM
KILL THE CAT!
HOO!
...AND THEN THINGS GET REALLY CRAZY.
YOW!
NOT JUST ANOTHER PRETTY FACE, ARE YOU?

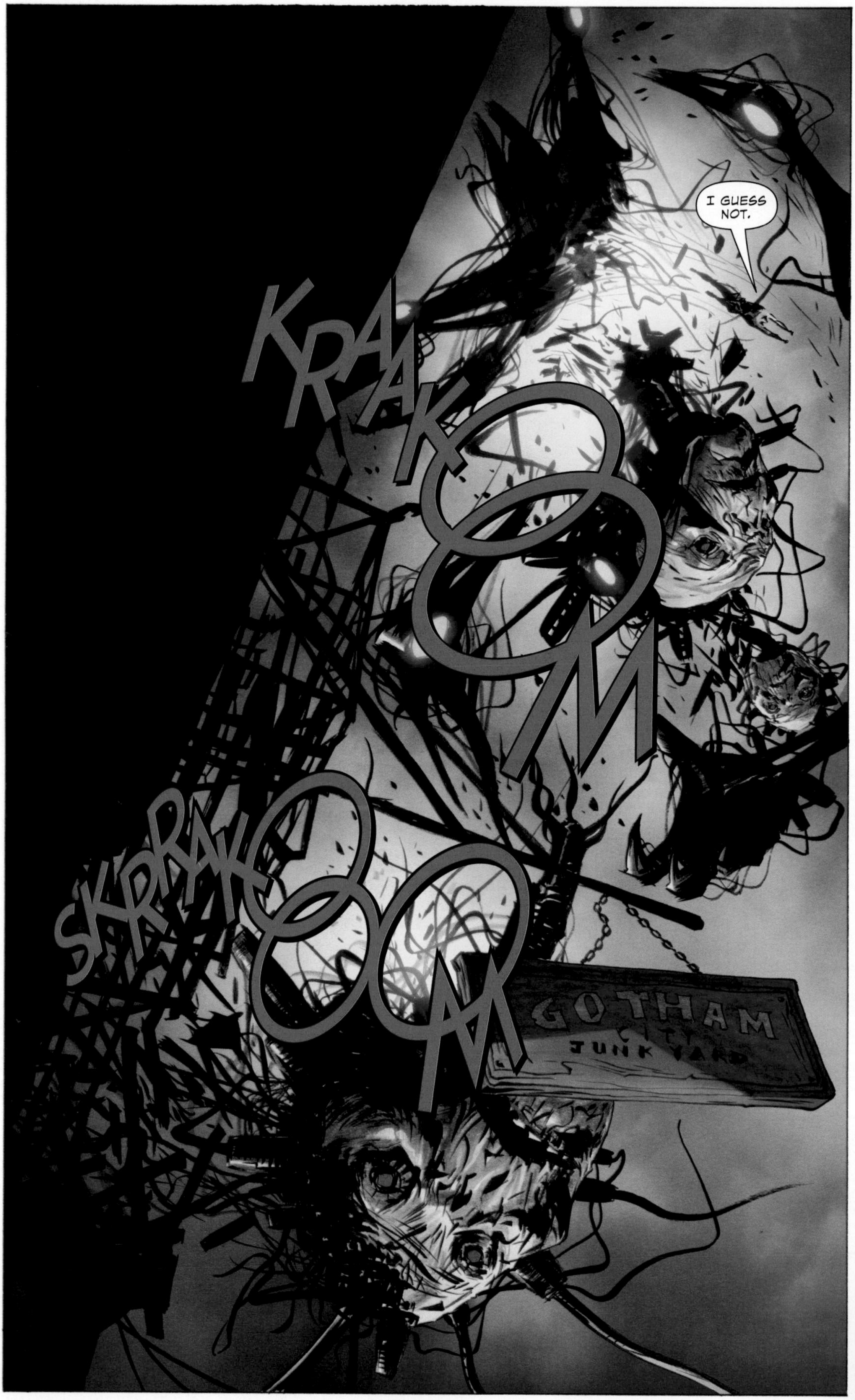
I GUESS NOT.
KRAKOOM
SKRRAKOOM
GOTHAM CITY JUNK YARD

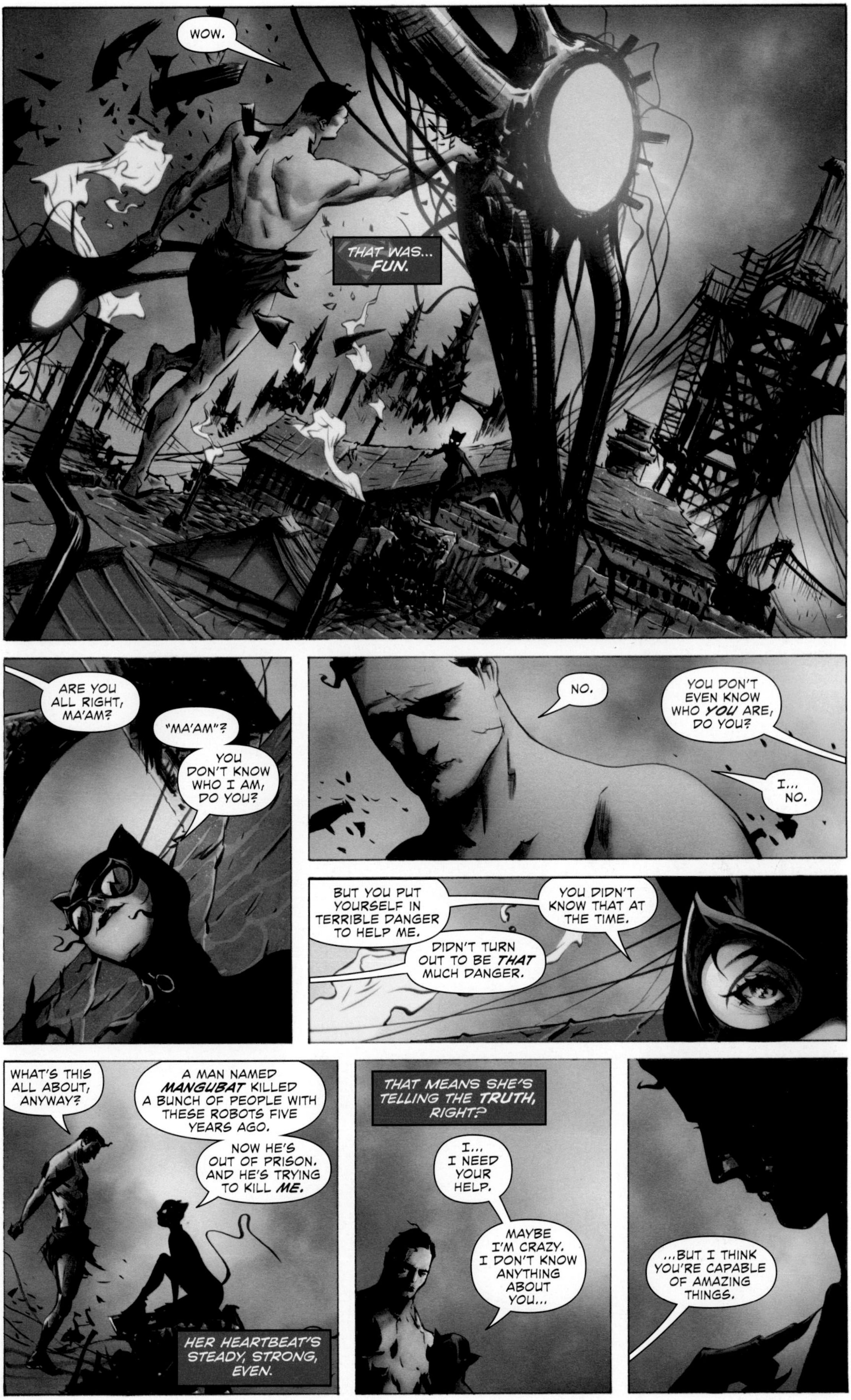
WOW.
THAT WAS... FUN.
ARE YOU ALL RIGHT, MA'AM?
"MA'AM"?
YOU DON'T KNOW WHO I AM, DO YOU?
NO.
YOU DON'T EVEN KNOW WHO YOU ARE, DO YOU?
I... NO.
BUT YOU PUT YOURSELF IN TERRIBLE DANGER TO HELP ME.
YOU DIDN'T KNOW THAT AT THE TIME.
DIDN'T TURN OUT TO BE THAT MUCH DANGER.
WHAT'S THIS ALL ABOUT, ANYWAY?
A MAN NAMED MANGUBAT KILLED A BUNCH OF PEOPLE WITH THESE ROBOTS FIVE YEARS AGO.
NOW HE'S OUT OF PRISON. AND HE'S TRYING TO KILL ME.
HER HEARTBEAT'S STEADY, STRONG, EVEN.
THAT MEANS SHE'S TELLING THE TRUTH, RIGHT?
I... I NEED YOUR HELP.
MAYBE I'M CRAZY. I DON'T KNOW ANYTHING ABOUT YOU...
...BUT I THINK YOU'RE CAPABLE OF AMAZING THINGS.

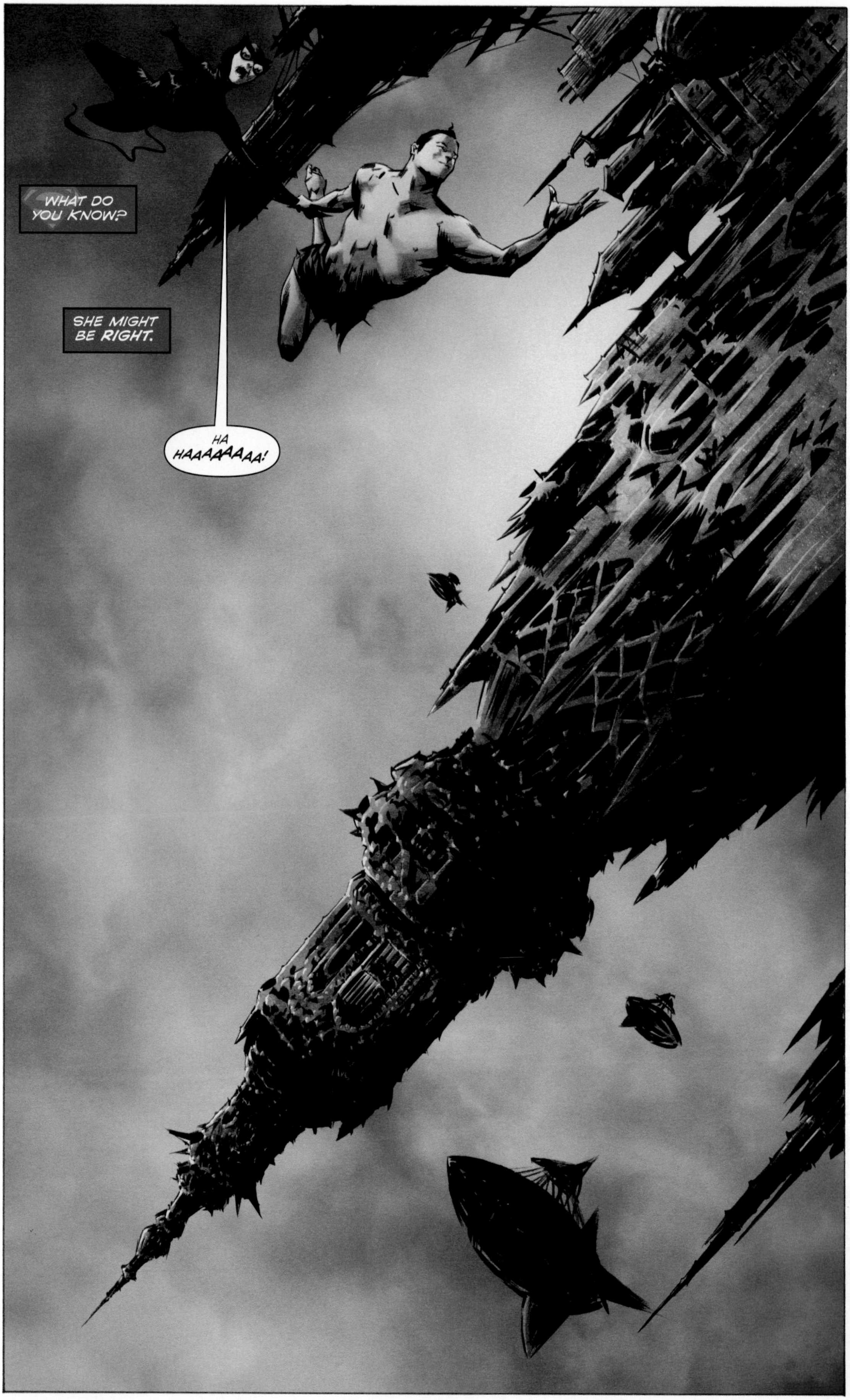
WHAT DO YOU KNOW?
SHE MIGHT BE RIGHT.
HA HAAAAAAAA!

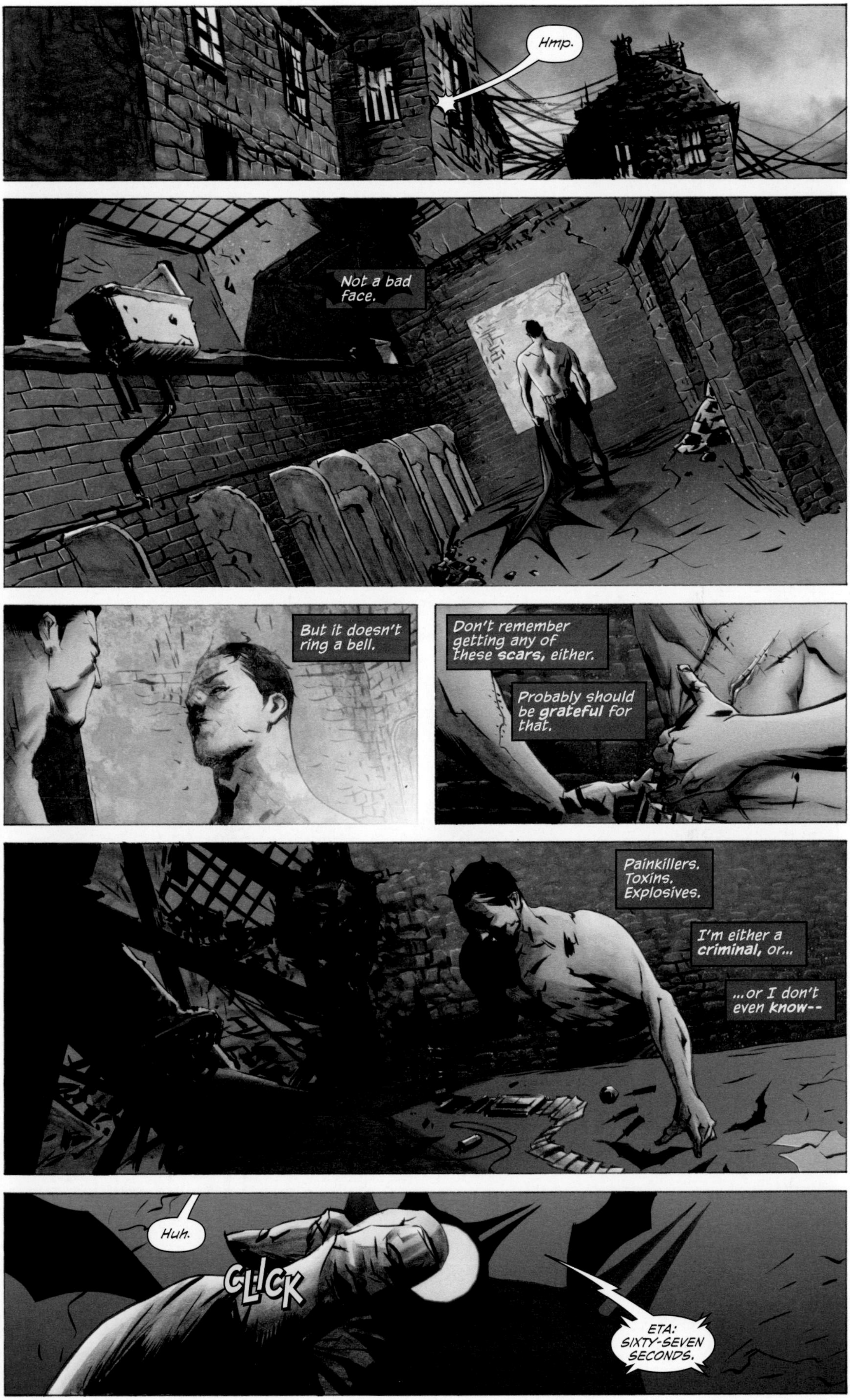
Hmp.
Not a bad face.
But it doesn't ring a bell.
Don't remember getting any of these scars, either.
Probably should be grateful for that.
Painkillers. Toxins. Explosives.
I'm either a criminal, or...
...or I don't even know--
Huh.
CLICK
ETA: SIXTY-SEVEN SECONDS.

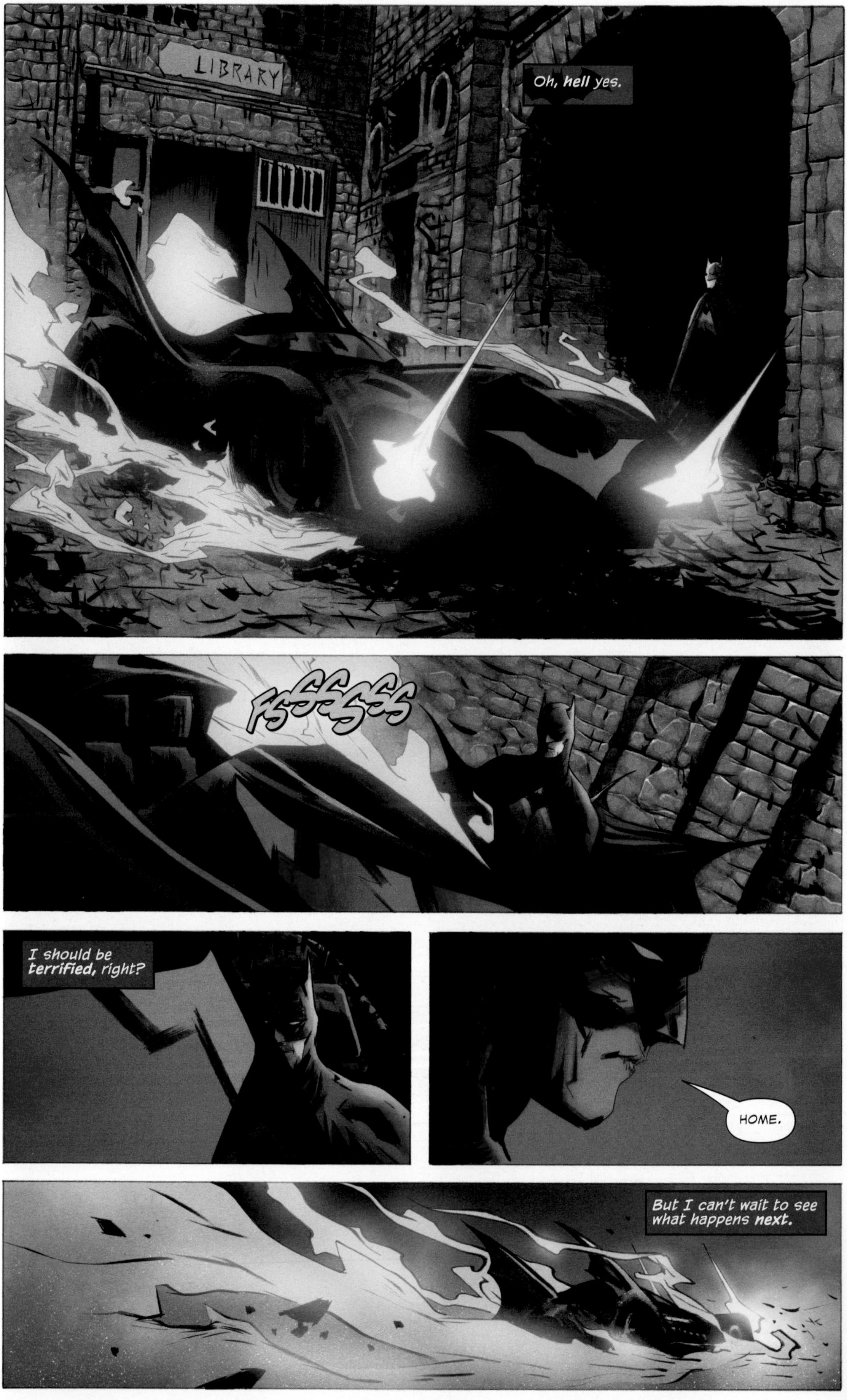
LIBRARY
Oh, hell yes.
FSSSSSS
I should be terrified, right?
HOME.
But I can't wait to see what happens next.

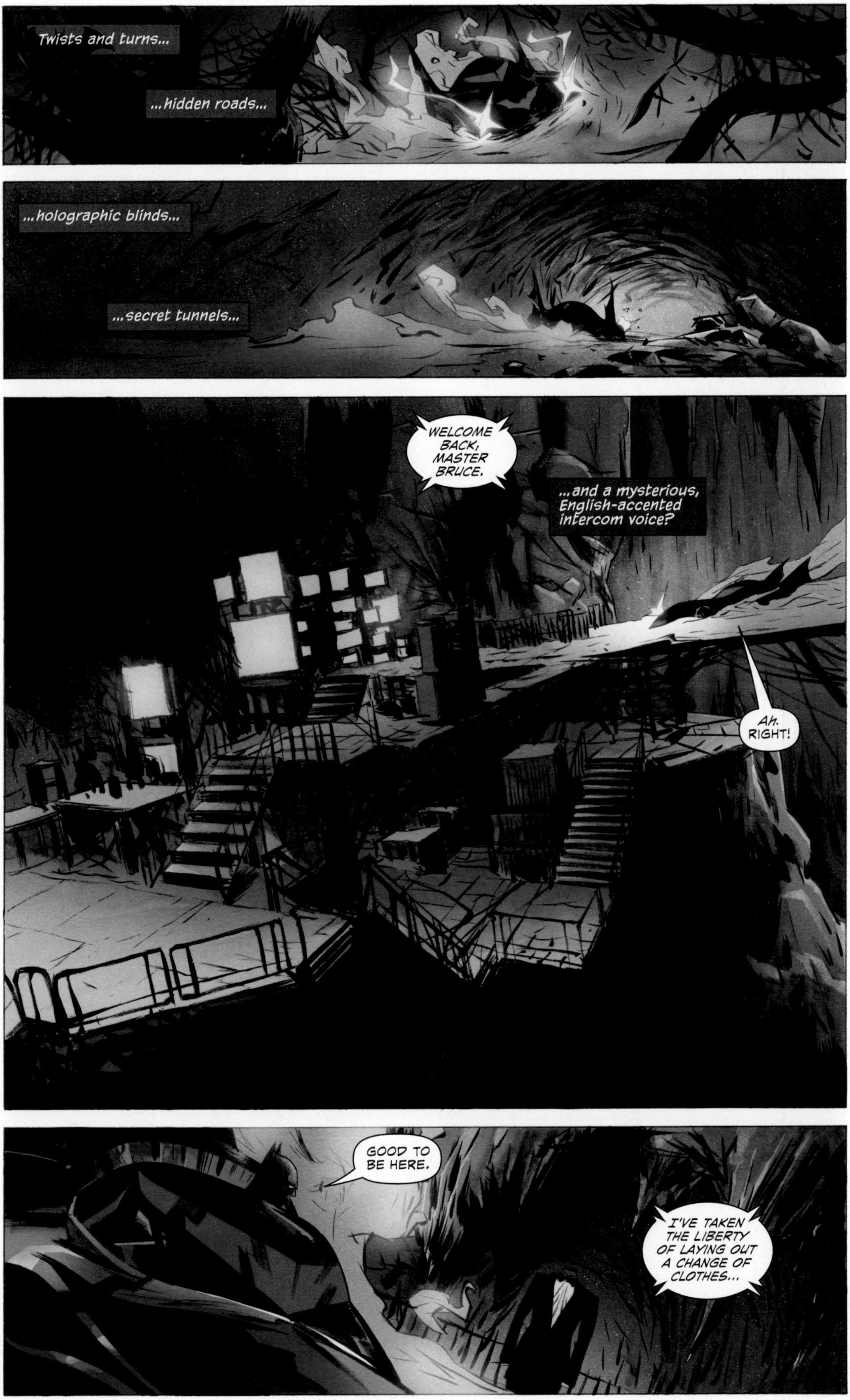
Twists and turns...
...hidden roads...
...holographic blinds...
...secret tunnels...
WELCOME BACK, MASTER BRUCE.
...and a mysterious, English-accented intercom voice?
Ah. RIGHT!
GOOD TO BE HERE.
I'VE TAKEN THE LIBERTY OF LAYING OUT A CHANGE OF CLOTHES...

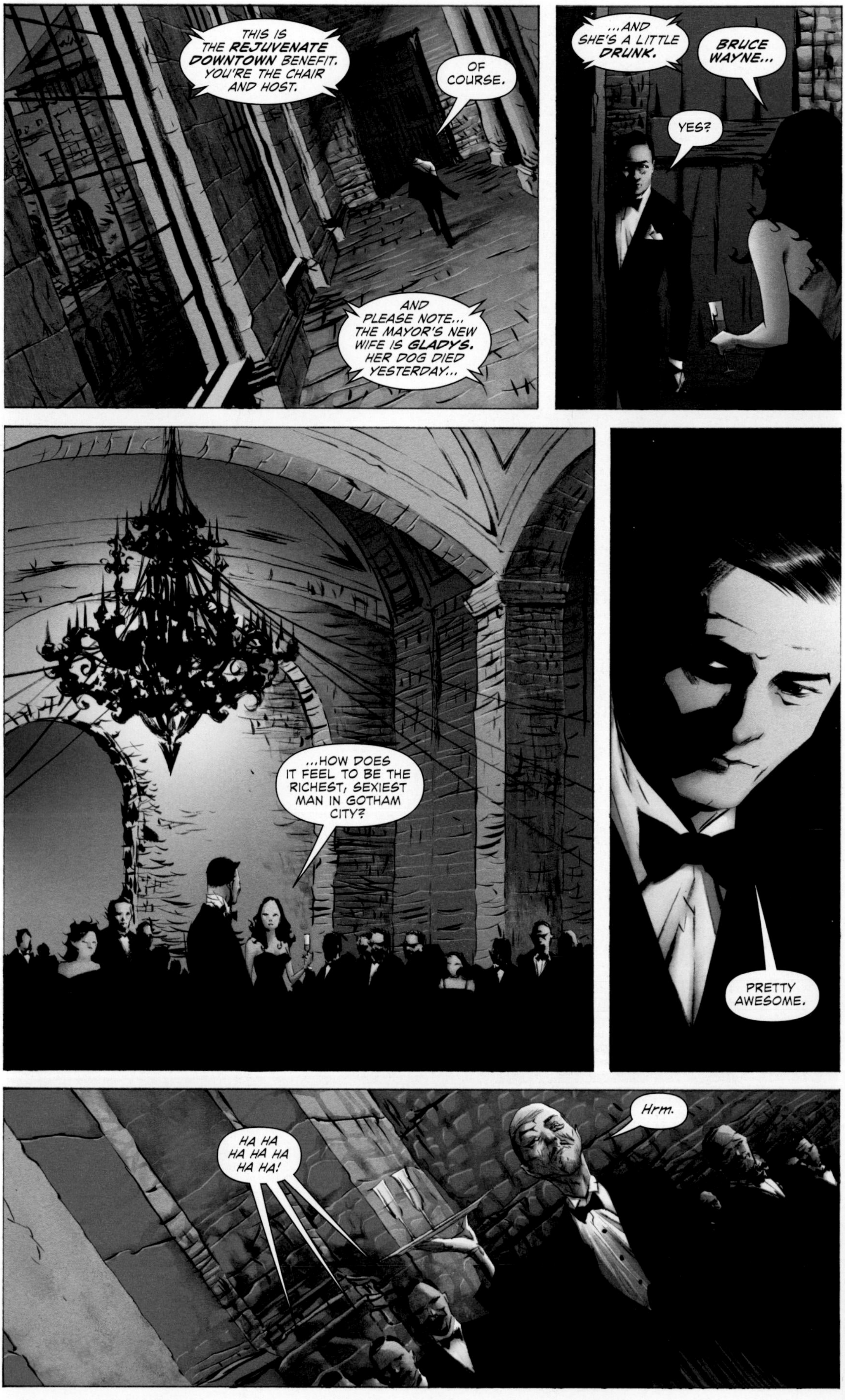
THIS IS THE **REJUVENATE DOWNTOWN** BENEFIT. YOU'RE THE CHAIR AND HOST.
OF COURSE.
AND PLEASE NOTE... THE MAYOR'S NEW WIFE IS **GLADYS.** HER DOG DIED YESTERDAY...
...AND SHE'S A LITTLE **DRUNK.**
BRUCE WAYNE...
YES?
...HOW DOES IT FEEL TO BE THE RICHEST, SEXIEST MAN IN GOTHAM CITY?
PRETTY AWESOME.
HA HA HA HA HA HA HA!
Hrm.

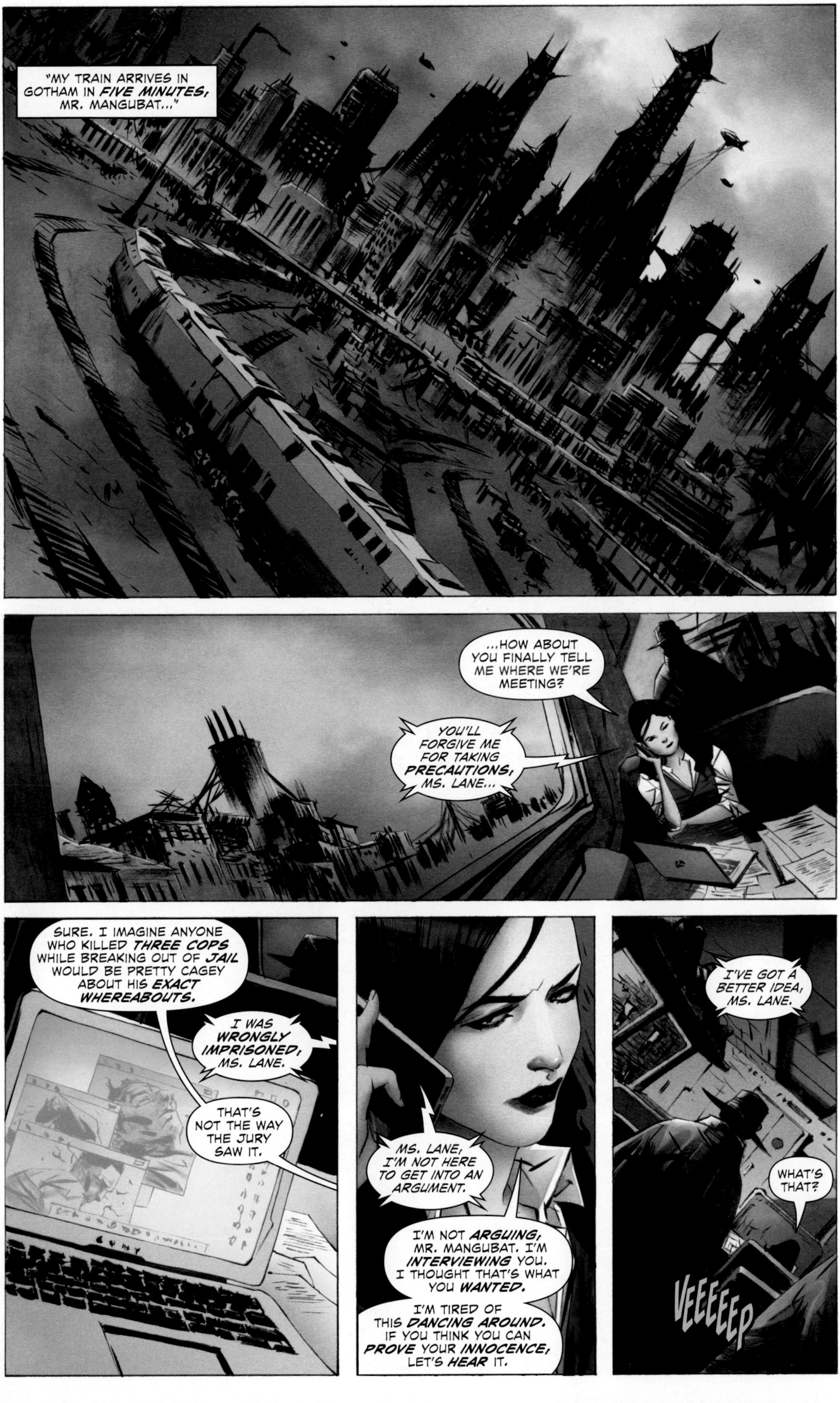
"MY TRAIN ARRIVES IN GOTHAM IN FIVE MINUTES, MR. MANGUBAT..."
...HOW ABOUT YOU FINALLY TELL ME WHERE WE'RE MEETING?
YOU'LL FORGIVE ME FOR TAKING PRECAUTIONS, MS. LANE...
SURE. I IMAGINE ANYONE WHO KILLED THREE COPS WHILE BREAKING OUT OF JAIL WOULD BE PRETTY CAGEY ABOUT HIS EXACT WHEREABOUTS.
I WAS WRONGLY IMPRISONED, MS. LANE.
THAT'S NOT THE WAY THE JURY SAW IT.
MS. LANE, I'M NOT HERE TO GET INTO AN ARGUMENT.
I'M NOT ARGUING, MR. MANGUBAT. I'M INTERVIEWING YOU. I THOUGHT THAT'S WHAT YOU WANTED.
I'M TIRED OF THIS DANCING AROUND. IF YOU THINK YOU CAN PROVE YOUR INNOCENCE, LET'S HEAR IT.
I'VE GOT A BETTER IDEA, MS. LANE.
WHAT'S THAT?
VEEEEEP

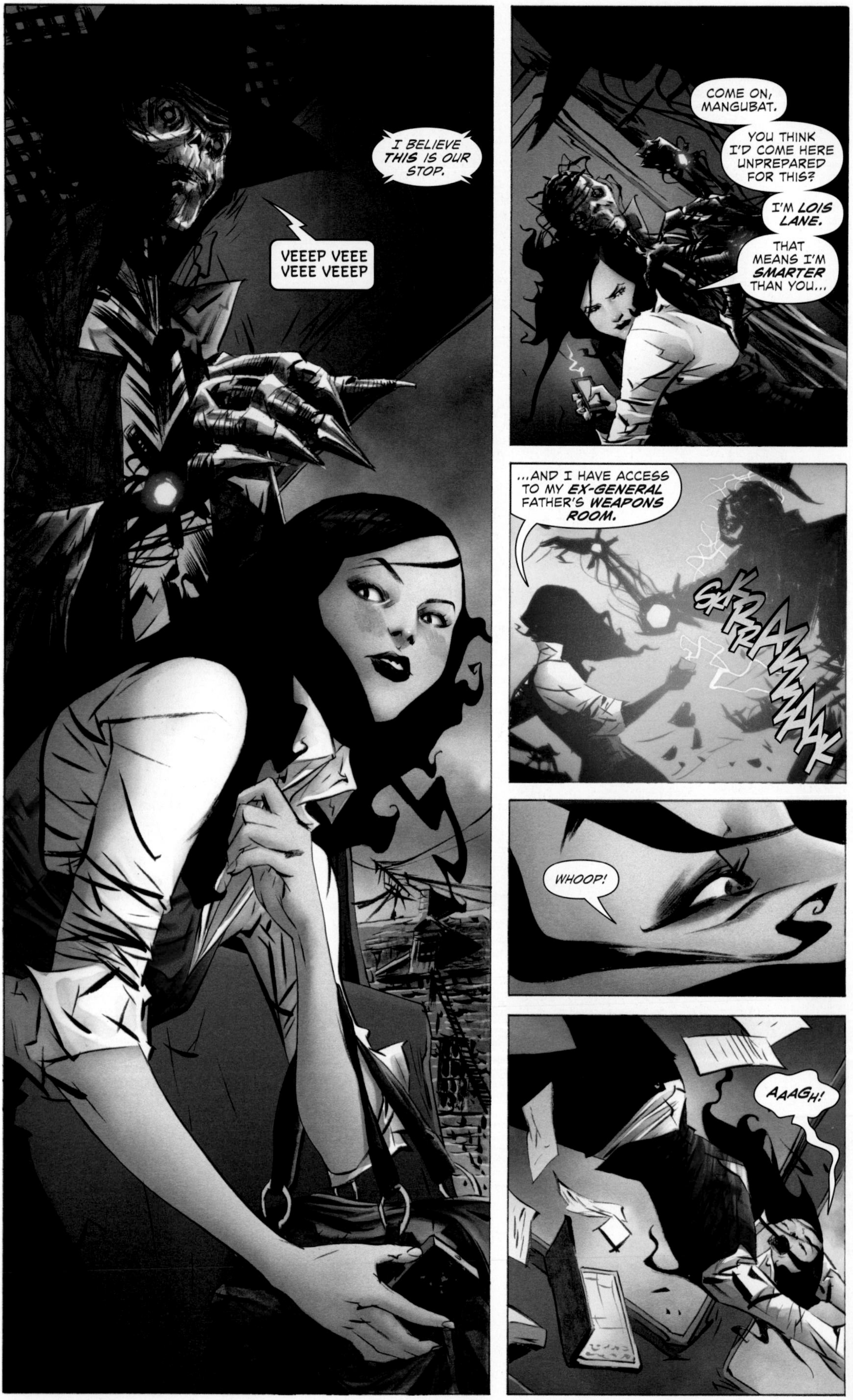
I BELIEVE THIS IS OUR STOP.
VEEEP VEEE VEEE VEEEP
COME ON, MANGUBAT.
YOU THINK I'D COME HERE UNPREPARED FOR THIS?
I'M LOIS LANE.
THAT MEANS I'M SMARTER THAN YOU...
...AND I HAVE ACCESS TO MY EX-GENERAL FATHER'S WEAPONS ROOM.
SKKRRAAWAAK
WHOOP!
AAAGH!

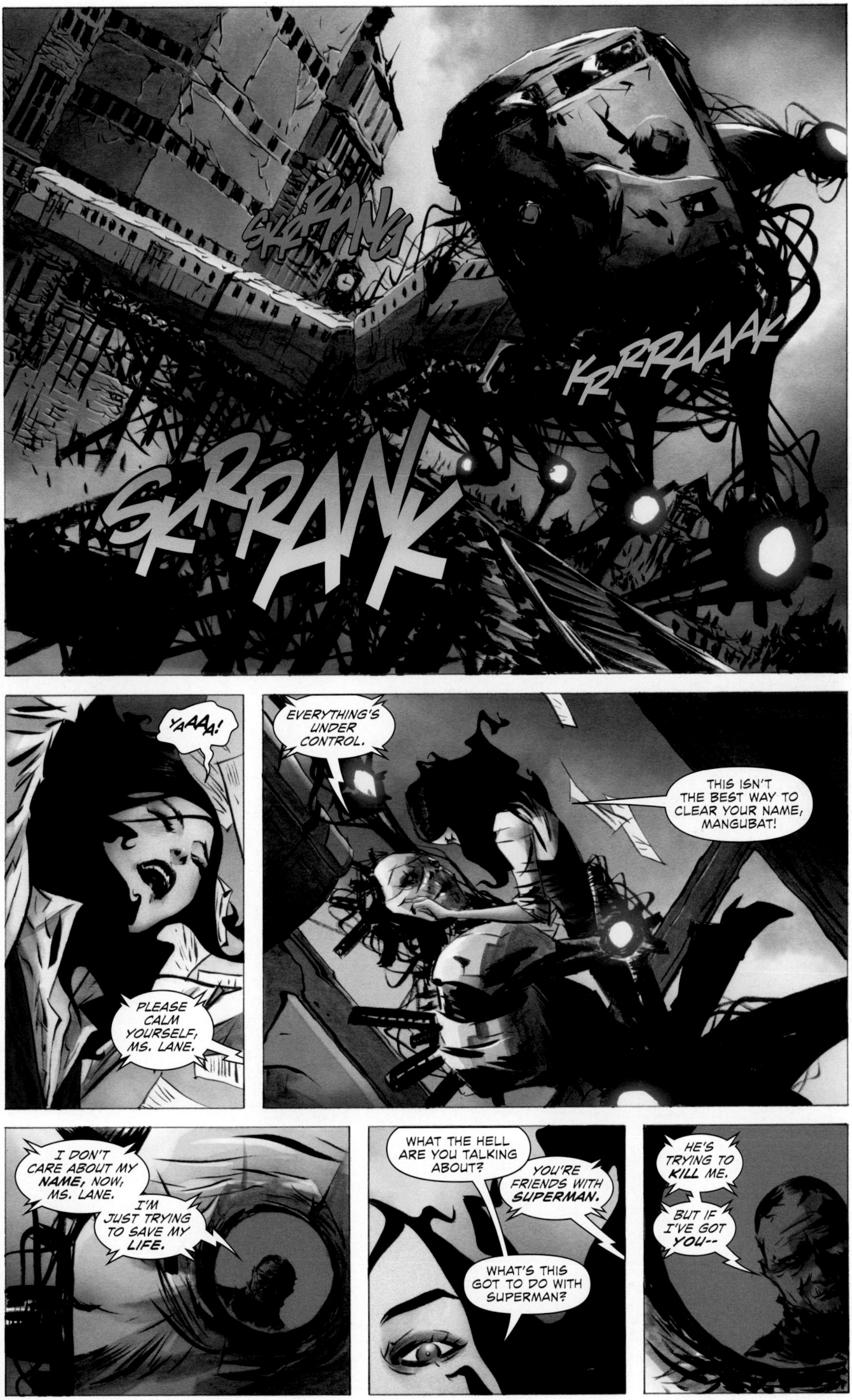
SKRANG
KRRRAAAK
SKRRANK
YAAAA!
PLEASE CALM YOURSELF, MS. LANE.
EVERYTHING'S UNDER CONTROL.
THIS ISN'T THE BEST WAY TO CLEAR YOUR NAME, MANGUBAT!
I DON'T CARE ABOUT MY NAME, NOW, MS. LANE.
I'M JUST TRYING TO SAVE MY LIFE.
WHAT THE HELL ARE YOU TALKING ABOUT?
YOU'RE FRIENDS WITH SUPERMAN.
WHAT'S THIS GOT TO DO WITH SUPERMAN?
HE'S TRYING TO KILL ME.
BUT IF I'VE GOT YOU--

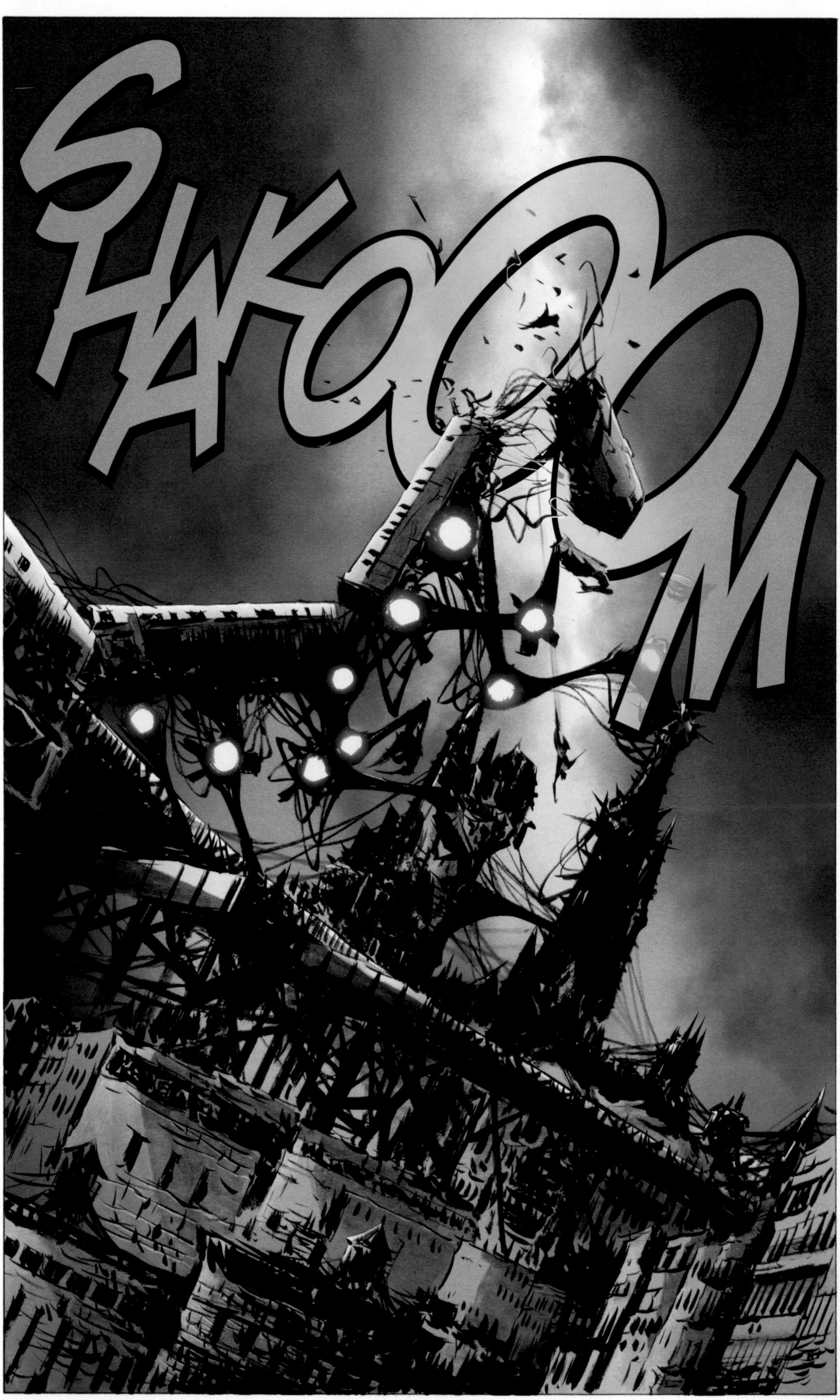
SHAKOOOM

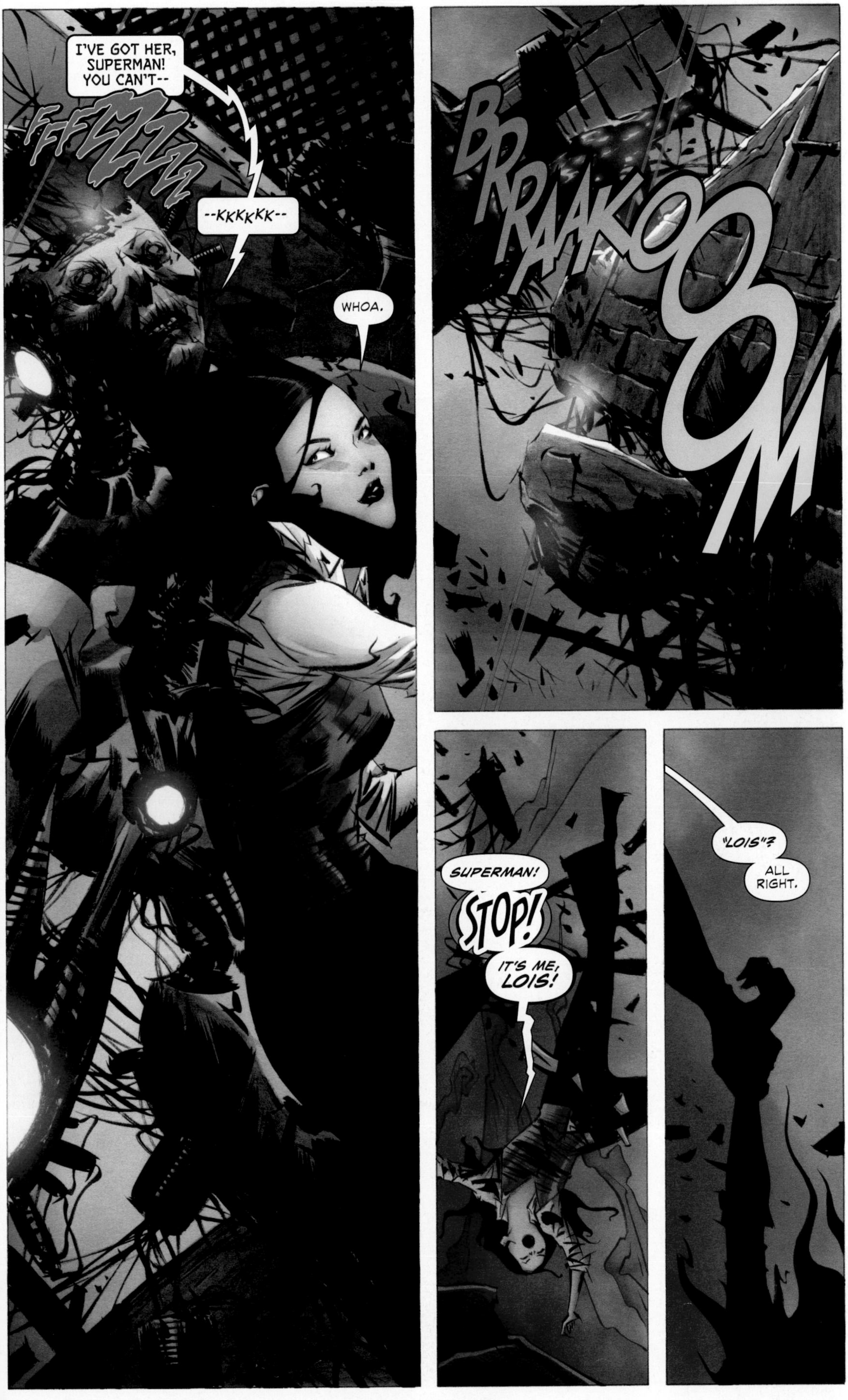
I'VE GOT HER, SUPERMAN! YOU CAN'T--
FFFZZZZZ
--KKKKKK--
WHOA.
BRRAAKOOOM
SUPERMAN!
STOP!
IT'S ME, LOIS!
"LOIS"?
ALL RIGHT.

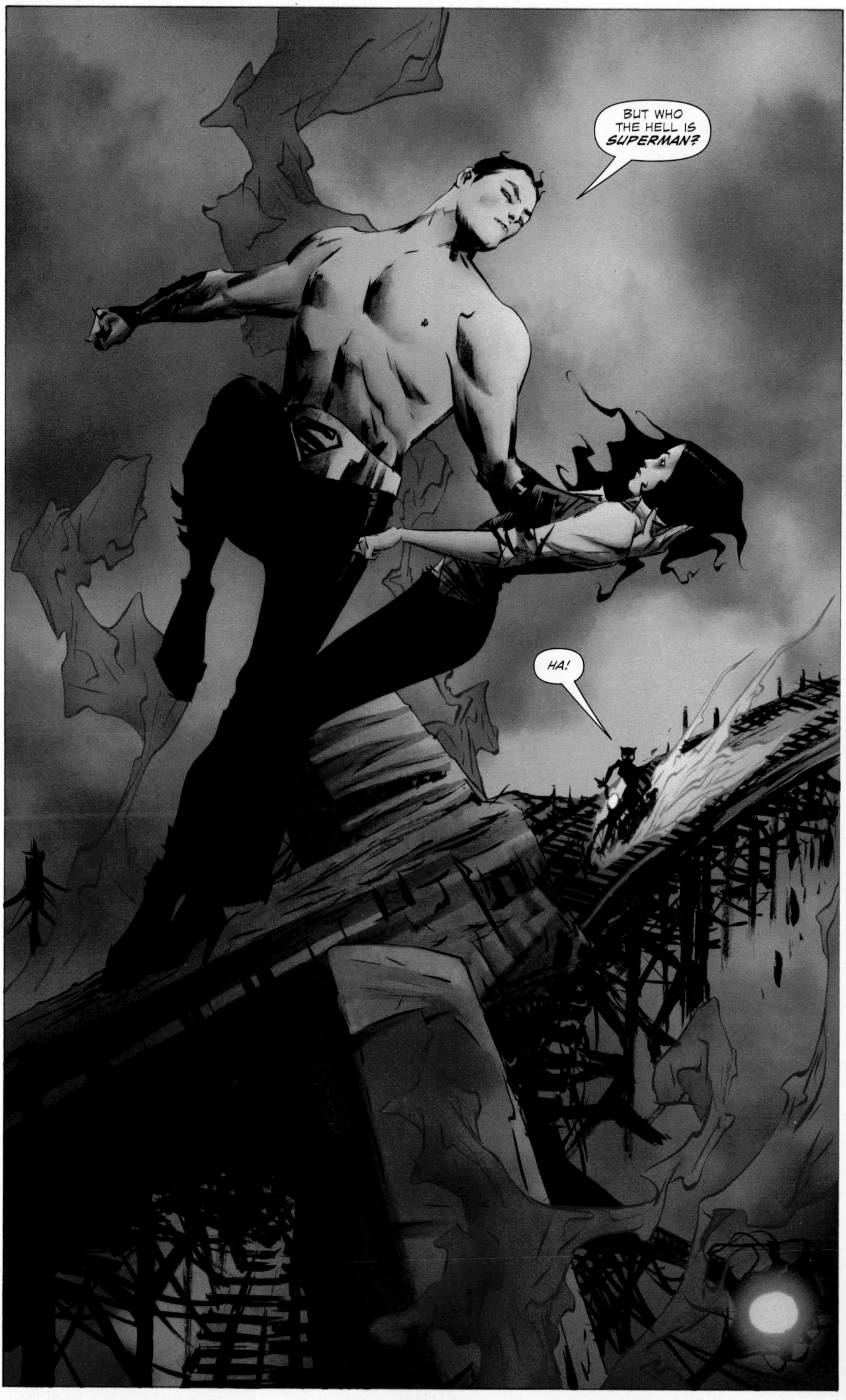
BUT WHO THE HELL IS SUPERMAN?
HA!

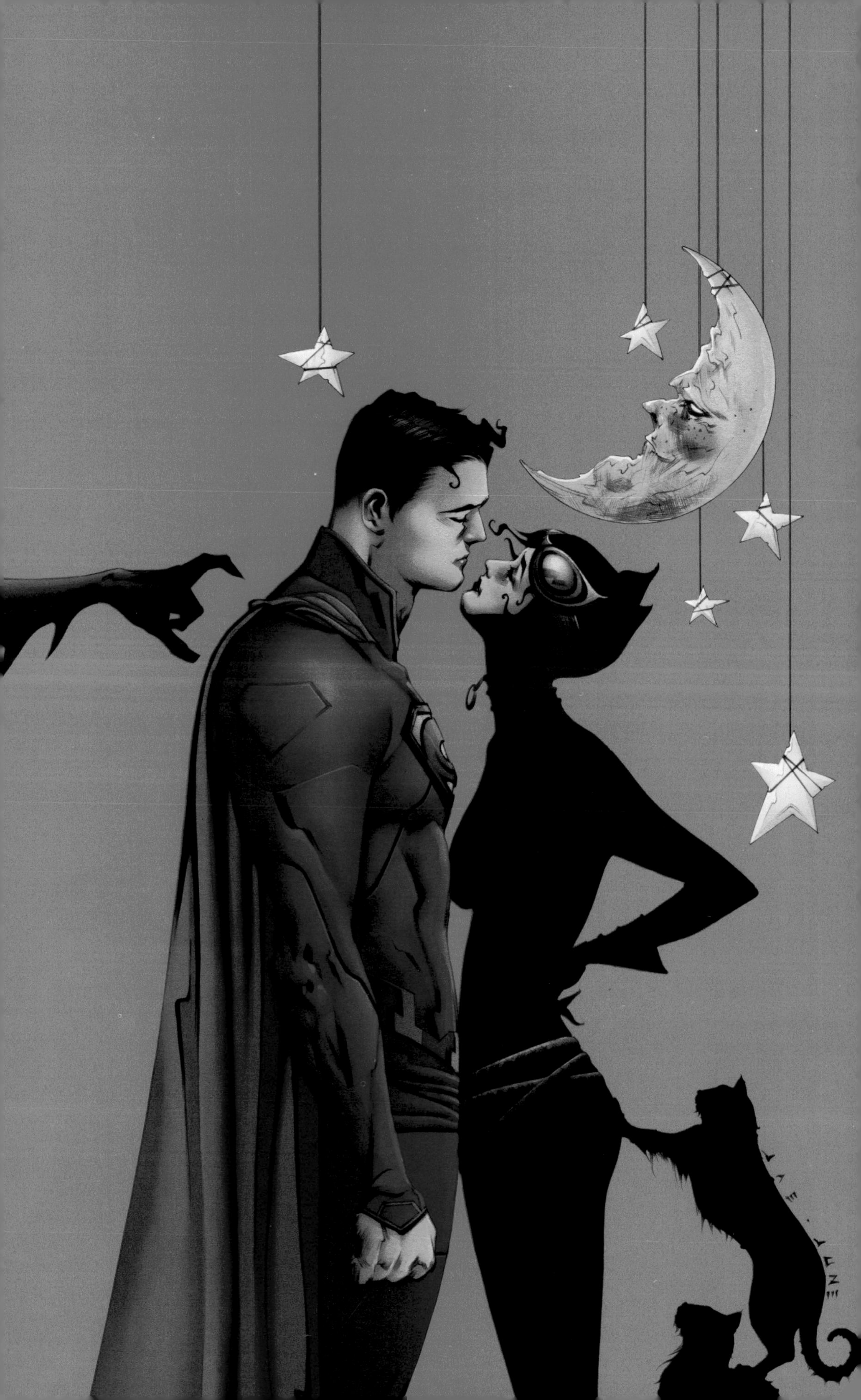

BLANK SLATE

GREG PAK writer DIOGENES NEVES MARC DEERING artists JUNE CHUNG colorist ROB LEIGH letterer cover by JAE LEE with JUNE CHUNG

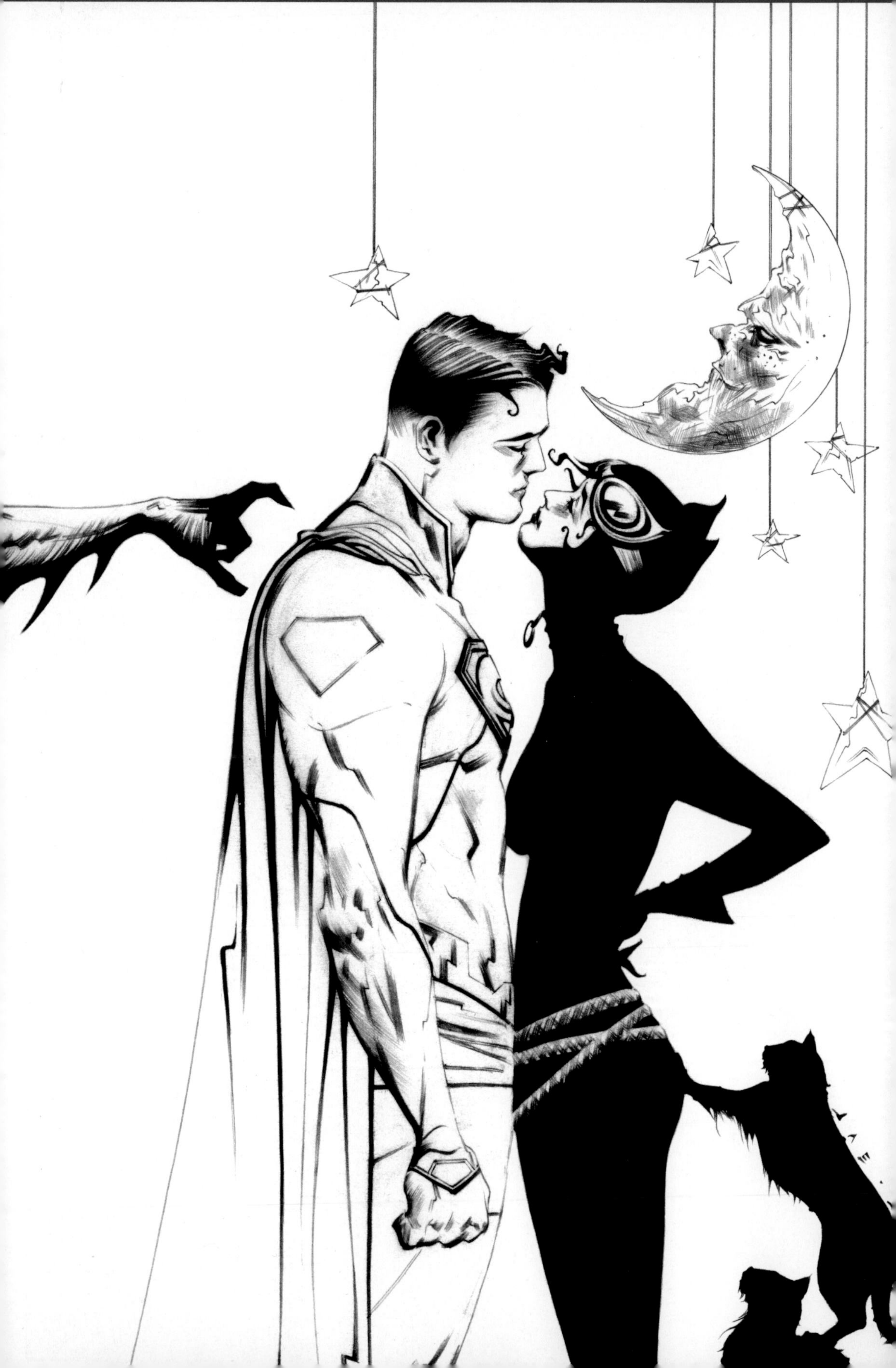

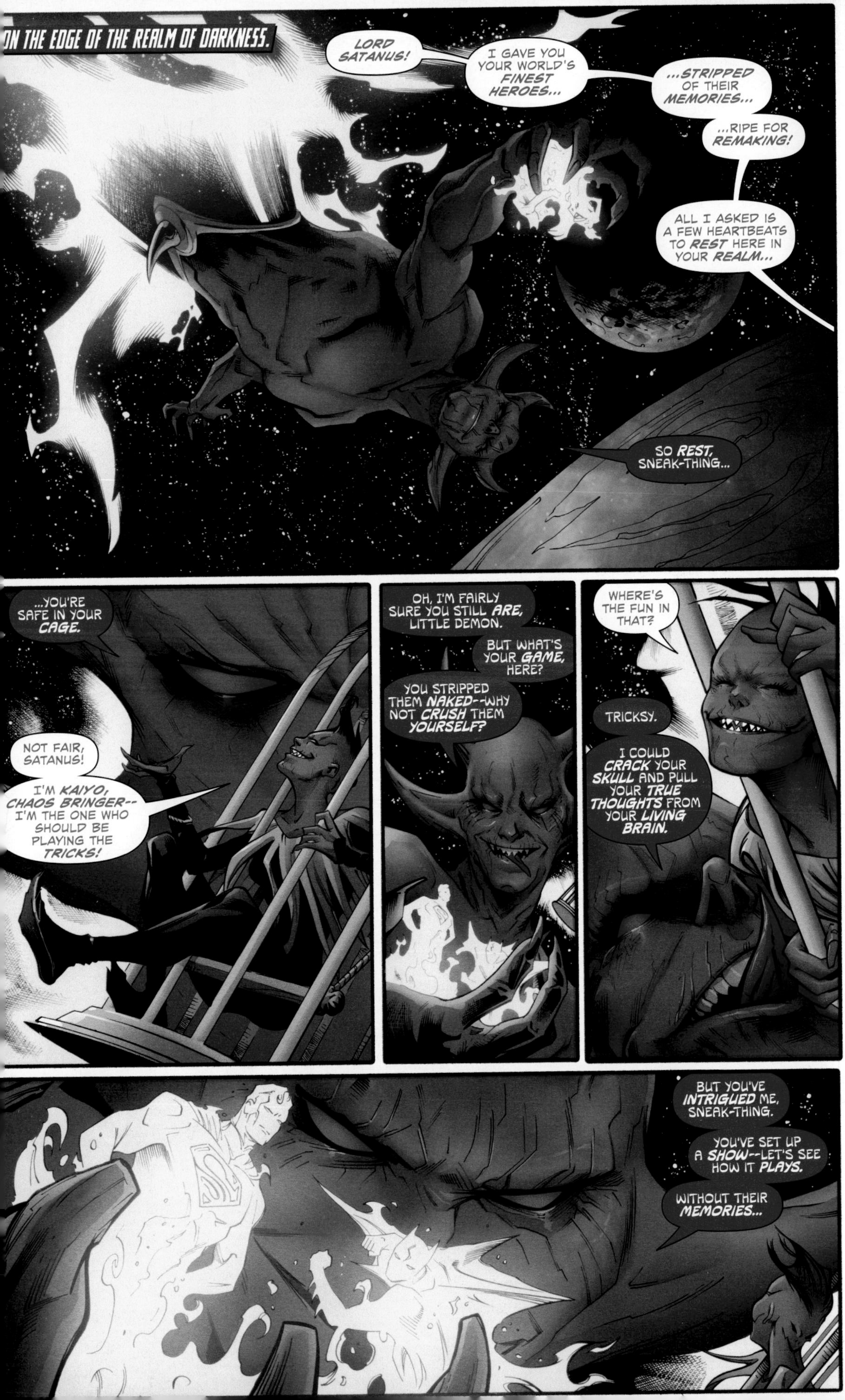
ON THE EDGE OF THE REALM OF DARKNESS.
LORD SATANUS!
I GAVE YOU YOUR WORLD'S FINEST HEROES...
...STRIPPED OF THEIR MEMORIES...
...RIPE FOR REMAKING!
ALL I ASKED IS A FEW HEARTBEATS TO REST HERE IN YOUR REALM...
SO REST, SNEAK-THING...
...YOU'RE SAFE IN YOUR CAGE.
NOT FAIR, SATANUS!
I'M KAIYO, CHAOS BRINGER-- I'M THE ONE WHO SHOULD BE PLAYING THE TRICKS!
OH, I'M FAIRLY SURE YOU STILL ARE, LITTLE DEMON.
BUT WHAT'S YOUR GAME, HERE?
YOU STRIPPED THEM NAKED--WHY NOT CRUSH THEM YOURSELF?
WHERE'S THE FUN IN THAT?
TRICKSY.
I COULD CRACK YOUR SKULL AND PULL YOUR TRUE THOUGHTS FROM YOUR LIVING BRAIN.
BUT YOU'VE INTRIGUED ME, SNEAK-THING.
YOU'VE SET UP A SHOW--LET'S SEE HOW IT PLAYS.
WITHOUT THEIR MEMORIES...

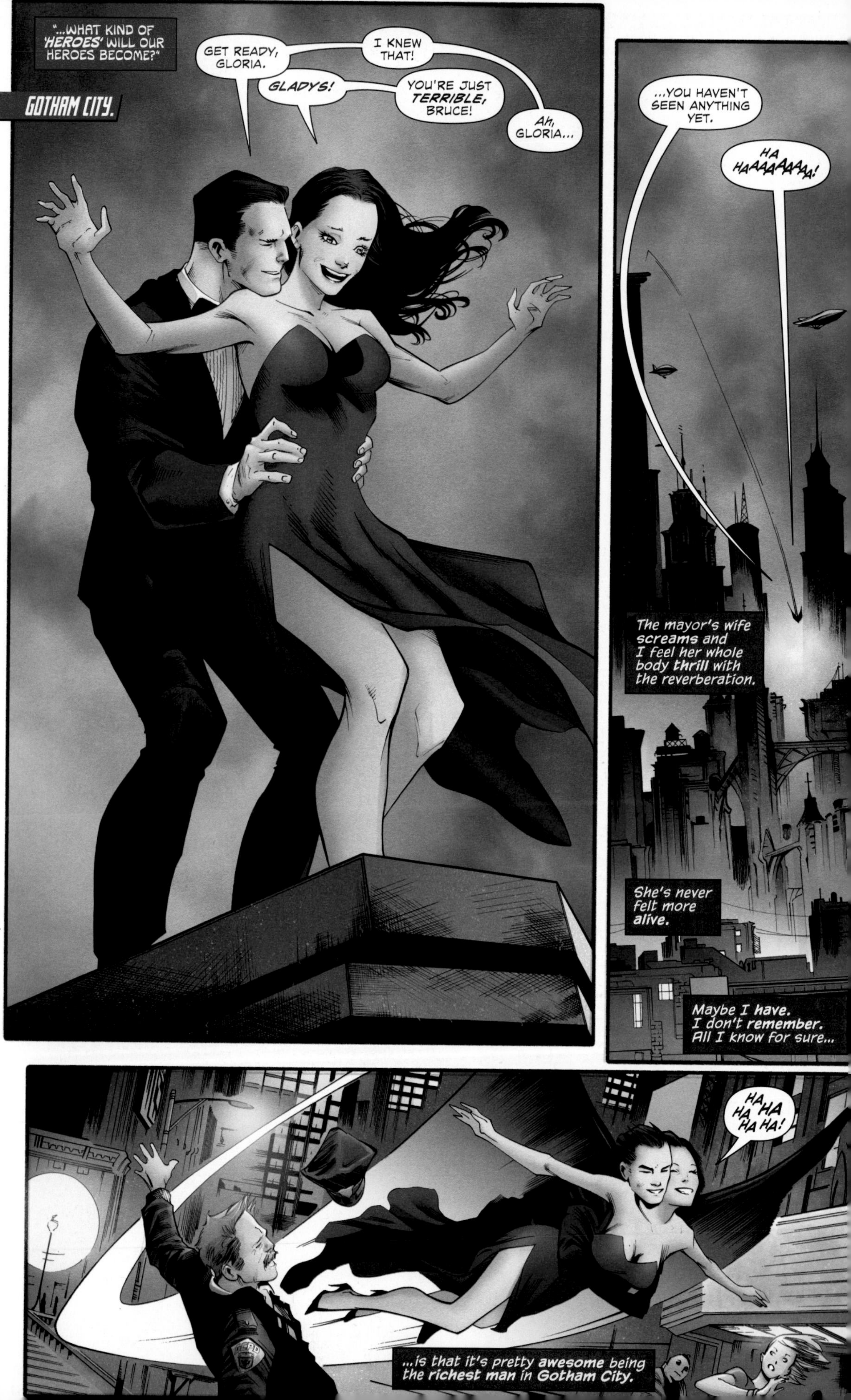
"...WHAT KIND OF 'HEROES' WILL OUR HEROES BECOME?"
GOTHAM CITY.
GET READY, GLORIA.
I KNEW THAT!
GLADYS!
YOU'RE JUST TERRIBLE, BRUCE!
Ah, GLORIA...
...YOU HAVEN'T SEEN ANYTHING YET.
HA HAAAAAAAA!
The mayor's wife screams and I feel her whole body thrill with the reverberation.
She's never felt more alive.
Maybe I have. I don't remember. All I know for sure...
HA HA HA HA HA!
...is that it's pretty awesome being the richest man in Gotham City.

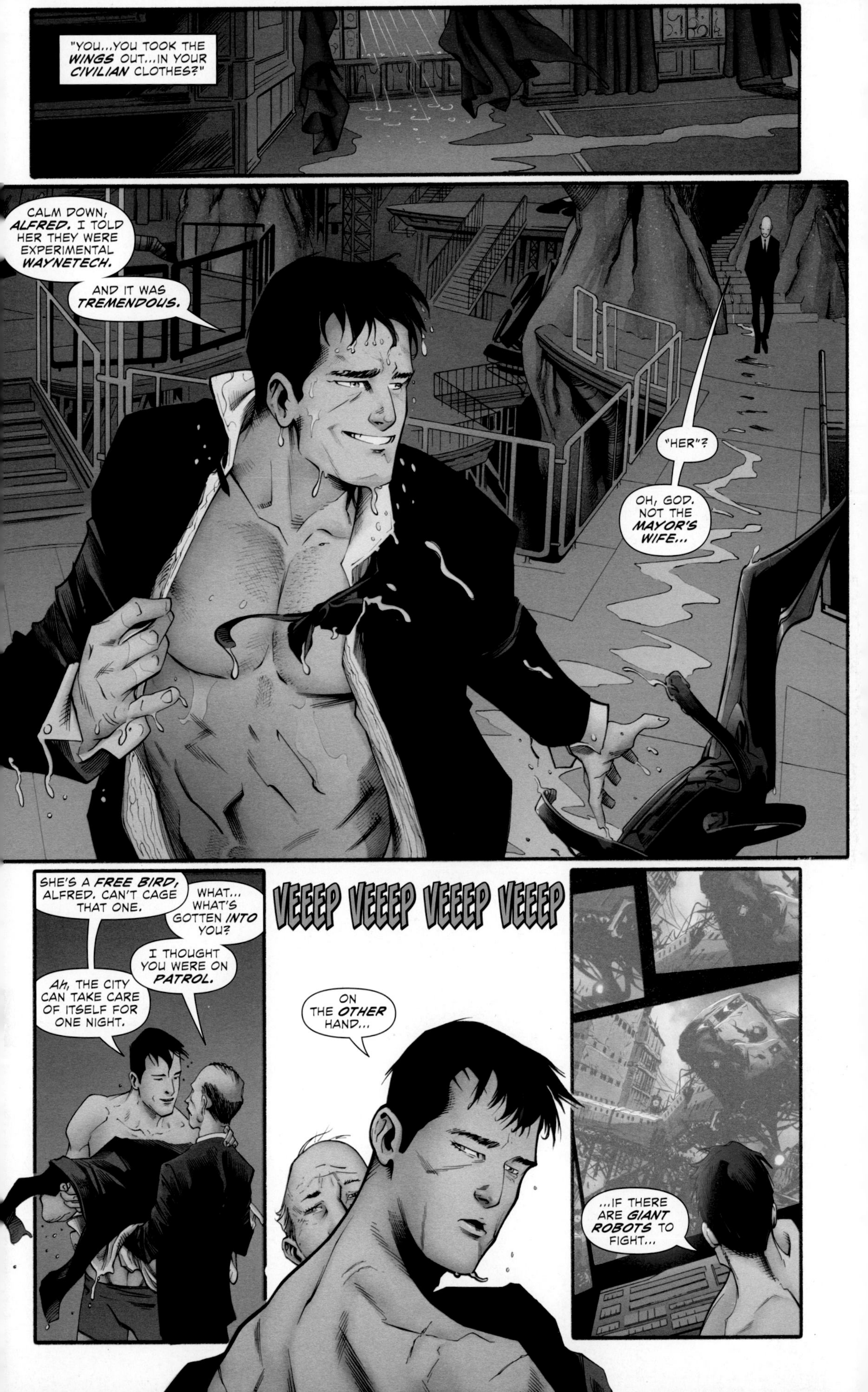
"YOU...YOU TOOK THE WINGS OUT...IN YOUR CIVILIAN CLOTHES?"
CALM DOWN, ALFRED. I TOLD HER THEY WERE EXPERIMENTAL WAYNETECH.
AND IT WAS TREMENDOUS.
"HER"?
OH, GOD. NOT THE MAYOR'S WIFE...
SHE'S A FREE BIRD, ALFRED. CAN'T CAGE THAT ONE.
WHAT... WHAT'S GOTTEN INTO YOU?
I THOUGHT YOU WERE ON PATROL.
Ah, THE CITY CAN TAKE CARE OF ITSELF FOR ONE NIGHT.
VEEEP VEEEP VEEEP VEEEP
ON THE OTHER HAND...
...IF THERE ARE GIANT ROBOTS TO FIGHT...

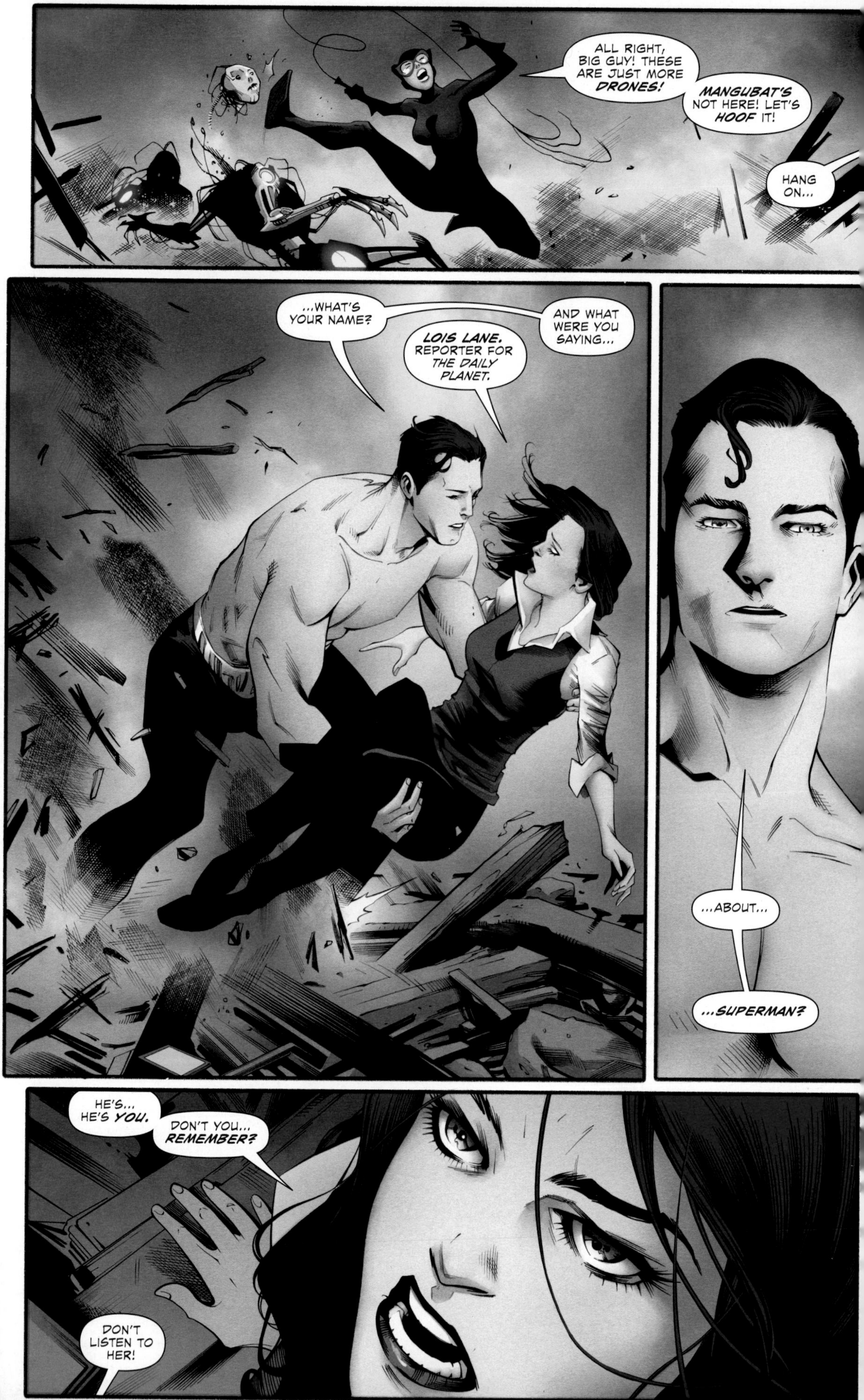
ALL RIGHT, BIG GUY! THESE ARE JUST MORE DRONES!
MANGUBAT'S NOT HERE! LET'S HOOF IT!
HANG ON...
...WHAT'S YOUR NAME?
LOIS LANE. REPORTER FOR THE DAILY PLANET.
AND WHAT WERE YOU SAYING...
...ABOUT...
...SUPERMAN?
HE'S... HE'S YOU.
DON'T YOU... REMEMBER?
DON'T LISTEN TO HER!

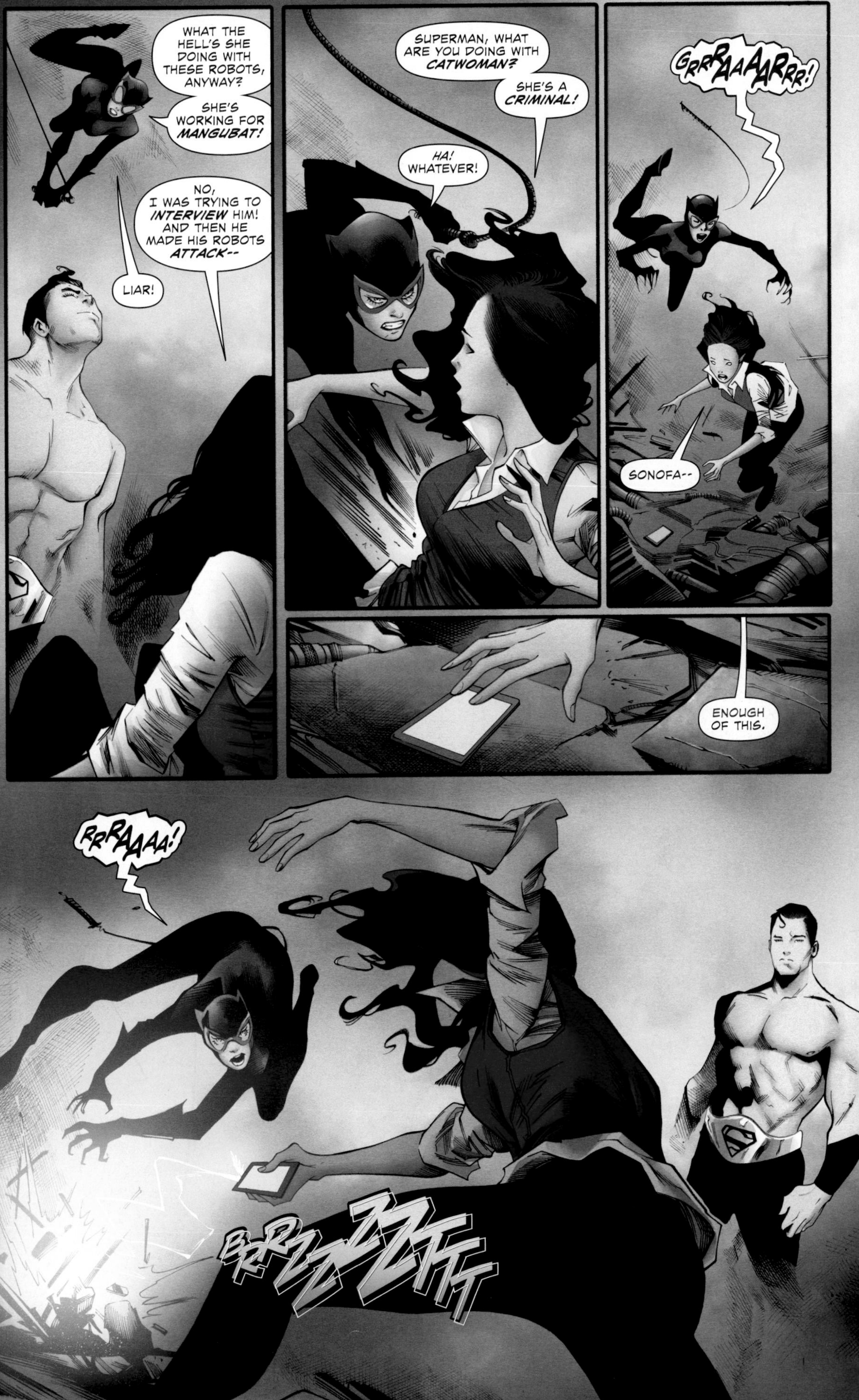

WHAT THE HELL'S SHE DOING WITH THESE ROBOTS, ANYWAY?
SHE'S WORKING FOR MANGUBAT!
NO, I WAS TRYING TO INTERVIEW HIM! AND THEN HE MADE HIS ROBOTS ATTACK--
LIAR!
SUPERMAN, WHAT ARE YOU DOING WITH CATWOMAN?
SHE'S A CRIMINAL!
HA! WHATEVER!
GRRRAAAARRR!
SONOFA--
ENOUGH OF THIS.
RRRAAAA!
BRRRZZZZZTTT

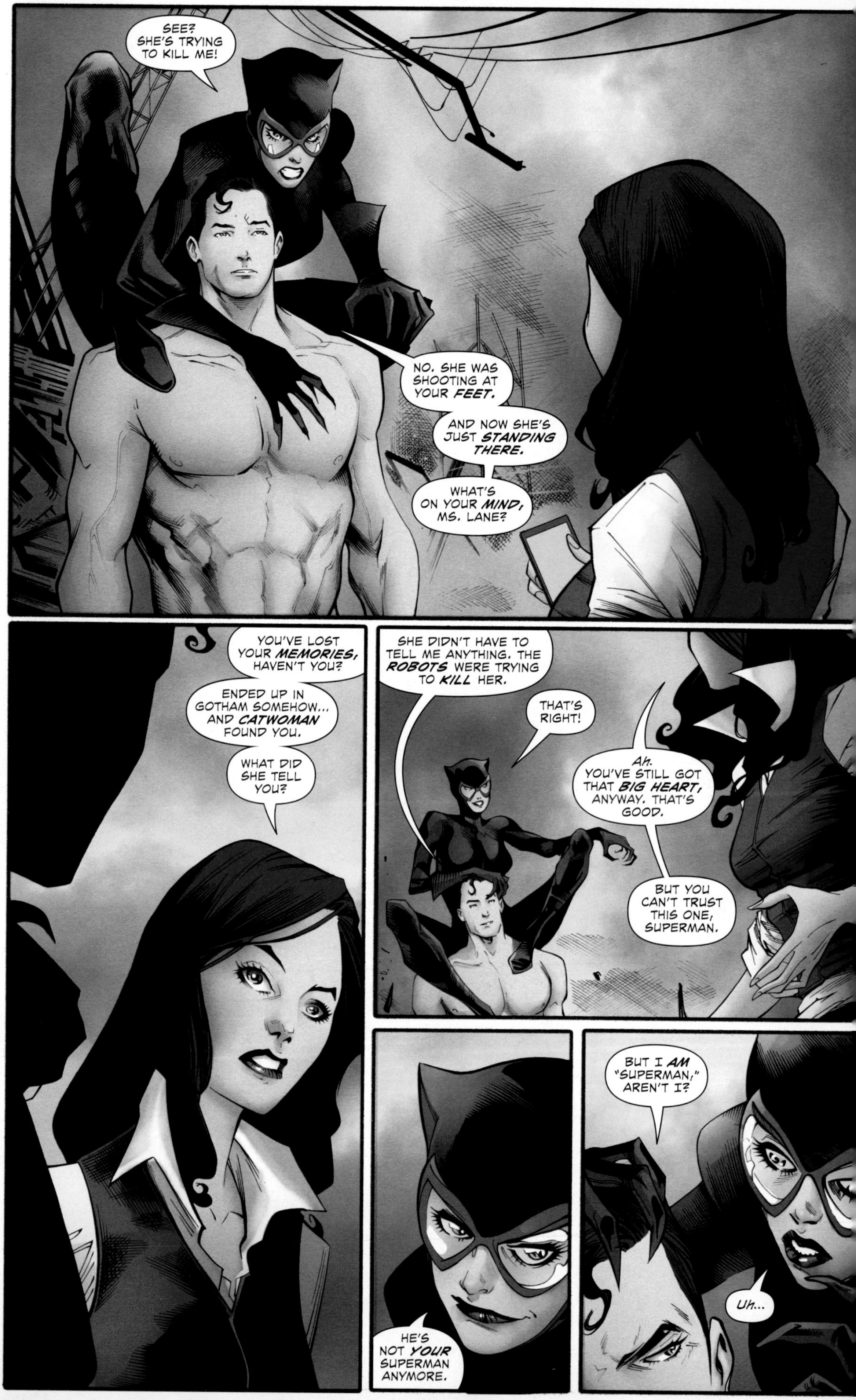
SEE? SHE'S TRYING TO KILL ME!
NO. SHE WAS SHOOTING AT YOUR FEET.
AND NOW SHE'S JUST STANDING THERE.
WHAT'S ON YOUR MIND, MS. LANE?
YOU'VE LOST YOUR MEMORIES, HAVEN'T YOU?
ENDED UP IN GOTHAM SOMEHOW... AND CATWOMAN FOUND YOU.
WHAT DID SHE TELL YOU?
SHE DIDN'T HAVE TO TELL ME ANYTHING. THE ROBOTS WERE TRYING TO KILL HER.
THAT'S RIGHT!
Ah. YOU'VE STILL GOT THAT BIG HEART, ANYWAY. THAT'S GOOD.
BUT YOU CAN'T TRUST THIS ONE, SUPERMAN.
HE'S NOT YOUR SUPERMAN ANYMORE.
BUT I AM "SUPERMAN," AREN'T I?
Uh...

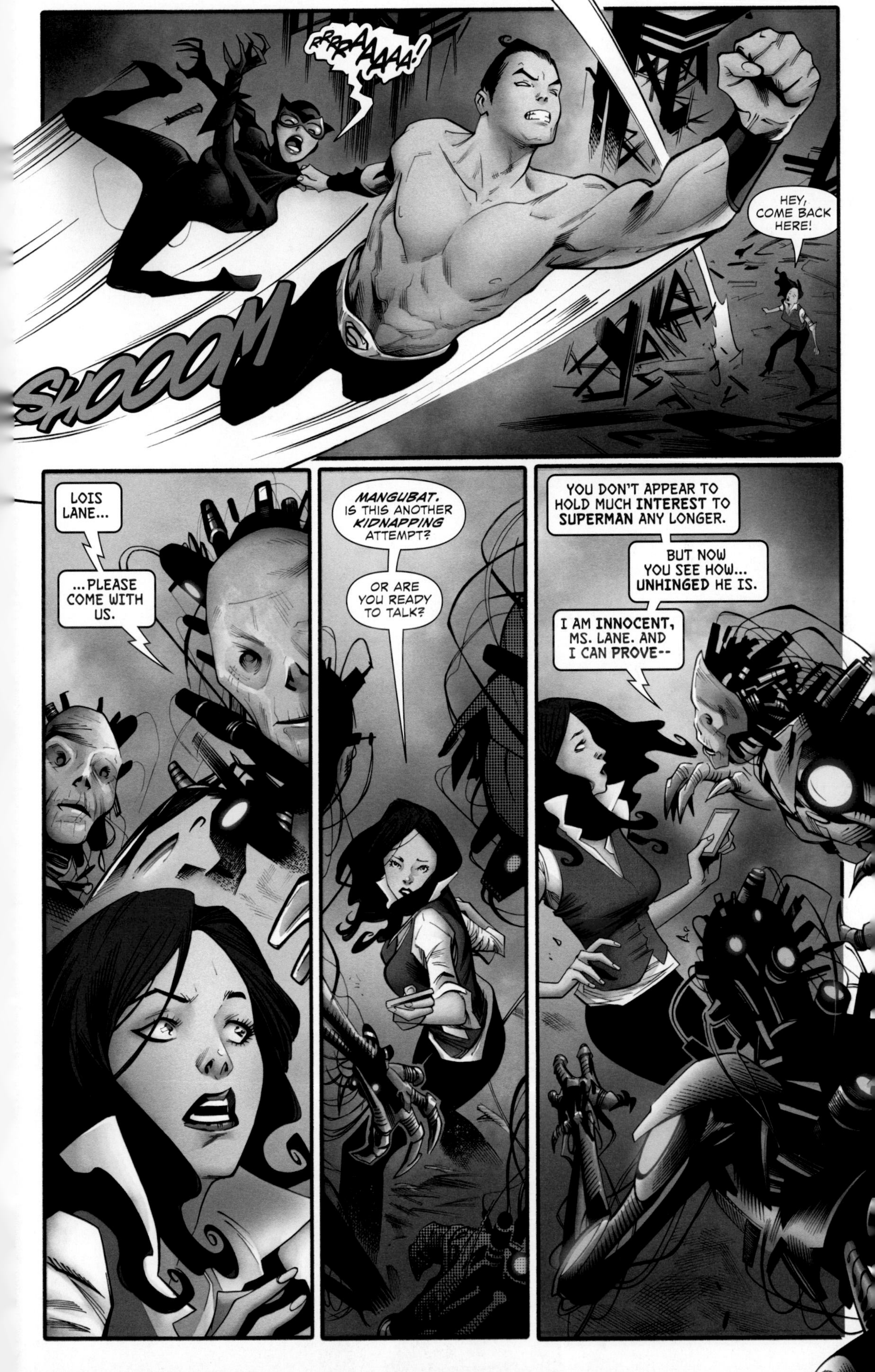
RRRAAAAA!
HEY, COME BACK HERE!
SHOOOOM
LOIS LANE...
...PLEASE COME WITH US.
MANGUBAT. IS THIS ANOTHER KIDNAPPING ATTEMPT?
OR ARE YOU READY TO TALK?
YOU DON'T APPEAR TO HOLD MUCH INTEREST TO SUPERMAN ANY LONGER.
BUT NOW YOU SEE HOW... UNHINGED HE IS.
I AM INNOCENT, MS. LANE. AND I CAN PROVE--

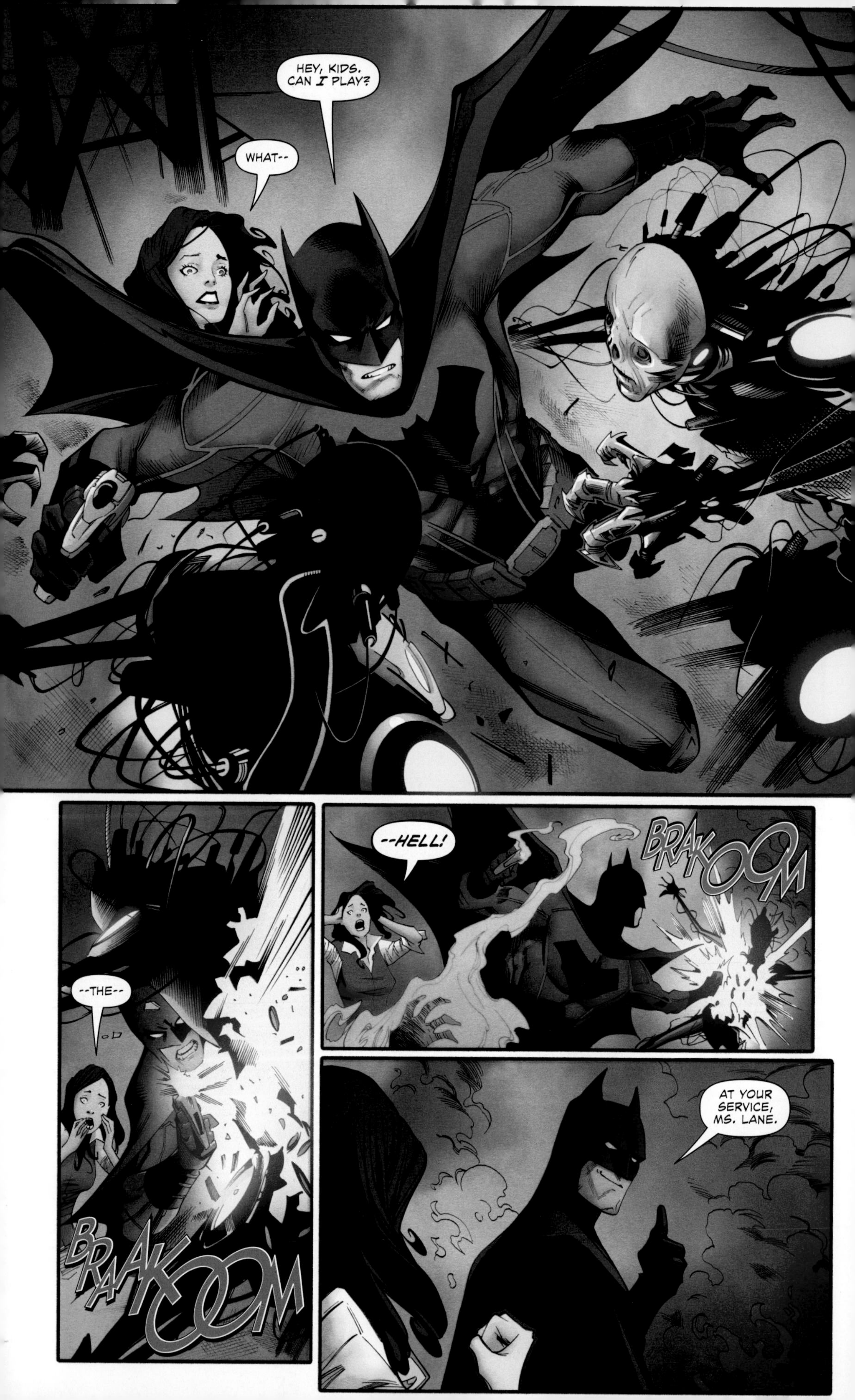
HEY, KIDS. CAN I PLAY?
WHAT--
--THE--
BRAKOOM
--HELL!
BRAKOOM
AT YOUR SERVICE, MS. LANE.

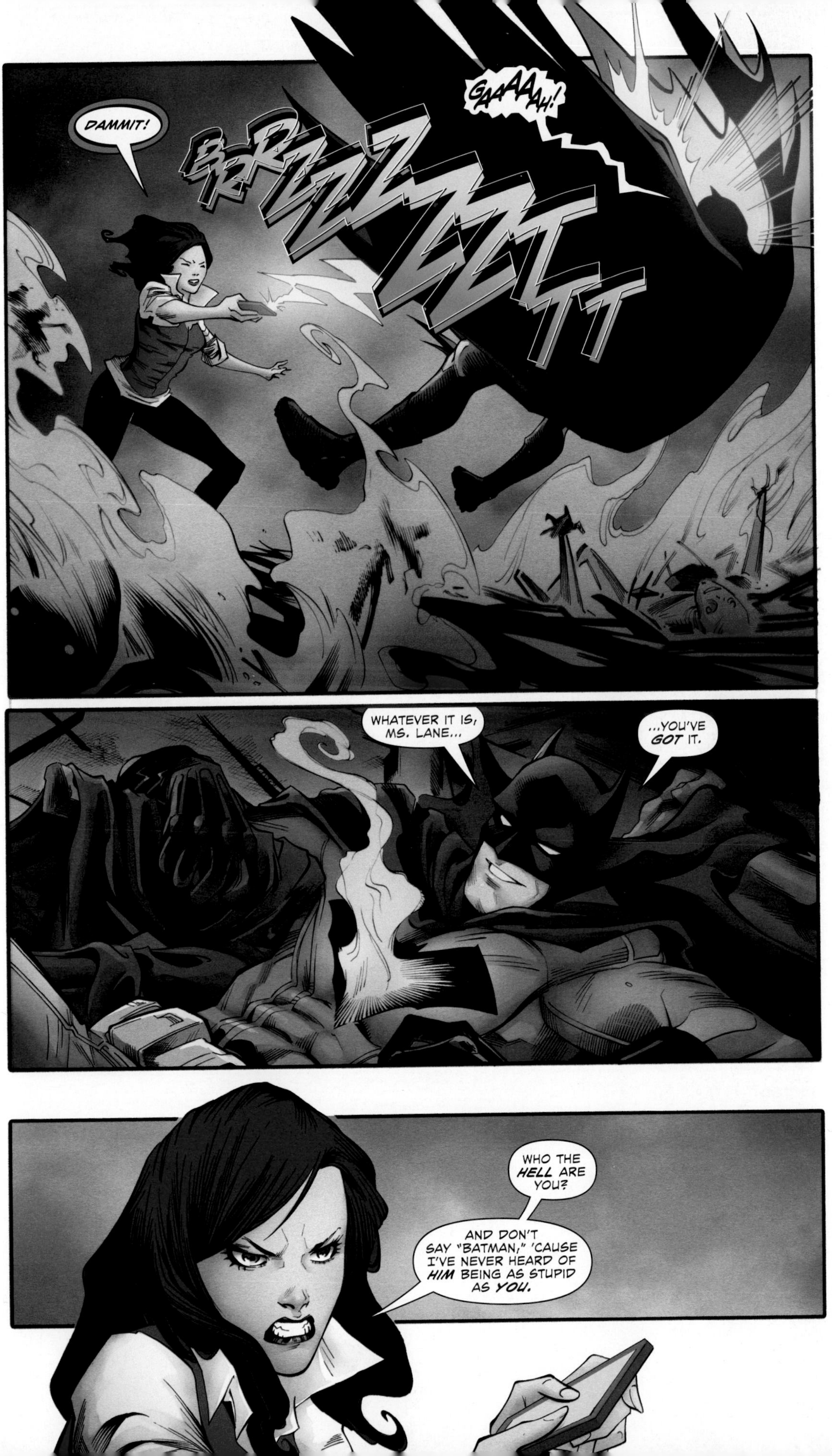
DAMMIT!
GAAAAAH!
WHATEVER IT IS, MS. LANE...
...YOU'VE GOT IT.
WHO THE HELL ARE YOU?
AND DON'T SAY "BATMAN," 'CAUSE I'VE NEVER HEARD OF HIM BEING AS STUPID AS YOU.

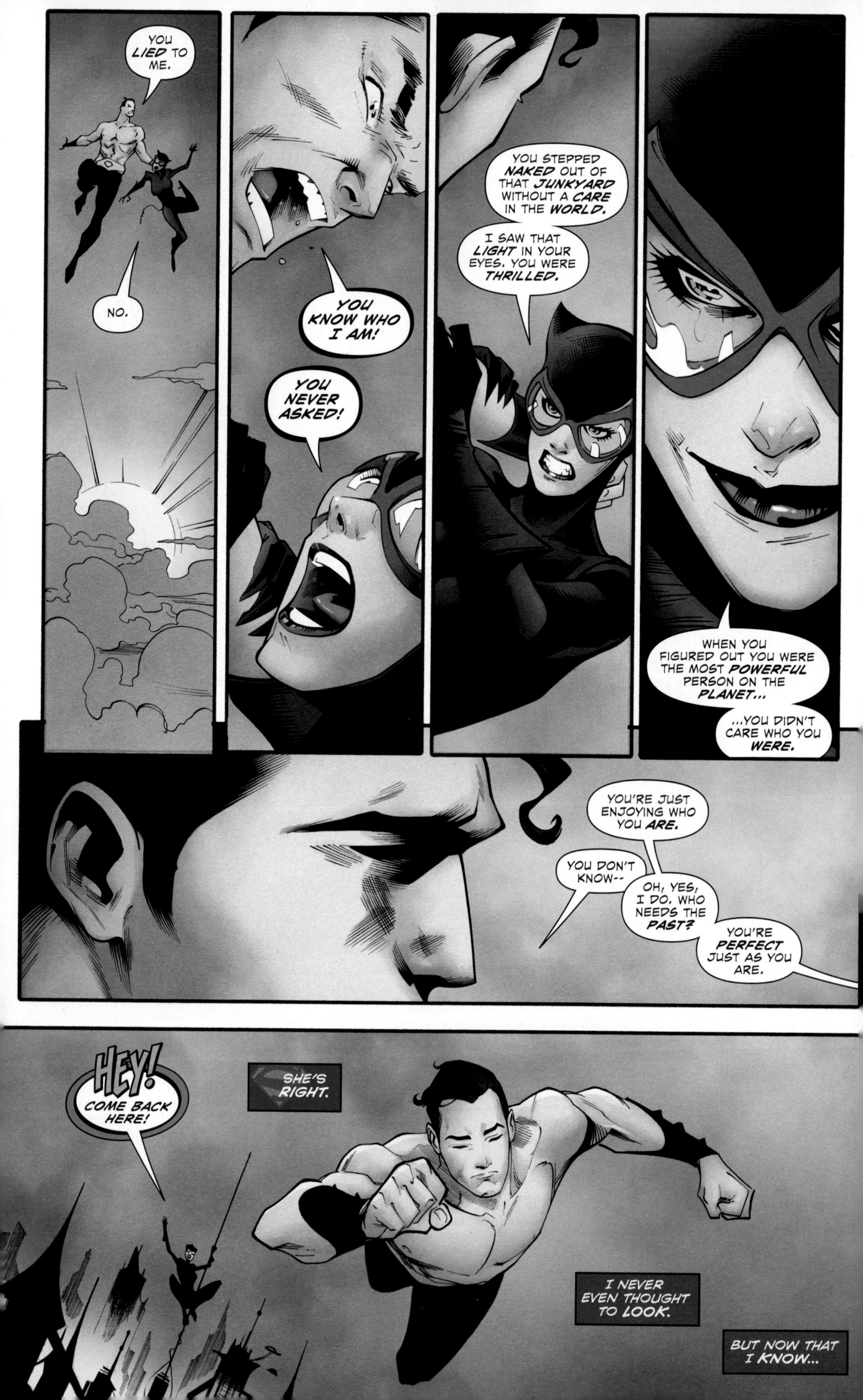
YOU LIED TO ME.
NO.
YOU KNOW WHO I AM!
YOU NEVER ASKED!
YOU STEPPED NAKED OUT OF THAT JUNKYARD WITHOUT A CARE IN THE WORLD.
I SAW THAT LIGHT IN YOUR EYES. YOU WERE THRILLED.
WHEN YOU FIGURED OUT YOU WERE THE MOST POWERFUL PERSON ON THE PLANET...
...YOU DIDN'T CARE WHO YOU WERE.
YOU'RE JUST ENJOYING WHO YOU ARE.
YOU DON'T KNOW--
OH, YES, I DO. WHO NEEDS THE PAST?
YOU'RE PERFECT JUST AS YOU ARE.
HEY! COME BACK HERE!
SHE'S RIGHT.
I NEVER EVEN THOUGHT TO LOOK.
BUT NOW THAT I KNOW...

...I SEE IT EVERYWHERE.

OFFICIAL SUPERMAN ACTION FIGURES

TOYMASTER

GAMESHOP

HEY! SUPERMAN! LONG TIME NO SEE!

Hn.

NICE NEW COSTUME. *DARK*. KIDS LIKE *DARK*.

TRICKY THING, THOUGH...

...WE GOTTA SELL *EDGY*... BUT *HEROIC*, YOU KNOW?

THRILL 'EM-- BUT DON'T *SCARE* 'EM. NOT *TOO* MUCH, ANYWAY.

WHAT IS ALL THIS?

I'M DOING LITTLE VIDS ABOUT YOUR *GREATEST EXPLOITS*-- BUT EXPLAINING THEM FROM YOUR POINT OF VIEW.

PEOPLE SEE YOU *FIGHTING MONSTERS*-- AND THEY THINK *YOU'RE* JUST ANOTHER MONSTER.

SO THIS SHOWS THEM HOW YOU'RE ALWAYS TRYING TO KEEP PEOPLE *SAFE*...

...AND HOW YOU'RE ALWAYS GIVING FOLKS THE *BENEFIT* OF THE *DOUBT*.

EVEN THE MONSTERS.

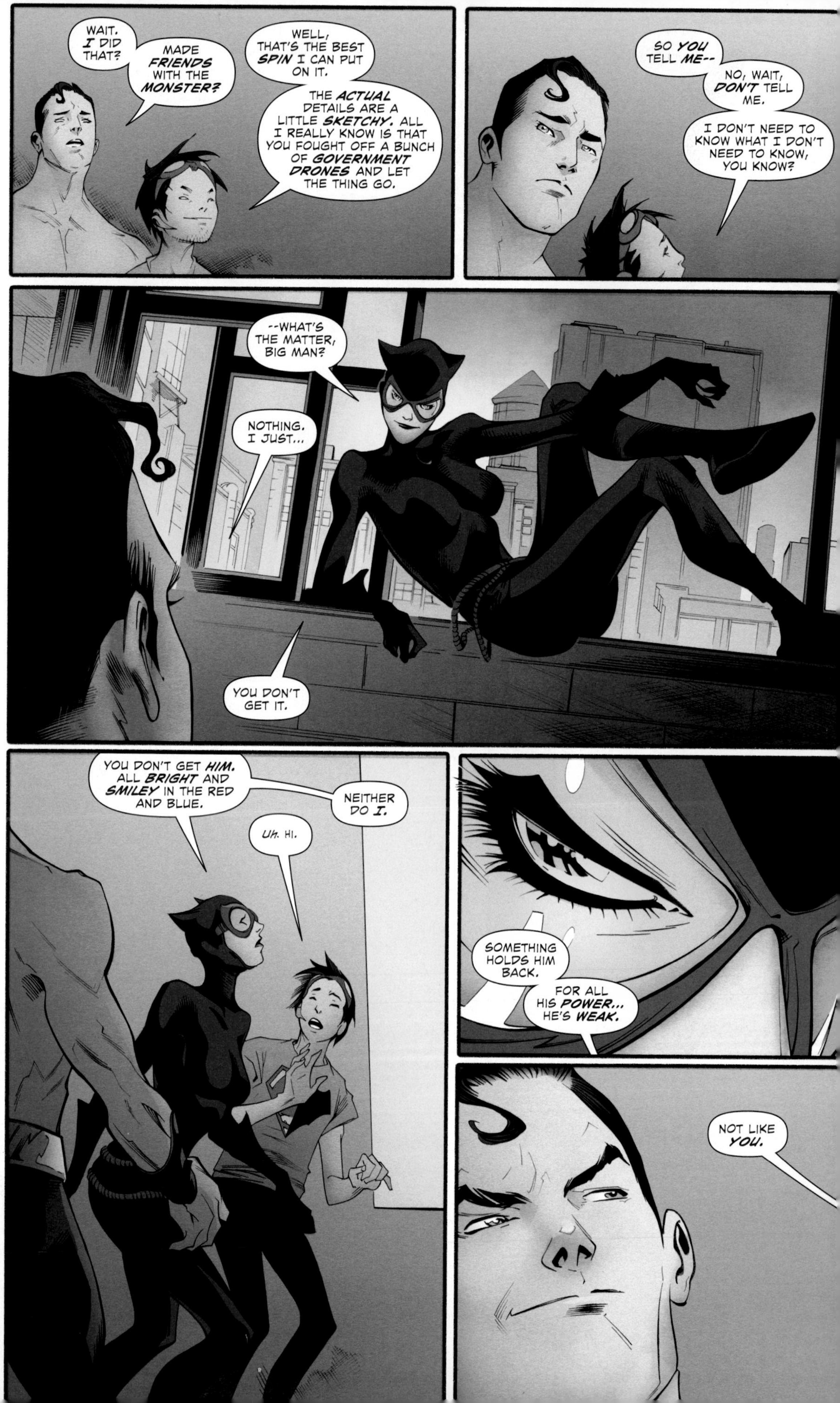
WAIT. I DID THAT?
MADE FRIENDS WITH THE MONSTER?
WELL, THAT'S THE BEST SPIN I CAN PUT ON IT.
THE ACTUAL DETAILS ARE A LITTLE SKETCHY. ALL I REALLY KNOW IS THAT YOU FOUGHT OFF A BUNCH OF GOVERNMENT DRONES AND LET THE THING GO.
SO YOU TELL ME--
NO, WAIT, DON'T TELL ME.
I DON'T NEED TO KNOW WHAT I DON'T NEED TO KNOW, YOU KNOW?
--WHAT'S THE MATTER, BIG MAN?
NOTHING. I JUST...
YOU DON'T GET IT.
YOU DON'T GET HIM. ALL BRIGHT AND SMILEY IN THE RED AND BLUE.
NEITHER DO I.
Uh. HI.
SOMETHING HOLDS HIM BACK.
FOR ALL HIS POWER... HE'S WEAK.
NOT LIKE YOU.

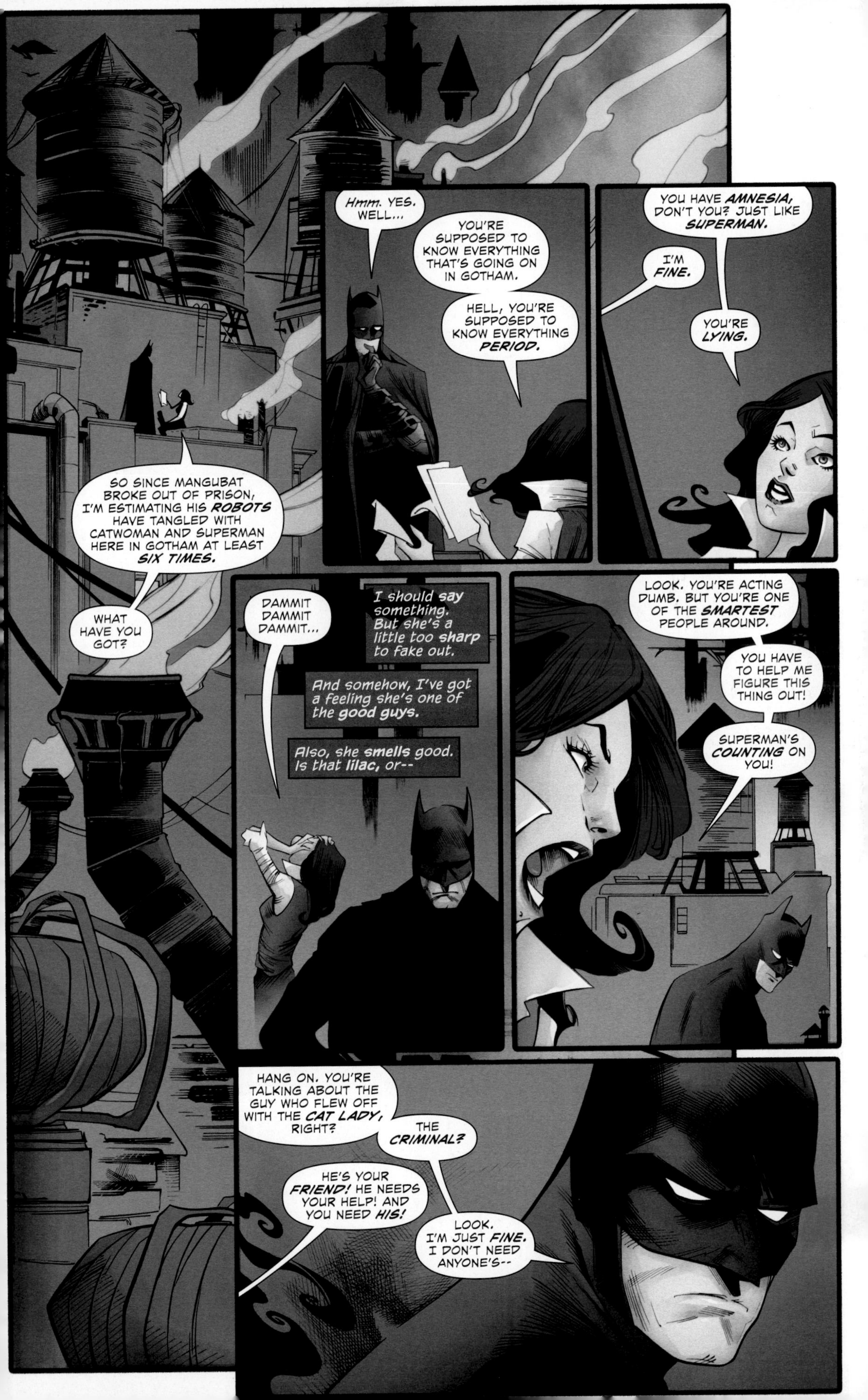
SO SINCE MANGUBAT BROKE OUT OF PRISON, I'M ESTIMATING HIS ROBOTS HAVE TANGLED WITH CATWOMAN AND SUPERMAN HERE IN GOTHAM AT LEAST SIX TIMES.
WHAT HAVE YOU GOT?
Hmm. YES. WELL...
YOU'RE SUPPOSED TO KNOW EVERYTHING THAT'S GOING ON IN GOTHAM.
HELL, YOU'RE SUPPOSED TO KNOW EVERYTHING PERIOD.
YOU HAVE AMNESIA, DON'T YOU? JUST LIKE SUPERMAN.
I'M FINE.
YOU'RE LYING.
DAMMIT DAMMIT DAMMIT...
I should say something. But she's a little too sharp to fake out.
And somehow, I've got a feeling she's one of the good guys.
Also, she smells good. Is that lilac, or--
LOOK. YOU'RE ACTING DUMB. BUT YOU'RE ONE OF THE SMARTEST PEOPLE AROUND.
YOU HAVE TO HELP ME FIGURE THIS THING OUT!
SUPERMAN'S COUNTING ON YOU!
HANG ON. YOU'RE TALKING ABOUT THE GUY WHO FLEW OFF WITH THE CAT LADY, RIGHT?
THE CRIMINAL?
HE'S YOUR FRIEND! HE NEEDS YOUR HELP! AND YOU NEED HIS!
LOOK. I'M JUST FINE. I DON'T NEED ANYONE'S--

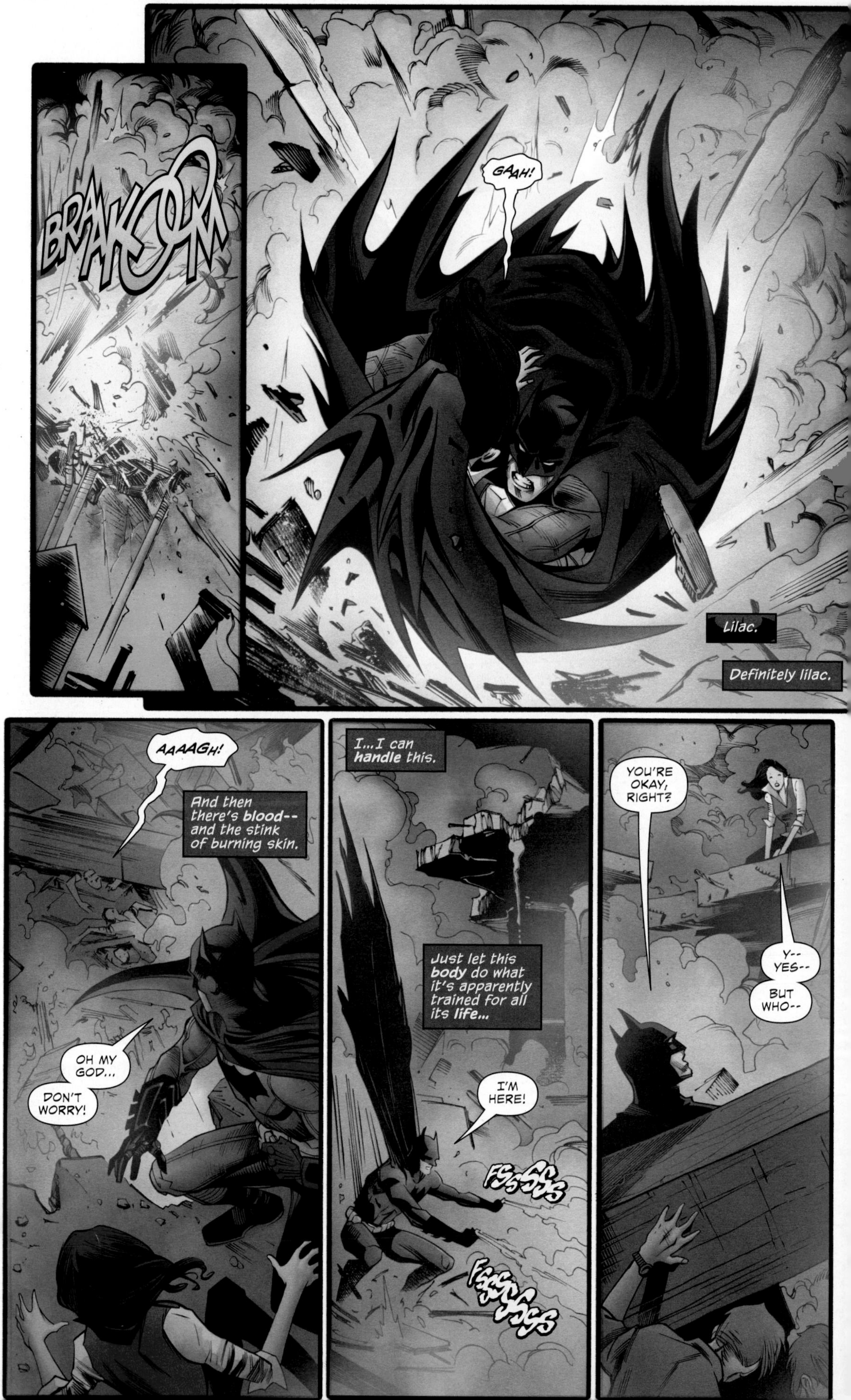
BRAKOOM
GAAH!
Lilac.
Definitely lilac.
AAAAGH!
And then there's blood-- and the stink of burning skin.
OH MY GOD...
DON'T WORRY!
I...I can handle this.
Just let this body do what it's apparently trained for all its life...
I'M HERE!
FSSSSS
FSSSSSSS
YOU'RE OKAY, RIGHT?
Y-- YES--
BUT WHO--

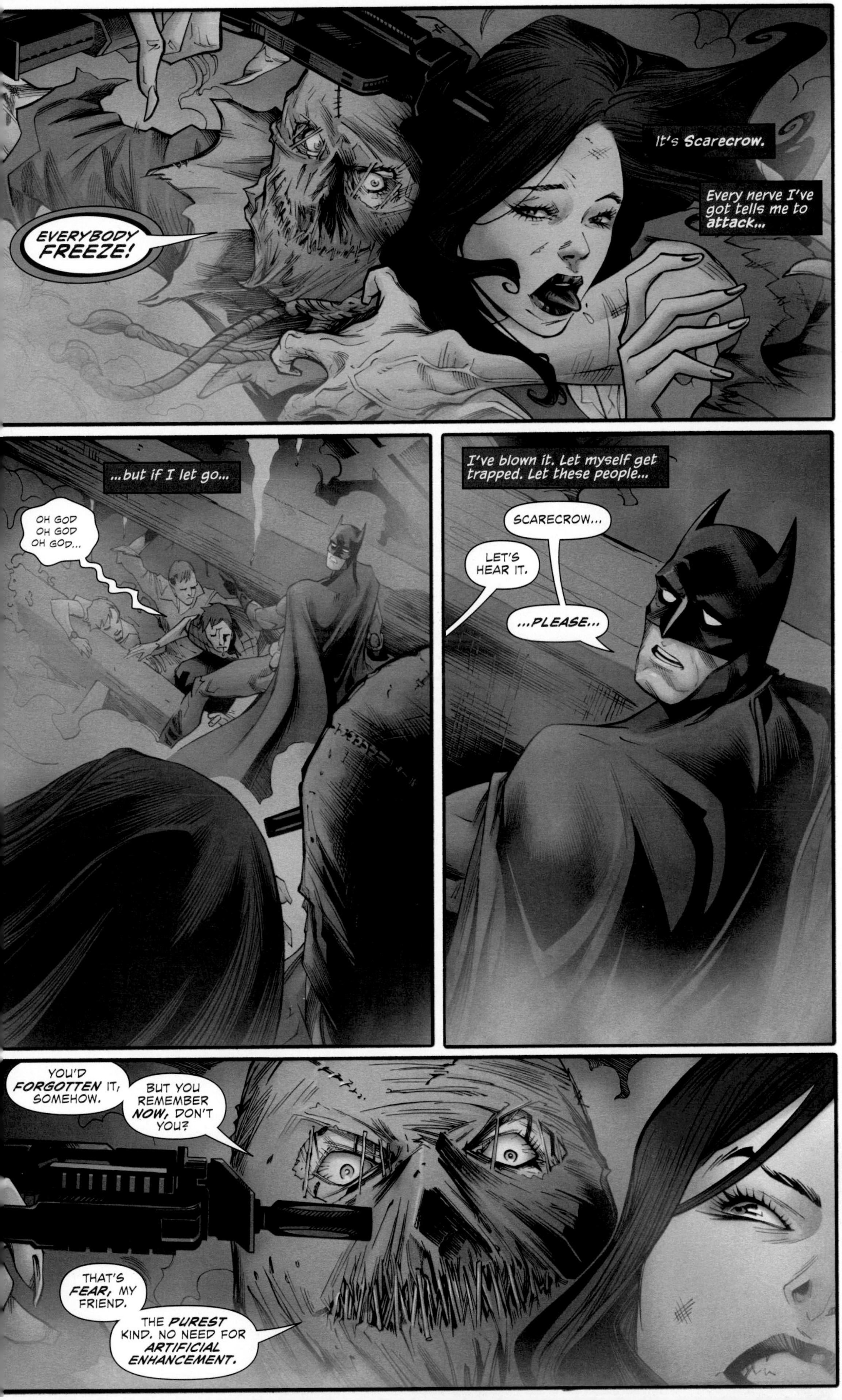
It's Scarecrow.
Every nerve I've got tells me to attack...
EVERYBODY FREEZE!
...but if I let go...
OH GOD OH GOD OH GOD...
I've blown it. Let myself get trapped. Let these people...
SCARECROW...
LET'S HEAR IT.
...PLEASE...
YOU'D FORGOTTEN IT, SOMEHOW.
BUT YOU REMEMBER NOW, DON'T YOU?
THAT'S FEAR, MY FRIEND.
THE PUREST KIND. NO NEED FOR ARTIFICIAL ENHANCEMENT.

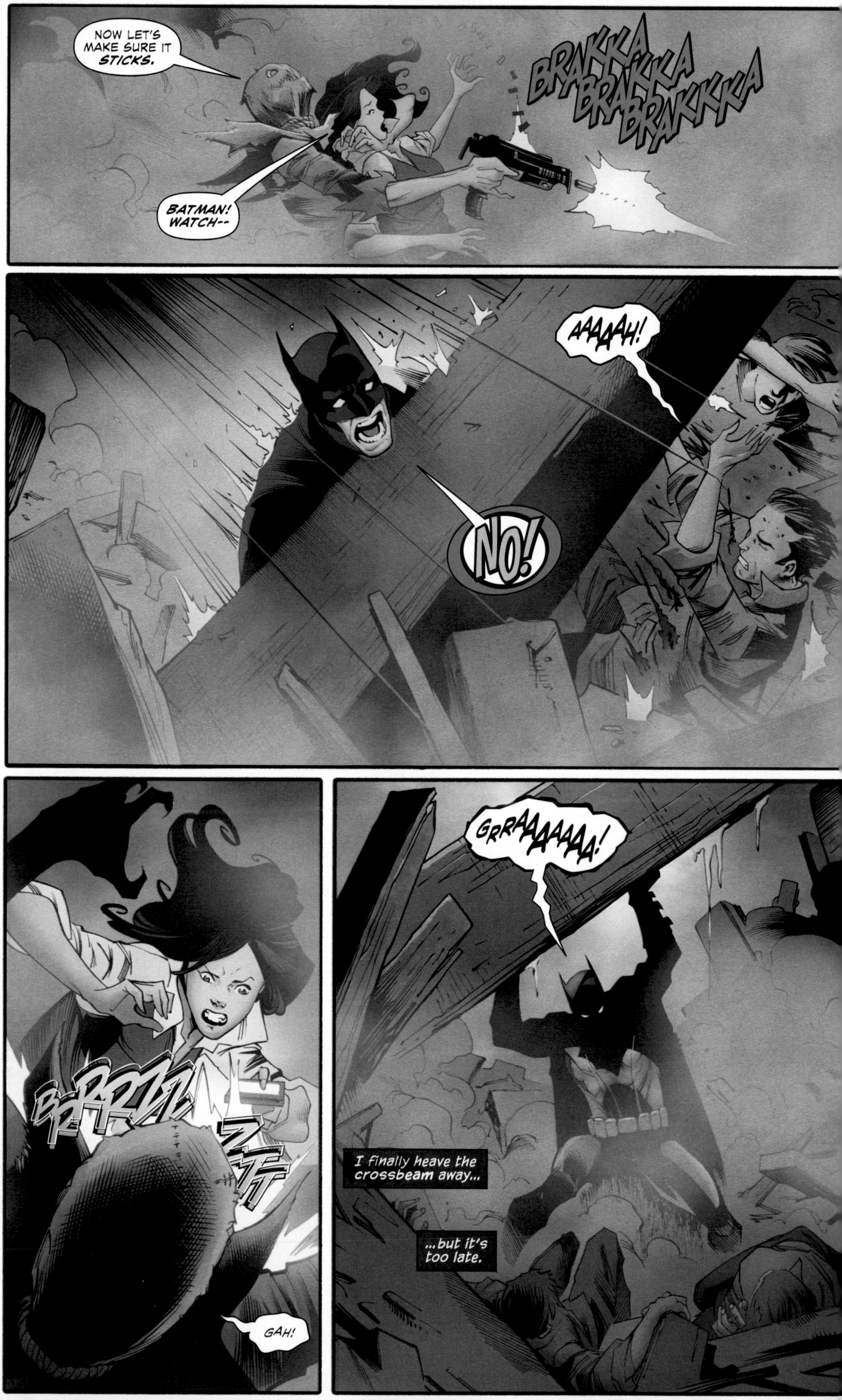
NOW LET'S MAKE SURE IT STICKS.
BRAKKKA BRAKKKA BRAKKKKA
BATMAN! WATCH--
AAAAAH!
NO!
BZRRZZZT
GAH!
GRRAAAAAAAA!
I finally heave the crossbeam away...
...but it's too late.

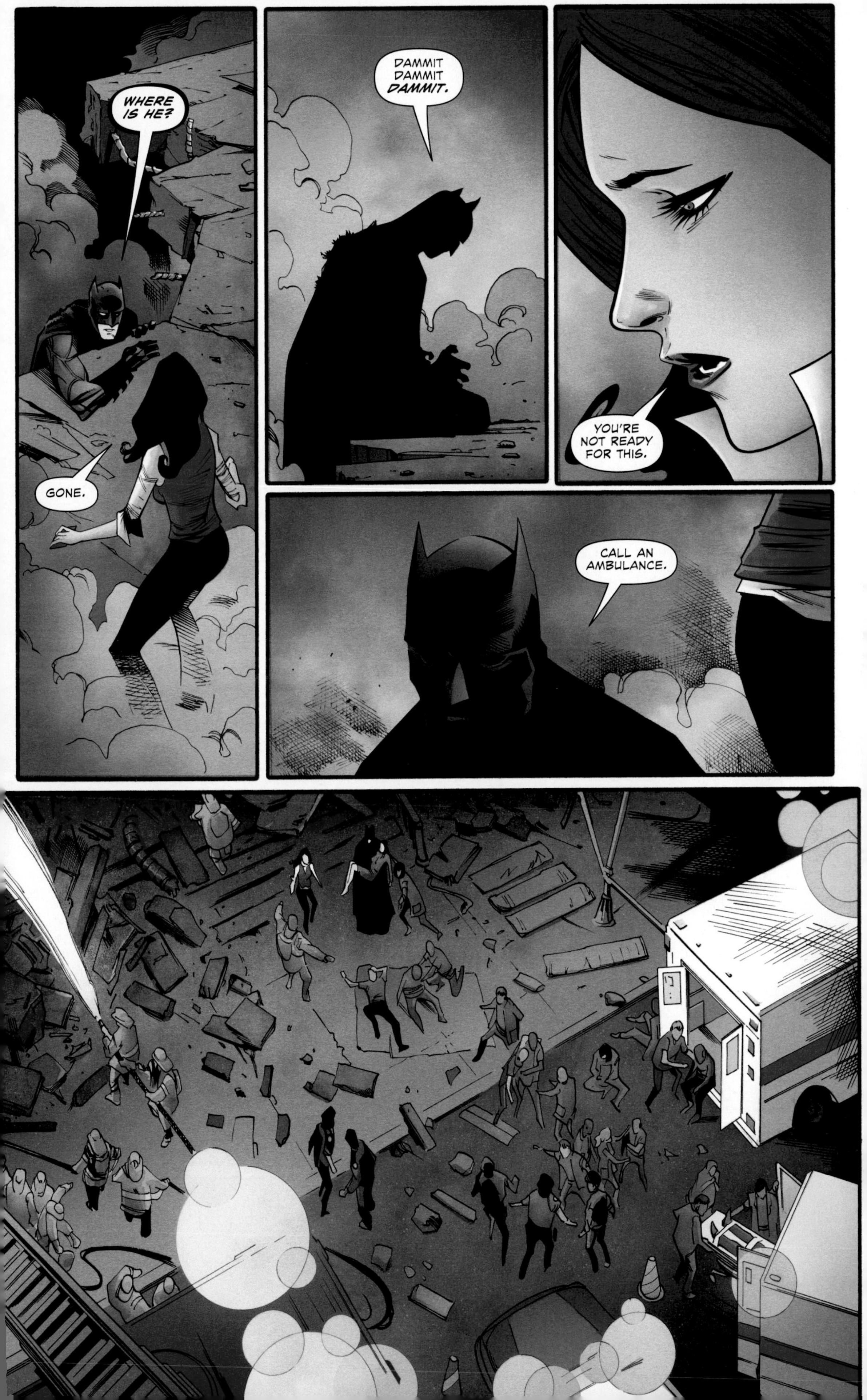
WHERE IS HE?
GONE.
DAMMIT DAMMIT DAMMIT.
YOU'RE NOT READY FOR THIS.
CALL AN AMBULANCE.

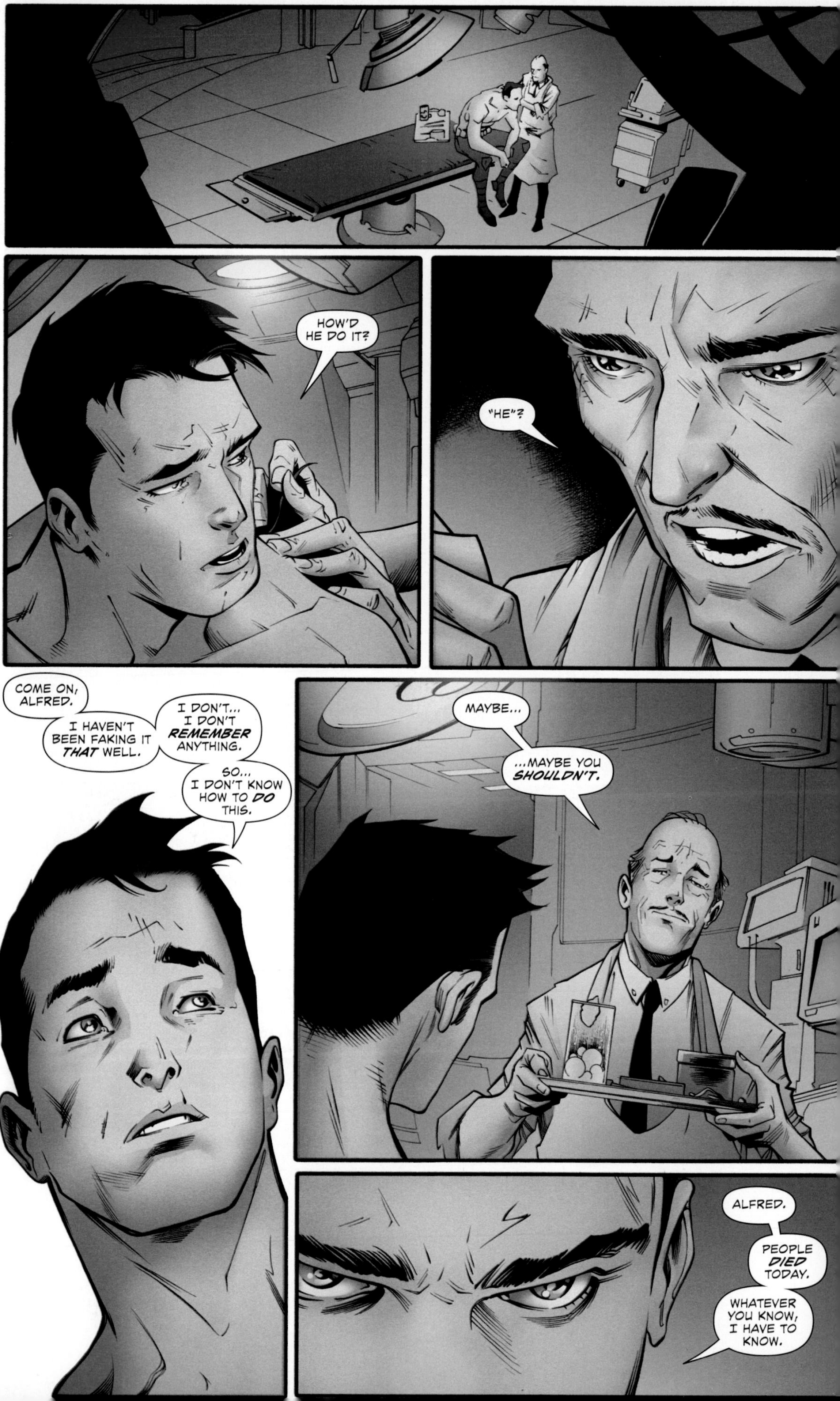
HOW'D HE DO IT?
"HE"?
COME ON, ALFRED.
I HAVEN'T BEEN FAKING IT *THAT* WELL.
I DON'T... I DON'T *REMEMBER* ANYTHING.
SO... I DON'T KNOW HOW TO *DO* THIS.
MAYBE...
...MAYBE YOU *SHOULDN'T.*
ALFRED.
PEOPLE *DIED* TODAY.
WHATEVER YOU KNOW, I HAVE TO KNOW.

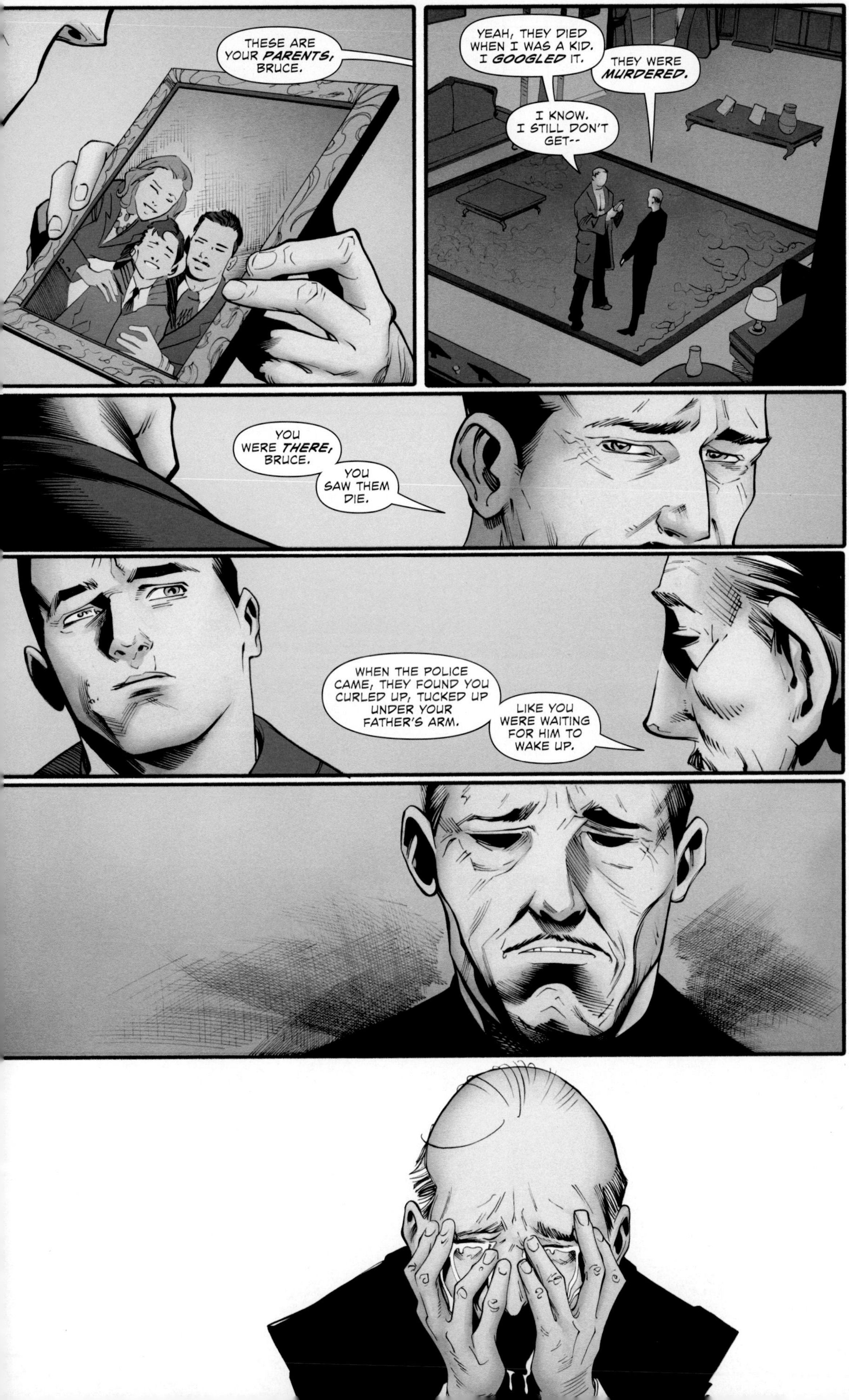

THESE ARE YOUR PARENTS, BRUCE.
YEAH, THEY DIED WHEN I WAS A KID. I GOOGLED IT.
THEY WERE MURDERED.
I KNOW. I STILL DON'T GET--
YOU WERE THERE, BRUCE.
YOU SAW THEM DIE.
WHEN THE POLICE CAME, THEY FOUND YOU CURLED UP, TUCKED UP UNDER YOUR FATHER'S ARM.
LIKE YOU WERE WAITING FOR HIM TO WAKE UP.

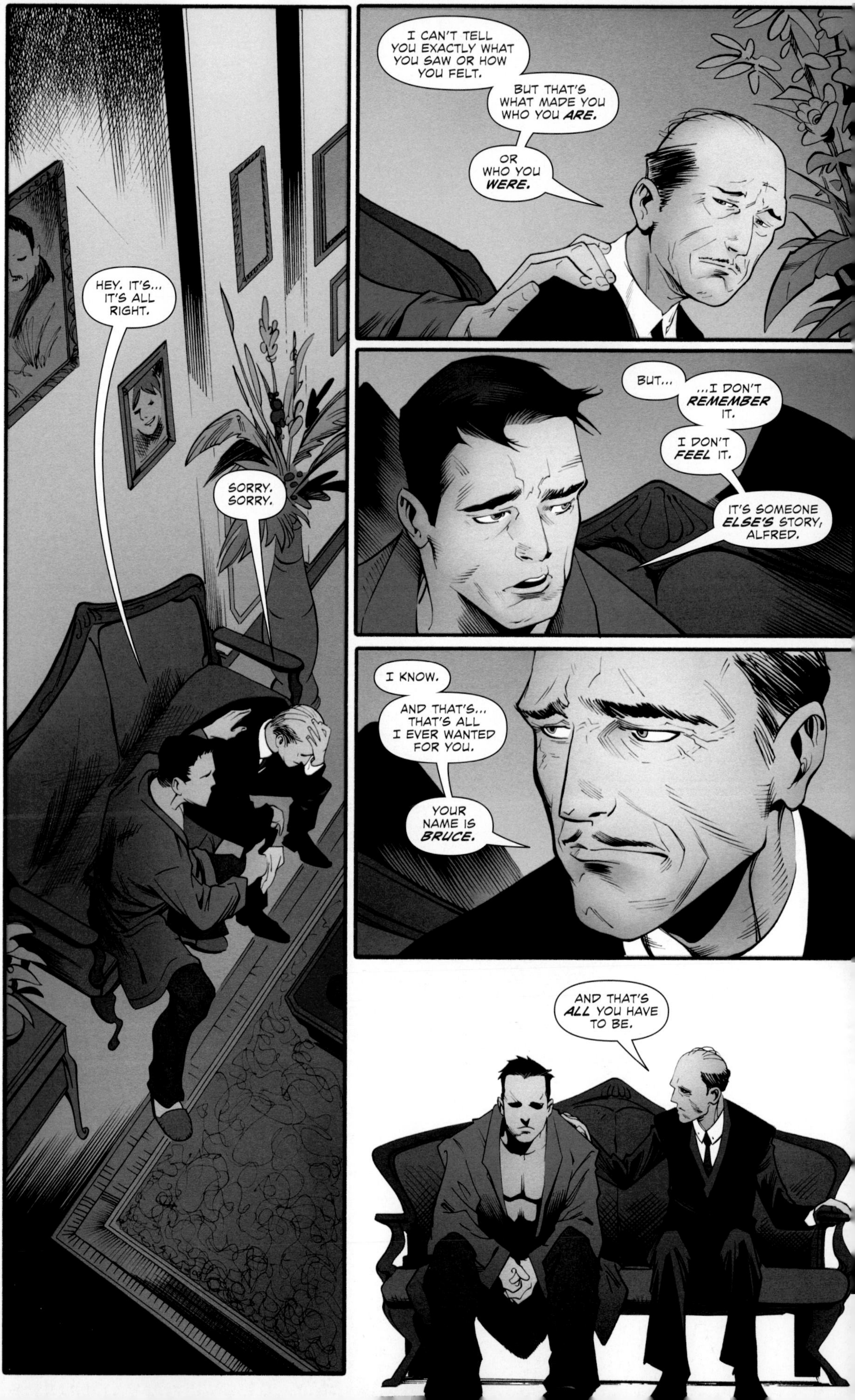
HEY. IT'S... IT'S ALL RIGHT.
SORRY. SORRY.
I CAN'T TELL YOU EXACTLY WHAT YOU SAW OR HOW YOU FELT.
BUT THAT'S WHAT MADE YOU WHO YOU *ARE.*
OR WHO YOU *WERE.*
BUT...
...I DON'T *REMEMBER* IT.
I DON'T *FEEL* IT.
IT'S SOMEONE *ELSE'S* STORY, ALFRED.
I KNOW.
AND THAT'S... THAT'S ALL I EVER WANTED FOR YOU.
YOUR NAME IS *BRUCE.*
AND THAT'S *ALL* YOU HAVE TO BE.

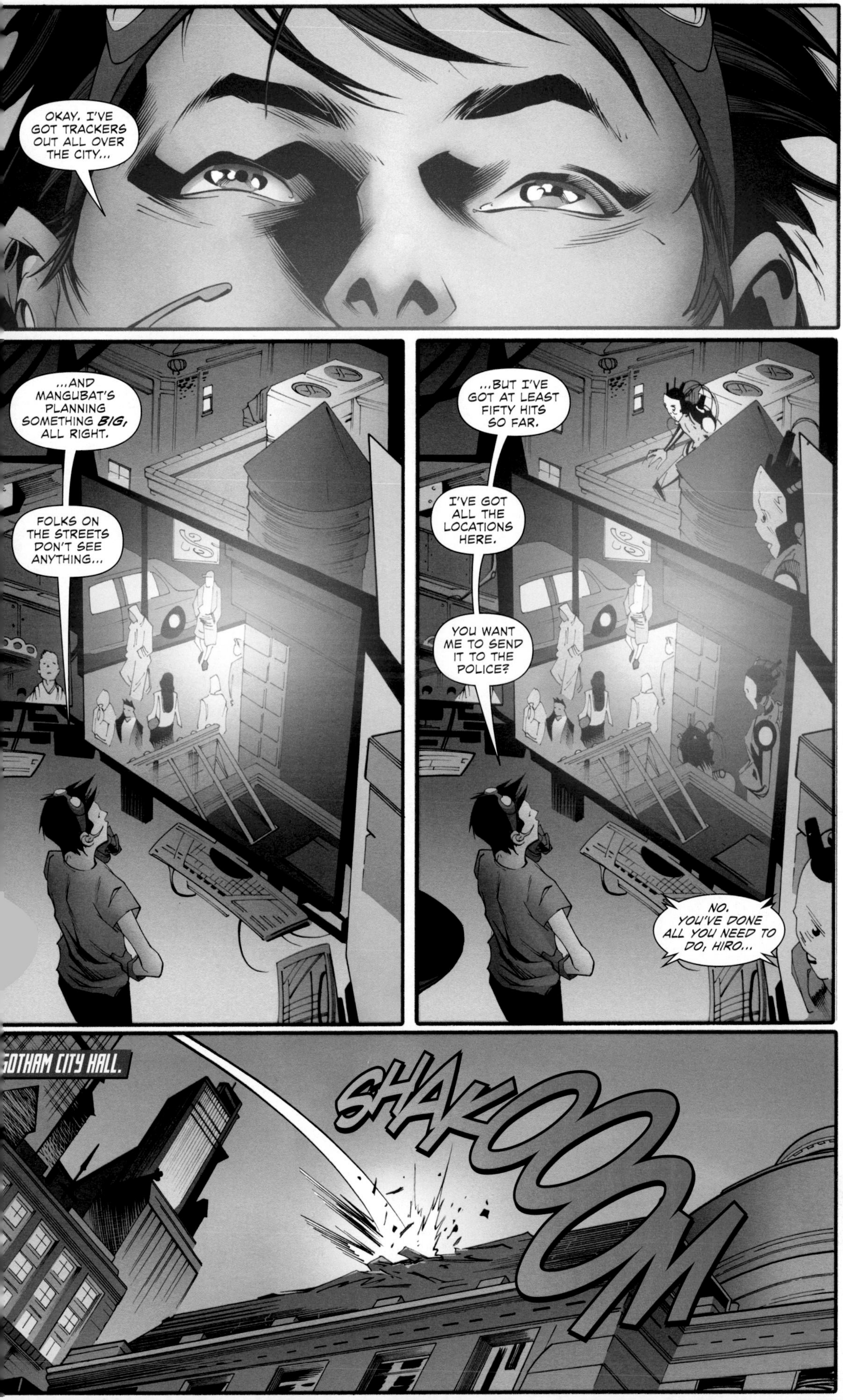
OKAY. I'VE GOT TRACKERS OUT ALL OVER THE CITY...
...AND MANGUBAT'S PLANNING SOMETHING *BIG*, ALL RIGHT.
FOLKS ON THE STREETS DON'T SEE ANYTHING...
...BUT I'VE GOT AT LEAST FIFTY HITS SO FAR.
I'VE GOT ALL THE LOCATIONS HERE.
YOU WANT ME TO SEND IT TO THE POLICE?
NO. YOU'VE DONE ALL YOU NEED TO DO, HIRO...
GOTHAM CITY HALL.
SHAKOOOM

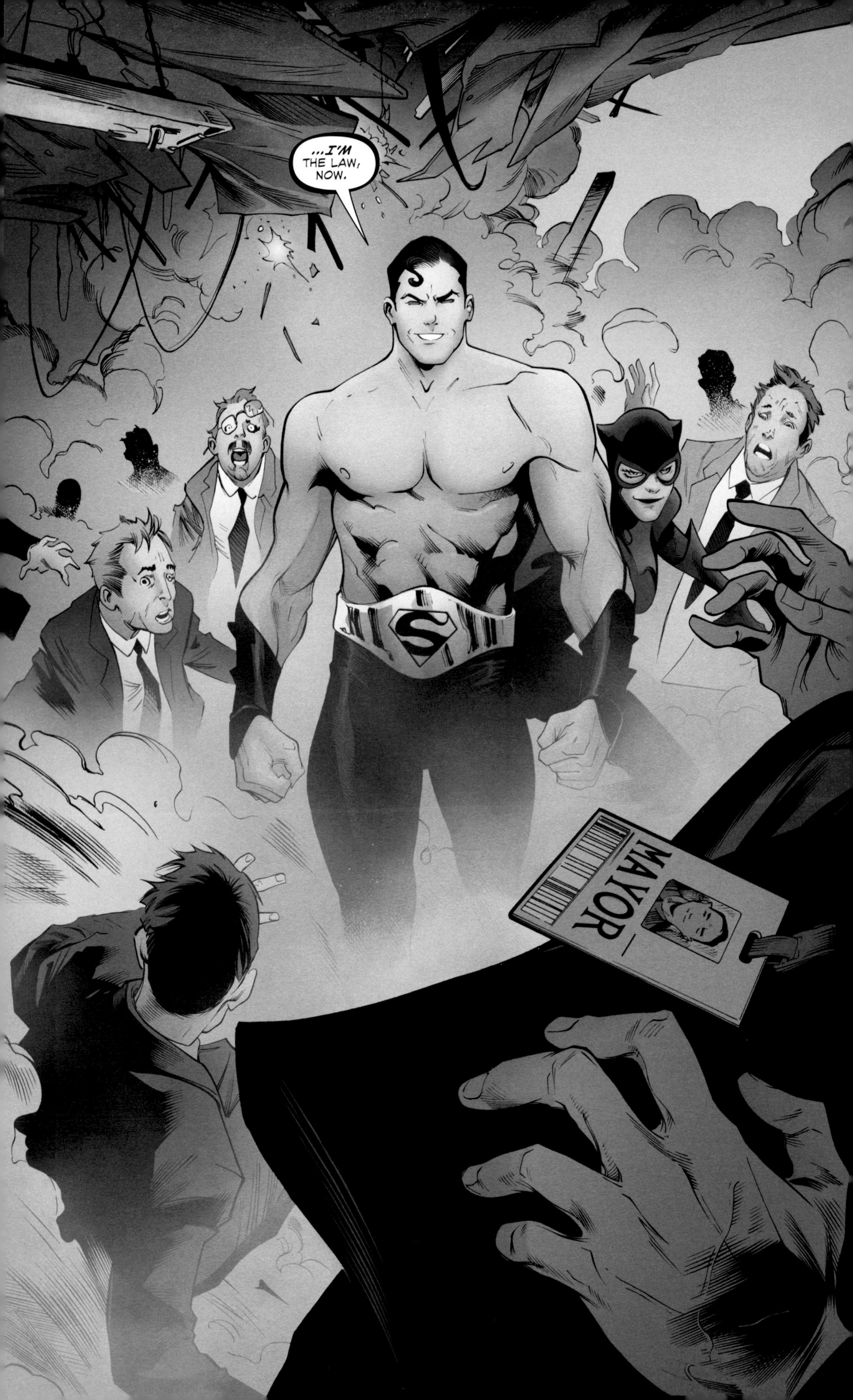
...I'M THE LAW, NOW.
MAYOR

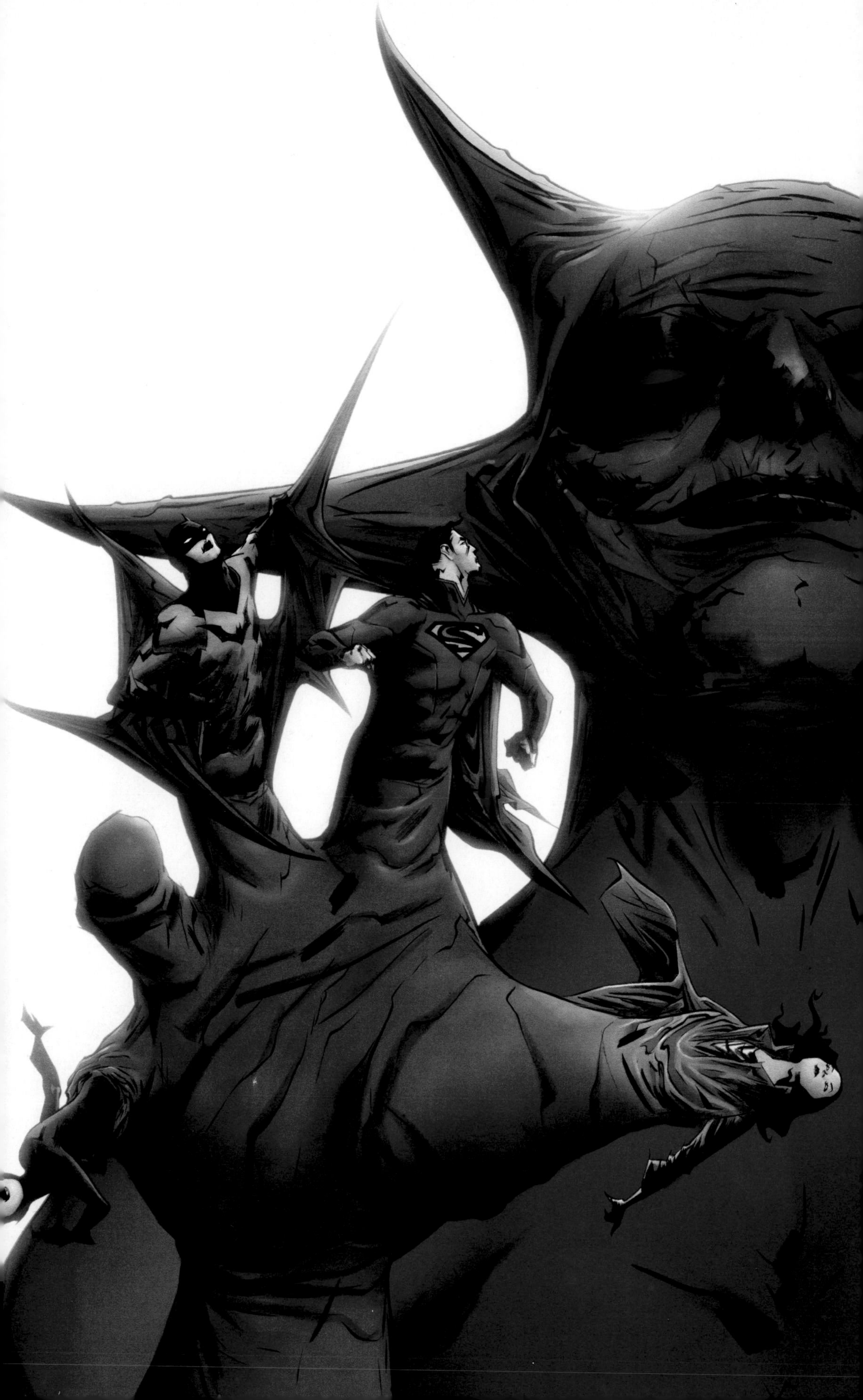

FORGET-ME-NOT

GREG PAK writer **PASCAL ALIXE DIOGENES NEVES MARC DEERING CLIFF RICHARDS** artists **ULISES ARREOLA** colorist **ROB LEIGH** letterer
cover by **JAE LEE** with **JUNE CHUNG**

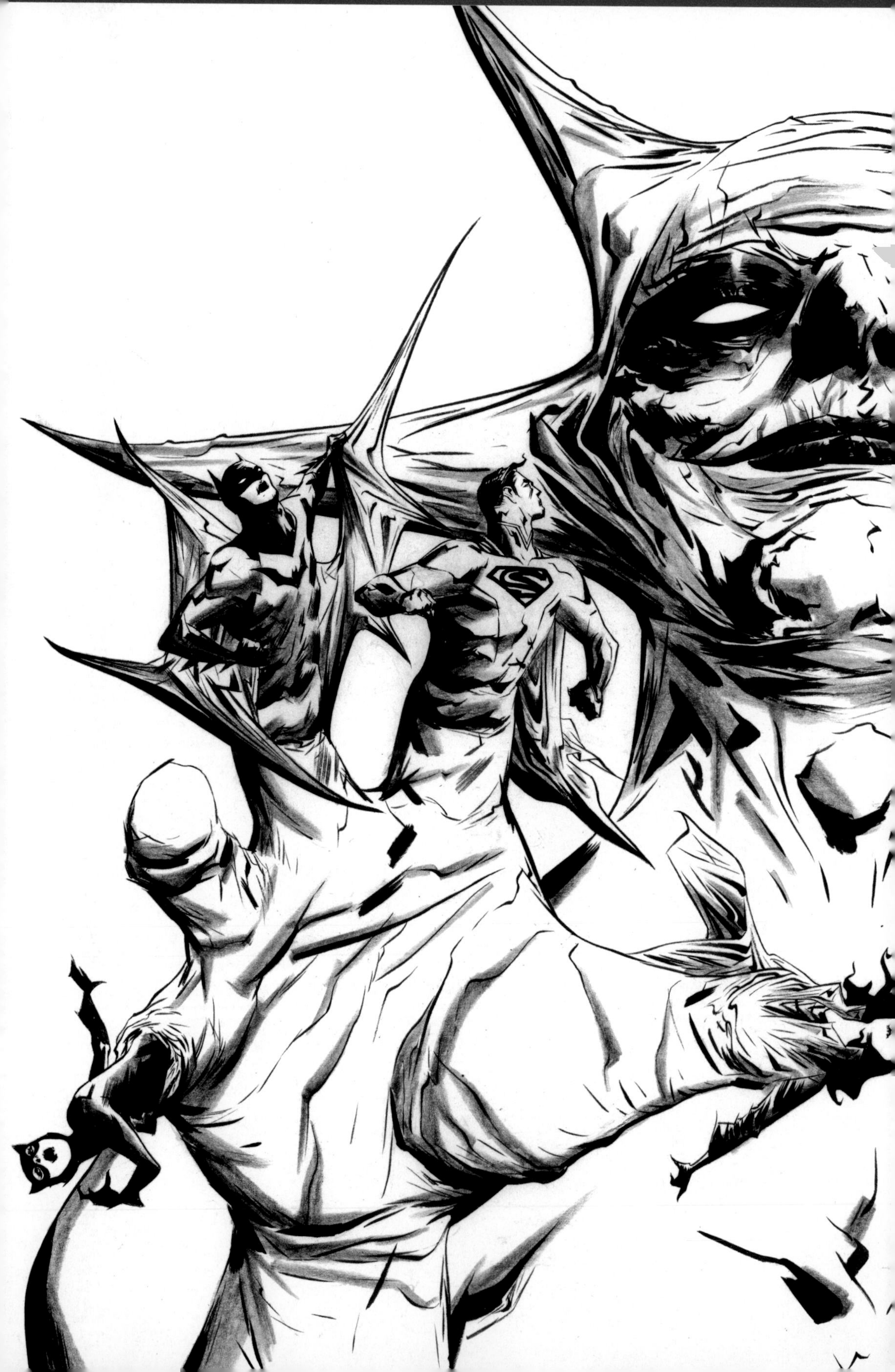

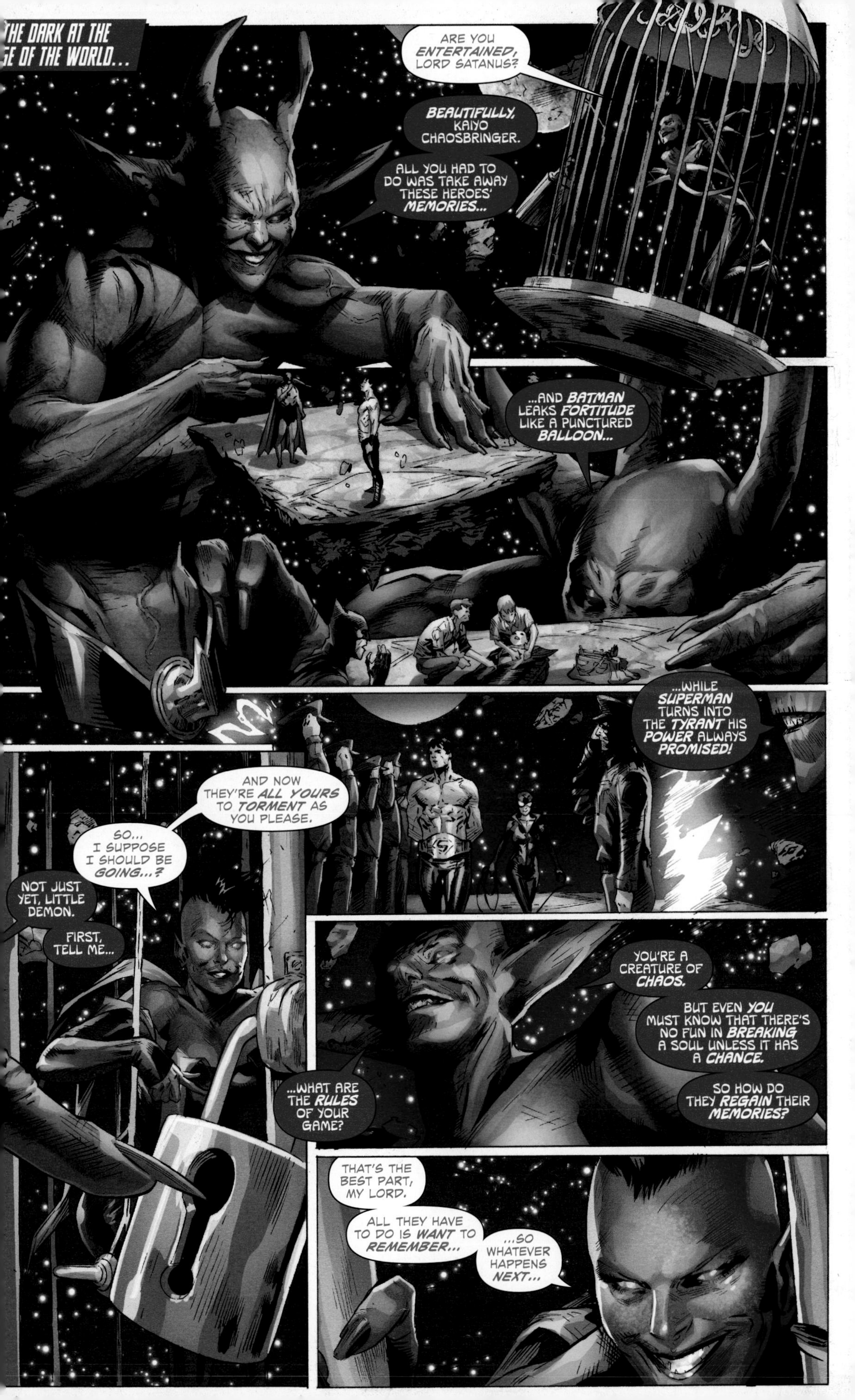
THE DARK AT THE
GE OF THE WORLD...
ARE YOU ENTERTAINED, LORD SATANUS?
BEAUTIFULLY, KAIYO CHAOSBRINGER.
ALL YOU HAD TO DO WAS TAKE AWAY THESE HEROES' MEMORIES...
...AND BATMAN LEAKS FORTITUDE LIKE A PUNCTURED BALLOON...
...WHILE SUPERMAN TURNS INTO THE TYRANT HIS POWER ALWAYS PROMISED!
AND NOW THEY'RE ALL YOURS TO TORMENT AS YOU PLEASE.
SO... I SUPPOSE I SHOULD BE GOING...?
NOT JUST YET, LITTLE DEMON.
FIRST, TELL ME...
...WHAT ARE THE RULES OF YOUR GAME?
YOU'RE A CREATURE OF CHAOS.
BUT EVEN YOU MUST KNOW THAT THERE'S NO FUN IN BREAKING A SOUL UNLESS IT HAS A CHANCE.
SO HOW DO THEY REGAIN THEIR MEMORIES?
THAT'S THE BEST PART, MY LORD.
ALL THEY HAVE TO DO IS WANT TO REMEMBER...
...SO WHATEVER HAPPENS NEXT...

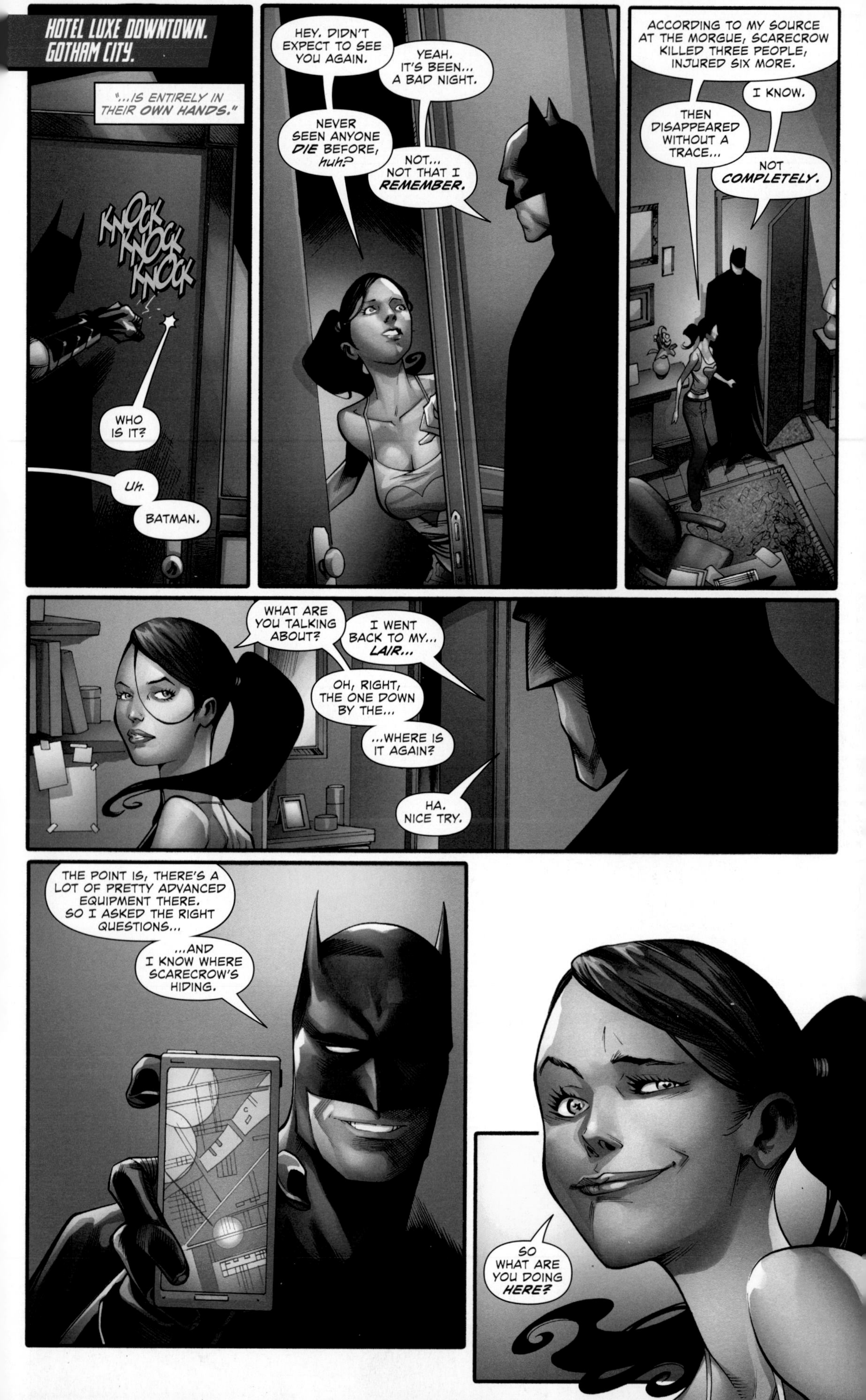
HOTEL LUXE DOWNTOWN. GOTHAM CITY.
"...IS ENTIRELY IN THEIR OWN HANDS."
KNOCK KNOCK KNOCK
WHO IS IT?
Uh.
BATMAN.
HEY. DIDN'T EXPECT TO SEE YOU AGAIN.
YEAH. IT'S BEEN... A BAD NIGHT.
NEVER SEEN ANYONE DIE BEFORE, huh?
NOT... NOT THAT I REMEMBER.
ACCORDING TO MY SOURCE AT THE MORGUE, SCARECROW KILLED THREE PEOPLE, INJURED SIX MORE.
I KNOW.
THEN DISAPPEARED WITHOUT A TRACE...
NOT COMPLETELY.
WHAT ARE YOU TALKING ABOUT?
I WENT BACK TO MY... LAIR...
OH, RIGHT, THE ONE DOWN BY THE...
...WHERE IS IT AGAIN?
HA. NICE TRY.
THE POINT IS, THERE'S A LOT OF PRETTY ADVANCED EQUIPMENT THERE. SO I ASKED THE RIGHT QUESTIONS...
...AND I KNOW WHERE SCARECROW'S HIDING.
SO WHAT ARE YOU DOING HERE?

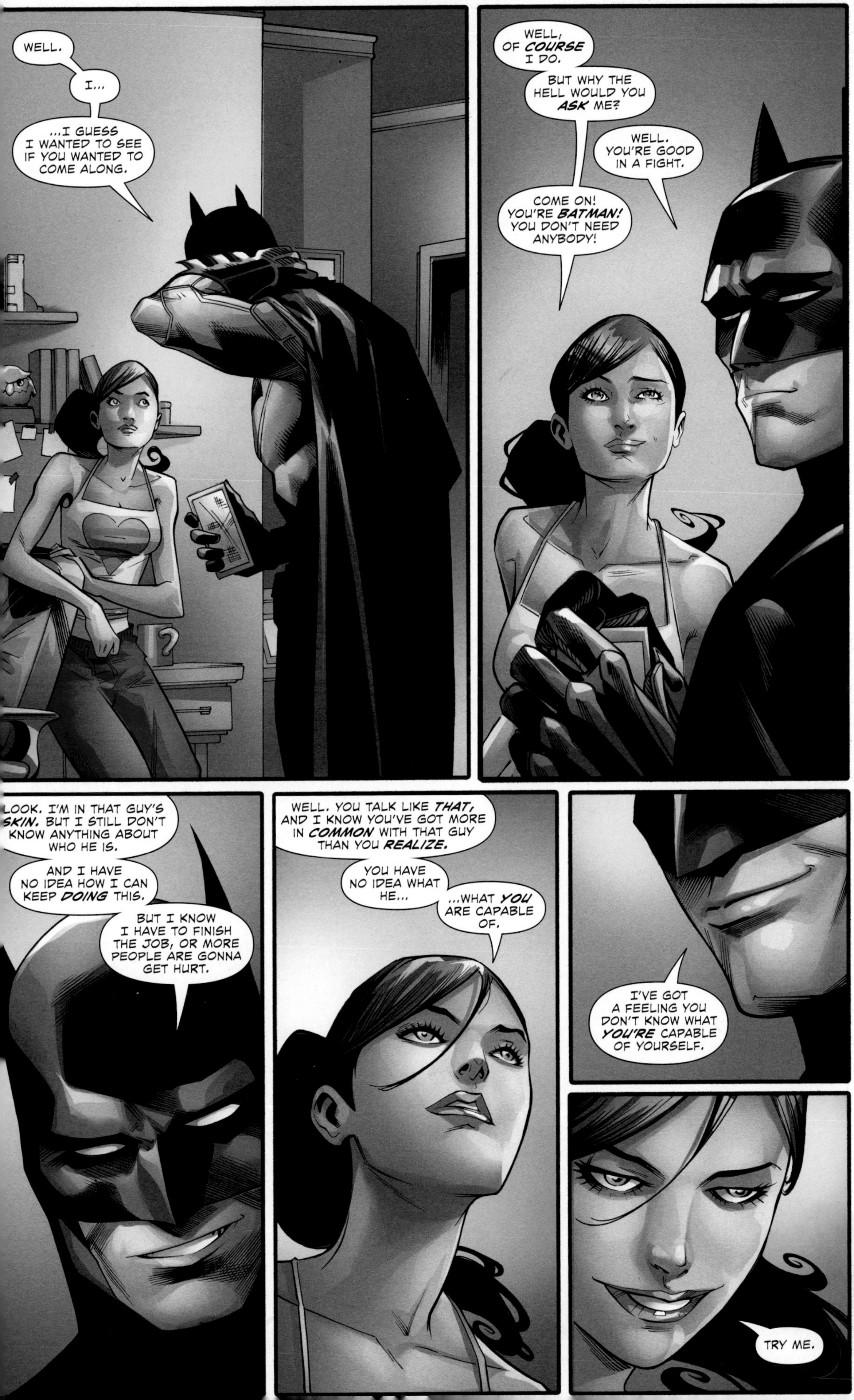
WELL.
I...
...I GUESS I WANTED TO SEE IF YOU WANTED TO COME ALONG.
WELL, OF COURSE I DO.
BUT WHY THE HELL WOULD YOU ASK ME?
WELL. YOU'RE GOOD IN A FIGHT.
COME ON! YOU'RE BATMAN! YOU DON'T NEED ANYBODY!
LOOK. I'M IN THAT GUY'S SKIN. BUT I STILL DON'T KNOW ANYTHING ABOUT WHO HE IS.
AND I HAVE NO IDEA HOW I CAN KEEP DOING THIS.
BUT I KNOW I HAVE TO FINISH THE JOB, OR MORE PEOPLE ARE GONNA GET HURT.
WELL. YOU TALK LIKE THAT, AND I KNOW YOU'VE GOT MORE IN COMMON WITH THAT GUY THAN YOU REALIZE.
YOU HAVE NO IDEA WHAT HE...
...WHAT YOU ARE CAPABLE OF.
I'VE GOT A FEELING YOU DON'T KNOW WHAT YOU'RE CAPABLE OF YOURSELF.
TRY ME.

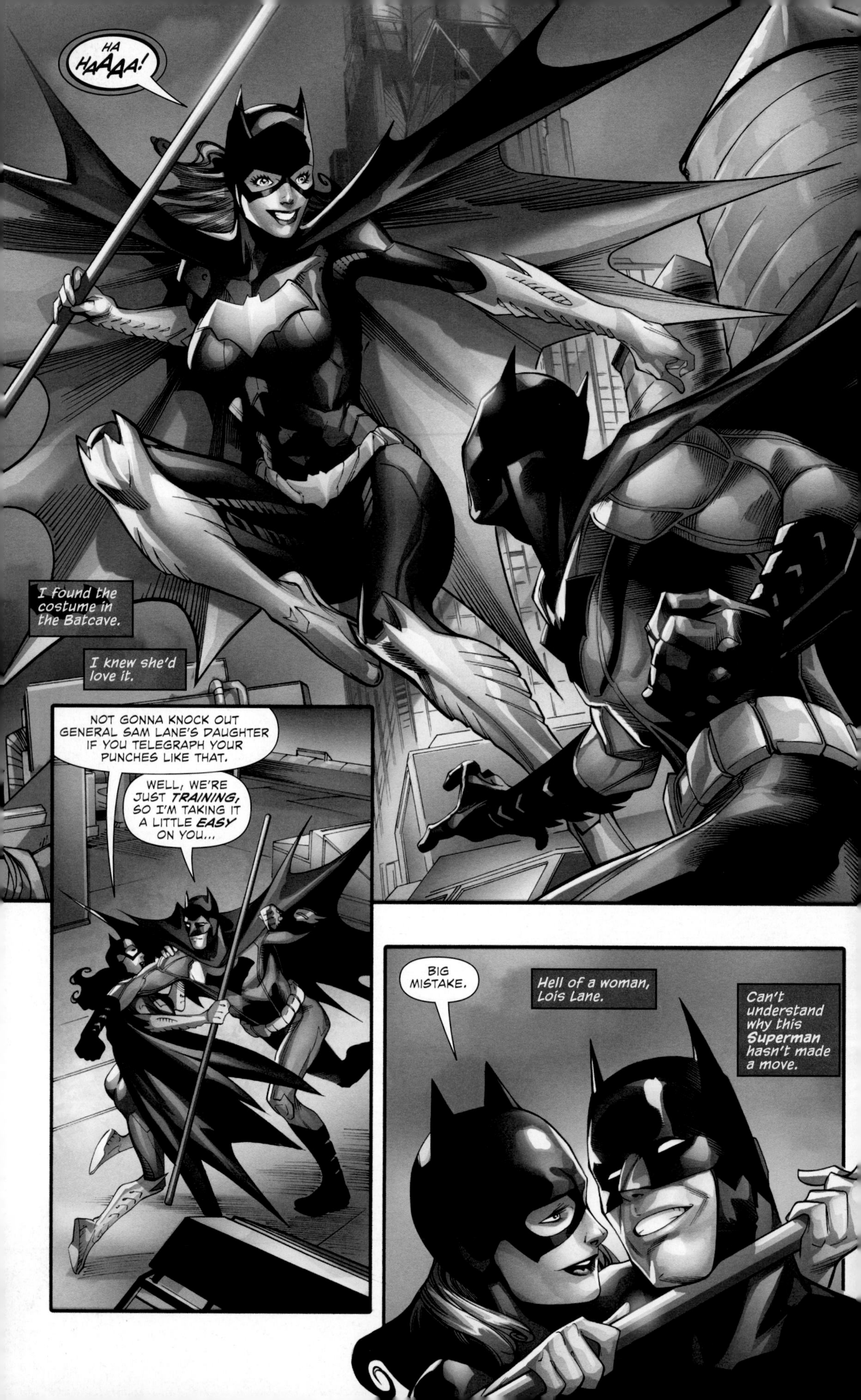
HA HAAAA!
I found the costume in the Batcave.
I knew she'd love it.
NOT GONNA KNOCK OUT GENERAL SAM LANE'S DAUGHTER IF YOU TELEGRAPH YOUR PUNCHES LIKE THAT.
WELL, WE'RE JUST *TRAINING*, SO I'M TAKING IT A LITTLE *EASY* ON YOU...
BIG MISTAKE.
Hell of a woman, Lois Lane.
Can't understand why this **Superman** hasn't made a move.

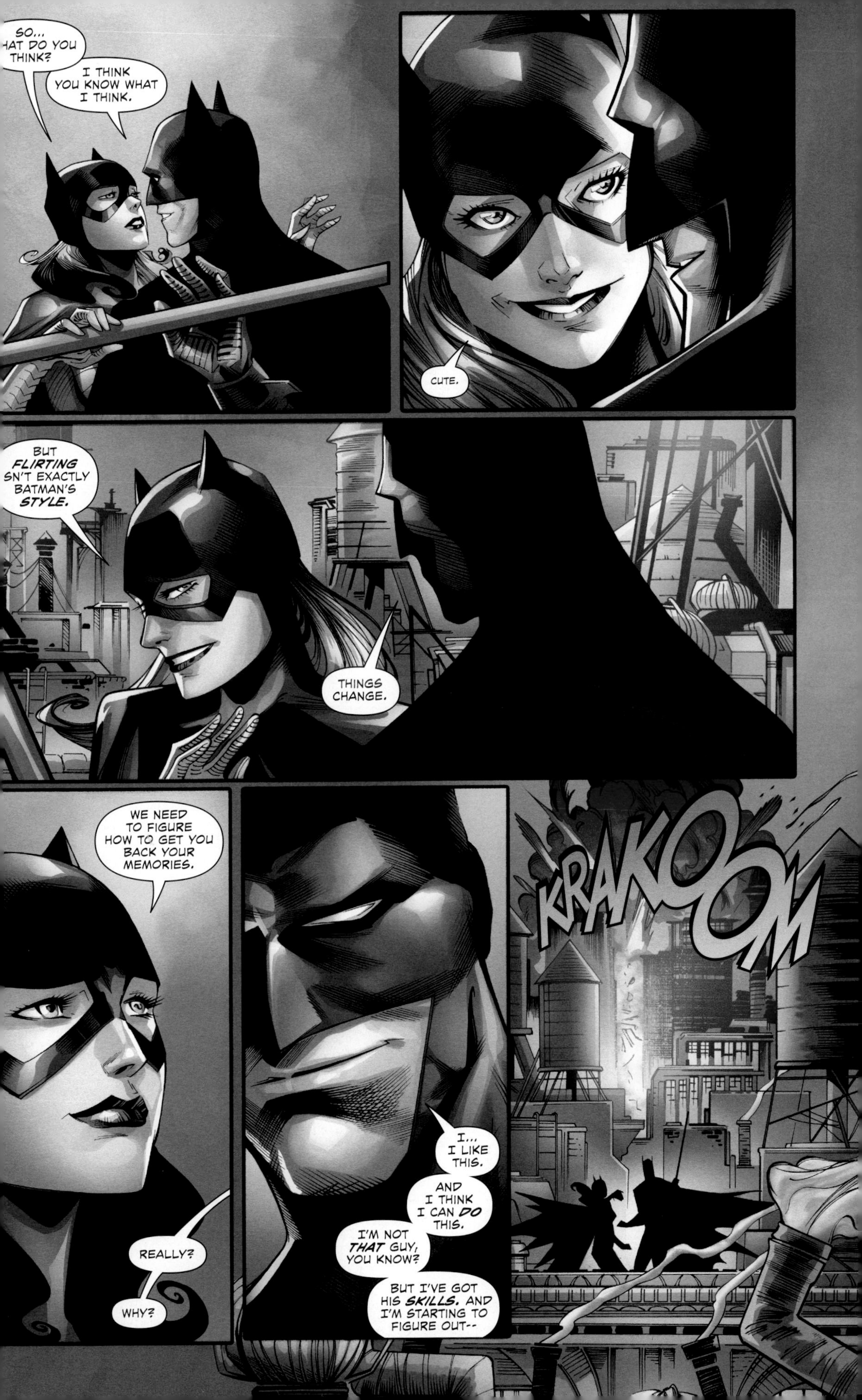
SO... HAT DO YOU THINK?
I THINK YOU KNOW WHAT I THINK.
CUTE.
BUT FLIRTING SN'T EXACTLY BATMAN'S STYLE.
THINGS CHANGE.
WE NEED TO FIGURE HOW TO GET YOU BACK YOUR MEMORIES.
REALLY?
WHY?
I... I LIKE THIS.
AND I THINK I CAN DO THIS.
I'M NOT THAT GUY, YOU KNOW?
BUT I'VE GOT HIS SKILLS. AND I'M STARTING TO FIGURE OUT--
KRAKOOM

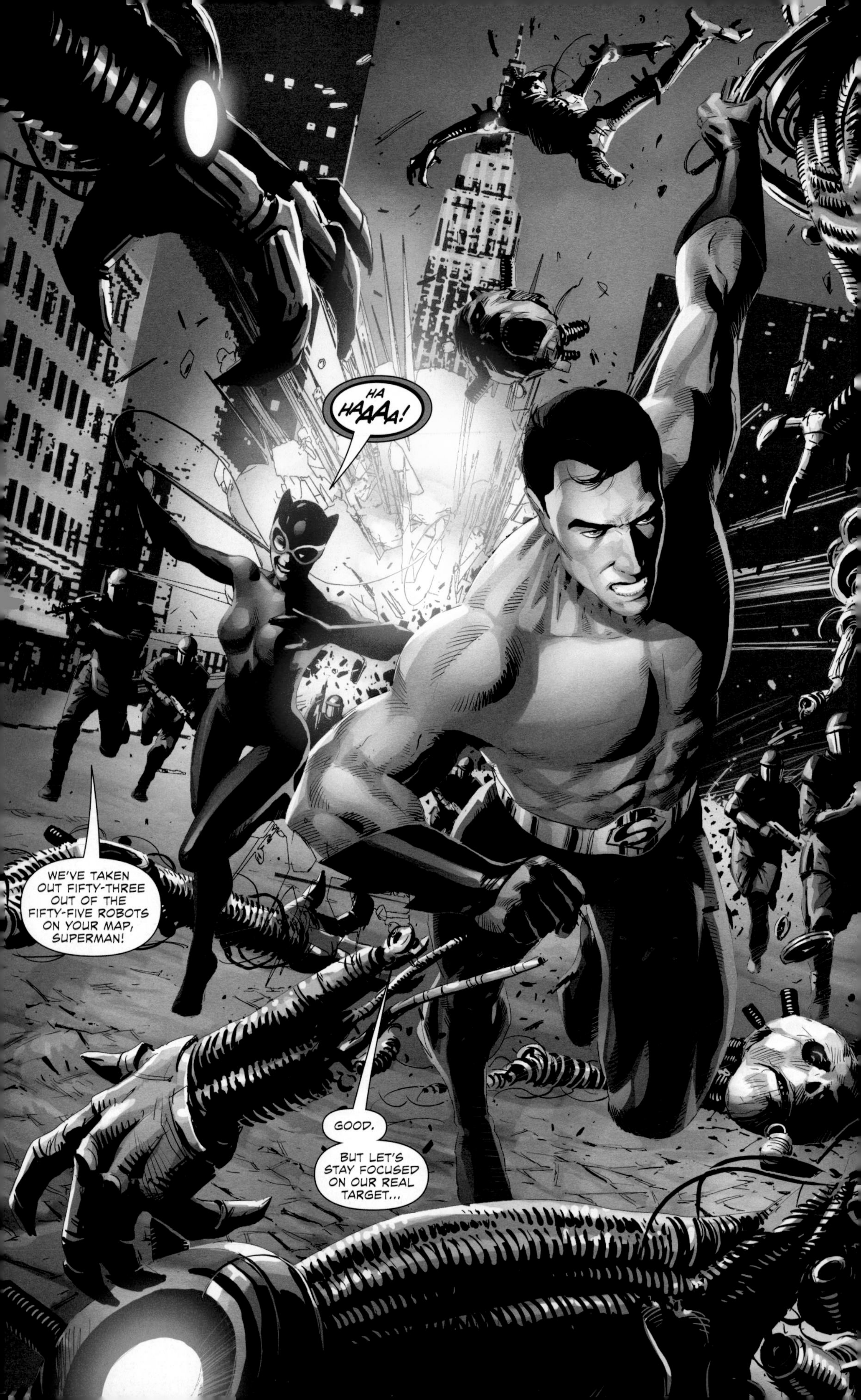
HA HAAAA!
WE'VE TAKEN OUT FIFTY-THREE OUT OF THE FIFTY-FIVE ROBOTS ON YOUR MAP, SUPERMAN!
GOOD.
BUT LET'S STAY FOCUSED ON OUR REAL TARGET...

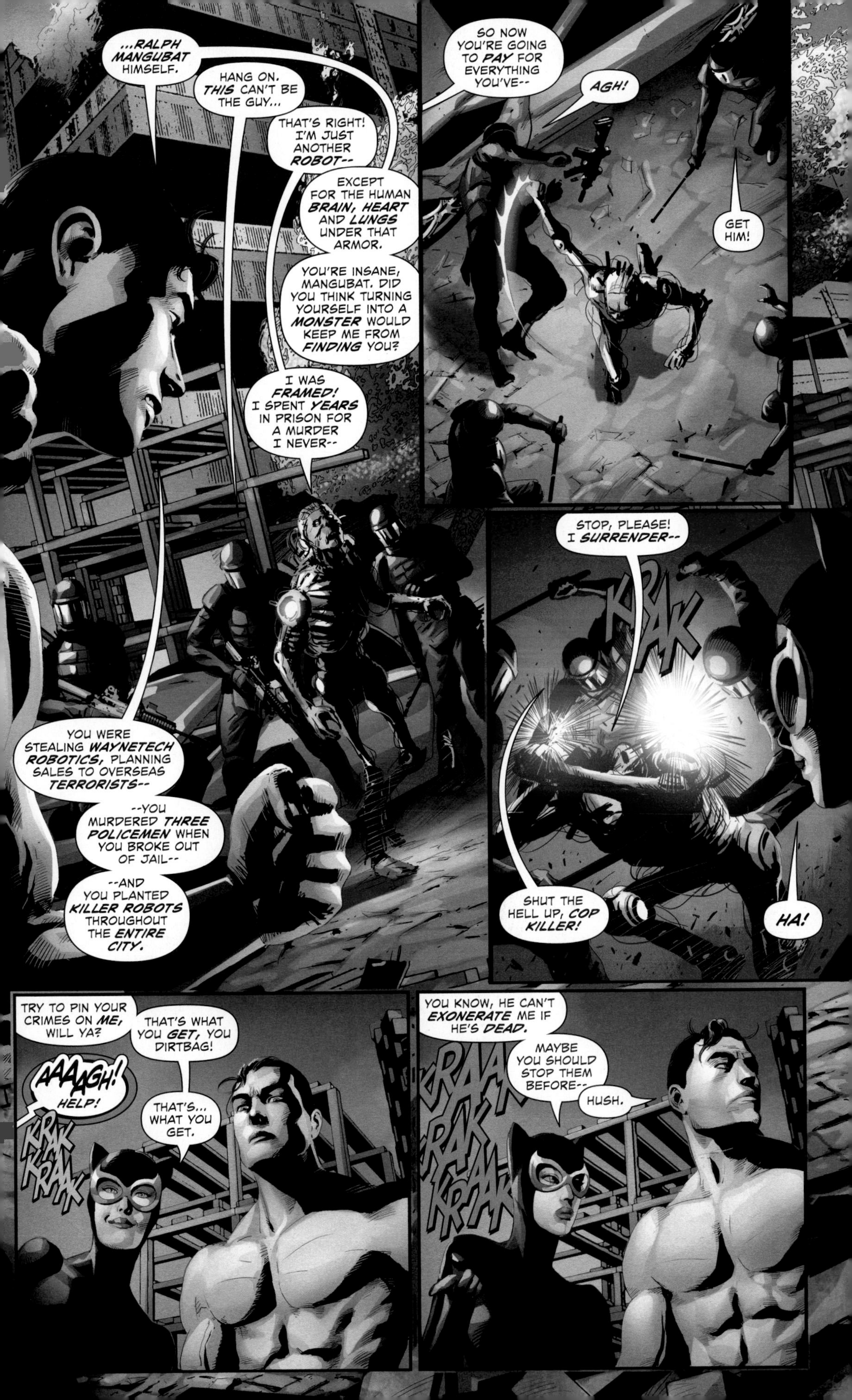
...RALPH MANGUBAT HIMSELF.
HANG ON. THIS CAN'T BE THE GUY...
THAT'S RIGHT! I'M JUST ANOTHER ROBOT--
EXCEPT FOR THE HUMAN BRAIN, HEART AND LUNGS UNDER THAT ARMOR.
YOU'RE INSANE, MANGUBAT. DID YOU THINK TURNING YOURSELF INTO A MONSTER WOULD KEEP ME FROM FINDING YOU?
I WAS FRAMED! I SPENT YEARS IN PRISON FOR A MURDER I NEVER--
YOU WERE STEALING WAYNETECH ROBOTICS, PLANNING SALES TO OVERSEAS TERRORISTS--
--YOU MURDERED THREE POLICEMEN WHEN YOU BROKE OUT OF JAIL--
--AND YOU PLANTED KILLER ROBOTS THROUGHOUT THE ENTIRE CITY.
SO NOW YOU'RE GOING TO PAY FOR EVERYTHING YOU'VE--
AGH!
GET HIM!
STOP, PLEASE! I SURRENDER--
KRAK
SHUT THE HELL UP, COP KILLER!
HA!
TRY TO PIN YOUR CRIMES ON ME, WILL YA?
THAT'S WHAT YOU GET, YOU DIRTBAG!
AAAAGH! HELP!
KRAK KRAAK
THAT'S... WHAT YOU GET.
YOU KNOW, HE CAN'T EXONERATE ME IF HE'S DEAD.
MAYBE YOU SHOULD STOP THEM BEFORE--
HUSH.
KRAAK KRAK KRAAK

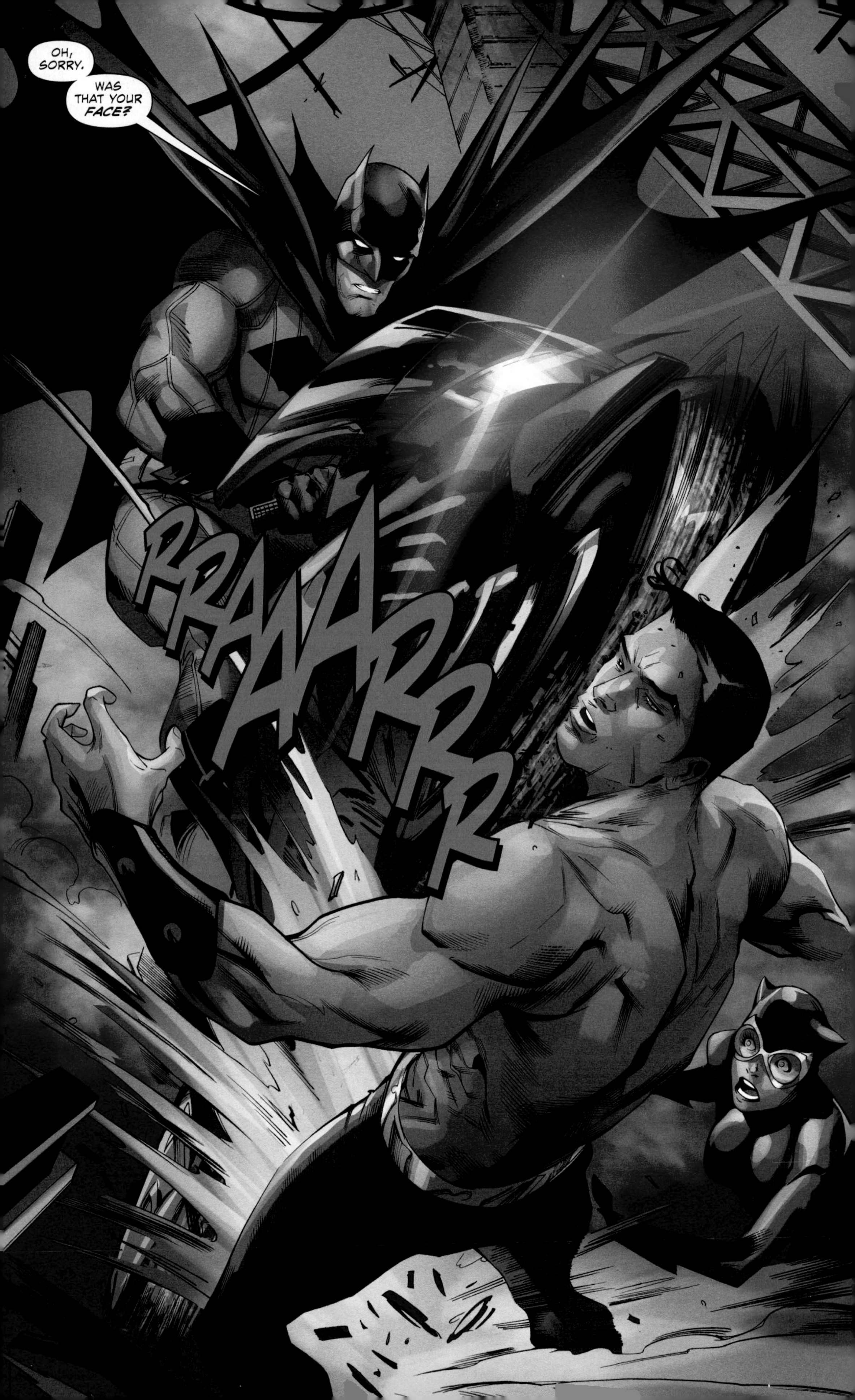
OH, SORRY. WAS THAT YOUR FACE?
RRAAARRR

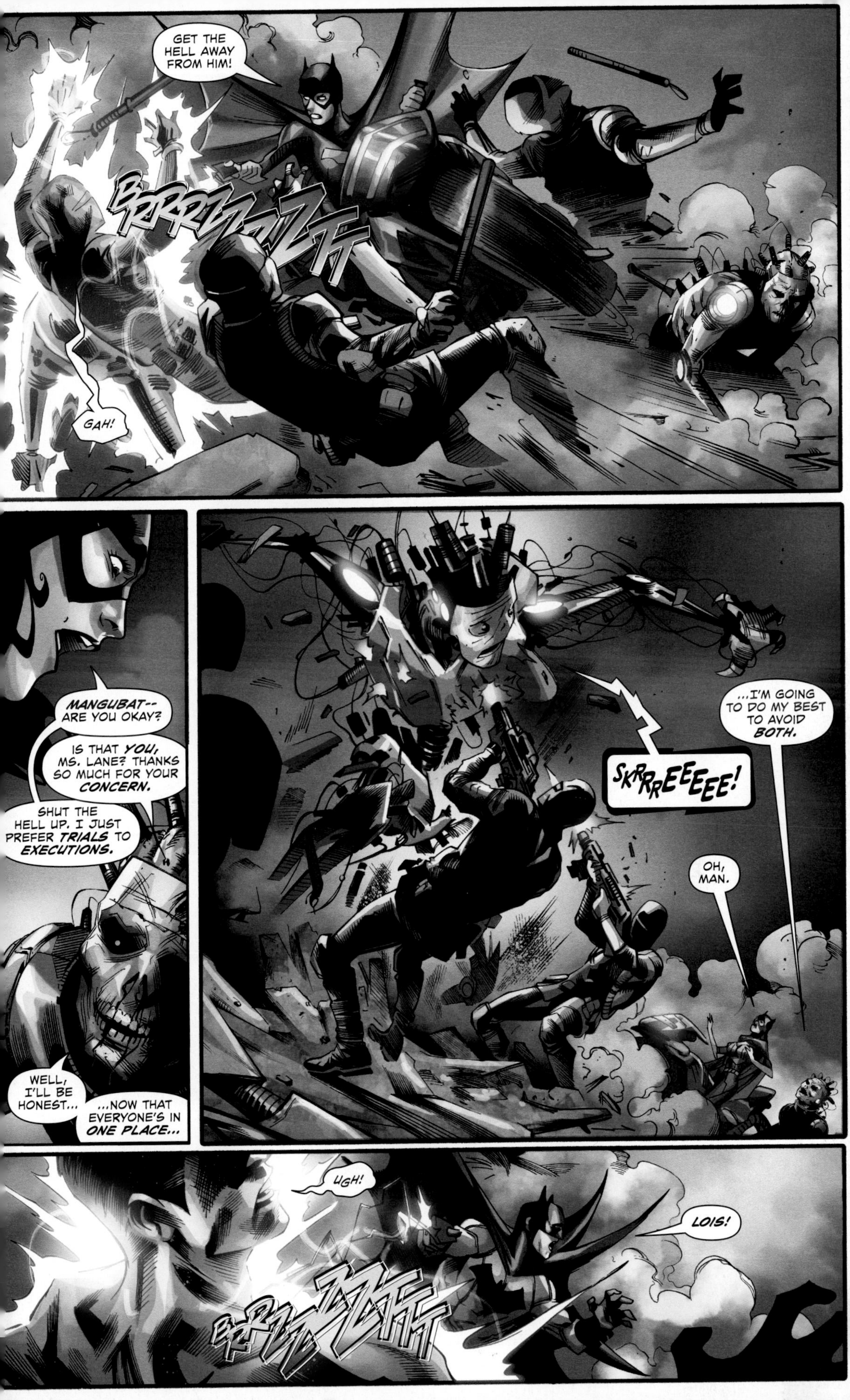

GET THE HELL AWAY FROM HIM!
GAH!
MANGUBAT-- ARE YOU OKAY?
IS THAT YOU, MS. LANE? THANKS SO MUCH FOR YOUR CONCERN.
SHUT THE HELL UP. I JUST PREFER TRIALS TO EXECUTIONS.
WELL, I'LL BE HONEST...
...NOW THAT EVERYONE'S IN ONE PLACE...
...I'M GOING TO DO MY BEST TO AVOID BOTH.
OH, MAN.
UGH!
LOIS!

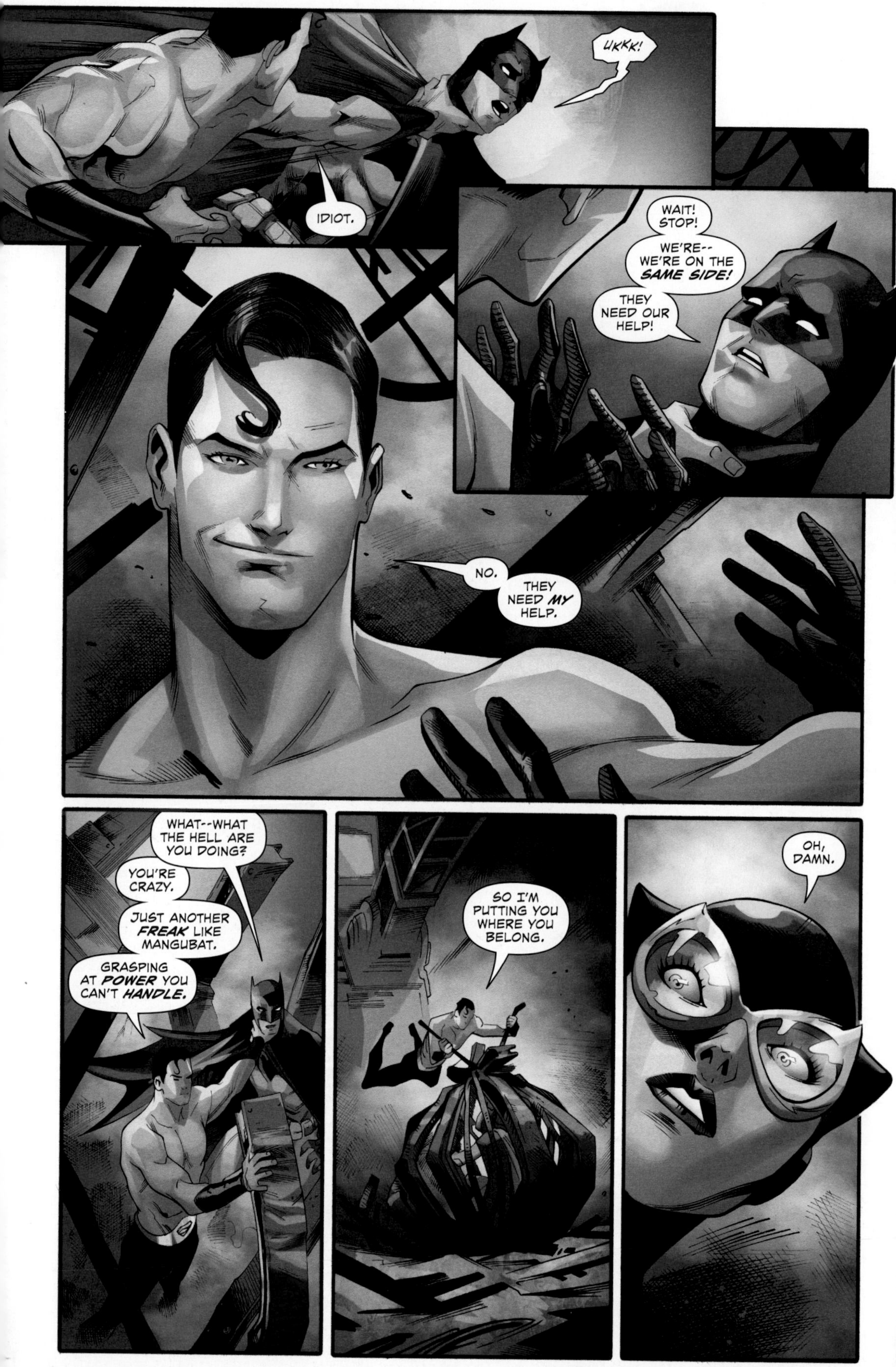
UKKK!
IDIOT.
WAIT! STOP!
WE'RE-- WE'RE ON THE SAME SIDE!
THEY NEED OUR HELP!
NO.
THEY NEED MY HELP.
WHAT--WHAT THE HELL ARE YOU DOING?
YOU'RE CRAZY.
JUST ANOTHER FREAK LIKE MANGUBAT.
GRASPING AT POWER YOU CAN'T HANDLE.
SO I'M PUTTING YOU WHERE YOU BELONG.
OH, DAMN.

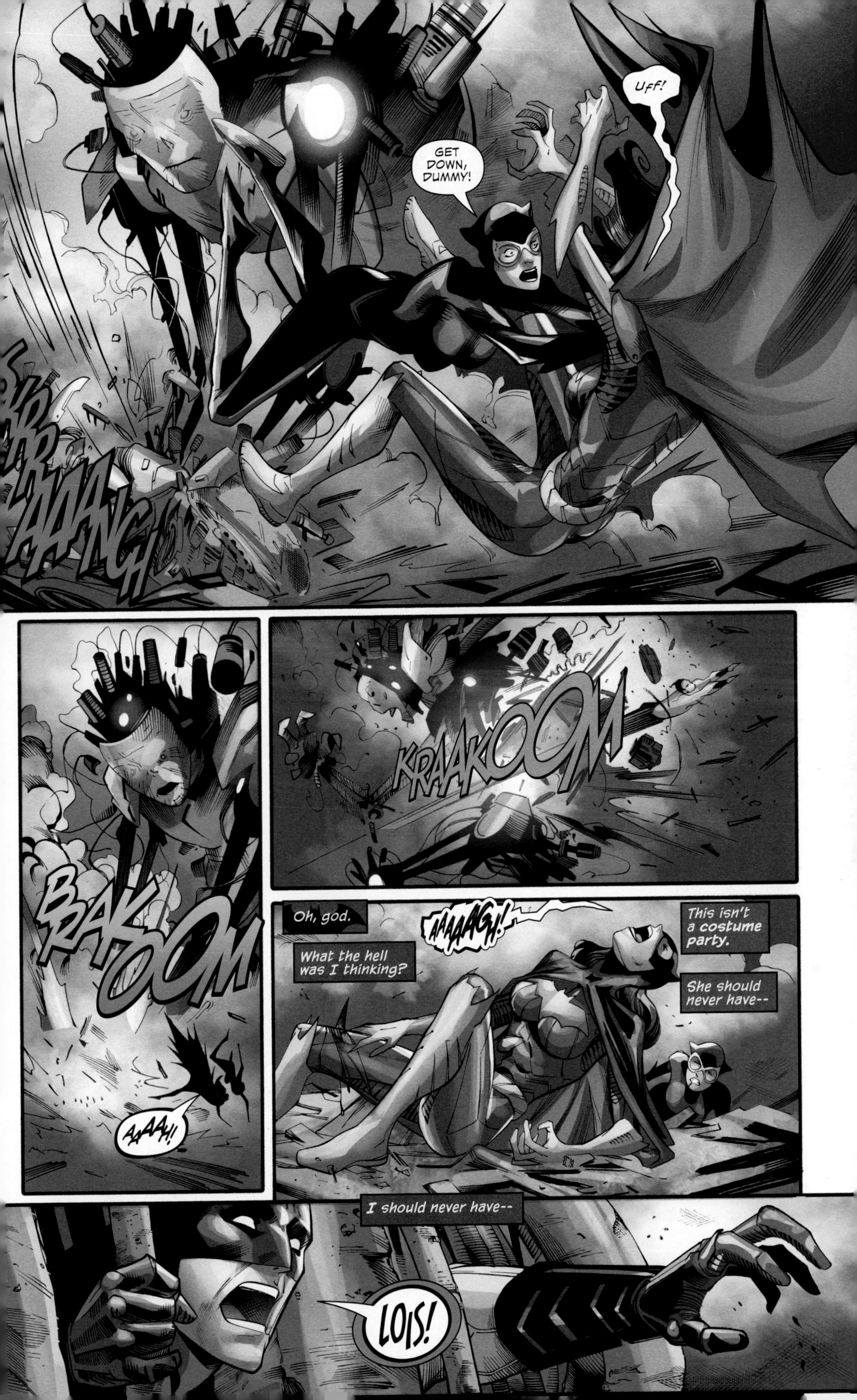

Uff!
GET DOWN, DUMMY!
SKRRRAAANCH
BRAKOOM
AAAH!
KRAAKOOM
Oh, god.
What the hell was I thinking?
AAAAAAGH!
This isn't a costume party.
She should never have--
I should never have--
LOIS!

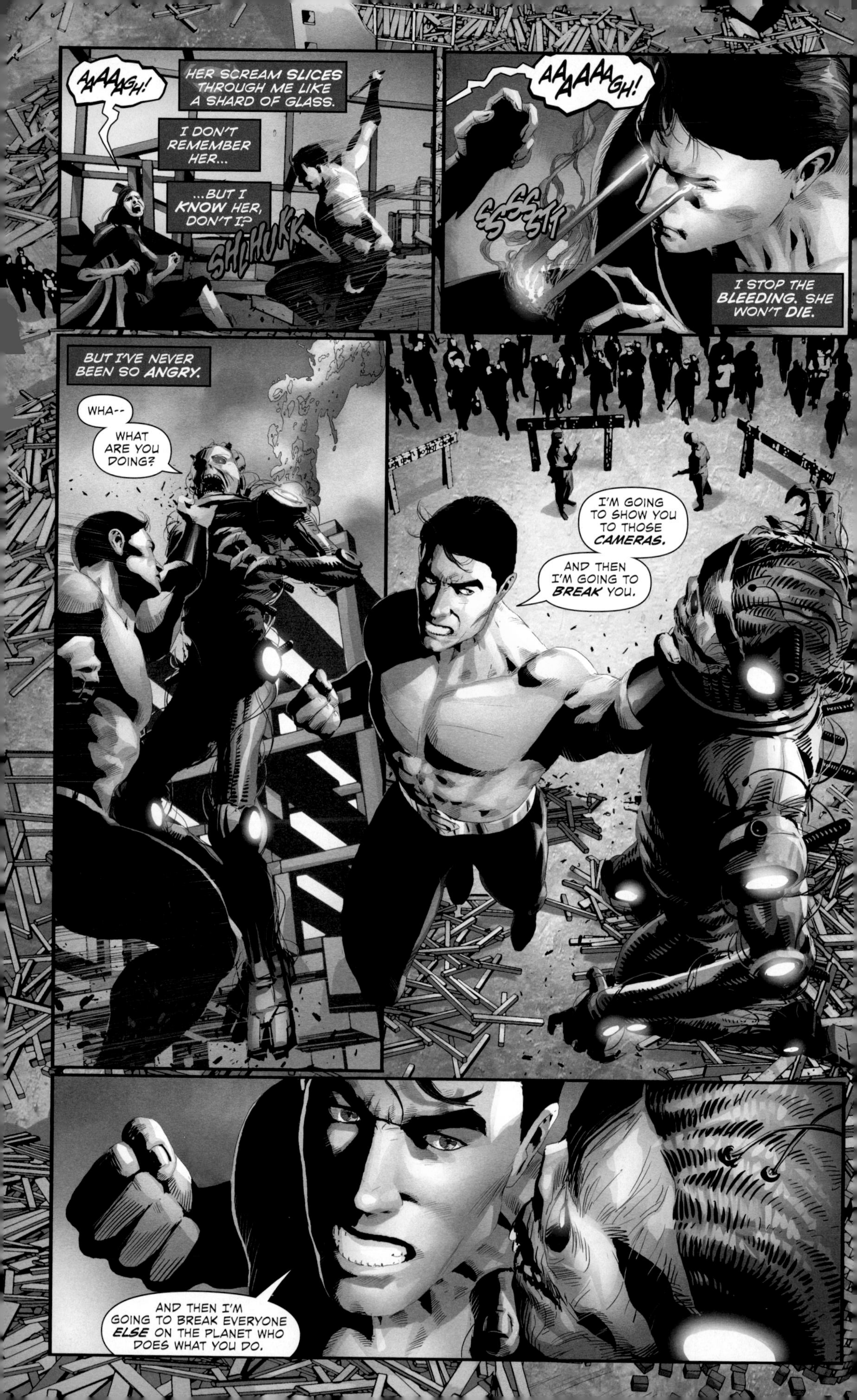
AAAAAGH!
HER SCREAM SLICES THROUGH ME LIKE A SHARD OF GLASS.
I DON'T REMEMBER HER...
...BUT I KNOW HER, DON'T I?
SHLHUKK
AAAAAAGH!
SSSSSTT
I STOP THE BLEEDING. SHE WON'T DIE.
BUT I'VE NEVER BEEN SO ANGRY.
WHA--
WHAT ARE YOU DOING?
I'M GOING TO SHOW YOU TO THOSE CAMERAS.
AND THEN I'M GOING TO BREAK YOU.
AND THEN I'M GOING TO BREAK EVERYONE ELSE ON THE PLANET WHO DOES WHAT YOU DO.

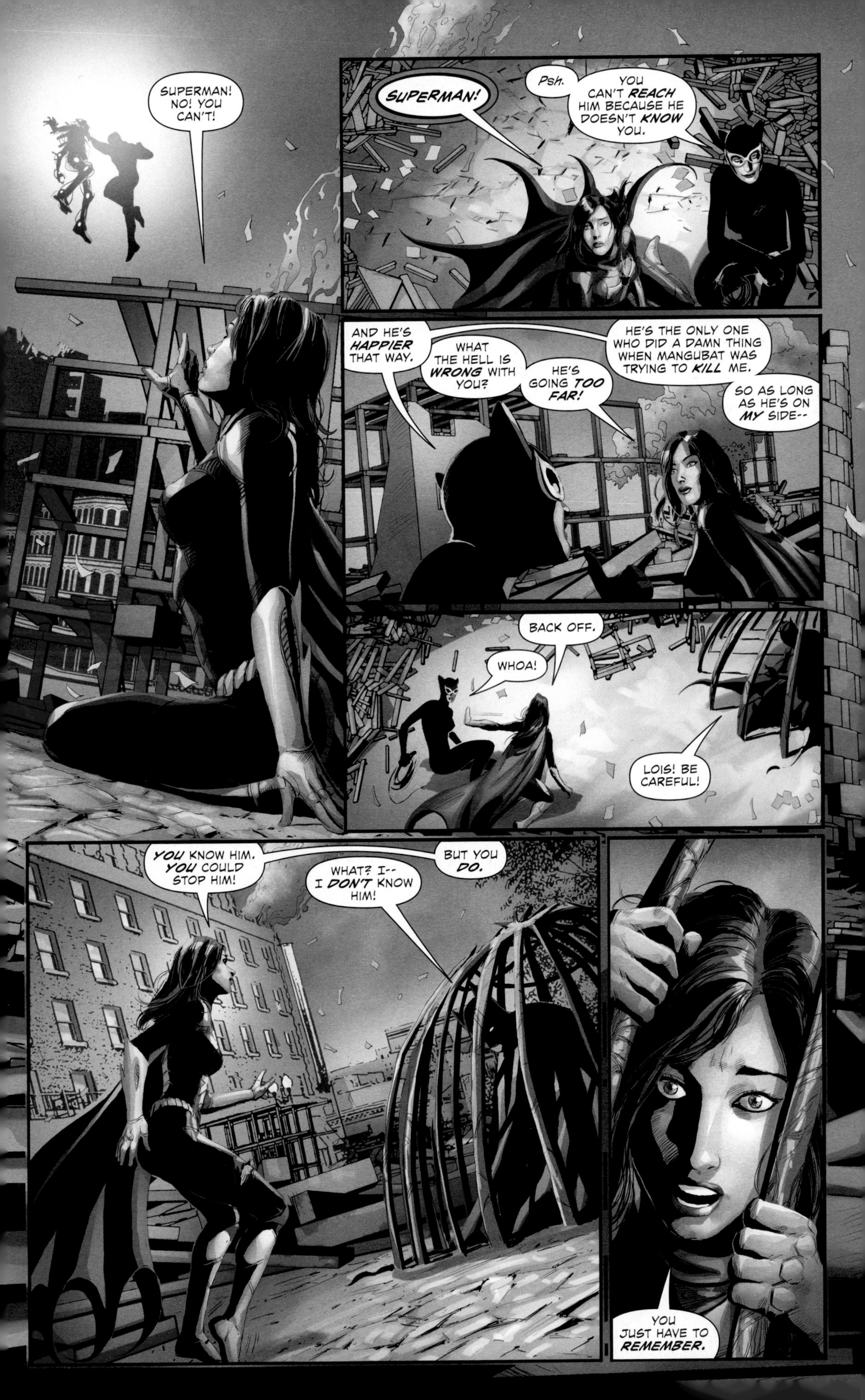
SUPERMAN! NO! YOU CAN'T!
SUPERMAN!
Psh.
YOU CAN'T REACH HIM BECAUSE HE DOESN'T KNOW YOU.
AND HE'S HAPPIER THAT WAY.
WHAT THE HELL IS WRONG WITH YOU?
HE'S GOING TOO FAR!
HE'S THE ONLY ONE WHO DID A DAMN THING WHEN MANGUBAT WAS TRYING TO KILL ME.
SO AS LONG AS HE'S ON MY SIDE--
BACK OFF.
WHOA!
LOIS! BE CAREFUL!
YOU KNOW HIM. YOU COULD STOP HIM!
BUT YOU DO.
WHAT? I-- I DON'T KNOW HIM!
YOU JUST HAVE TO REMEMBER.

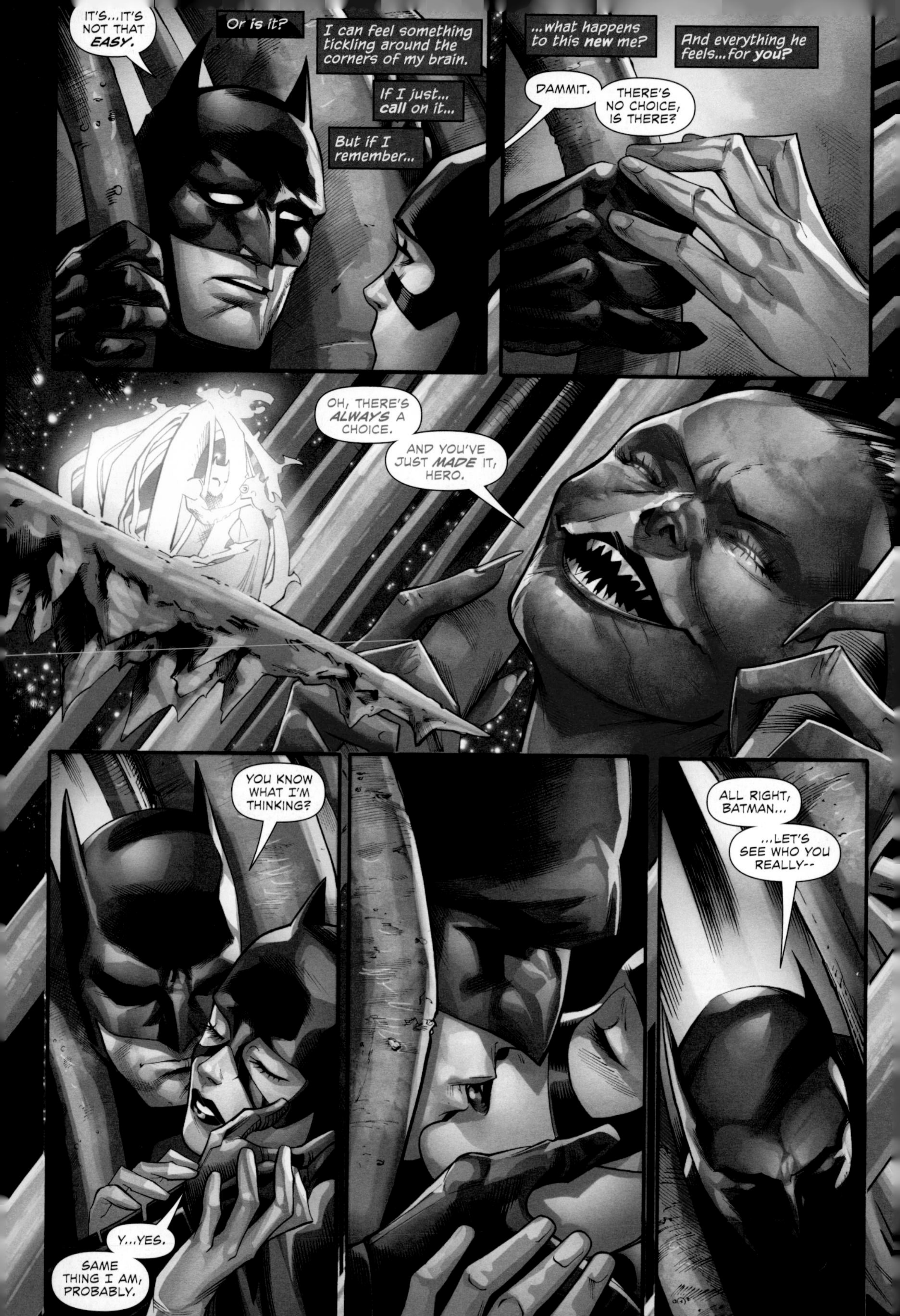

IT'S...IT'S NOT THAT EASY.
Or is it?
I can feel something tickling around the corners of my brain.
If I just... call on it...
But if I remember...
...what happens to this new me?
And everything he feels...for you?
DAMMIT.
THERE'S NO CHOICE, IS THERE?
OH, THERE'S ALWAYS A CHOICE.
AND YOU'VE JUST MADE IT, HERO.
YOU KNOW WHAT I'M THINKING?
Y...YES.
SAME THING I AM, PROBABLY.
ALL RIGHT, BATMAN...
...LET'S SEE WHO YOU REALLY--

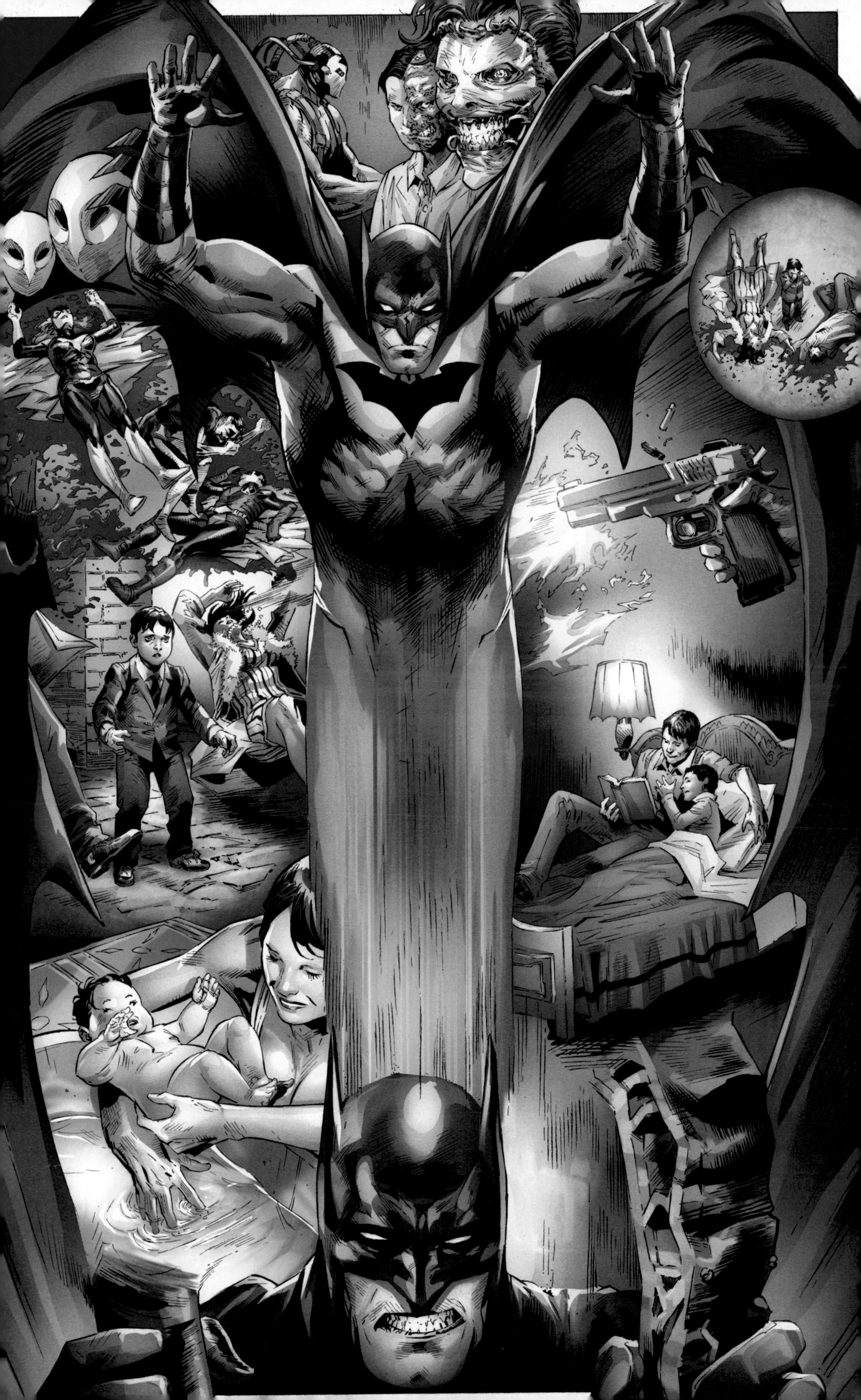

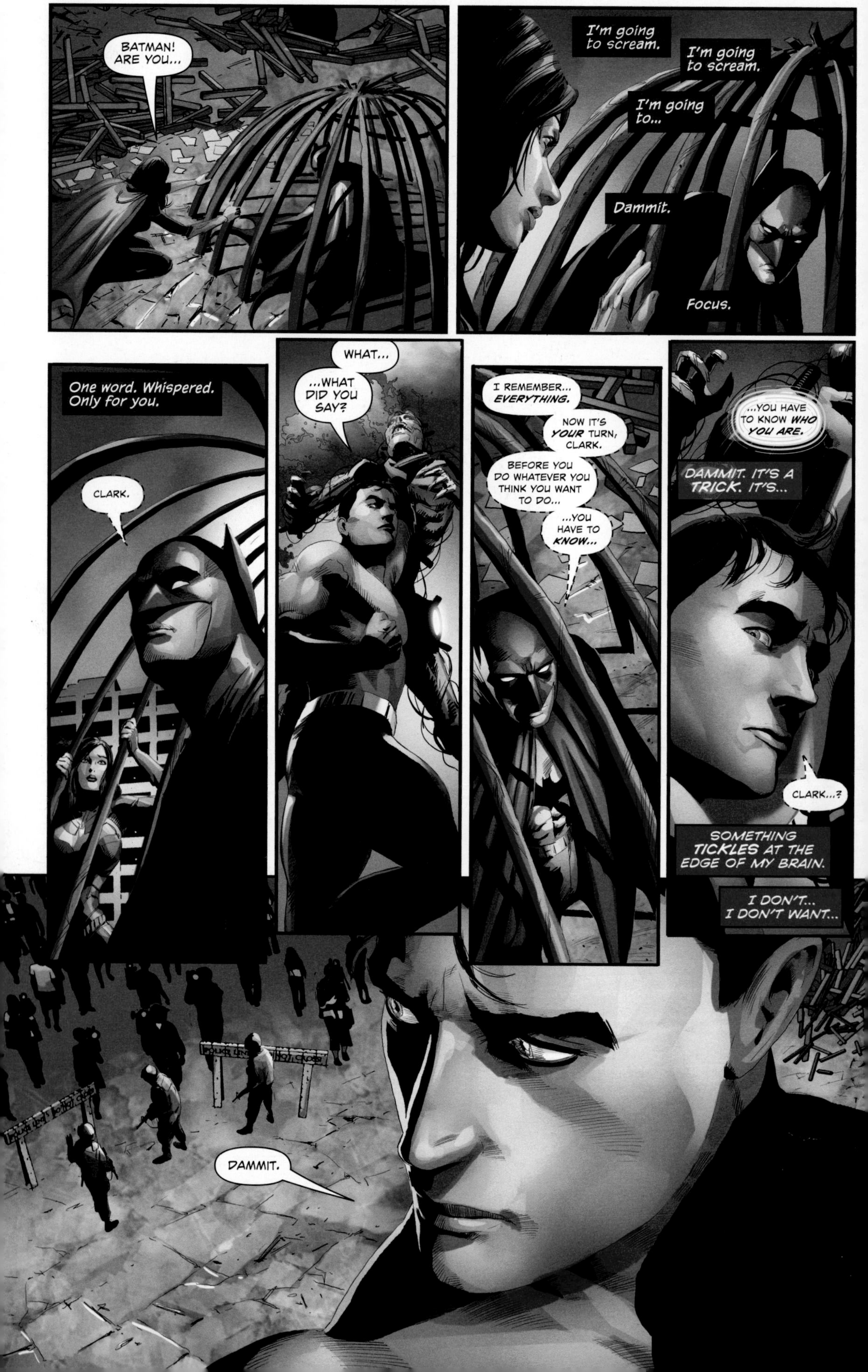

BATMAN! ARE YOU...
I'm going to scream.
I'm going to scream.
I'm going to...
Dammit.
Focus.
One word. Whispered. Only for you.
CLARK.
WHAT...
...WHAT DID YOU SAY?
I REMEMBER... EVERYTHING.
NOW IT'S YOUR TURN, CLARK.
BEFORE YOU DO WHATEVER YOU THINK YOU WANT TO DO...
...YOU HAVE TO KNOW...
...YOU HAVE TO KNOW WHO YOU ARE.
DAMMIT. IT'S A TRICK. IT'S...
CLARK...?
SOMETHING TICKLES AT THE EDGE OF MY BRAIN.
I DON'T... I DON'T WANT...
DAMMIT.

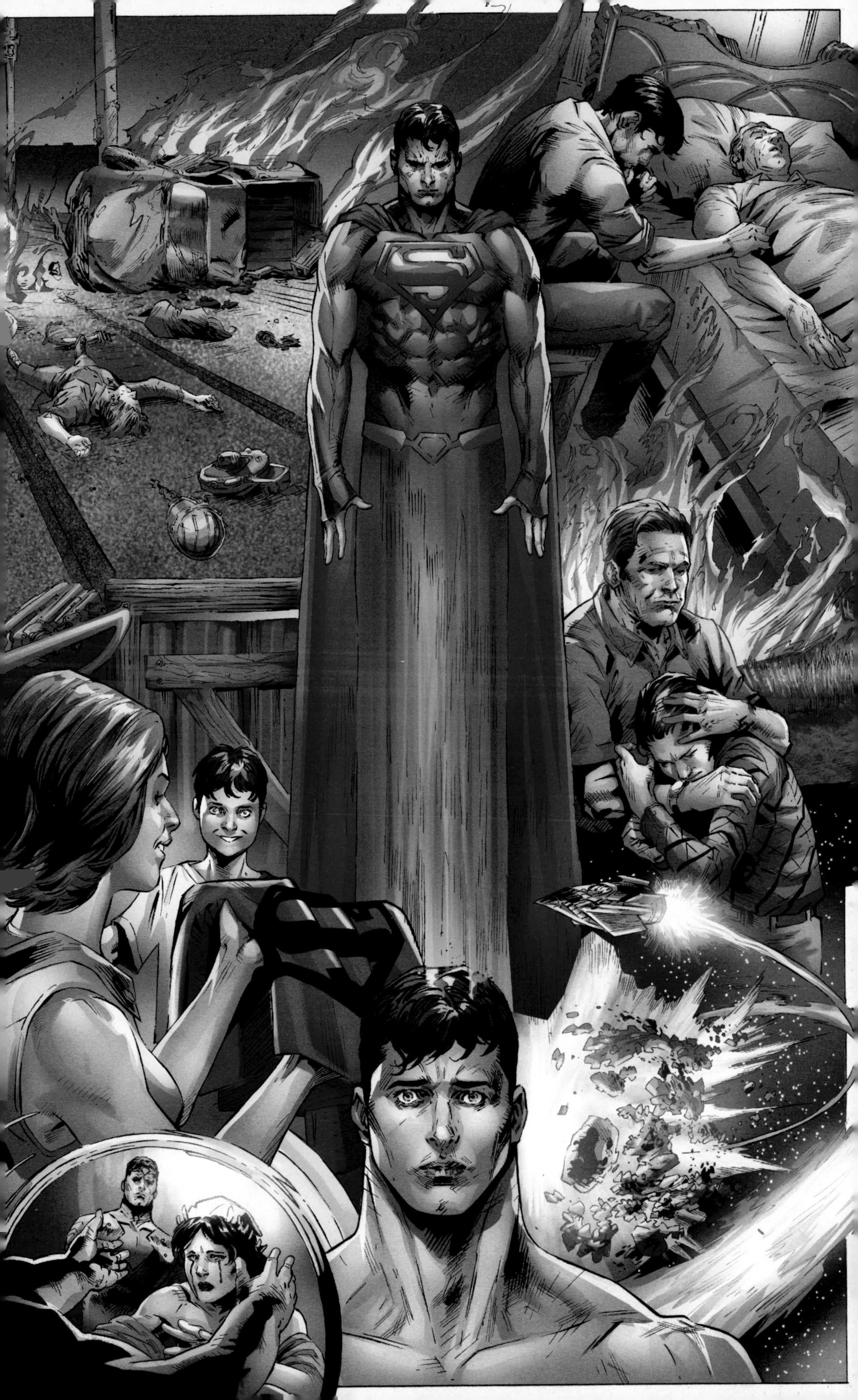

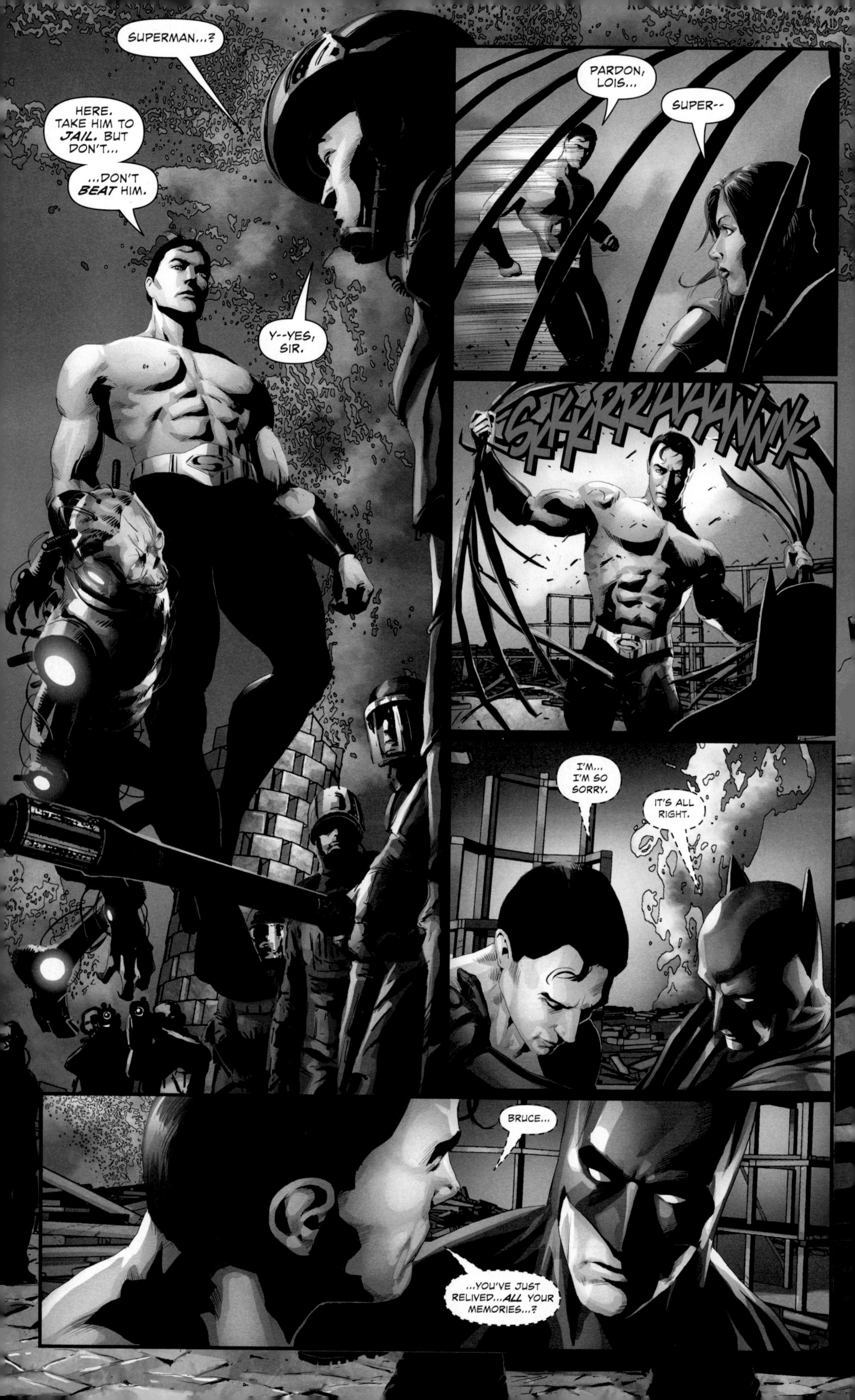
SUPERMAN...?
HERE. TAKE HIM TO *JAIL.* BUT DON'T...
...DON'T *BEAT* HIM.
Y--YES, SIR.
PARDON, LOIS...
SUPER--
SKKRRRAAANNNK
I'M... I'M SO SORRY.
IT'S ALL RIGHT.
BRUCE...
...YOU'VE JUST RELIVED...*ALL* YOUR MEMORIES...?

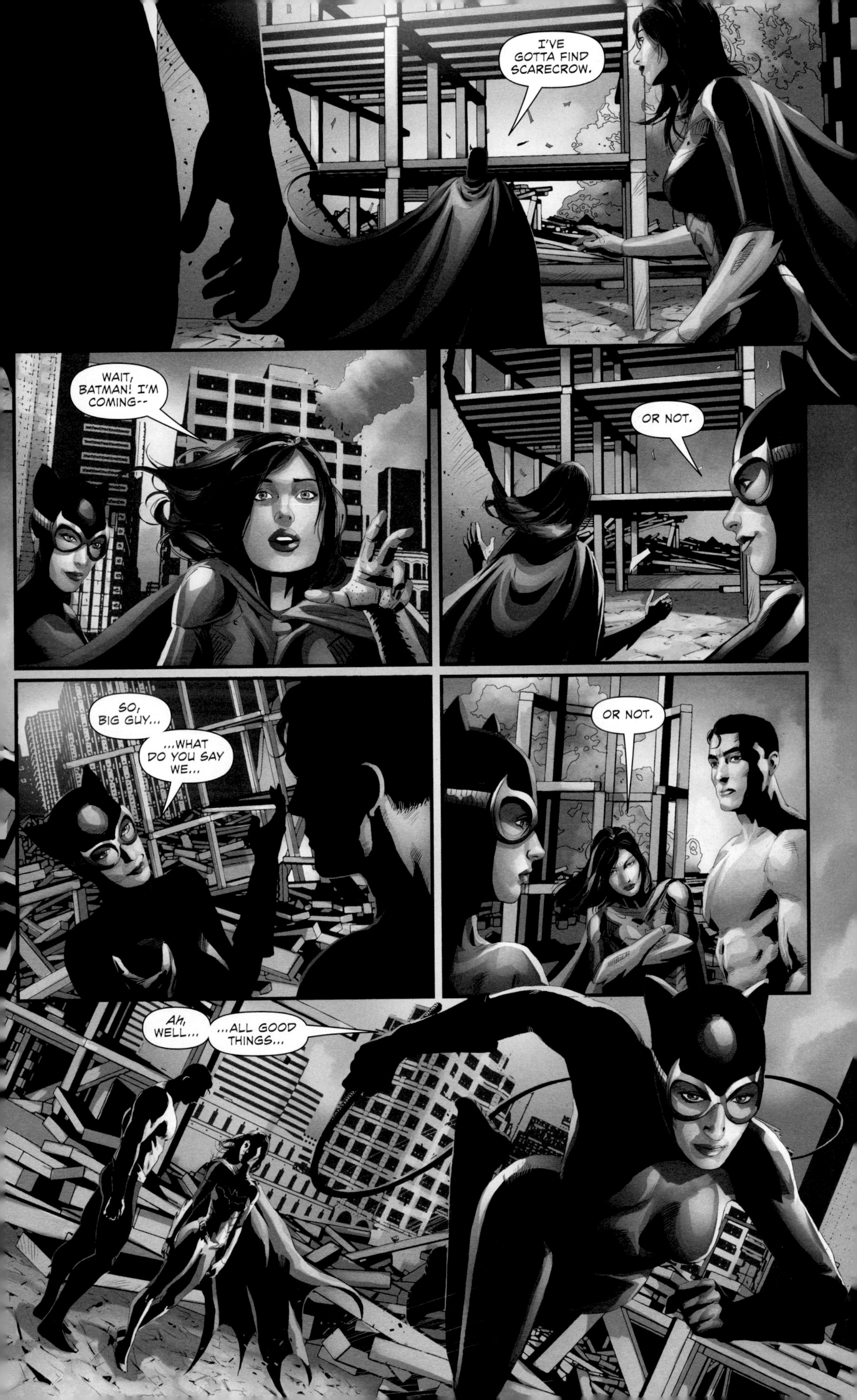
I'VE GOTTA FIND SCARECROW.
WAIT, BATMAN! I'M COMING--
OR NOT.
SO, BIG GUY...
...WHAT DO YOU SAY WE...
OR NOT.
Ah, WELL...
...ALL GOOD THINGS...

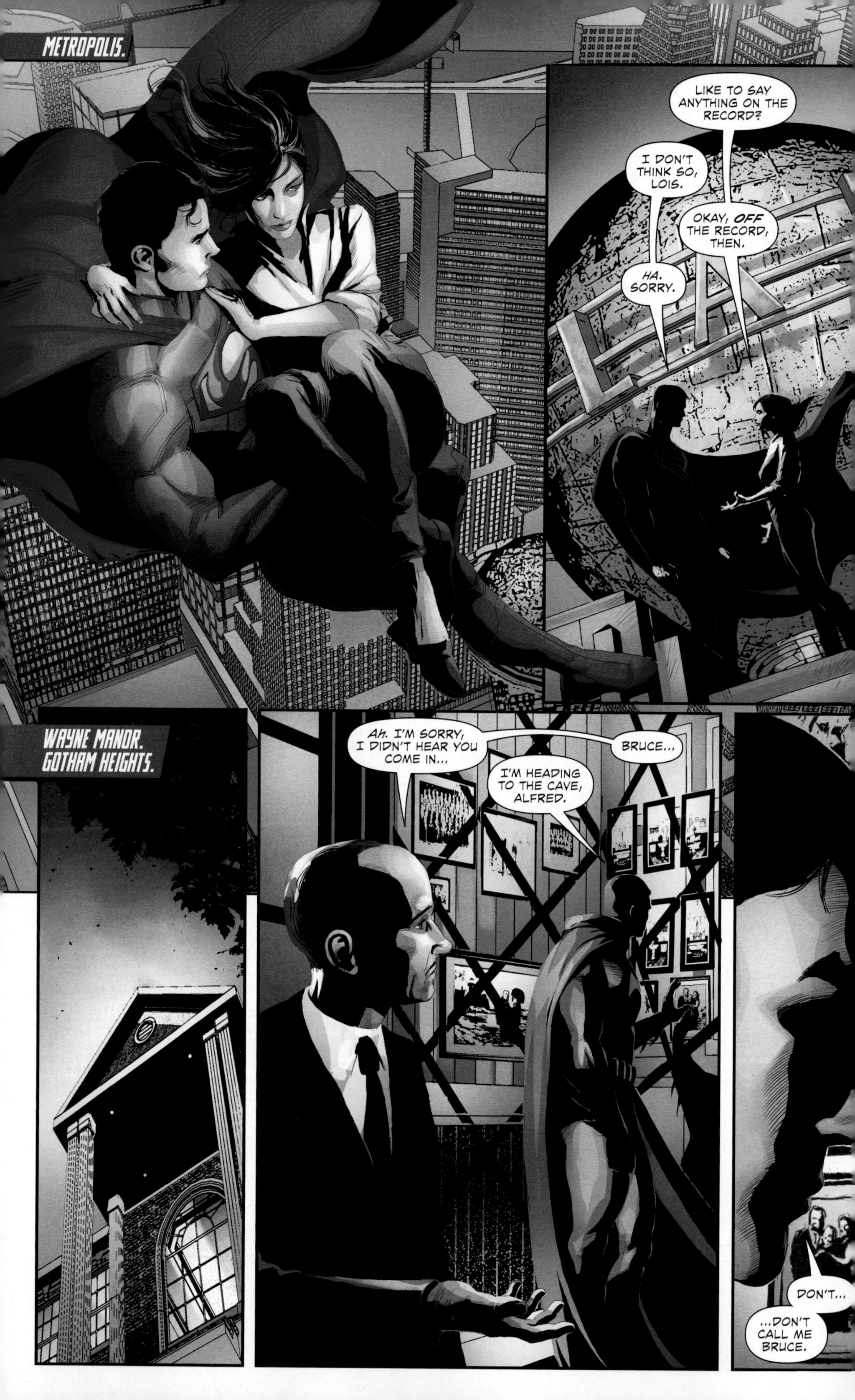
METROPOLIS.
LIKE TO SAY ANYTHING ON THE RECORD?
I DON'T THINK SO, LOIS.
OKAY, OFF THE RECORD, THEN.
HA. SORRY.
WAYNE MANOR. GOTHAM HEIGHTS.
AH. I'M SORRY, I DIDN'T HEAR YOU COME IN...
BRUCE...
I'M HEADING TO THE CAVE, ALFRED.
DON'T...
...DON'T CALL ME BRUCE.

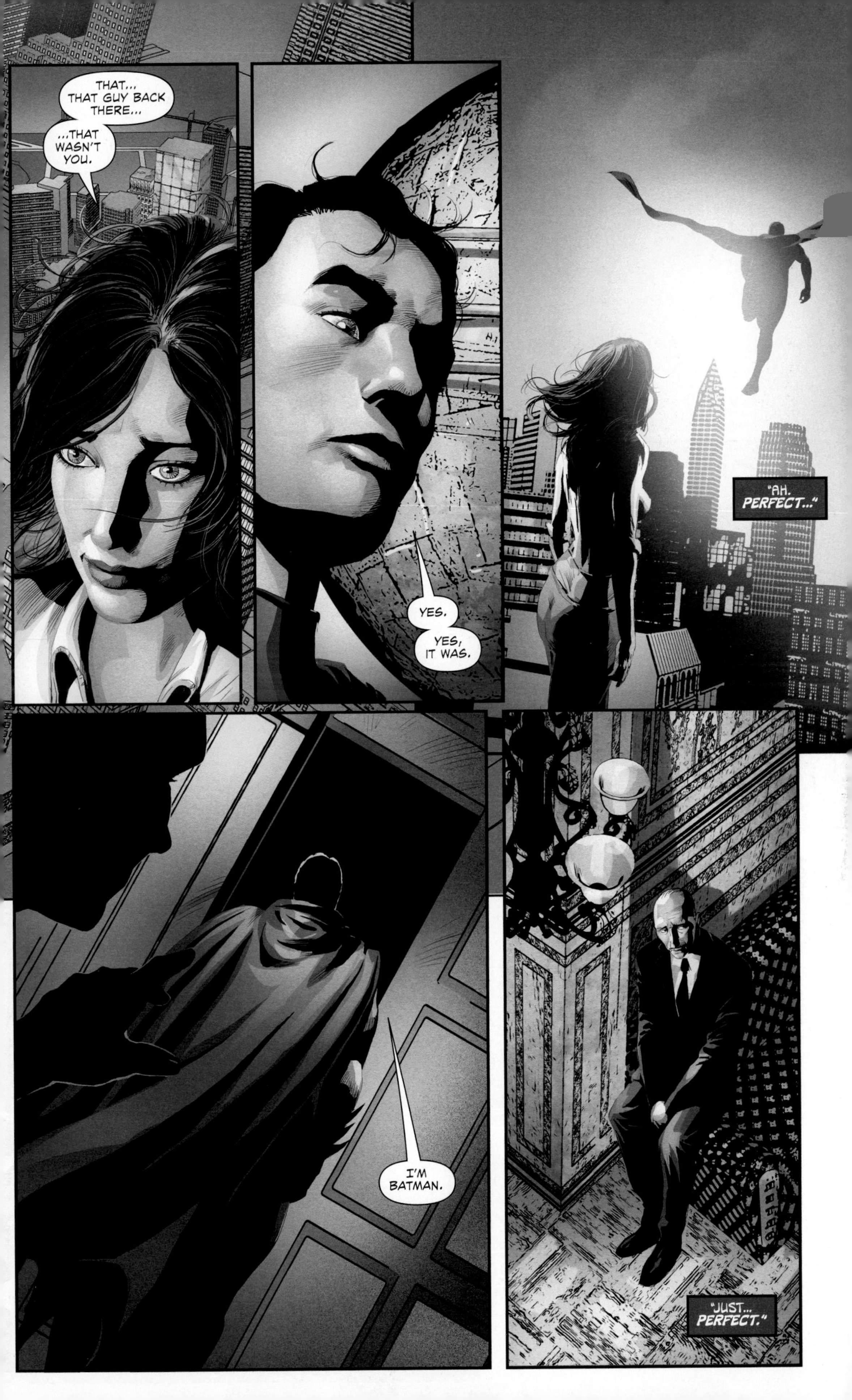

THAT... THAT GUY BACK THERE...
...THAT WASN'T YOU.
YES.
YES, IT WAS.
"AH. PERFECT..."
I'M BATMAN.
"JUST... PERFECT."

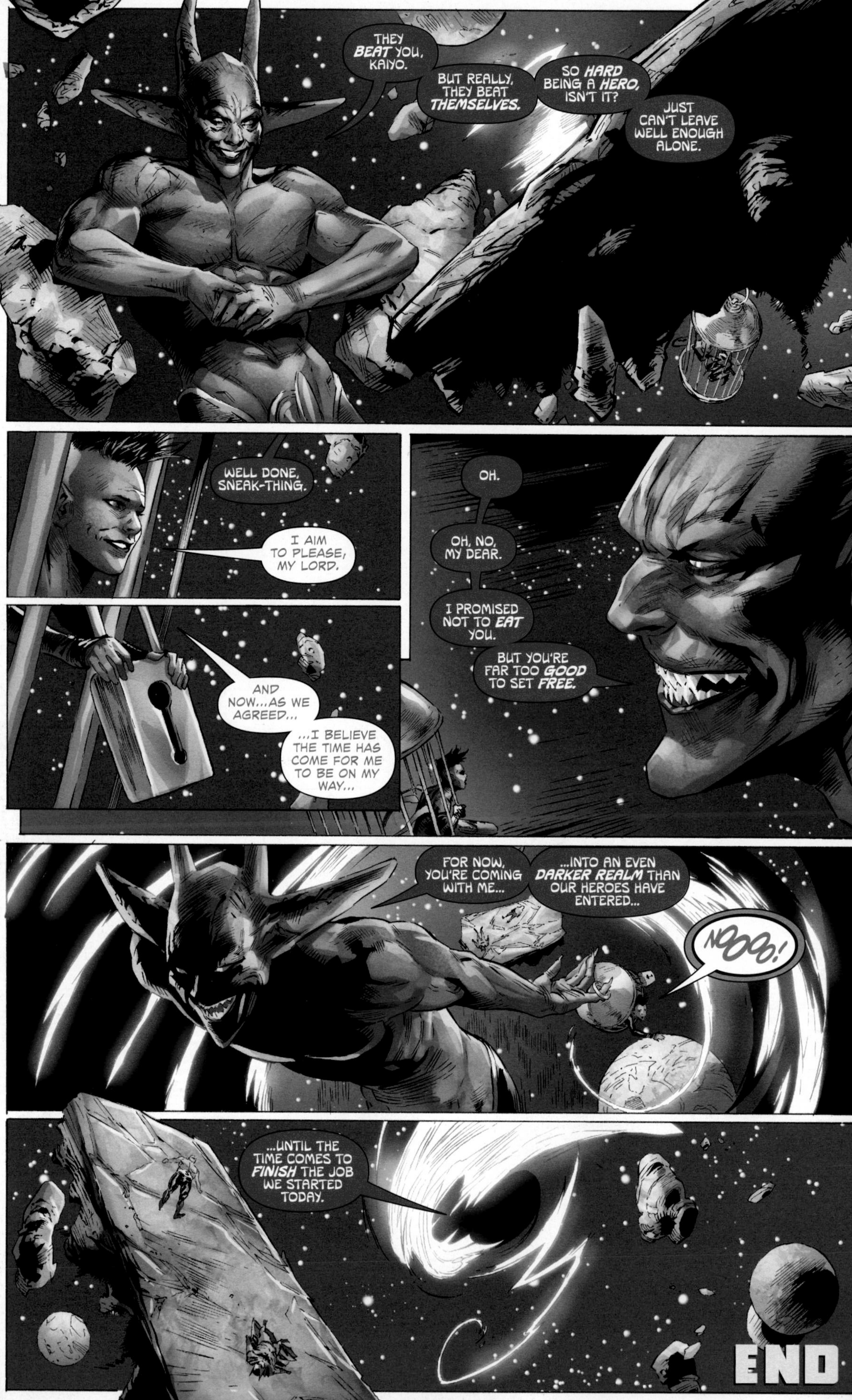
THEY BEAT YOU, KAIYO.
BUT REALLY, THEY BEAT THEMSELVES.
SO HARD BEING A HERO, ISN'T IT?
JUST CAN'T LEAVE WELL ENOUGH ALONE.
WELL DONE, SNEAK-THING.
I AIM TO PLEASE, MY LORD.
AND NOW...AS WE AGREED...
...I BELIEVE THE TIME HAS COME FOR ME TO BE ON MY WAY...
OH.
OH, NO, MY DEAR.
I PROMISED NOT TO EAT YOU.
BUT YOU'RE FAR TOO GOOD TO SET FREE.
FOR NOW, YOU'RE COMING WITH ME...
...INTO AN EVEN DARKER REALM THAN OUR HEROES HAVE ENTERED...
NOOOO!
...UNTIL THE TIME COMES TO FINISH THE JOB WE STARTED TODAY.
END

BATMAN/SUPERMAN 10
MAD variant by Tom Richmond

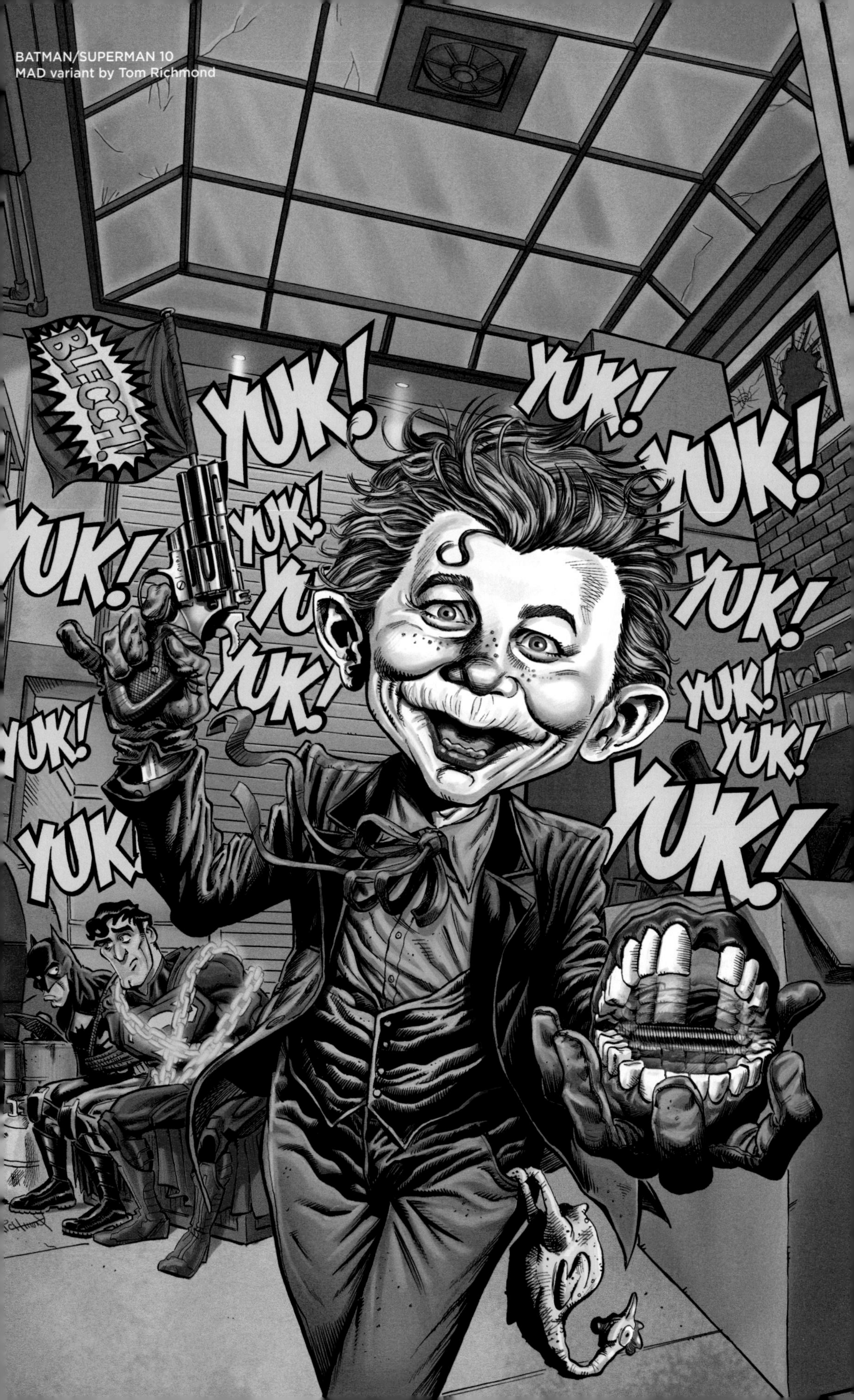
BLECCH!
YUK!
YUK!
YUK!
YUK!
YUK!
YUK!
YUK!
YUK!
YUK!
YUK!
YUK!
YUK!
YUK!

BATMAN/SUPERMAN 11
BATMAN '66 variant by Mike and Laura Allred

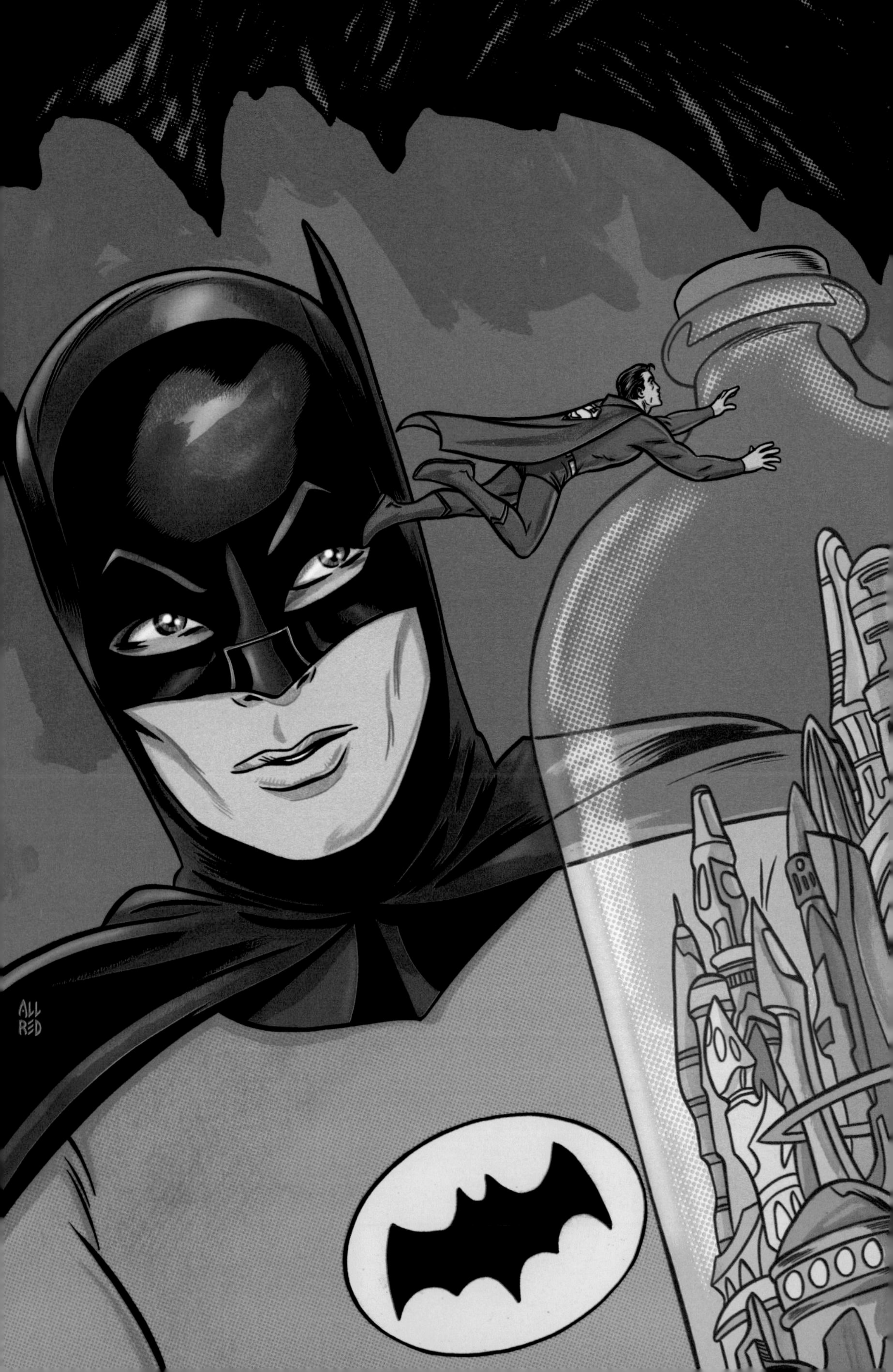
ALL RED

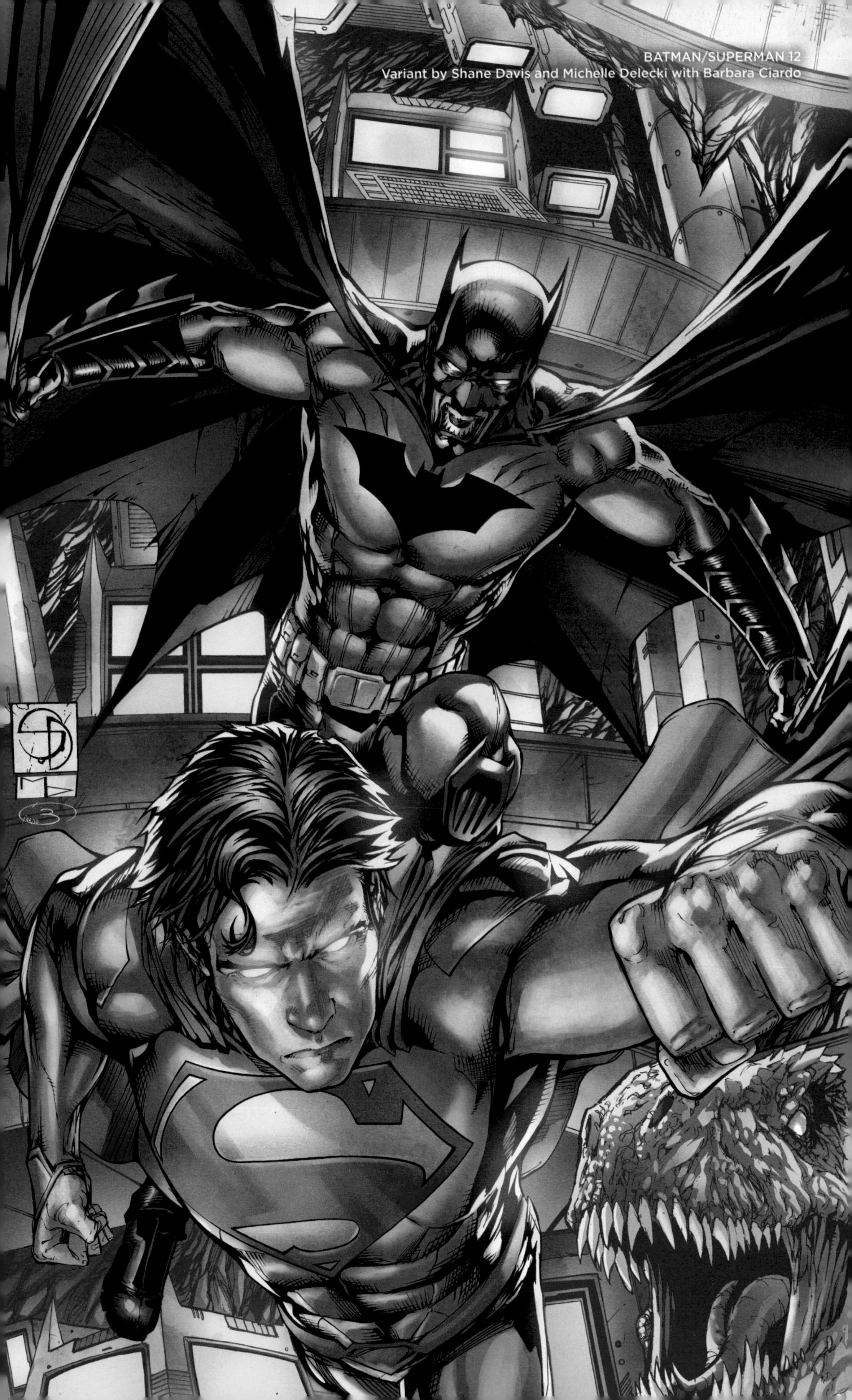

BATMAN/SUPERMAN 12
Variant by Shane Davis and Michelle Delecki with Barbara Ciardo

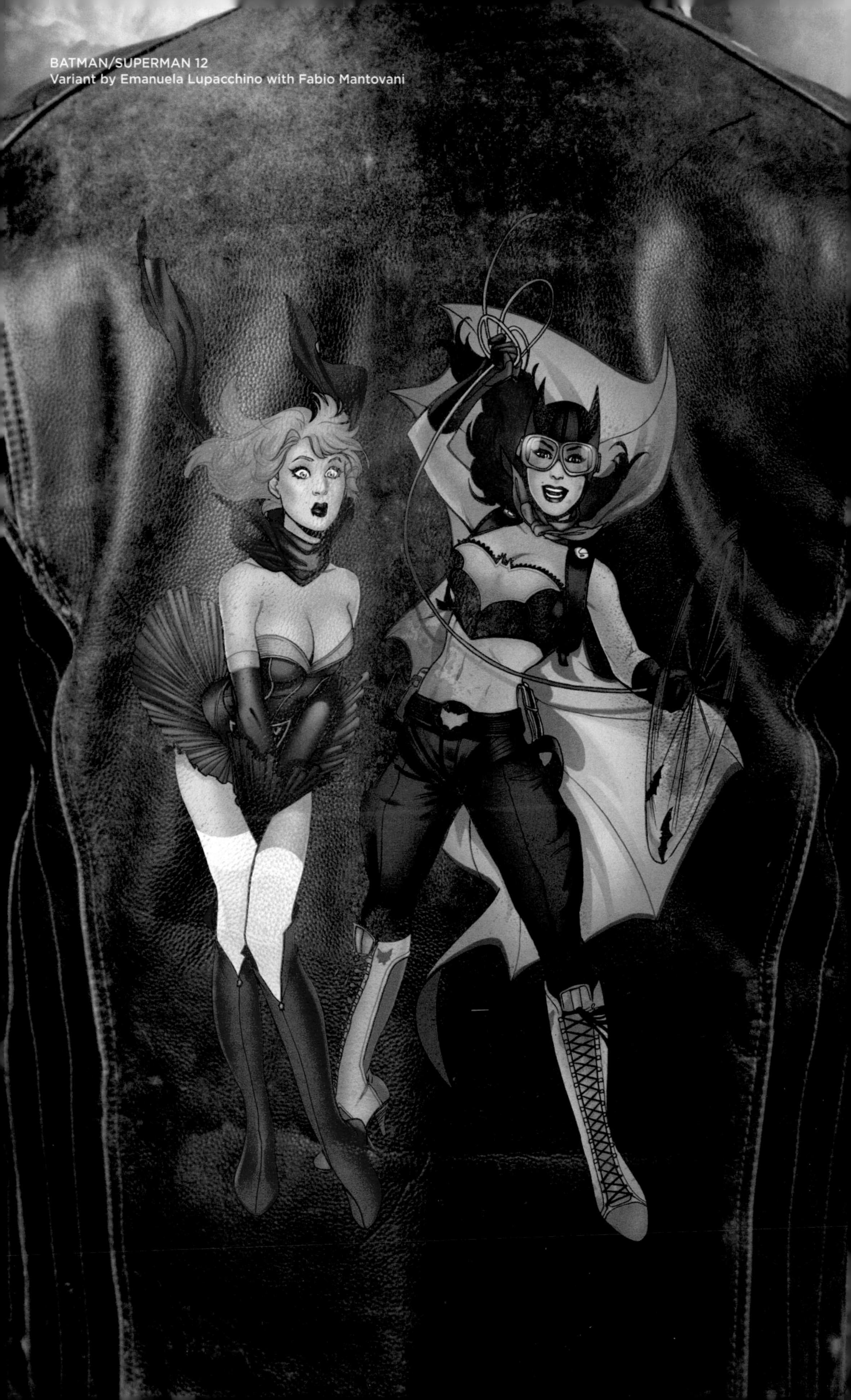

BATMAN/SUPERMAN 12
Variant by Emanuela Lupacchino with Fabio Mantovani

BATMAN/SUPERMAN 13
Batman 75th Anniversary variant by Dan Jurgens with Alex Sinclair

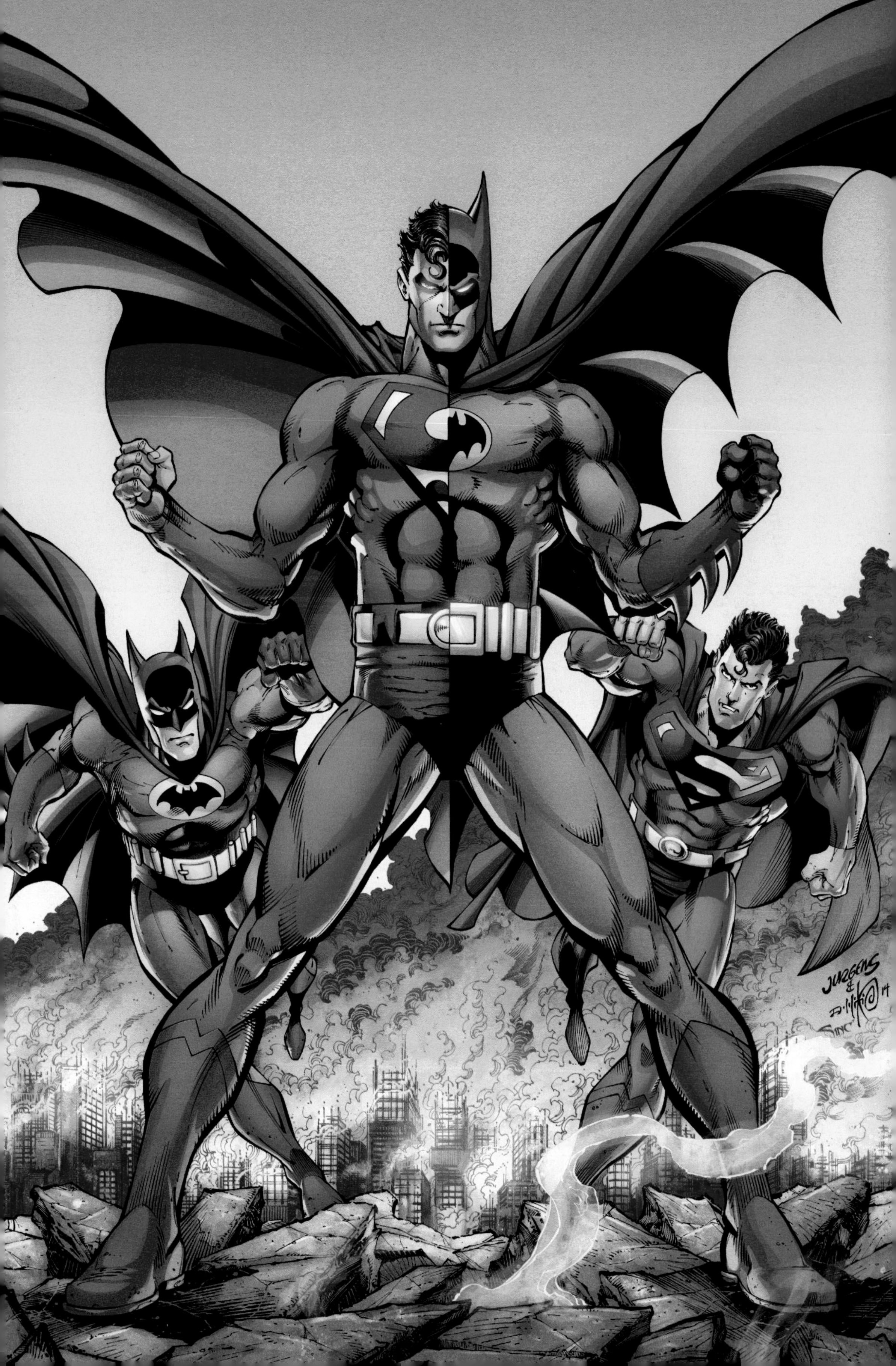

JURGENS

BATMAN/SUPERMAN 13
Variant by Ben Oliver

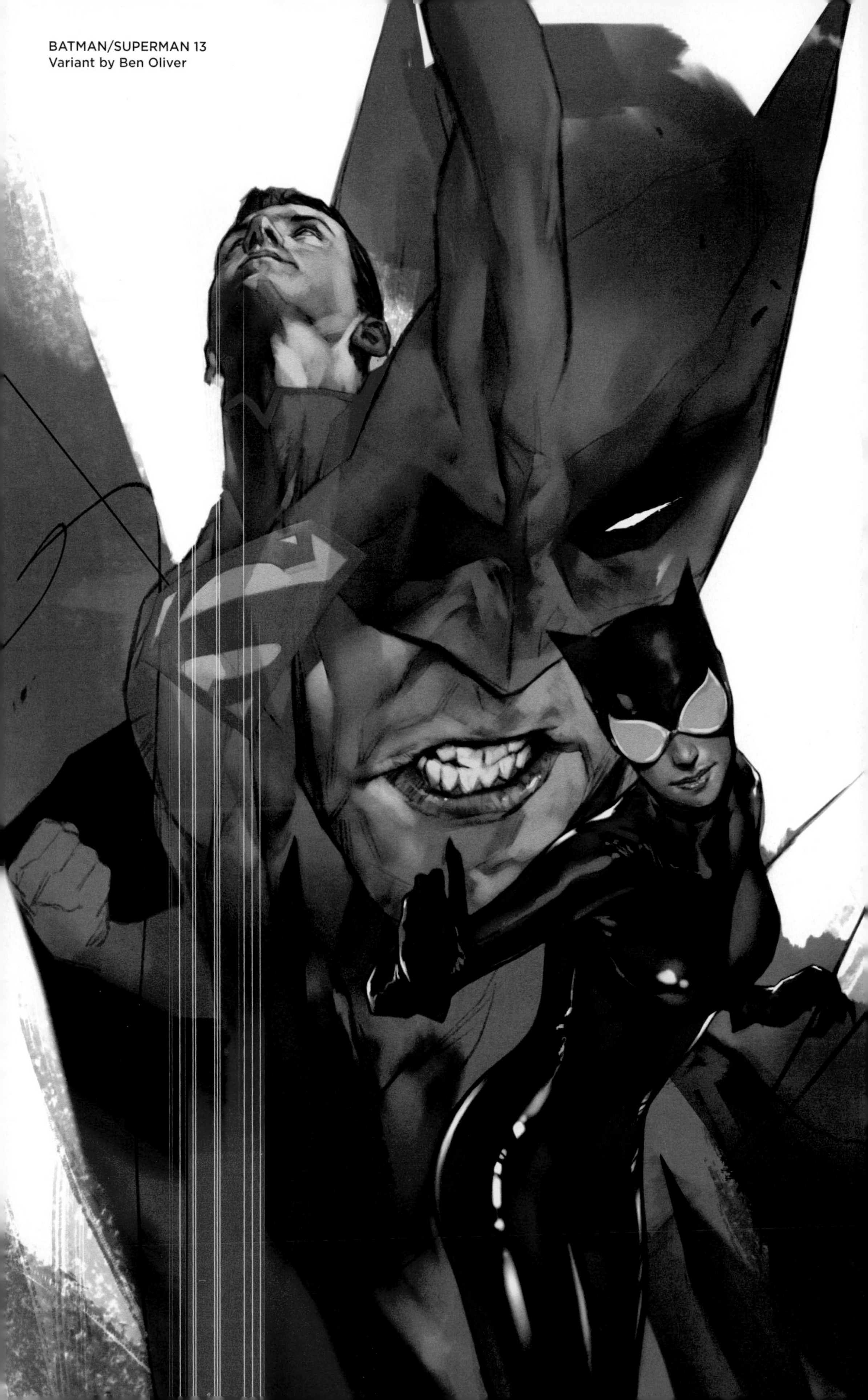

BATMAN/SUPERMAN 14
Variant by Paulo Siqueira

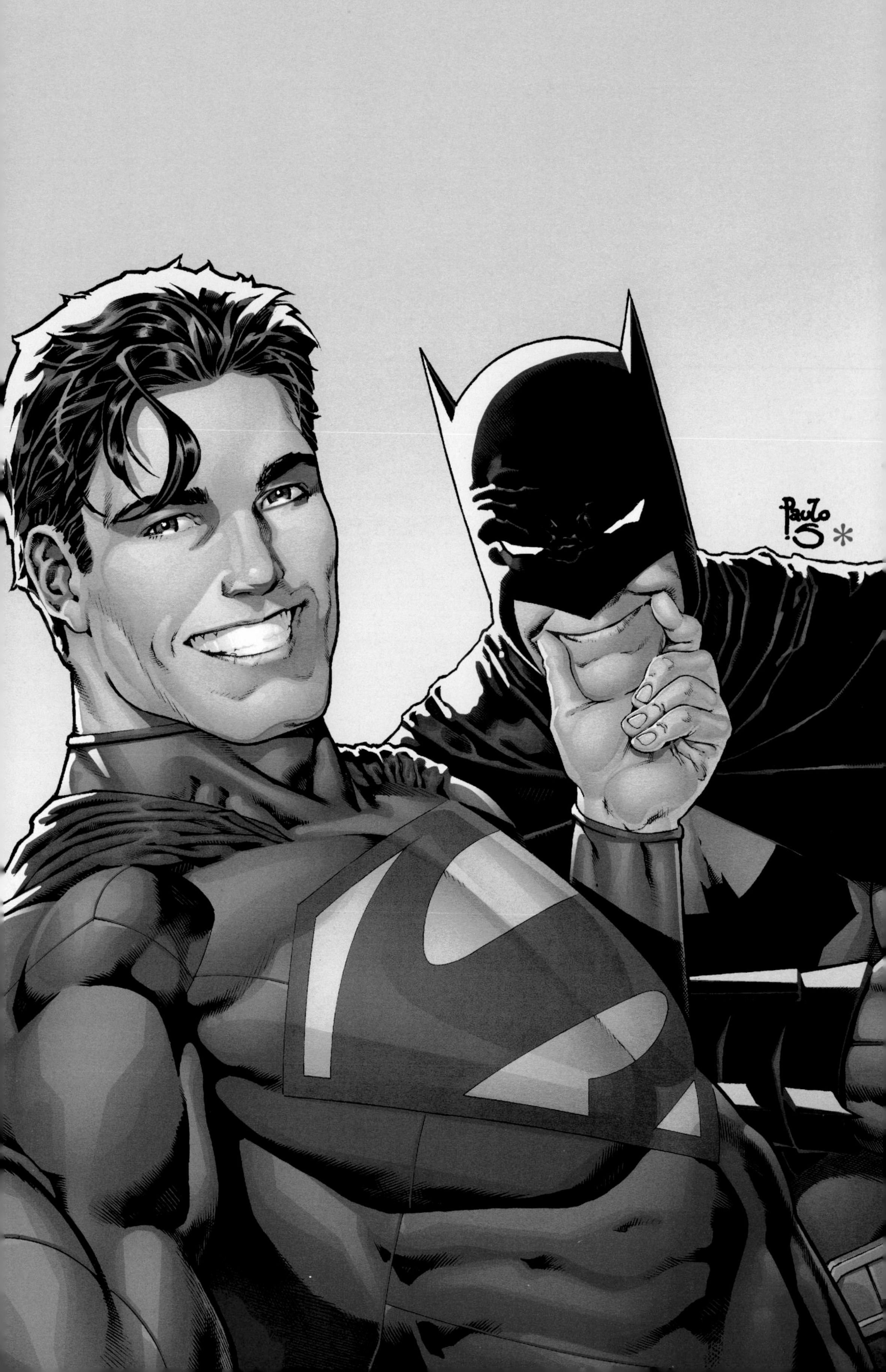

BATMAN/SUPERMAN 14
Variant by Matteo Scalera with Matt Hollingsworth

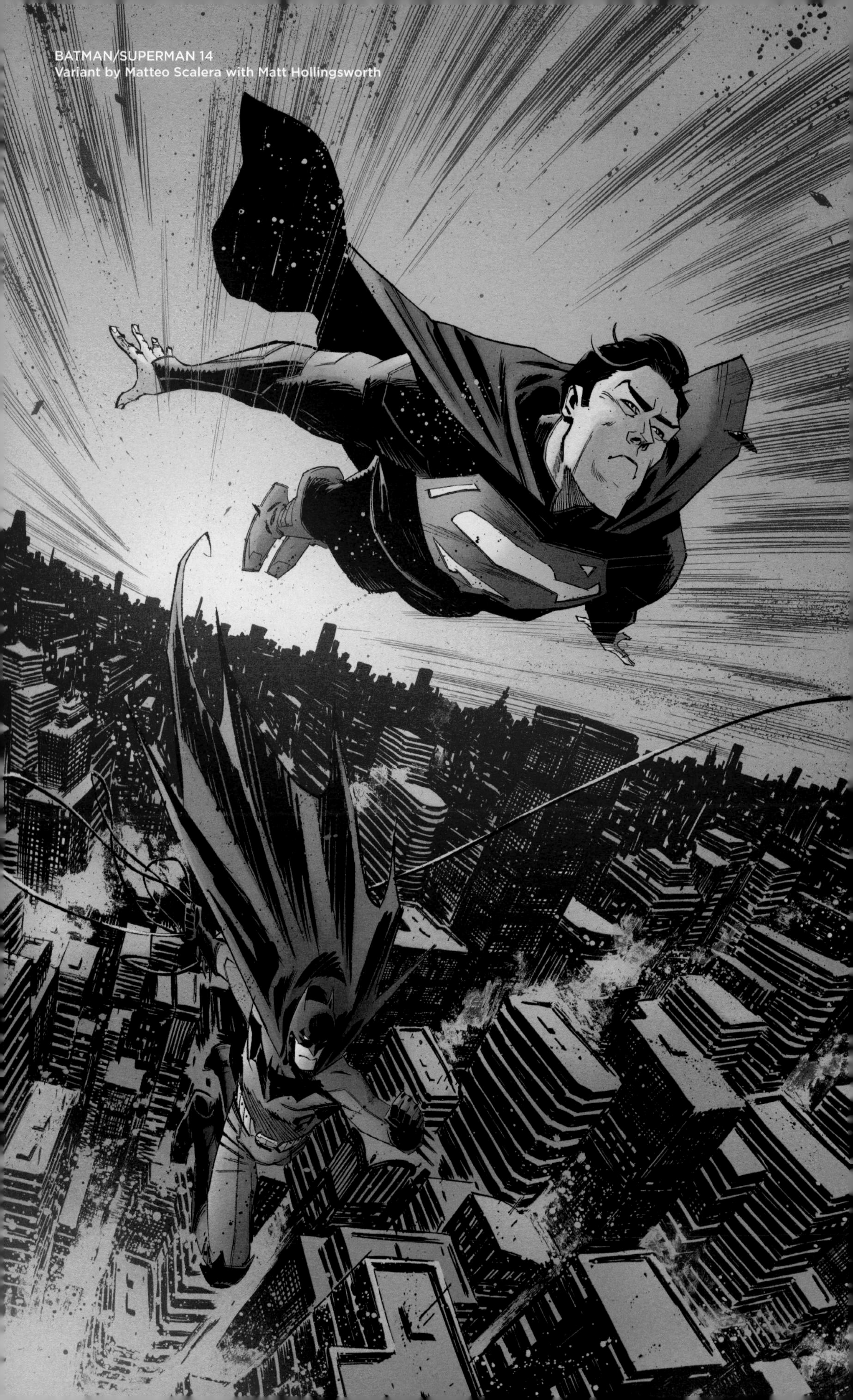

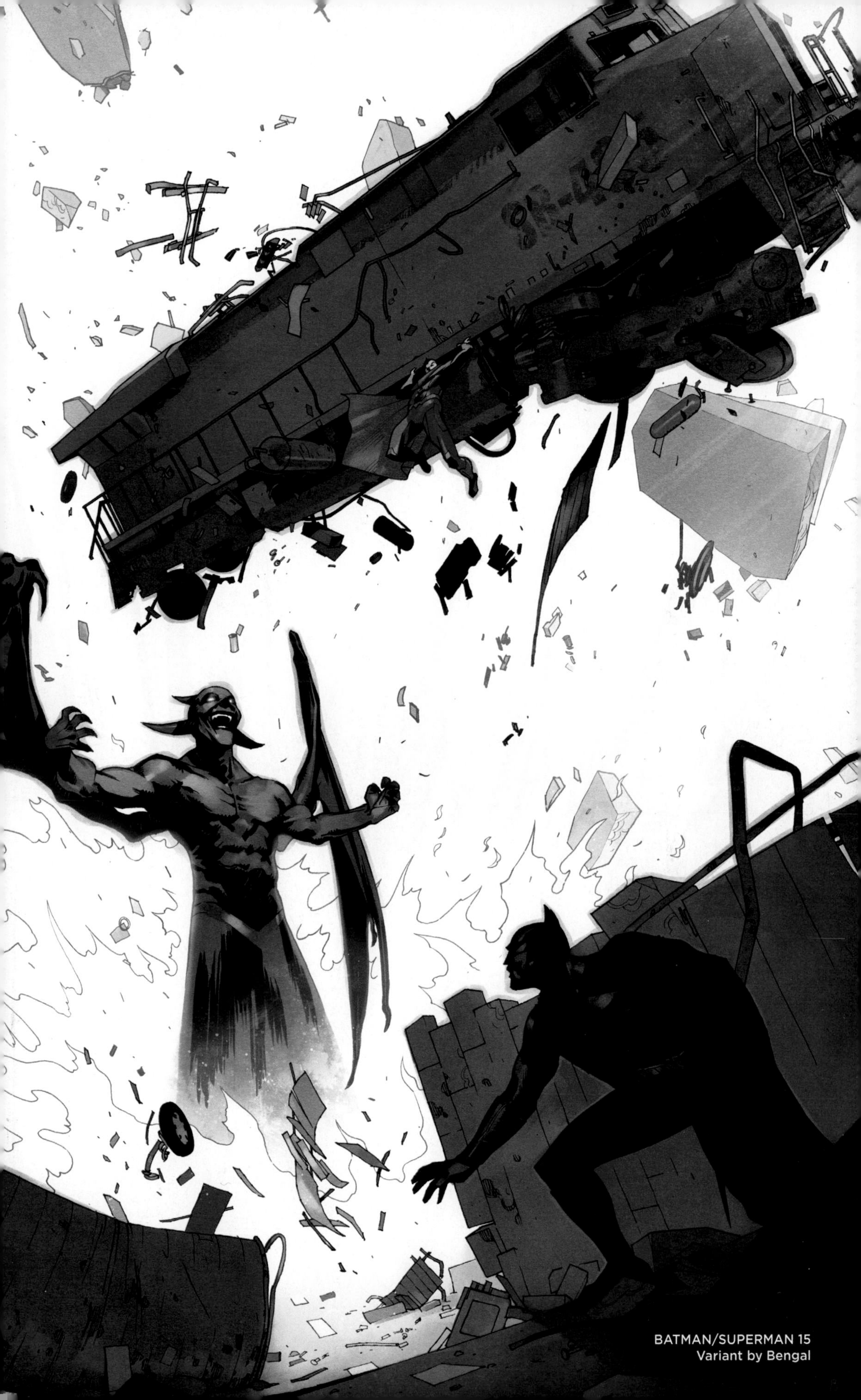

BATMAN/SUPERMAN 15
Variant by Bengal

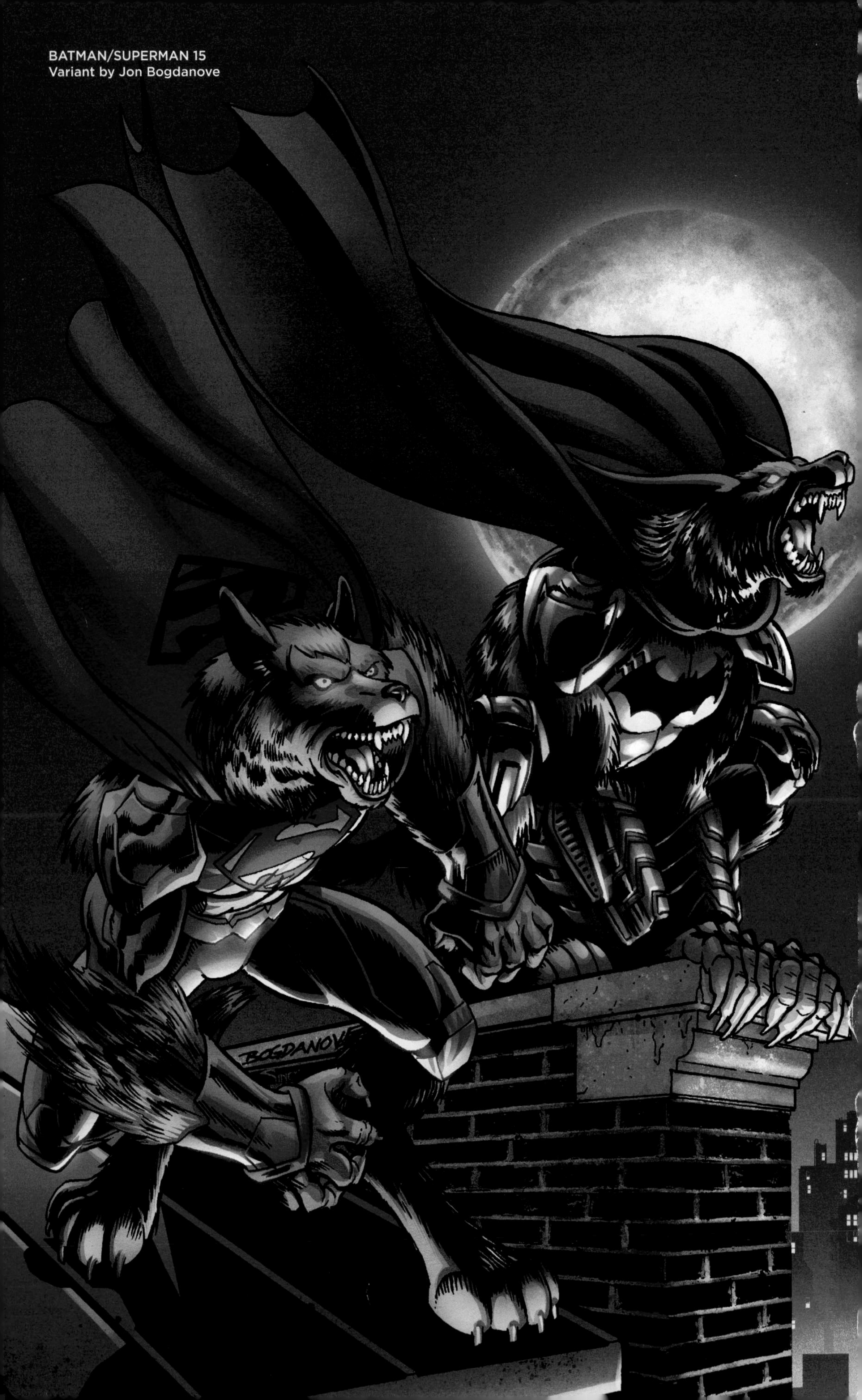
BOGDANOVE

BATMAN/SUPERMAN 15
Variant by Jon Bogdanove